MEMPHIS STATE UNIVERSITY
Y0-EHC-633

INDEX TO POETRY IN PERIODICALS
1920-1924

INDEX TO POETRY IN PERIODICALS

1920-1924

An Index of Poets and Poems
Published in American Magazines and Newspapers
Prepared By
The Editorial Board
Granger Book Co., Inc.

GRANGER BOOK CO., INC.
Great Neck, New York

International Standard Book Number 0-89609-224-0
Library of Congress Catalog Card Number 81-80120

Printed in the United States of America

CONTENTS

PREFACE

The INDEX TO POETRY IN PERIODICALS, 1920-1924, continues the systematic indexing of verse published in American magazines and newspapers initiated by the edition for 1915-1919. It is intended to provide access to material not otherwise retrievable.

This volume contains more data than its predecessor, both in the number of poems included (almost 16,000 as against 9441) and in the number of periodicals indexed (302 as against 122). This is attributable to greater facility in locating more recent materials, and, apparently, more verse having been published in the later period.

While every magazine devoted to poetry and almost every general magazine and newspaper which regularly published verse is indexed, this work is not encyclopedic or all-inclusive; it is believed, however, that there are no significant omissions.

EXPLANATORY NOTES

LIST OF PERIODICALS INDEXED

Each of the 302 periodicals indexed is listed at the front of the book together with a short alphabetical abbreviation or symbol which refers to it.

Periodicals which are not extant have been annotated with dates of publication and other historical data where possible. Every effort consistent with an index of this type has been made to provide such material; more exhaustive labor to this end must be left to histories of American magazines.

Alternative titles of periodicals are shown in brackets when known.

INDEX TO POETS & POEMS

Each poem in the Index is listed under its author. Under the full name of the author, the entry provides:

(1) Title of poem(s)
(2) Symbol which refers to the periodical in which the poem appears
(3) Date of issue of the periodical.

Anonymous authors are included in the Index. Authors identified by initials are listed under such initials at the beginning of the alphabetical sequence for each letter. The last initial is used as the "sur-initial" for alphabeting purposes; thus, for example, an attribution given as C.A.D. is listed as "D.,C.A."

Various forms of an author's name as they may appear in two or more periodicals have been reconciled and are shown only in the most usual or readily identifiable form. However, an author may appear under more than one name form if certainty as to identity is not absolute. Cross-references from pseudonyms to full legal names are given when known.

Articles at the beginning of titles are retained but disregarded in the alphabeting. Thus, each poem beginning with an article is alphabeted by the word following the article.

The date of issue of the periodical in which the poem appears follows the symbol and is given in the short numerical mode (with only the last digit of the year shown) [e.g. November 22, 1919 is given as 11/22/9]. If the precise issue of the periodical cannot be determined, a question mark is used for the uncertain factor (e.g. if the particular week in which a poem appeared in a weekly publication is unknown, the entry will read 11/?/9; if the particular month of a monthly periodical is uncertain, the citation will be given as ?/9).

LIST OF PERIODICALS INDEXED AND KEY TO SYMBOLS

ADV	ADVENTURE
AJA	AJAX. 1916-1921?
AIN	AINSLEE'S. 1898-1926, then merged with True Western Stories
ALE	ALEXANDRIA GAZETTE
ALL	ALL STORY WEEKLY [MAGAZINE]. 1905-1920, then merged in Golden Argosy
ALS	ALL'S WELL. 1920-1935, superseded Reedy's Mirror [REM]
AME	AMERICA. 1909-
AMF	AMERICAN FORESTRY. 1895-
AMH	AMERICAN HEBREW. 1879-?
AMJ	AMERICAN JOURNAL OF CLINICAL MEDICINE. 1894-
AMK	AMERICAN LEGION WEEKLY
AML	AMERICAN MAGAZINE. 1906-, formerly Frank Leslie's Popular Magazine [see also LES]
AMM	AMERICAN MERCURY. 1924-
AMN	AMERICAN MESSENGER. 1843-1923
AMP	AMERICAN POETRY MAGAZINE. 1919-1933
AMS	AMERICAN-SCANDINAVIAN REVIEW
ARG	ARGOSY. 1882- (various titles)
ARI	ARIZONA LYRICS
ART	ART REVIEW
ASI	ASIA. 1917-1942, previously Journal of American Asiatic Association, 1898-1917
ATC	ATLANTA CONSTITUTION
ATM	ATLANTIC MONTHLY
AVE	AVE MARIA. 1865-?
BAA	BALTIMORE AMERICAN
BAU	BEAUTY
BEA	BEACON. 1921-
BEL	BEACON LIGHT
BOO	BOOKMAN. 1895-1933, then American Review
BOP	BOSTON POST
BOT	BOSTON [EVENING] TRANSCRIPT
BOY	BOY SCOUT'S MAGAZINE. 1913-
BRE	BREEZY STORIES
BRI	BRIEF STORIES
BRO	BROOM. 1921-1924
BRW	BROWNIES' BOOK
BRY	BROWNING MAGAZINE
BUC	BUCANNEER. 1924-1925
BUF	BUFFALO EVENING ENQUIRER
BUS	BUFFALO SATURDAY NIGHT

CAP	CAPRICE. 1922-1923
CAR	CARTOONS MAGAZINE
CAS	CASEMENTS. 1923-1924?
CAW	CATHOLIC WORLD. 1865-
CED	CEDAR RAPIDS REPUBLICAN
CEN	CENTURY MAGAZINE. 1870-
CHA	CHAT
CHD	CHICAGO DAILY TIMES
CHE	CHICAGO [EVENING] NEWS
CHL	CHICAGO LITERARY TIMES. 1923-1924
CHN	CHICAGO [DAILY] NEWS
CHT	CHICAGO TRIBUNE
CIC	CHRISTIAN CENTURY. 1884-
CIE	CHRISTIAN ENDEAVOR WORLD. 1886-
CIH	CHRISTIAN HERALD. 1878-
CIJ	CHRISTIAN SCIENCE JOURNAL. 1883-
CIM	CHRISTIAN SCIENCE MONITOR
CIR	CHRISTIAN REGISTER. 1821-?
CIT	CHURCHMAN. 1845-
CIU	CINCINNATI TIMES
CIV	CIRCLE. 1924-1938
CLC	C L OF C INDEX
CLA	CLARKSDALE DAILY REGISTER
CLS	CLASSIC
CLT	CLAY. 1922-1923
CLU	CLUB FELLOWSHIP MIRROR
COL	COLLIER'S [WEEKLY]. 1888-
COM	COMMONWEAL
CON	CONGREGATIONALIST. 1816-
COS	CONSERVATIVE
COT	CONTACT. 1920-1923
COV	CONTEMPORARY VERSE. 1916-1929
CSA	COSMOPOLITAN. 1886-
CTY	COUNTRY BARD. 1918-1945, then American Bard
CUU	CRISIS. 1910-?
DAI	DAILY PROGRESS
DAR	DAR MAGAZINE
DAV	DAVENPORT TIMES
DEL	DELINEATOR. 1873-1937
DEP	DEPAUX MAGAZINE
DER	DES MOINES REGISTER
DES	DESIGNER WOMAN
DET	DETROIT SATURDAY NIGHT
DEU	DETROIT SUNDAY NEWS
DEV	DEVILS LAKE JOURNAL
DEW	DEW DROPS
DIA	DIAL. 1880-1929
DOU	DOUBLE DEALER. 1921-1926

DRA	DRAMA. 1911-1931
DRE	DREAM WORLD
EDI	EDICT
EME	EMERSON QUARTERLY
EVM	EVERYBODY'S MAGAZINE. 1899-1929, then united with Romance
EXT	EXTENSION
FAR	FARM JOURNAL. 1877-
FIL	FILM FUN. 1915-?, previously Judge's Library, 1887-1913 then Magazine of Fun, 1913-1915
FLY	FLYING
FOG	FORGE. 1924-1929
FON	FORTHNIGHTLY REVIEW. 1865-
FOR	FORUM. 1886-1930
FOT	FORT WORTH RECORD
FOU	FOUR. 1923-1925
FRE	FREEMAN. 1920-1924
FUG	FUGITIVE. 1922-1925
GAL	GALLEON. 1924-1925
GAR	GARGOYLE. 1922-1922?
GLE	GLEANER. 1913?-?
GOH	GOOD HOUSEKEEPING. 1885-
GRA	GRANITE MONTHLY. 1877-1930
GRE	GREEN BOOK MAGAZINE
GRI	GRINNELL REVIEW
GUA	GUARDIAN. 1924-1925
GUI	GUIDE
GUL	GUILD PIONEER. 1923-?
GYP	GYPSY. 1925-1937
HAB	HARPER'S BAZAAR
HAM	HARPER'S MAGAZINE
HAR	HARRISON SEARCHLIGHT
HEA	HEACOCK'S
HOL	HOLLAND'S MAGAZINE
HOM	HOME DEPARTMENT MAGAZINE
HUE	HUE AND CRY. 1923-1929?
IND	INDEPENDENT. 1848-1928
INI	INDIANA QUARTERLY
INL	INDUSTRY ILLUSTRATED. 1921-1927, then united with Industrial Engineering
INT	INTERLUDES. 1924-1933
JAP	JAPAN REVIEW. 1916-1922
JEF	JEWISH FORUM. 1918-
JOH	JOHN MARTIN'S BOOK
JUD	JUDGE. 1881-1937, absorbed Leslie's Weekly, 1922 [LES]
JUN	JUNIOR CHRISTIAN ENDEAVOR
KAN	KANSAS CITY STAR
KNO	KNOX ALUMNUS

LAD	LADIES' HOME JOURNAL. 1883-
LAL	L'ALOUETTE. 1921, 1924-1938?
LAR	LARIAT. 1923-1929
LES	LESLIE'S ILLUSTRATED WEEKLY. ?-1922, absorbed by Judge, 1922 [JUD]
LIB	LIBERATOR. 1918-1924, superseded Masses
LIC	LINCOLN LORE
LIF	LIFE. 1883-1936
LIH	LITERARY WORLD
LIK	LITTLE FOLKS
LIR	LITTLE REVIEW. 1914-1929
LIT	LITTLE WANDERER
LIV	LIVE STORIES
LIW	LIVING CHURCH. 1878-
LOS	LOS ANGELES SATURDAY NIGHT
LOT	LOS ANGELES TIMES
LYR	LYRIC. 1917-1919, 1921-?
LYW	LYRIC WEST. 1921-1927
MAA	MCCALL'S MAGAZINE. 1870
MAC	McCLURE'S MAGAZINE. 1893-1929
MAG	MAGNIFICAT
MEA	MEASURE. 1921-1926
MEC	MEMPHIS COMMERCIAL APPEAL
MEN	MENORAH JOURNAL. 1915-?
MES	MESSENGER
MID	MIDLAND. 1915-1933, then merged with Frontier
MIH	MILITARY ARTS
MII	MILITARY SENTINEL
MIL	MILWAUKEE ARTS MONTHLY. 1922-1923, later Prairie [PRA]
MIN	MINARET. 1915-1926
MNJ	MINNEAPOLIS JOURNAL
MOD	MODERN POETRY
MOR	MODERN REVIEW. 1922-1924, combined with S4N, 1926
MOS	MOTHER'S MAGAZINE
MOT	MOTION PICTURE CLASSIC
MOZ	MOTION PICTURE MAGAZINE
MUC	MUCH ADO
MUN	MUNSEY'S MAGAZINE. 1889-1918, then Munsey, 1918-1929
MUS	MUSE AND MIRROR. 1922-1932, absorbed by Frontier, 1932
NAT	NATION. 1865-
NAU	NATIONAL MAGAZINE. 1865-1933
NAW	NAUTILUS MAGAZINE. 1898-
NEG	NEGRO WORLD
NEN	NEW NUMBERS. 1914-?
NEP	NEW PEN. 1921-1922
NER	NEW REPUBLIC. 1914-
NES	NEW YORK [EVENING] POST. Includes Literary Review
NET	NEW YORK [EVENING] SUN

NEU	NEW YORK HERALD
NEV	NEW YORK TRIBUNE
NEW	NEW YORK TIMES
NEY	NEW YORK TIMES BOOK REVIEW & MAGAZINE
NEZ	NEWARK NEWS
NOA	NORTH AMERICAN REVIEW. 1815-1940
NOM	NOMAD. 1922-1924
NOW	NORTH WESTERN RAILWAY MAGAZINE
OCO	OCONOMOWOC ENTERPRISE
ONW	ONWARD
OPE	OPEN ROAD. 1919-?
OPP	OPPORTUNITY. 1923-?
ORE	OREAD MAGAZINE
ORI	ORIENT. 1923-1927, then New Orient
OUT	OUTLOOK. 1870-1935
OVM	OVERLAND MONTHLY. 1868-1935
OWE	OWENWOOD MONTHLY
PAG	PAGAN. 1916-1922
PAL	PALMS. 1923-1940
PAN	PARACLETE
PAR	PARISIENNE MONTHLY MAGAZINE. 1915-1921
PAS	PARIS REVIEW
PAU	PARNASSUS. 1927-1937, superseded Rhythmus [see RHY]
PEA	PEARSON'S MAGAZINE. 1899-1925
PEG	PEGASUS. 1923-1924
PEW	PENNSYLVANIA GRIT
PEO	PEOPLE'S FAVORITE MAGAZINE
PER	PERSONALIST. 1920-?
PHI	PHI BETA KAPPA KEY
PIR	PICTORIAL REVIEW. 1899-1939
PIT	PITTSFIELD (MASSACHUSETTS) EAGLE
PIW	PICTURE WORLD
PLA	PLAYBOY. 1919-1924
POA	POET AND PHILOSOPHER
POB	POET LORE. 1901-1953
POE	POETRY: A MAGAZINE OF VERSE. 1912-1971
—	POET'S SCROLL. See SCR
POM	POETRY SOCIETY OF SOUTH CAROLINA YEARBOOK
POR	POETRY REVIEW. 1912
POT	POET'S GUILD
PPM	POPULAR MAGAZINE [FOR BOYS]. 1903-1930
PRA	PRAIRIE. 1923-?, formerly Milwaukee Arts Monthly [MIL]
PUB	PUBLIC LEDGER
PUR	PURDUE ALUMNUS
QUW	QUEEN'S WORK
RAC	RACING PIGEON
RAD	RADIO DIGEST
REB	RED BOOK

RED	RED CROSS MAGAZINE. 1906-1920
REM	REEDY'S MIRROR. 1891-1920, superseded by All's Well [ALS]
REW	REVIEWER. 1921-1925, absorbed by Southwest Review, 1926, [SOW]
RHY	RHYTHUMUS. 1923-1924, superseded by Parnassus [PAU]
ROC	ROCK ISLAND ARGUS
ROS	ROSARY MAGAZINE. 1891-
ROT	ROTARIAN
S4N	S4N. 1919-1925, then combined with Moden Review [MOR]
SAB	ST NICHOLAS MAGAZINE. 1873-?
SAC	ST ANTHONY'S MESSENGER
SAD	SALEM EVENING NEWS
SAF	SAN FRANCISCO NEWS LETTER
SAT	SATURDAY EVENING POST
SAU	SAUCY STORIES
SAX	SAXBY'S
SCA	SCANDINAVIAN REVIEW
SCM	SCRIBNER'S MAGAZINE. 1887-1939, then united with Commentator
SCR	[POET'S] SCROLL. 1922-1934
SEA	SEATTLE WOMAN
SEW	SEWANEE REVIEW. 1892-
SHA	SHADOWLAND
SIG	SIGN
SMA	SMART SET. 1900-1930
SMI	SMITH'S MAGAZINE
SNA	SNAPPY STORIES. 1916-?
SON	SONNET. 1917-1921
SOO	SOUTH ATLANTIC QUARTERLY. 1902-
SOU	SOUTHERN LITERARY MAGAZINE
SOV	SOUTHERN METHODIST UNIVERSITY
SOW	SOUTHWEST REVIEW. 1924-, formerly Texas Review, 1915-1924 [TER], absorbed Reviewer, 1926 [REW]
SPE	SPECTATOR
SPO	SPOKANE CHRONICLE
SPR	SPORTS AFIELD. 1887-?
SPT	SPRINGFIELD (MASSACHUSETTS) REPUBLICAN
STA	STAG FOLIO
STC	STARS AND STRIPES
STE	STEP LADDER
STJ	STRATFORD JOURNAL. 1916-1920. See entry below
STM	STRATFORD MONTHLY. 1924-1925. See entry above
SUB	SUNBEAM
SUM	SUNDAY POST MAGAZINE
SUN	SUNSET. 1898-
SUR	SURVEY. 1909-1937
SVG	SURVEY GRAPHIC. 1921-1948
TAL	TALMUD MAGAZINE

TEL	TELLING TALES
TEM	TEMPO. 1921-1923?, then absorbed by Larus, -1927
TER	TEXAS REVIEW. 1915-1924, then Southwest Review [SOW]
TOD	TODAY'S HOUSEWIFE
TOM	TOMORROW. 1924
TOU	TOUCHSTONE
TOV	TOWN AND COUNTRY
TOW	TOWN TOPICS
TRU	TRUTH
UNI	UNITY
UNV	UNIVERSITY OF CALIFORNIA CHRONICLE
UPR	UNPARTISAN REVIEW
VAN	VANITY FAIR
VER	VERMONTER. 1895-?
VIO	VIOLINIST
VOI	VOICES. 1921-?
WAN	WANDERER. 1923-1924
WAV	WAVE. 1922-1924
WAY	WAYFARER
WIL	WILLIAMSPORT SUN
WIN	WINDSOR MAGAZINE
WOM	WOMAN'S MAGAZINE
WOW	WOMAN'S WORLD. 1865-1940
WRA	WORLD OUTLOOK
WRE	WORLD TOMORROW
WRL	WRITER'S DIGEST
WRM	WRITER'S MONTHLY
YAR	YALE REVIEW
YOA	YOUNG'S MAGAZINE
YOB	YOUTH: POETRY OF TODAY. 1918-1919
YOC	YOUTH'S COMPANION. 1827-1929

INDEX TO POETRY IN PERIODICALS
1920-1924

AE See George William Russell

Abarbanel, David
Sonnet. LIB 9/2
Abbe, Julia
Kitchen characters. SOV 1923
Abdullah, Achmed
Poems of central Asia. BOO 12/4
Aber, Caroline E.
Mary mother. AMP 12/3
Aber, Loureine
All us dead ones. VOI 3-4/4
Bereft. POE 10/1
City wed. POE 10/1
Cut loose. LIB 5/2
Death. POE 10/1
Death. POE 3/4
Elevator man. POE 10/1
From city lanes. POE 10/1
Girl. POE 10/1
The gymnast. DOU 11/3
Kinship. POE 3/4
Listen to the years flying. POE 3/4
Music. VOI 3-4/4
My littleness. DOU ?/3
Old man. POE 10/1
Stars on a night. POE 3/4
Trees. POE 3/4
Waters hold back a chant. VOI 3-4/4
Your arms. POE 3/4
Aberle, Will
Old cloak. WAN 6/3
The phantom ship. WAN 8/3
Typhoon. WAN 9/3
Aborn, Maude
A garden. GRA 7/1
Abreder, Hermina E.
Broadway faces. AMP 12/2
Adair, Ivan
The poet's soul. COV 6/2
Song. COV 6/2
Adams, Andrew McIver
A leave taking. MUN 3/2
The married lover. MUN 2/2
The new husbandman. MUN 5/2
To a beautiful lady on tour. MUN 7/2
Adams, Bill
Billy Peg-leg's fiddle. OUT10/26/1
Adams, Elizabeth Challis
What can I do? CIJ 6/4
Adams, Elizabeth Kemper
Respite. SCM 6/3
Adams, Franklin P.
Codicil to a will. HAM 9/1
Hypothesis. HAM 1/3
Song of synthethic verility. HAM 2/0
To a lady troubled by insomnia. BOO 5/1
The true-love. BOO 6/4
Adams, J. Donald
The miracle. DIA 9/1
Tinder. DIA 8/0
Adams, John Alden
April in the woodland. MUN 4/2
Adams, John R.
Two stages of self-delusion. WAN 9/4
Adams, Leonie
April morality. NER11/23/1
The barouche. MEA 12/4
Bird and bosom --apocalyptic. NER 7/23/4
Crest. NER 2/13/4
Discourse with the heart. MEA 12/4
A gull goes up. NER 5/21/4
Home-coming. LIB 10/1
On Sensis' mummy. NER 4/4/3
Our lady of victory. MEA 12/4
Quiet. LIB 9/1
Spire St. Patrick's & the moon. MEA 12/4
Those not elect. NER 11/7/3
Thought's end. NER 2/21/3
A wind of fall. LIB 9/1
Adams, Letitia M.
Songs. GRA 4/2
Adams, Pauline
Death and the lady. NER 9/12/3
The monarch of the forest. AMP10-11/3
Adams, William C.
The story of Pemigewasset. GRA 2/1
Addison, Medora
After. LYW 4/24
Candle light. LYW 9/2
Cargoes. FOR 8/4
Coward: stars and stones. COV 1/29/4
The cripple. COV 12/2
Defeat. VOI 12/2
Dream builders. VOI S/2
The dreamer. COV 12/2
Dreamers and a sword. COV 3/2
The end. LYW 4/24
Fear. COV 12/2
Grafton Road. COV 8/3
Heretic. COV 3/2
Inarticulate. VOI 12/2
Lamplight. COV 12/2
Love's reticence. COV 3/2
Masquerade. LYR 8/3
Motherhood. POE 2/2
My April. COV 12/2

My sons. COV 5/1
The open gate. LYR 6/3
The quest. COV 5/1
Rich man, beggar man, thief. FOR 3/4
Riches. COV 5/1
Trapped. LYR 2/2
Walls. COV 3/2
Wanderlust. LYR 2/2
Wasted hours. COV 3/2
Your hands. COV 12/2
Your love. LYR 4/2
Yours. VOI W/2

Adler, Frederick H.
A greeting from the world. AMP 1-2/4

Adler, Frederick Herbert
Epitaphs. MEA 10/4

Adler, Mortimer J.
The fearless. POE 1/1

Aiken, Conrad
Asphalt. DIA 6/0
Battersea bridge. CEN 6/1
Concert pitch. NER 6/7/2
Dragon spring. YAR 4/2
The figure head. CEN 6/1
The house. BOO 10/2
Improvisations: lights & snow. BRO 6/2
Midnight. CEN 6/1
The milestone. MEA 3/1
An old man sees himself. DIA 3/1
The open window. CEN 5/1
Portrait of a girl. BRO 12/1
Poverty grass. RHY 2/3
Susanna. NER 8/24/1
Third movement.."Pilgrimage.." MEA 5/1
Twilight, Rye, Sussex. CEN 6/1
The vampire, 1914. NER 4/9/4

Aikins, Ruth
To Rosamond's eyes. LAR 4/3

Ainslie, Caroline
Accomplishment. LYW 10/4
Defiance. VOI 5-6/4
Fishing at Celilo. LAR 12/3
In the woods. LYW 11/3
Lonely street. LYW 10/1
Reproof. LYW 10/2
Shu-Shula. LYW 11/3
Throught the storm. LYW 4/3

Alden, John
On hearing the clavichord. SCM 9/4

Aldington, Richard
An earth goddess. NOA 1/0
Exile. DIA 10/3
A garden homily. NES 8/5/2
Madrigal. POE 6/3
Nightingale. DOU 7/2
The River Kennet. YAR 10/3
Six songs for Puritans. DIA 8/2
A sophistry of duration. NES 11/4/2

Aldis, Dorothy
April. POE 8/4
Bridges. POE 8/4
Grapes. POE 8/4
Intangible. POE 8/4
Realization. COV 6/4
Sonnet: "Lovers, stir not." POE 8/4
Sunday supper. COV 6/4
Tenderness. COV 6/4

Aldis, Mary
The happening. POE 1/3
The other one comes to her. POE 1/3
Search. POE 1/4
She remembers. POE 1/3
She thinks of the faithful one. POE 1/3
They meet again. POE 1/3
To one who asks. POE 1/1
To you. STE 3/4
The wandering one makes music. POE 1/3
The wandering one. POE 1/3

Aldrich, Marie
Gypsy dance. CTY S-A/4

Aleksander, Blok
The poet. EME 4/3

Alexander, Bessie Rowe
Forgiveness. CIC10/19/2

Alexander, Hall
Dreams for Freudian analysis. PAG 4-5/0

Alexander, Hartley
Amerindian air. NAT 2/16/1
The blizzard. SCM 1/2
The cities of white men. SCM 1/2
The great drum. SCM 1/2
I am running. MID 9-10/1
Mirage. SCM 1/2
The origin of death. SCM 1/2
The pines are thinking. BOO 1/3
Pioneers. LAR 4/3
The sun's last ray. SCM 1/2
The wet grass of morning. SCM 1/2

Alexander, Jane Barbara
When I am plunged in sunlight. BOO 10/3

Alexander, Sandra
To B.S.. LYR 4/3
Your hands. LYR 8/2

Algert, Bernadine
Apres-midi. LYW 10/1

Blue waters. TER 10/1
Chinoiserie. LYW 10/1
Complaint of a vagabond. LYW 2/2
Devil to a ghost. TER 10/1
Mirror. TER 4/2
Mist. LYW 10/1
Night trail. TER 4/2
Ravine (spring). TER 4/2
Reply. TER 10/1
Song of a ballerina. LYW 2/2
To common-sense. TER 10/1
Valentine. LYW 2/4
When warriors die. TER 10/1
White locusts. TER 4/2

Allbright, B. F.
To my uncle. LAR 6/3

Allen, Dorothy Hoskins
Harlequin married. LYW 2/4

Allen, Effie Alger
The first red man. POE 2/3
A legend of the Mississippi. POE 2/3
Night on the river. AMP 4/2
The phantom steamer. POE 2/3
Sunshine lake. AMP A/1

Allen, Eleanor
The cry of Gandahari. OVM 5/4
New gods. LAR 10/3
Old China. LAR 7/3
To one who sings. LAR 11/3
A wish. LAR 3/4
Wonder. LAR 7/3

Allen, Grace
Echo answers beauty. COV 3/4
Whoso knoweth beauty without... COV 1/3

Allen, Hervey
Black roses. NOA 1/3
Carolina spring song. POM 1922
Confession. COV 5/1
Dead men-to a metaphysician. BOO 5/2
Despair. COV 5/1
Gargantua. MEA 2/2
Hag-hollerin' time. POE 4/2
Macabre in macaws. POE 4/2
Moments. COV 4/2
Palmette town. POE 4/2
Portentia. REW 5/2
Refuge. COV 10/2
Relativity. NES 6/3/2
Shadows. POE 4/2
Sunshine. POE 4/2
Upstairs downstairs. POE 4/2
Walls. VOI 6-7/3
The wanderer. COV 6/4
The wingless victory. NER 8/18/0

Allen, Joe
Lines. LAR 2/4
Smoke. LAR 2/4

Allen, Laura Shelley
To him that overcometh. CIJ 8/4

Allen, Mary Pierson
"Inasmuch." COV 6/3

Allen, Rae
A natural error. AIN 2/2
Shore leave. AIN 5/2

Allen, William C.
At evening time. CON 5/17/3

Allen, Willis Boyd
The shrine. SCM 10/0

Allen-Siple, Jessie
"Blarney" CTY S-A/1
A California idyll. CTY S-A/1
Censure. CTY Win/4
A corner for men. CTY W/1
The dolly dress. CTY W/1
Home's where the heart's at re. CTY S-A/1
How I know its fall. CTY S-A/4
The meadow lark. CTY S/2
Room at the top. CTY S/2
Sailing home to me. CTY Spr/3
Sing me to sleep. CTY Aut/2
Songs of praise. CTY W/1
Sweet little brier rose. CTY S/2
The truth. CTY S-A/4
The trysting place. CTY Win/3
The vision. CTY Win/4
Wah all yo' is. CTY Win/3
When ma gets sick. CTY S-A/4
Where they allus is. CTY Sum/3

Allers, Dorothy
After the end. INT 1-3/4
Cathedral. INT 1-3/4
Longing. INT10-12/4
Withered leaves. INT 7-9/4

Allie, Arthur
An angry word. AMP 4/2
The river. AMP 4/2

Alling, Kenneth Slade
The angle worm. VOI 11/4
Beauty. MEA 10/2
The bee. MEA 10/1
The beetle. VOI 11/4
The bird. MEA 7/3
Bluejay. COV 3/1
Boast. MEA 11/3
Escapes. MEA 5/1
February thaw. MEA 3/2
Ferns. MEA 7/3
The final sunset. MID 2/1
First ice. NES12/21/1
The freight train. LES 3/4/2
Ghouls. MEA 6/2
Low tide. MEA 11/3
Nude. MEA 7/4

On the passing...fire horse. NES ?/1
Pater. MEA 1/4
Pebbles. VOI 5-6/4
Sands. COV 8/2
Sleep-a fragment. COV 3/1
Snow. COV 1/0
Something like a wind. MEA 10/1
Spring death. MEA 3/4
Spring water. VOI 5-6/4
Stones gathered for a chimney. MEA 10/1
Summer night. MEA 10/1
That strange thing. COV 5/0
This flesh. MEA 9/4
Three flowers. COV 5/0
Three poems: rain. COV 3/1
To a Maryland yellow-throat. MEA 7/3
To a woman. MEA 8/2
To one who asked. MEA 5/3
To----. MID 8/1
Toul sector, October... MEA 2/2
The unscarred fighter remember. MEA 3/2
Winter water. VOI 5-6/4

Allsopp, Fred W.
Authors' land. SCR 9/4
Autumn leaves. SCR 12/4
Mysterious power. SCR 11/4
The road home. SCR 10/4
Too good to be mortal. SCR 11/4

Allured, S. S.
The west that was. LAR 12/3

Almack, John C.
The lanes of Oregon. CTY S-A/1
The road to Miramar. AMP 12/3
Romany way. AMP 2-3/3

Almy, Frederic
On the use of boards. SVG 12/3

Altrocchi, Julia Cooley
Autumn and spring. STM 11/4
Disseverance. LYW 10/3
The dreamers of death. POE 11/0
Easter morning in the woods. CIV 5/3
The heart of a woman. STE 10/3
The hollow soul. AMP 5-6/4
The lost balloons. BRI 8/4
October. STE 10/3

Alwood, Lister Raymond
The first robin. DEU 4/17/1
Igcognito. DEU 6/27/1
An interlude. DEU 5/2/0
Maker of little songs. DEU 5/22/1
A rhyme of vers libre. DEU 1/16/1
Spring-in the city. DEU 4/3/1
To a leaf. DEU 5/9/0
White bees. DEU 5/9/0

Ames, Lucile Perry
Age. PAG 12/1
Dream-ash. PAG 1/2
Misty-trail. PAG10-11/1
To a pink peach tree. LAR 3/4
The white monk. COV 3/3

Ammidown, H. F.
To Monadnock. GRA 3/2

Ammons, Mildred Hudson
Comrade. OVM 5/4

Andelson, Pearl
At play. VOI A/1
Chapter. POE 12/2
Excursion. DIA 2/3
Late winter wood. VOI 12/2
Madonna. VOI A/1
Out of weariness. POE 12/2
Philosophic dialogue. POE 12/2
Sea girl. POE 12/2
Thin refuge. POE 12/2
Tide out. VOI A/1
A trivial day in early autumn. POE 12/2
Worker in marble. POE 12/2

Anderson, Claiborne Hauks
Cobwebs and iron. REW

Anderson, Dorothy
A litany. COV 1/1
Mist in the city. COV 3/4
A trysting. COV 3/4

Anderson, Marguerite L.
Playmates. AMP 4/2

Anderson, Maxwell
The beggar god-II, the god... MEA 12/1
The beggar god-III, he gathers. MEA 12/1
The beggar god-IV, He broods... MEA 12/1
Emptying ashes. NER 1/19/1
Epilogue. MEA 11/4
Hylas. COV 4/0
Judith of Minnewaukan. MEA 9/1
Looking out upon the world. COV 10/0
Lucifer. MEA 1/2
Night in the queen's garden. COV 10/0
Noon in a wood. MEA 5/2
Oil-derricks at dawn. COV 10/0
Prayer after youth. NER 12/3/4
"She said, though you should." NER 7/5/2
St. Agnes' morning. NER 3/16/1
Thrall to dust. COV 10/0
"The time when I was plowing" NER 6/21/2
"Whether the dark has ushered. NER 5/21/4

"Who has burned his wings." MEA 9/2
"You who have dreams born ..." NER 3/26/4

Anderson, Mildred Dyke
Knowledge. AMP 8-9/3
Portrait. AMP 8-9/3

Anderson, Robert Gordon
Leader of men. SCM 2/0

Anderson, Sherwood
Testament on the two glad men. DOU 4/2
Testament. DOU11-12/4

Andre, Walt
Dies Irae. Wan 10/3

Andrew, Thekla Hollingsworth
Heart's desire. MUN 6/2

Andrews, Anabel C.
Absent. GRA 12/0

Andrews, Andrew L.
Easter-1923. NOM Spr/3
Requiem. NOM S/2
Upon attending service at Trin. NOM Aut/2
Virtue. S4N/1-2/3

Andrews, Beatrice B.
Adder tongue lilies. STE 6/3

Andrews, George Lawrence
Dawn. SOU 7/3
Her voice. AMP 8-9/3
A jilted lover speaks. NOM Sum/4
The lost path. ART 4/2
Memory. CAW 6/4
Nightfall. MAG 10/3
The old. PAU #2/4
Silver on gray. SOU 8/3
Sunrise in the hills. CIH 6/23/3
Three poplars. CIV 9-10/4
Unconquered. SOU 4/4
Wild geese. WIN 9/4

Andrews, Loring
Emancipation. PAG A-S/1
A woman I met. S4N 12/2

Andrews, Mary Raymond Shipman
The calling road. SCM 12/2
Cardinal Mercier. SCM 3/2
Creation. SCM 3/1
Homesick. SCM 12/0
Pax Vobiscum. SCM 8/1
Pulp-wood. SCM 7/3

Annett, Albert
Autumn. GRA 11/0
January. GRA 1/1

Anonymous
Age. SCR 9/2
At parting. FRE 4/5/2
Cobweb boy. NAT11/28/3
The Dempsey & Carpentier fight. NAT 6/12/1
Department store demonstrator. NAT12/28/2
Holiday. NAT12/28/2
Incredible facts. NAT12/28/2
A lady of eight years - to my. CTY Sum/3
Moment mystical. PAG 4-5/0
The municipal lodging house. NAT12/28/2
The night wind. NAT12/28/2
Out of work. NAT12/28/2
Papers. NAT12/28/2
Paradox. DEP 12/3
Preludes to a pantomime. NAT 5/1/0
Sufficiency. DEP 12/3
Summer rain. PAG O-N/1
Thoughts. LAR 10/3
Three unnamed poems. CAP 1-2/3
Uses. NAT12/28/2
Windows and smells. NAT12/28/2

Anthony, Edward
Romance in a barber shop. HAM 12/2

Anthony, Helen Emerson
An old stone wall. INT10-12/4
The sea. INT 7-9/4

Anthony, Jeannette B.
Freedom. CIJ 3/4

Appleby, Elizabeth
Quatrains. DEP 10/4

Arata, Oliver S.
Canzonet. POA 9/1
Thomas A. Edison. LAR 12/3

Armfield, Maxwell
Battle. DOU 10/1
Vision at noon. NER 8/30/2

Armstrong, Elizabeth A.
Happiness. AMP 8/2

Armstrong, Hamilton Fish
Lines for the hour. NES 3/2/0

Armstrong, Martin
All is one. BRO 6/2
The buzzards. CEN 11/0
Man seeks to cage delight. POE 11/3
Rhapsody. CEN 12/0

Armstrong, Nelchen
The white road. LYW 6/2

Arnault, Antoine-Vincent
The leaf. LYR 10/3

Arno, Beth
After sundown. AMP Aut/1

Arnold, Amy Herron
Four sonnets. YAR 4/4
My June. SCR 2/4
Tea. SCR 8/4
Upon a rainy day. SCR 8/4

Arnold, Anne

"All through the night." AMP 10/2
Fulfillment. AMP 2/2
My garden. GOH 8/2

Arnold, Ethel H.
God's goodness. CIJ 8/4

Ashburn, Frank D.
Four sonnets. YAR 4/4
The pagan. YAR 3/4
Two sonnets. YAR 11/3

Ashe, William E.
Miami in December. HEA 10/4

Ashleigh, Charles
Death bed. LIB 3/2
Oriental nocturne. CEN 11/1
Vespers. LIB 3/2

Ashley, Comelia
The new year. AMP 12/3
The Yucca path. AMP 8/2

Ashley, Margaret Lee
Basking. COV 7/4
The old piano. COV 1/4
The planting. COV 7/4
The song of Edric. COV 12/4

Ashwin, E. Allen
Translations from the Anacreon. DIA 4/1

Aswell, James B.
Mortuary. MIN 7-8/4

Athay, Ruth Davies
Yuccas. LAR 6/3

Atherton (see Dennen), Grace

Atkins, Lois
Hill-charm. LYW 12/3

Atkinson, Arthur W.
To the northern lights. LYW 2/2

Atkinson, John Hampton
Heliotrope and jarjoram. AMP 2/2
Heliotrope and marjoram. AMP 9-10/4

Atsu-Ko Saisho
When beauty dies. FRE 11/9/1

Atwood, Slyvia
Little houses. NEN 3/28/1

Aughiltree, Ruth
Discovery. LYW 4/4
The farmer prays. CTY S-A/4
I can't stay by my fireplace. CTY Win/4

August, S. G.
Silent. STE 7/2

Auslander, Jacob
I come singing. NER 3/24/0

Auslander, Joseph
Abandoned. MEA 5/2
Abyss. NER10/10/3
After Hiroshige. COV 4/3
April's bewildering. AMP 5/3
Beauty will wound us. COV 4/2
Beauty. COV 8/1
Bellerophon. FUG 12/3
Blind searcher. MEA 2/2
The bright blasphemy. LYW 4/2
Broken things. VOI W/2
Candles and torches. MEA 7/2
Cesar Franck. VOI 6-7/3
Companion of quiet. BOO 9/3
Covenant. COV 10/3
Credo. FUG 12/3
Crying, "Thalassus!" VOI W/2
The dark edge of the dawn. COV 8/1
Dead leaves. COV 11/1
Downpour. COV 5/1
Ebb-tide. NER 4/12/2
Enigma. POE 3/4
Ennuye. BOO 10/4
Essences. FUG 2/4
Feather and bells. NER 2/28/3
Forget! NES 3/29/4
Frailty, thy name is-. MEA 2/2
Ghoul. MEA 2/4
Haunted solitude. ATM 4/3
Heat on the Gulf. VOI 6-7/3
Herodiade. POE 3/4
I cannot bind your spirit. LYR 10/2
I greet you! VOI Spr/2
I have heard music. VOI 8-9/3
I have waited for you long. POE 5/2
I know it will be quiet... MEA 5/2
I struck a word. NER 5/23/3
In envy of cows. NER 5/9/3
In time of desolation. NER 1/16/4
Instead of tears. POE 3/4
Interval. NER 9/26/3
Is this the lark! MEA 5/2
Jeweled breathing. CAS 1/3
Just now. FUG 12/3
Little Lou. POE 5/2
Lone gulls. COV 11/2
Love and the garlands. MEA 7/1
Marie Antoinette. LYR 4/4
O my wild charger of dreams. VOI Aut/2
Oakum. COV 10/3
Of course they had to visit... NER 5/17/2
One instant. COV 8/1
Out of the fog. AMP Aut/1
Paint me the glory of a furrow. SON 1-2/0
Passing-passing. LYW 11/2
Prisoners of dusk. LYR 6/3
The recoil. VOI Aut/2

Shrift on All Soul's Day. NES10/27/3

Baldwin, Eleanor
The old man of the mountain. GRA 12/1
Resignation. OUT 12/3/4
The rider of the wind. SCM 5/4

Baldwin, Faith
Books. SCM 7/3
The downtown church. IND 8/16/4
Exile. VOI Aut/2
Grey magic. VOI Spr/3
Lassitude. AMP 5-6/4
Legend. MAC 10/2
The moon in a mirror. MEA 1/3
My sister's sons. COV 6/0
The petty soul. OUT 5/3/1
Portrait. MEA 5/2
The silent singer. LYW 3/4
Sonnets in memoriam. MEA 9/2
The street of fine houses. LYW 7-8/3
Warning. IND 9/27/4

Baldwin, Helen
The boatmen on the Yang-tse. CEN 4/0
The cartman of Kalgan. CEN 4/0
The last journey. CEN 4/0
The shepherd of Hanoerpaar. CEN 4/0
The warrior's bride. CEN 4/0

Baldwin, Summerfield
To one who ought to be a Catho. CAW 8/2

Ballentine, Ella Jean
To the song sparrow. LAR 12/3

Bancroft, Margaret
Rondeau. AMP 9-10/4

Banerji, Suresh Chandra
Ana Pavlowa. COV 3/4

Bangert, Carl F.
The flight - and return. AMP 6-7/3

Bangs, Janet Norris
April. POE 4/4
Care. POE 10/2

Bank, Enos R.
God's gallery. INT 4-6/4
The new year. INT 1-3/4

Banker, Caroline Fornay
In Orient-land. AMP 9-10/4

Bankhead, John Stickney
Mother. SCR 1/4

Banks (Jr.), Theodore H.
Victory. EVM 3/1

Banks, Gay Walton
Preserve the shot tower. CIV11-12/4

Banks, Kathrina
Lake Tahoe. UNV 7/4

Banks, Sam J.
Autumn. BOT10/29/4

Banning, Kendall
The strangers of the inn. GRI 6/1

Banning, Martha Thomas
The booby. NET Win/3

Banning, Waldo
Youth. COV 3/3

Barber, Bruce
The stream's secret. MUN 4/2

Barber, Emma Cowan
The west. LAR 12/3

Barber, Katherine A.
From a letter. SOV 1923
I have a love. CAS 1/3
My days. CAS 1/3
Veranda chairs. CAS 1/3

Barber, Mary Finette
The elusive. COV 1/4

Barclay, Rhoda L.
The play-actors. AMP 6-7/3

Barclay, Robert E.
Questions. COV 8/0

Bard, Albert S.
Gallstones and balloons. NER 10/1/4

Bardin, James C.
When the wind blows in the fir. COV 8/2

Barker, S. Omar
At timberline. COV 6/4
Foreknowledge. LYW 6/3
Life. COV 6/4
Little trails. LAR 3/4
Mountain lakes. COV 6/4
Mountains. OVM 6/4
Pierrot in the hills. LAR 3/4
To an unknown ancestor. STM 10/4
A word at parting. OVM 6/4

Barker, Semele
Willows in winter. LAR 3/4

Barkley, Alice
Acacia. SCR 5/3
Alice. SCR 12/2
As the poppies. LAR 10/3
At dawning. SCR 2/3
Bonfires. LAR 2/4
Candle, teach me! LAR 8/3
Changing clouds. SCR 10/4
The Christmas tree speaks. SCR 12/4
Contrast. SCR 9/2
Daffodils. LAR 2/4
Dear friend. SCR 5/4
Dewdrops. SCR 3/3
Early Sunday morning. SCR 4/4
Every morn, I've given all sav. SCR 3/4

For autumn colors. SCR 11/4
Give, give, give. SCR 5/3
Green. SCR 5/3
Grey rain. LYW 3/3
Happiness. SCR 10/3
Heartless. SCR 12/2
Hollyhocks. SCR 10/3
How can I sing? SCR 5/4
I cannot let the old year die. SCR 12/2
I have a singing heart. SCR 2/3
I will walk proudly. SCR 9/3
I would not bind you. SCR 7/4
If you loved me enough. SCR 11/3
July--the artist. SCR 8/4
July. SCR 8/4
Little songs. SCR 5/3
A lullaby. SCR 5/3
A May song. SCR 5/4
Meditation. SCR 9/3
My heart is singing. SCR 5/3
My heart. SCR 8/4
My little hill. SCR 9/4
Naming candles. SCR 9/3
Orange. SCR 2/4
Pangs of the body. SCR 2/4
Poppies. SCR 9/3
The rain sings the song of my. SCR 3/3
Red. SCR 3/3
Sapphire seas. SCR 6/4
Say that you want me. SCR 1/4
Silver stars are not for me. SCR 7/4
Sunflowers. SCR 10/3
Theresa. SCR 9/2
Through the darkness spinning. SCR 12/2
What are men to me? SCR 2/3
Which? SCR 2/3
Whitsunday. SCR 5/3
Why should I want you? SCR 11/3
Yellow. SCR 3/3
Your name. SCR 1/4

Barkley, Frederick R.
Crow's nest. DEU 4/24/0
First night en route. DEU 4/17/1

Barnard, Edward W.
A ballade of ye twentie-fyfthe. FRE12/28/1

Barnes, Djuna
Crystals. NER 6/20/3
First communion. DIA 8/3
Pastoral. DIA 4/0
To the dead favorite of Liu Ch. DIA 4/0

Barnes, Eleanor
Wind in April. LIC 4/3

Barnes, Florence
Love and fate. MIN 5-6/4

Barnes, Peter
Dream kisses. COV 8/1

Barnett, Henry
Off the China coast. COV 2/1

Barnett, Mavis Clare
Miltonic. EME 3/4
Of a little sister. EME 3/4
The old men of the poorhouse. PAR #2/3
Silence. COV 12/2

Barney, Anna Louise
Arachne. CTY Sum/3
Crossing the bay. CTY W/1
I shall come back to you. AMP 2/2
Lover's lane. CTY Win/4
Memory. CTY S-A/4
Portrait. STE 10/3
September. AMP Aut/1
Storm fragments. AMP 2-3/3
The valley. CTY S-A/1
When all my ships. CTY Aut/2
Wild sunflowers. LAR 4/4

Barney, Danford
The guest. PAR #2/3

Barney, Natalie Clifford
To travel or not to travel. DIA 4/3

Baron, H. S.
Dreams. S4N 12/2

Baron, Jacques
L'Azur. LIR A-W/4

Barr, Elizabeth N.
Bath-sheba. STM 8/4

Barr, F. Stringfellow
L'envoi. GRI 8/0

Barr, Henrietta C.
A dune song. LYW 7-8/3
Immortality. LYW 7-8/2

Barr, Ronald W.
At parting. SCR 3/4
Atonement. SCR 11/3
Au revoir. SCR 7/4
Cherry blossoms. SCR 4/4
Dream rosary. SCR 1/4
Elegy (to Constance Olive Pain. SCR 1/4
La fille de joie. SCR 10/3
La golondrins. SCR 2/4
Lorraine. SCR 6/4
Memorial Day (1922). SCR 5/4
The organ grinder. LYR 8/4
Paulette, Leander to-. SCR 3/4
Semper fidelis. SCR 2/4
Shadows. SCR 2/4

Barrett, Lucile
Autumn's trail. HAM 10/1

Barrett, Mary
The pool. WAN 10/3
Savage noon. WAN 8/3
Barrett, Wilton Agnew
Lost river. EVM 11/0
Barrington, Pauline
The hill. LYW 4/1
The house. LYW 4/1
Interim. LYW 4/1
Los Angeles. LYW 11/1
The mirror. LYW 4/1
Wings. LYW 4/1
Barrow, Elfrida De Renne
Colors. POE 5/3
Concerning the world. POE 5/3
Dawn dream. REW 10/3
Death. POE 4/2
Futility. POE 5/3
God's acre. POM 1922
Habit and custom and I. POE 5/3
Hush. POE 5/3
I wonder. POE 4/2
Impressions. POE 4/2
Insomnia. POE 5/3
Presentment. POE 5/3
Recognition. POE 4/2
Traveling. POE 5/3
Twilight. POE 4/2
The wall between. POE 5/3
Winter sunset. CAS 1/3
Barrows, Marjorie
Suzanne's garden. STE 3/2
Barry, Bernice M.
Denial. AMP 4-5/3
Duty. AMP 12/3
Barry, Iris
Lamentation. POE 9/2
Nocturne. POE 9/2
An unposted letter. POE 9/2
Virgin moon. POE 9/2
Bartlett, Alice Hunt
Hunger. AMP 5-6/4
Patrollers of the skies. FLY 9/2
Radio. AMP 4-5/3
Bartlett, Frances
"The back shore." BOT 8/5/2
The spirit of Oxford. BOT 3/14/3
Bartlett, Ruth Fitch
She looks beyond tomorrow. HAM 10/4
Barton, Clara Virginia
Oregon. OVM 5/4
Barton, Ralph
The Declaration of Independenc. CSA 4/3
Bassett, Ruth
Baby's puff. GRA 10/2
God-thanks. GRA 5/2
Roses. AMP 3-4/4
Storms. GRA 7/2
This I know. AMP 12/3
Well seasoned. LYW 12/2
Batchelor, Jean M.
The letter. LYW 12/1
Lines for a sun dial. MEA 12/4
Trade's temple. GRA 12/1
Bates, Katharine Lee
At Camden. VOI Spr/2
At the tomb of Rachel. JEF 11/4
Autumn feather. FOR 10/3
The bodyguard. AIN 10/2
Brief life. YAR 10/0
Cedar hill. NOA 5/0
Christmas, 1923. CIT12/15/3
The debt. ATM 9/3
The dream. OVM 7/4
February 3, 1924. BOT 2/6/4
First love. COV 5/2
The flight of Asmodaeus. DOU 6/2
The glebe. NES 12/7/4
Robert Bridges and Thomas Hard. CAS 3/3
Sarah Threeneedles(Boston 1698. DOU 4/2
Shut out. VOI Aut/1
The spirit weaveth wings. STE 6/2
The stone mason. CIC11/23/2
Tired feet. CIT11/17/3
Too far. STE 12/4
Under the maples. PAR 1/4
Where time's long river. LYR 11/1
Batten, Therese K.
Dawn. CIJ 5/4
Baudelaire, Charles
The cracked bell. FUG 6/6/3
The former life. FUG 6/6/3
Ill luck. FUG 6/20/3
Spleen. FUG 6/20/3
Baxter, David
The blizzard Marde Gras. LAR 3/4
March. LAR 3/4
Baxter, Nelle Skinner
The dreamer. AMP 9-10/4
Baxter, Sylvester
The sage. CON 6/20/2
Sea-change. NET 3/21/0
The skeptic. CON 6/20/2
Beach, Gladys M.
Thoughts by a dying campfire. LAR 4/4
Beall, J. W.
Poetry. CIV 9-10/4
Beall, M. E.
The old book shop. AMP 2-3/3

Bealle, Alfred Battle
The adventurer. POE 5/0
Grasses and sand. POE 5/0
To an old man sitting in a cha. NOM Spr/3
Beals, A. M.
A memory. LAR 4/4
Beals, Carleton
The Apollo of Veii. BRO 3/3
Mexico. NER 8/25/0
Stigmatae. BRO 3/3
Bean, J. Herbert
Butterfly. LAL 10/4
Beaucaire, Anne
Alchemy. LAL 10/4
Devastation. CIV11-12/4
Even-song. SCR 8/4
On the dusk of night. CIV 5-6/4
A page of triolets. CIV 5-6/4
To a water-lily. LAL 10/4
Beaumont, Gerald
Castles in Spain. REB 4/3
The old school gang. REB 3/3
Beck, J. O.
On the mountain peaks. PUR 1/2
Beck, John Oscar
A towering sycamore. AMP11-12/4
Becket, Gene
Appeal. HEA 2/4
Beckhard, Arthur J.
The lights come on. GRA 5/1
Beddow, Elizabeth Russell
Florida coast. NOM Spr/3
October. NOM Sum/2
Recluse. NOM Spr/4
Beebe, Frances
The first death. LYW 9/3
Beebe, Lucius
Absence. VOI Spr/3
Corydon. YAR 10/3
Encore. AMP Aut/1
Euterpe. YAR 12/3
Island of the dead. VOI Spr/3
Quid restat. YAR 1/4
Beebe, Theodore B.
The parting. AMP Aut/1
Beede, Lillian Barker
My desert cross. LYW 2/3
Beeler, Florence Ashley
The coming of the sandman. AMP 2/2
From early morn till dewy eve. AMP 10/2
The lighthouse. MUS 11/4
One hour. MUS 12/4
Storm. AMP Aut/1
Beghtol, Charles
When I build my house. OVM 3/4
Behre, Edwine
At dawn. PAG 12/1
March night. LYW 3/2
Sketches from the Tyrol. LYW 12/2
Bein, Richard
Fragments from the Chinese. CAS 3/3
Bek, Herschell
Eternal remembrance. LYW 4/4
Mood. PAG 12/1
Poem. WAN 9/4
Summer heat. WAN 7/4
Tropic dawn. WAN 2/4
Belding, Alice
Fancy. AMP 5-6/4
Belknap, P.H.
The comfortable people. AIN 4/0
Bell, Jessica
Armistice Day. CTY S-A/1
Autumn. CTY S-A/1
A dream home. CTY S-A/1
A girl in a garden. AMP 12/2
John Burroughs. CTY S-A/1
Libation. AMP 8-9/3
Lilac weather. CYT Spr/2
Star gold. CTY Aut/2
Today in June. AMP 5-6/4
When plum trees are blooming. CTY Sum/2
Bellamann, Henry
Aline Carter. BRO 12/2
The artist. POE 11/1
Carrie Dyer. BRO 12/2
Charleston motifs. POM 1922
Concert pictures. MID 5/0
Cups of illusion. TEM Win2-3
Decorations for an imaginary... BRO 12/1
Edges. POE 11/1
Edna Bentley. BRO 12/2
Esther Cain. BRO 12/2
Fly-leaf. BRO 12/2
Funebre. TEM Aut/1
Gardens on the Santee. MEA 4/1
Gargoyles of Notre Dame. POE 11/1
The gate. MID 11/0
God. POE 11/1
The Gulf Stream. LYR 6/4
The gypsy. POE 10/4
Hedges. BRO 6/2
Heroic elegy. TEM Aut/1
High trees. POE 4/2
Homesickness. CEN 12/2
How quiet was my sea. MID 11/0
In a Charleston garden. REW 4/2
In modo barbaro. TEM Aut/1
Inland waterways. POM 1922
A last word. BRO 6/2
Leaf answers. REW 10/3
Louise Taylor. BRO 12/2

Lullaby. POE 11/1
Mary Larkin. BRO 12/2
Moonlight. MID 11/0
Nets on the water. SOU 7/3
Now is purple. MEA 1/2
Pause. SOU 7/3
Peaks. POE 11/1
Poppies. SOU 7/3
Portrait sonnets, I, II, III,. VOI Aut/1
The pursuit. MEA 8/2
Question. MEA 1/2
The return. TEM 6/1
Sand hills. MEA 4/1
Sea thought among the hills. FUG 12/3
Sequentials. SOU 7/3
Skylines. FUG 12/3
Songs of discontent. VOI 6-7/3
A sound in the mullberry trees. YAR 10/2
The stranger. LYR 7/2
Sue Kittrell. BRO 12/2
Thinning mist. VOI Sum/2
Through a hundred gates. AMP Aut/1
Toward the winds. LYR 5/2
When the world goes home. NOA 4/1
Winter burial. NOA 4/1

Bellemin, Frank J.
The Alamo. LAR 2/3
Beethoven. LAR 2/3
Builders. LAR 3/4
Keeping on the job. LAR 3/3

Belloc, Hilaire
Tarantella. CEN 4/1

Bellows, Donald
Horizons. SMA 1/3

Bemis, Katharine Prescott
Four heart flowers. LAR 11/3
The road to Spain. AMP10-11/3

Bendall, Wilfird H.
Sixth poem. BRO 10/3

Benedict, Ida
Horizons. DET 12/8/3

Benedict, Libbian
Explanation. NAT 5/28/4

Benet, Laura
Enemies. BOO 12/1
Falling water. VOI 9-10/4
Hope. AIN 6/2
Humor. NES ?/1
Islands. NAT 5/28/4
Tadpoles. DOU 2-3/4
Tancock Island. VOI 9-10/4

Benet, Stephen Vincent
All night lone. NER 2/7/3
Azrael's bar. BOO 2/1
The ballad of William Sycamore. NER 11/8/2
Carol. NAT 4/16/4
Days pass. VAN 4/2
Difference. NER 6/15/1
Flood tide. YAR 10/0
July. BOO 7/1
King David. NAT 2/14/3
Lost. NES 3/1/4
Men pass. VAN 4/2
New style. NAT 4/16/4
Oh, tricksy April. NER 4/26/2
Operation. COV 12/0
Under green trees. AIN 1/0
X-ray. NER 5/21/4

Benet, William Rose
Adversary. CEN 5/1
Animalcule. NES 7/29/2
The beating heart. NER11/16/1
Cesar Franck. VOI 6-7/3
Doppelganger. NER 2/1/2
Dust on the plains. CEN 3/0
The faun in the snow. NER 4/12/2
Fire and glass. CEN 1/2
The fugitive. NER 6/1/1
The gray plower. OUT10/22/4
Heat on the Gulf. VOI 6-7/3
"Junkets," immortal. NES 2/26/1
Moon rider. NER 3/7//3
Primum Mobile. NER 7/18/3
The south wind. BOO 5/2
Stage directions. NER 1/3/3
To Henry J. Ford, Illustrator.. BOO 1/0
To a falcon. BOO 4/4
Turpin at Vauxhall. BUC 12/4
The wood-cutter's wife. SCM 8/4

Bennett, John
The wandering minstrel's song. POM 1922

Bennett, Joy
Thoughts. LYW 2/2
To you. LYW 2/2

Bennett, Matthew
Consolation. MES 12/4
Regret. MES 12/4
They. MES 11/4

Bennett, Raine
The golden lake of Naishapur. WAN 9/3
In Fabre's garden. LYW 10/3
An old lady sits by the window. WAN 6/3
Prophesy. WAN 6/4
When the muezzin calls. WAN 9/3
The wolf. WAN 3/4

Bennett, Sara E.
Rhythm. COV 6/1

Benninger, Annie
Songs. WAN 11/3

Benshimol, Ernest
Sonnet of life. COV 7/3
Under the cypress. COV 7/3
Benson, Arthur Christopher
Dedication (of Lord Vyet & oth. GRA 6/3
Lord Vyet. GRA 6/3
Benson, Louis F.
A carol of Christmas... COV 12/4
Hymn for Arbor Day. COV 12/4
A melody for love and life. COV 12/4
Benson, Stella
If you were careless. POE 9/0
Wild trees in February. BOO 8/2
Bentley, Booth
Formosa. POE 2/3
Benvenuta, Sister Mary
To pain. CAW 6/1
Berenberg, David P.
Echoes. MEA 2/4
John Peters. MES 10/4
Nocturne. GUL 6/3
Pedagogue. NOM Aut/3
Recognition. NOM Aut/3
Semiramis. GUL 5/3
Sic transit. GUL 5/3
Silences. LIB 10/2
Two sonnets. MEA 2/2
Words. MES 8/4
Your halo. MEA 1/2
Berkshire, Thomas Randall
Death. COV 3/4
The last dance. COV 3/4
The old man. COV 3/4
Berry, Annabel Ledlie
Blindness. LAL 5/4
Berry, Elizabeth Robbins
Our unknown dead. BOT 6/5/0
Berry, Raymond Alvin
The buoys of prayer. LYW 7-8/3
Besse, J. N.
In the "jungle," Second Avenue. LAL 9/4
Best, Marshall Ayres
Harvard class poem. BOP 6/20/3
Bete, Clara R.
A caged fancy. AMP 8/2
Betts, Craven Langstroth
Roosevelt. TEM Aut/1
Betts, Thomas Jefferson
Ballade of forgotten wars. SCM 8/0
Beyers, Anna F.
Keep out bitterness. AMP 10/2
Mystery. AMP 12/3
Beyers, Meredith
Bits of curl. POE 6/2
Fat man. POE 6/2

Bialik, Chaim N.
The house of eternity. GUA 12/4
Tonight I waited. GUA 12/4
Bibesco, Elizabeth
A poem. NER 4/9/4
Bichols, Beth Cheney
Songs from the sea. AMP 8/3
Bickley, Beulah Vick
Ancestry. COV 2/2
At twilight hour. CTY Aut/2
The dreamer. AMP Aut/1
First class mail. CTY Win/4
The gardener. CTY S-A/1
The great American (T.R.). CTY W/2
Heaven. AMP 9-10/4
In memory. CTY W/2
Joy for a little house. AMP 9-10/4
Mastery. AMP 2/2
Mid-western stars. CTY Spr/2
My bargain. CTY S-A/4
My star flower. TEM 6/1
A scarlet tanager. AMP 8-9/3
The spirit of the hearth. CTY S-A/1
Tis love that calls you home. CTY Spr/2
Biddle, Francis X.
I was a ship. LIB 4/2
November 11th. LIB 3/2
Billings, Warren T.
The church without walls. GRA 11/1
Billy (pseud.), Uncle
Archangel Bill. COV 11/3
Canto three. COV 11/3
Jesus's joke. COV 2/2
Jimmy Jones in heaven. COV 11/3
Binkley, James Malcolm
Grant just these two. SCR 9/2
Remembrance. SCR 9/2
Binns, Archie
Going home. TEM 4/1
Passing at night. MEA 12/1
Birch-Bartlett, Helen
Belshazzzar. POE 2/0
The bringer of gifts. POE 2/0
Drift. POE 2/0
Epilogue. POE 2/0
First class mail. CTY Win/3
The lake. POE 2/3
Lola wears lace. POE 2/3
The moonlight dance. POE 2/3
Premonitions. POE 2/0
Quest for beauty. AMP 12/2
Re-encounter. POE 2/0
Remembrance. POE 2/0
Smoke-stack dragons. CTY Win/3
Bird, James

The cat bird. STE 6/3
A greeting from a bookfellow. STE 8/3
Vita et mors. STE 9/3

Bird, Stephen Moylan
Harpalyce. VOI Aut/2
Higher dawn. COV 10/2
Llewellyn. VOI Aut/2
The witch. COV 10/2
Your hair. COV 10/2

Bishop, Flora J.
The bunny. WAN 8/4
Moods of a lake. SOV 1923

Bishop, John Peale
The death of a dandy. VAN 4/2
Epithalamium. S4N 3-4/3
The hunchback. POE 6/1
Twelfth night. SCM 12/3

Bishop, Morris
Dementia praecox. POE 10/4
Ecclesiastes. POE 3/2
A New Hampshire boy. POE 3/2
The old photograph. POE 10/4
Some words to Moliere. NES 6/3/2

Bishop, Ralph Parker
Amaryllis. LYW 4/4
Words. LYW 4/3

Bissell, W. T.
Sonnet. YAR 2/4

Bjorkman, Edwin
Felicia. REW 12/1
The pond. REW 5/2
Song of the bowl. REW 12/1

Black, MacKnight
Advice. FOR 8/4
Before new birth. LYR 11/4
"Dead on the field of..." COV 2/3
Give not with your hands. NAT 8/6/4
Indulgence. COV 2/3
March earth. LYR 11/4
November earth. SVG 11/3
Poets. COV 11/4
The return. SVG 4/3
The secret strength. VOI 5-6/4
Setting out. COV 2/3
Shadow drum. COV 1/4
South wind. COV 1/4
Storm. COV 1/4
Suspension bridge pier... COV 11/4
Three poems. COV 8/3
Three workers. COV 11/4
To a truck driver. VOI 7-8/3
Witness. COV 12/2

Blackburn, Irma Grace
Beauty's feet. SCR 11/4
A man is rich. OVM 12/4
White hands of winter. BUC 12/4

Blackman, Kate
Love's departure. LYW 4/3
Song of the reeds. LYW 2/2

Blackney, Lena Whittaker
I shall go back. ALS 7/3

Blair, Marlow Dilwin
The lost lady. COV 8/4

Blake, Adeline O'Bryon
Nearing shore. CIV11-12/4
Spring clouds. CIV 1/4

Blake, Adeline O'Byron
Lady ocean. CIV 3/4

Blake, Alice
Gray lady. WAN 10/3
Sonnet. WAN 2/4

Blake, Bertha H.
On the jetties, Miami Beach. STE 2/4

Blake, Pansy
Kisses on my hair. AMP 12/2

Blake, William B.
Comparisons. SCR 2/4
My valentine. SCR 2/4

Blake, Winifred Ballard
Vision. POA 9/1

Blanchard, Ames
When learning palls. COV 6/0

Blanchard, Amy E.
A day. EVM 11/0

Blanchard, Grace
School time. GRA 9/3

Blanchard, Margaret
True living. CIJ 11/3

Bland, Henry Meade
Hills of Sutter. OVM 7/4
Writing the ballade. WRM 8/4

Blanden, Charles Granger
Apple blossoms. CHT 7/26/2
The bell. CHT11/16/1
Caravans. CIC 2/25/3
The changelings. CHT10/20/1
Chicago. CHT 1/31/2
Daffodils. CHT 6/1/2
The dancing shadow. OVM 3/4
Day break. ALS 5/2
The deserted house. CHT11/20/1
Deserts. CIC12/11/4
Duality. CHT11/26/1
For him who calls his heart... CIC 11/2/2
From matin song to vesper bell. CIC 9/13/3
Fulfillment. CHT 3/1/2
Fusion. CHT 10/8/1
The ghost. LYR 3/3
Hours. CHT 7/15/2
In March. CHT 3/14/2
In a forest. CHT 7/28/2
The invisible singer. CIC

9/27/3
Lincoln. CIC 2/22/3
Lincoln. CIC 5/22/4
Little windows. CHT 8/7/2
Lowly lives. LYR 3/3
Naked trees. CHT 4/6/2
New altars. ALS 2-3/3
Oasis. CIC 10/2/4
Octave. CHT 7/12/2
Overtones. CHT 8/29/1
The passing throng. CHT 1/24/2
The poet. LYR 11/2
Prayer. CIC 6/9/4
Quatrain. CIC 7/24/4
The reef of care. CHT11/27/1
The road to Bethany. OVM 12/4
Roosevelt. CHT10/27/1
Shadows. CHT 7/31/2
Shrines. CHT 4/17/2
Song (...to Shillington). CHT 5/17/2
Song. CHT 9/21/1
Song. CIC10/18/3
Song. PEG 3/3
Sonnet. CIC 5/3/3
The Statue of Liberty speaks. ALS10-11/2
Sunset leaves. CHT11/10/1
A tear bottle. CHT 8/27/1
To a mocking bird. LYR 6/3
To a ruby-throated hummingbird. CHT 7/22/2
Torrey pines. OVM 6/4
Truth. ALS 4/2
Ultima Thule. CHT11/25/1
The unknown God. CIC 1/18/3
The weaver. CHT 8/30/1
The winds of dawn. CHT 11/7/1
Winter joys. CIC 2/23/2
Wullie Campbell's dream. CHE 5/2
Yesterday. CHT 8/3/1

Blanding, Henriette de S.
Exile. COV 6/3

Blanker, Fredericka
Walls. FOR 11/4

Blankner, Frederocl V.
To cypresses. DOU11-12/4

Bliss, Gordon
Intimations. CIC 5/29/4

Bliss, Martha Hart
Prophets. SVG 4/3

Block, Louis James
The gold and crimson sun. STE 6/2
Outlooks. CAP 5/3

Block, Ralph
After Rachmaninoff. POE 3/0

Bloom, Charles Norman
Frailty. BOO 8/4
Wind-jammers. VOI 5-6/4

Blumenthal, Minnie Edith
Italian lullaby. INT 7-9/4

Blunden, Edmund
Almswomen. CEN 4/1
Changing moon. LYW 7/4
Country sale. YAR 7/2
Rural economy (Flanders, 1917). LYR 6/3
The shadow. YAR 7/2

Blunt, Hugh F.
At the foot of the Cross. MAG 11/4
Bethlehem. MAG 12/1
For Our Lady's crowning. MAG 8/3
God's handmaid. MAG 3/2
Her pathway. MAG 6/2
The holy house. MAG 10/1
In Maytime. MAG 5/2
A little child shall lead. MAG 12/4
My rosary. MAG 10/3
A rhymer's prayer. MAG 9/4
To Saint Joseph. MAG 3/2

Blunt, Wilfrid Seawen
The wind and the whirlwind. NAT12/10/4

Boal, Frances
Trop tard. COM12/10/4

Bock, Frances MacFarland
Up from the dry arroyo. AMP 2-3/3

Bodenheim, Maxwell
Advice to my young wife. CEN 11/2
Ah! critics. CHL 8/1/3
And if I say. NES 3/10/3
Boarding-house episode. DIA 2/0
Challenge. DOU 3-4/3
City streets. NAT 3/21/3
City-girl. LIB 7/2
Concerning roses. POE 9/3
Cry, naked and personal. MIL 12/2
Dear Minna. NAT 5/10/2
Decadent cry. DIA 4/3
Definitions. REW 4/3
Dress-model. DOU 12/1
Emotional monologue. POE 5/1
Ending. DIA 2/0
Envious poet. NAT 7/4/3
Feminine talk. POE 5/1
Fifth Avenue. DIA 2/0
Flapper. BOO 11/2
Garbage-heap. DOU 4/2
Helena protests. NES12/29/3
Imaginary people. DOU 2/2
The incurable mystic answers... DOU 10/2

Inevitable. MOR Aut/2
Instructions for a ballet. DIA 3/2
Intense comment. BOO 10/4
Landscape. BOO 9/2
Mabel Callahan. REW 4/4
Negro criminal. BOO 10/1
Negro laborer. NAT 7/5/2
New York City. NAT 2/21/3
Office girl. NAT 7/4/3
Old actor. DOU 2/2
Old theme. POE 10/4
Philosophical dialogue. POE 5/1
Pine trees. NES 5/14/1
Poems to Minna. NAT 5/28/4
Poet's love letter. NAT 12/3/4
Portrait. BRO 3/3
Rattlesnake mountain fable. YAR 10/0
Realistic creator. BOO 5/3
Rhymed conversation with money. BOO 11/3
Sappho answers Aristotle. POE 5/1
The scullion and the queen. COV 4/4
The servant of the prince. NAT 3/26/4
Sonnet to Minna. NAT10/29/4
Sonnet to Minna. DOU 2-3/4
Sonnet to my wife. DOU 1/2
Sonnet. DIA 2/0
Summer evening:New York subway. DIA 8/1
Sunlight on the avenue. POE 10/4
The sword converses with a phi. DOU 10/2
To a baby. NAT 8/22/3
To a country girl. YAR 7/2
To a playing child. NES 9/13/4
Truck drivers. DOU 7/2
Two sonnets to my wife. MEA 12/1
Two women on a street. DIA 2/0
Underworld note. DOU 3/2
The universe and the green dra. DOU 1/4
Village-clerk. DOU 12/1
A visitor from Mars smiles. NAT 4/4/3
When fools dispute. DIA 2/0

Bodine, William Lester
Lake Geneva. NOW 7/3

Bodkin, Muriel Cameron
Chalice. FOR 12/4

Bogan, Louise
The alchemist. NER 2/22/2
The catalpa tree. VOI 12-1/4
The changed woman. RHY 6-7/3
The crows. NES 4/15/2
Decoration (for W.). NER 8/24/1
Elders. POE 8/2
The frightened man. MEA 2/3
A girl to Juan. MEA 5/4
Knowledge. POE 8/2
Last hill in a vista. MEA 11/2
Leave-taking. POE 8/2
Medusa. NER12/21/1
Memory. NER 5/10/2
Portrait. LIB 4/2
Resolve. POE 8/2
The romantic. MEA 2/3
Song for a slight voice. CEN 11/4
Song. VOI 12/2
Stanza. MEA 11/2
Statue and birds. NER 4/12/2
The stones. MEA 6/3
A tale. NER10/19/1
To a dead lover. POE 8/2
Trio. MEA 6/3
Women. MEA 2/2
Words for departure. MEA 4/1

Boissevain, Mynhart J.
Adagio. LYW 7-8/2

Boll, Helene M.
The birth of a thought. PAR #4/4
Close at my heart. PAR #4/4
Credo. CIV 5-6/4
Fire. PAR #2/3
Joy. MAC 11/3
Symbols. CIV 9-10/4
Twice. PAR #4/4
Twilight. LAL 5/4

Bolling, Bertha
Pan's garden. SCM 12/4
The spirit of the dawn. SCM 12/2

Bond, George D.
Late autumn. SOV 1923

Bond, Josiah
Arizona. ARI 11/2
Crystal robes. ARI 11/2
Drilling song. ARI 11/2
From days of old. ARI 11/2
The holy birthday. ARI 11/2
Homer. ARI 11/2
The merciful nimrods. ARI 11/2
Our first born. ARI 11/2
Why evolution is slow. ARI 11/2

Bone (tr.,), L. Addison
Evening. STE 10/4

Bonner (Jr.), Leonard
Inspiration. GRA 5/1

Bonner, Amy
Poise. POE 5/1
Revelations. POE 5/1

Boogher, Susan M.

Cumulative death. HAM 2/1
Fugitive. POE 11/0
The seeker. REW 10/4

Booth, Edward Townsend
To a New England girl. POE 4/1
To an authentic priest. POE 4/1

Bordersen, Helen Hicks Bates
Mona Kinsella. AMP 6-7/3

Borland, Evelyn Bourne
Confession. OVM 2/4
The hour of my delight. OVM 6/4

Borland, Hal
The old chief. GUA 12/4

Borland, Harold G.
The flute player. LYW 6/2

Borland, Mary
The bowl. FOR 11/3
Evening. FOR 9/4
Into the woods. COV 8/4
Loneliness. COV 1/4
Petra, the lost city. FOR 3/4

Bornholdt, Florence Parker
For I was wed today. LYW 4/1
The Malibu Hills. LYW 4/1
My art looks up. LYW 9/1

Borst, Beatrice West
A cycle. LYW 12/2
My neighbor's journey. LYW 11/3
The soul of a woman. LYW 12/2

Borst, Richard Warner
In a mail order house. MID 3/1
Under the live oak tree. LYW 5/4
The waiting supper. OVM 7/4

Bosschere, Jean
The offering of Plebs. BRO 2/2

Bossee, Mary E.
A cousin to Tithonus. POM 1922
A cousin to Tithonus. SOU 8/3

Bostick, Louise Stedman
Song of a mountain flower. LYW 11/1
Sunset. LYW 5/4
The visitor. LYW 11/1

Boston, Everett
Psalms of the sea: dreams. DOU11-12/4
Psalms of the sea: the rivals. DOU 10/4
Psalms of the sea. DOU 7/4
Psalms of the sea: the reason. DOU 8-9/4

Boston, Grace
What have you done! AMP 9-10/4

Bostwick, G. G.
Sanctuary. LYW 10/3

Botroff, Christo
My prayer. STE 2/4

Boulton, Hilda Brann
Beggars. LYW 3/3

Boutelle, Grace Hodsdon
It vanished. POE 8/1

Boutwell, Edgar
Conscience. DOU 10/2
Work. DOU 10/2

Bowdoin, Peter
"Love in whose name." MEA 5/3

Bowen, Helen
Scent of sage. SCM 3/4

Bowen, Stirling
April. LIB 6/2
Autumn. LIB 10/2
Cages. BOO 12/1
Cartoons of the French Rev... MEA 6/1
Chinatown. DEU12/12/0
The city children. DEU 4/17/1
The cobbler's daughter. MEA 12/3
Danton. BOO 1/3
The deserted room. LIB 11/1
Evening song. LIB 8/2
Gallery night. DEU 2/20/1
The gold rush, 1849. LIB 9/1
Impressions. DEU 5/18/0
In the golden age. LIB 10/1
Marat. BOO 1/3
The milkman's boy. MEA 12/3
A mulatto girl-in police court. LIB 11/1
Napoleon. BOO 1/3
Nocturne. DEU 6/20/0
On the hilltop. DEU 1/30/1
The poet. BOO 3/4
The private secretary. BOO 3/4
The rainbow's end. LIB 9/1
Revelation. DEU 5/2/0
The school teacher. BOO 3/4
Snow. DEU 1/2/1
Sonnet (for G.B.). DEU 3/21/0
Spring song. DEU 8/22/0
To a girl of Chinatown. DEU10/10/0
Two sonnets. DEU 1/18/0
Voltiare. BOO 1/3

Bower (see Frazee-B), Helen

Bower, Helen
Wanderlust. LIB 2/2

Bowles, O. J.
Aerial. LYW 10/1
Clouds. LYW 10/1
Walls. LYW 11/2

Bowman, Forrest
Consummation. DEU 3/28/0
Disillusion. DEU 1/16/1
Le reve. DEU 2/8/0

Bowman, J. E.
Poet and pilgrim. GRA 5/1

Bowman, Louise Morey

Bread and fire. BOO 7/4
Florence. POE 9/4
Rome. POE 9/4
Venice. POE 9/4

Boyce, Faith
The house of our dreams. SOU 7/3
Shadows. SOU 7/3

Boyd, Marion M.
Gravity. BOO 11/4
Indian summer. COV 10/0
Wistful doubting. COV 5/4

Boyd, Vaida Stewart
Stampede. BUC 12/4

Boyesen, Bayard
Lake. BRO 11/1

Boyesson, Bayard
In the forest. AIN 4/0

Boyle, Kay
Monody to the sound of zithers. POE 12/2
Morning. BRO 1/3

Boyne, Madge
Dawn. SCR 11/4
My world. SCR 12/4
Wealth. SCR 12/4

Brackett, Charles
The florist shop. CEN 1/0

Bradbury, Brooks
Vice versa. LYR 5/3

Bradford, Gamaliel
All the same. LYR 5/4
The anniversary. SCM 10/1
The blot. COV 1/4
Books and peace. STE 1/4
The butterflies. OUT 1/2/4
Cherry-buds. TEM Aut/1
The cicada. AMP 8/2
The comfortable grave. COV 11/0
A common case. VOI Aut/1
Damned. LYR 5/4
Dreams. LYR 12/4
The fabric. COV 4/2
Facility. LYR 1/4
The fisherman. COV 1/4
Flight of kisses. LYR 8/3
God's humour. LYR 5/4
Her great-grandmother. COV 4/3
Hymn to ignorance. NES 6/3/2
Illimitable. COV 4/2
Life's honey. COV 4/3
Love's perversity. LYR 8/3
Mare amoris. LYR 10/2
Mary Stuart. CAS 3/3
Morality. LYR 8/3
My art. LYR 5/4
My delight. COV 11/0
My grave. LYR 5/4
My trees. LYR 5/4
Peace with God. LYR 5/4
The problem. COV 4/3
Rain. NES 8/23/4
Rhyme. AMP 2/2
Roses. BOO 8/2
Sin's assaults. LYR 5/4
Song of the sea rover. MIN 5-6/3
The surprise. OUT 1/4/2
The thing to do. COV 4/2
The thyroid gland. FOR 11/4
Two poems. MIN 9-10/3
Wholesome hell. COV 11/0
Why? LYR 2/4

Bradley, Mary Davis
Lullaby. LAR 11/3

Bradley, Mary D.
Bethel. LAR 5/3

Bradley, Virginia Burton
Gathering figs. LYW 11/1

Brady, Emeline Margaret
The portrait, to Lola. LYW 12/1

Brady, Kathryne Helen
Dawn. SCR 8/4
Shadow souls. SCR 8/4
Sunset. SCR 3/4
Triumph. SCR 4/4

Braganca, Anita
Keats. HAM 10/1

Brainerd, Clarence J.
Dead old dad. CTY S-A/4
The land of bards. CTY Spr/4
The yellow streak. CTY Sum/3

Braithwaite, William Stanley
Damsons. EME 6/3
Eyes. LYW 7-8/2
The gift. LYR 2/4
The hanging house. LYW 7-8/2
I saw the first ploughing. EME 6/3
Mockery. LYR 9/4
An old moon. LYW 3/3
Old winds. LYR 10/2
The one-way door. LYR 6/4
The warning. LYR 10/2

Braley, Berton
The dash after the period. CSA 5/3
Empty. SCM 12/3
Enchantment. HAM 4/0
Renascence. HAM 1/0

Branch, Anna Hempstead
Inheritance. NES 7/5/4

Branch-White, Florence
Bird man. AMP 3-4/4
Rain. AMP 3-4/4
Slumber. AMP 3-4/4
The uniform. AMP 3-4/4
You. AMP 3-4/4

Brandt, Zelma Corning
To Henrietta Rodman. SVG 6/3

Branford, F. V.
The idiot. DIA 4/4
Branham, Juliet
After operation. CEN 10/3
A cocotte to a firefly. BOO 1/4
Issue. COV 2/4
Branson, Anna M.
The dreamer. SCM 9/4
Brant, Irving
A-wing. BOT10/14/2
The wild rose. MID 2/1
Brayton, John
Supplicant. OVM 9/4
Breese, Alan
In you. LIB 1/2
The snow again. LIB 12/1
Bregy, Katherine
The sword. COV 8/4
Brehm, Albert G.
Sympathy. AMP 6-7/3
Bremer, Anne
Bare boughs. WAN 8/3
Compensation. WAN 8/3
The journey. WAN 8/3
Mist. WAN 8/3
Sketch. WAN 8/3
Snow. WAN 8/3
Still life. LYW 11/3
Breton, Nicholas
Attar of roses. MUN 3/2
Ballade of fish in the sea. MUN 6/2
To Phyllida in the city. MUN 7/2
Brewer, Wheaton Hale
Equinox. LYW 10/2
Red embers. LYW 10/2
Sea thought. LYW 4/4
Brewster, Margaret Cable
An epitaph. SCM 5/0
Bridges, Downham
Argument. SON 2/1
Enigma. SON 2/1
Manumission. SON 2/1
Refuge. SON 2/1
Bridges, Robert
Buch der lieder. YAR 7/3
Bridgman, Amy Sherman
Cold. COV 1/1
Bright, Verne
Beauty. CYT S-A/4
Chant for a swift runner. WAN 10/4
Free. LAR 6/3
Gray April. SCR 3/4
I have been glad. OVM 5/4
Manila. WAN 3/4
Sappho in Lesbos. BUC 11/4
Sone for an Oregon spring. LAR 2/4
Zamboango. SCR 5/4
Brinkman (tr.), Florence
At parting. FRE 4/5/2
Cries of the raven. FRE 4/5/2
Epitaph to a warrior. FRE 4/5/2
From the west window. FRE 4/5/2
Marching to war. FRE 4/5/2
Ode to Nanking. FRE 7/12/2
Brintnall, Edna Goit
Chinatown. LYW 11/1
Deathless. LYW 1/3
Brisbin, Marshall Ney
Life. LAR 9/3
Broadus, Kemper Hammond
Blizzard. POE 5/2
Burnt out. POE 5/2
Brockman, Lucy N. W.
Cadences. AMP 9-10/4
Gain. AMP 4-5/3
Loss. AMP 4-5/3
Mysteries. AMP 9-10/4
The solstices. AMP 4-5/3
A suite. AMP 4-5/3
The sycamores of Iowa. AMP 9-10/4
Brockman, Zoe Kincaid
Land of dreams. AMP 10/2
Lines. AMP 2/2
Brody, Alter
Clocks. BOO 8/3
Grandmother. POE 12/2
Invincible. BOO 8/1
Nocturne from a window. CLT Spr/2
On the screen. CLT Spr/2
Spring. DIA 5/0
Bromberger, Anna
In the subway. GUL 7-8/3
Brooke, William E.
Spoil. SVG 2/4
Brooks, Clarissa
Biblio-philanthropy. STE 4/4
A knitting song. STE 10/3
Of love and death. STE 7/2
Brooks, Fannie
The beginning. CTY Spr/3
Compensation. CTY Spr/2
Makin' hay. CTY S-A/1
Snowflakes. CTY W/2
The thief. CTY Aut/2
Brooks, William E.
The song in the night. SVG 12/1/2
Brown (Jr.), Howard H.
Nocturne. YAR 5/4
Brown, Abbie Farwell
Berries. EME 2/3
The cave. COV 8/1
Ciphers. COV 10/0
Grandser. COV 7/3

Pirate treasure. COV 10/0
Silhouette. LYR 2/4
The tempting Polly. COV 12/1

Brown, Alice
The adventurer. NOA 1/1
Apples. HAM 2/1
Autolycus. YAR 1/4
Enchantment. COV 6/0
The ever changing. HAM 7/1
Heliotrope. HAM 9/1
The trees. HAM 2/0

Brown, Alison
Homing. AMP 3-4/4

Brown, Alta Wrenwick
But love, ah!, love! AMP 9-10/4

Brown, Ellen Lucy
The oriole. GRA 9/2

Brown, Georgiana
Love's old charms. WOW 4/0

Brown, Grace Evelyn
Nocturne. AMP 8/2
River wraiths. VOI Aut/2
Window. NOM Win/2

Brown, Joan
Modesty. MIN11-12/4

Brown, Leah
The beauty of nature. POA 9/1

Brown, Marion Francis
Boscobel. VOI 12/4
Brush fires. AMP11-12/4
Compromise. LYR 10/4
God bless flappers. HEA 9/4
Identity. AMP 8/2
Life's debtor. LYR 12/4
Poignancy. AMP11-12/4
Saturation. AMP 1-2/4
Wayfarer's prayer. AMP 8/2
When spring comes back to Gile. AIN 3/2

Brown, Sarah-Margaret
From Chicago "L" POE 2/2
Tryst. POE 8/3

Brown, Sydney B.
I gathered violets in your eye. AMP 3-4/4

Brown, Sydney Barlow
Question. AMP 4-5/3
Romance. AMP 10/2

Browne, Harriet Augusta
Famine. AMP 4-5/3

Browne, Jonathan
Frustration. VOI 5-6/4
A late remonstrance. VOI 5-6/4

Browne, P. W. Stella
Epitaph by Pierre Louys. FRE 2/28/3
Memorial Day. SVG 6/3
On a statue of Lincoln. SVG 2/3
Refuge. SVG 1/3
Shepherd's song by Pierre Louy. FRE 2/28/3

Brownell, Baker
Be a sport. DIA 5/3
School teacher. POE 5/3
Soil. POE 5/3
The wave. DIA 12/0
Words. POE 5/3
Work-horse. POE 5/3

Bruncken, Herbert Gerhard
Are you with me here? MIN 5-6/4
At the grave..Edward MacDowell. MIN11-12/4
Rondeau. MIN 9-10/3
The town clock. MIN 5-6/3

Bryan, Amanda
Lilies. REW 10/3

Bryan, George S.
Anathema. BOO 10/2
Cats and men. BOO 3/4

Bryan, Jack
Tranquility. DEP Fall/3

Bryant, Gladys
Bound. WAN 11/4
An old woman, weeping. WAN 2/4
Reflection. LIB 2/2
The return. LIB 10/1

Bryant, Louise
Aftermath. LIB 11/1
Russian memories. DIA 5/0

Bryden, J.
Memory. CAS 3/3

Bryher, Winifred
Episode. NOA 5/0
Wild rose. POE 12/0

Bryne, M. St. Clare
In after days. MAC 10/2

Bryning, Winifred Livingstone
Messengers of hope. BOT 2/4/2

Bryther, Winifred
Gulls. POE 11/4
Out of boyhood. POE 11/4
Thessalian. POE 11/4

Buchanan, Allison
The unloved. POE 3/2

Buchanan, Jean
Fifth Avenue Heather. AMP 1-10/4

Buck, Howard
Plush. POE 8/4

Buckley, Nancy
Alien. OVM 11/4
The artist speaks. POA 1/2
"At shut of evening flowers." LYW 4/2
Christmas prayer. MAG 12/4
Dawn-magic. AMP 5-6/4
Emanuel. MAG 11/4
The hills of Connemara. OVM

10/4
Homing. MAG 8/4
"Laughter and longing." LYW 4/3
Lilacs. OVM 2/4
Mater Dolorosa. MAG 9/4
The spinner. MAG 7/2

Bugbee, Perley R.
The hillside's chief. GRA 5/1
A meteor headstone. GRA 12/0
A winter's night. GRA 3/2

Bulknap, Helen Runyon
Correspondences. LYW 10/1

Bull, Lois M.
Three fantasies. AMP 12/2

Bullen, John Ravenor
Far distant bells. POA 9/1

Bunch, Audred
A daughter of the dust. LAR 4/3
Foreboding. OVM 5/4
I don't say what I think. LAR 2/4
Sacrament. LYW 6/3

Bunin, Ivan Aleksieevich
A song. FRE 8/17/1

Bunker, John
The inn. CAW 11/0
The old woman. COM11/12/4

Bunner, Alice C.
Premonition. SCM 12/2

Bunner, Anne
The sixty-ninth of "Fragments" SCM 10/0

Bunten, Florence Hines
The night path. SCM 2/3

Burcham, Mildred
The road. SCR 1/4

Burgess, Bangs
A mountain spring. OVM 7/4

Burgess, Dorothy
Alien. MEA 12/4
As the waves sink into sand. LYR 12/4
Fall panel. VOI 3-4/4
October twilight. LYR 11/4
There is no wonder now. LYR 12/4
Vision. LYR 8/4
Water I'll have. OUT 9/10/4

Burgess, Gelett
Ballade of the derby hat. HAM 5/3

Burgess, Robert Louis
Flute. WAN 11/3
Girls. MEA 5/3
I rejoice that the swallow. LYW 6/3
The Lady Elizabeth smokes. STE 3/4
Like a young plum tree. PAG 9-10/1
Melissa. POE 10/3
Peasant. FRE 9/5/3
To my lady the universe. MEA 8/4
Worship. STE 1/4

Burke, Barbara
Freckles. PAL Spr/3

Burke, Francis
Ambition. DEU 5/2/0
Disconsolate. DEU 5/2/0

Burke, John J.
A wounded bird. AMP 5-6/4

Burke, Kenneth
Two portraits. S4N 12/2
Ver renatus orbis est. COT Adver#

Burlingame, Roger
Interval. SCM 5/0
Romance. SCM 11/4

Burman, Ben Lucien
Ballad of Piney Ridge. CEN 3/4

Burn, Audrey
Mystic spring. BUC 12/4

Burnaby, Hugh
On the Thames. SCM 12/0

Burnell, Judge
Woes of the Fontanas. LAR 2/4

Burnham, Eleanor McC.
A promise. AMP 6-7/3

Burns, Aubrey
The sky at dawn. SOV 1923
Sunsets and dawns. SOV 1923
Texas silhouette. SOV 1923

Burns, Mary Paul
The poet muses. AMP 6-7/2
Twilight. AMP 6-7/2

Burnshaw, Stanley A.
Aesthetes. VOI 11/4
After storm: August. VOI 11/4
Communion. SCR 5/4
Core of night. VOI 11/4
Dark clouds. SCR 5/4
October noon. CIV 9-10/4
Remains. LYR 6/4
Starlight. SCR 4/4

Burr, Amelia Josephine
Blue water. BOO 2/0
Enough for me. OUT 3/16/1
Florence. SCM 7/3
Island. OUT 7/6/1
Life eternal. LAD 2/4
The little son. SCM 4/1
The rainy day. COV 5/0
Sanctuary. SCM 6/4
To a scarlet lizard. OUT 1/7/0
Trincomalee. LYR 11/1
Two songs. COV 1/1
Typhoon. BOO 6/1
The victor. OUT 3/31/0

Warning. OUT ?/1
The wedding journey. EVM 11/0
West of Suez. SCM 9/1

Burroughs, Jack
A child questions me. HAM 11/1

Burt, Jean Brooks
The things divine. LAR 4/3

Burt, Maxwell Struthers
"Beauty persists." SCM 7/2
Duetto: summer. SCM 7/1
"I know a lovely lady who is d. SCM 3/3
Mountain dawn. HAM 2/2
Mountain prayer. SCM 12/2
The river. SCM 4/2
Threnody in major and minor. SCM 6/4
To this house. SCM 12/4
Walled gardens. HAM 9/1
When I grew up to middle-age. SCM 12/1

Burton, Clara Moore
Baby's eyes. CTY Win/4
The early dandelion. CTY Spr/2
Grand-Pop's girl. CTY Sum/3
Harvest apples. CTY S-A/4
Love versus ambition. CTY Aut/2
My tree. CTY Win/4
The whip-poor-will's song. CTY Spr/2

Burton, Letitia E.
Enlightenment. CIJ 1/4

Burton, Richard
Birds' nests. EME 6/3
By night and day. HAM 8/2
The carpenter lad. CIC 6/12/4
Early evening in April. NER 5/12/0
If I had time! CIC10/19/2
Learning and loving. PER 10/1
Shakespeare reads King James... CIC 9/11/4
Spring in the park. LYW 3/4
Tanaquil. PAL Sum/3

Busch (Jr.), Briton Niven
Inarticulate. COV 9/0
Insomnia. COV 2/2
Wild duck. MEA 3/2

Busey, Garreta Helen
Sent with an anonymous bouquet. BOO 12/4

Bush-Banks, Olivia Ward
The great adventure. MES 10/3

Bushnell, Mable Cone
The way. CIJ 7/4

Bushnell, Nelson S.
The inn. MAG 6/3
The pianist. AMP 8/2

Buss, Kate
Gargoyle. POE 11/1
Personae mutae. NER10/22/4

Butchard, Reuben
In Rocky Mountain land. CIC 9/13/3

Butts, Dorothy
Audience. POE 11/1
Difference. POE 11/1
Listening. POE 11/1
May basket. POE 11/1
The parade. POE 11/1
Please. POE 11/1
To the hills...Northampton. POE 11/1
The transient. POE 11/1
A vanity. POE 11/1

Bye, Jean Palmer
Singing voice. AMP Aut/1

Byers, Velma
Mid-summer rose garden. LAR 7/3
Remembering. LAR 7/3

Bynner (and Kiang Kang-hu), W.
A green stream. POE 2/2
Harmonizing a poem... POE 2/2

Bynner (tr.), Witter
Answering Vice-Prefect Chang. POE 2/2
At Ch'u-Cho on the western str. FRE12/21/1
At Chin-ling ferry. OUT 8/30/2
The beautiful Hsi-Shih. POE 2/2
Bidding General Yen farewell... FRE 8/1/3
Bringing in the wine. FRE 5/9/3
By the Purole cliff. BOO 12/1
A drawing of a horse by Genera. NES10/29/1
Drinking alone under the moon. FRE 5/2/3
Early autumn. FRE 7/4/3
Farewell to Li Ts'ao... FRE12/21/1
A farewell to my friend Ch'en. VOI Spr/3
A friendship. DIA 5/1
Fruits of circumstance. DOU 6/2
The garden of the golden valle. BOO 12/1
The gold-threaded robe. FRE 1/4/2
A greeting on the Huai River. FRE12/21/1
Hard traveling in Shu'. NAT 5/3/2
Hard traveling. FRE 5/23/3
A hearty welcome to vice prefe. NES10/29/1
I climb to look-out cemetery... BOO 12/1
In a retreat among bamboos. POE 2/2

6/20/3
As to moonlight. NAT 2/7/3
At his funeral. BOO 2/3
Beside a brook at Mokanshan. LYR 4/4
The big white bird. FUG 2-3/3
The blind signer. NER 7/11/3
A buffalo dance..Santo Domingo. NAT 9/24/4
By the lake. CEN 2/3
Carvings of Cathay. NER 1/28/0
Castle in Spain. DIA 4/0
A chanty. COV 2/0
Chinese translators... NAT 12/5/3
Christians. FRE10/18/2
The city. BOO 12/4
A dancer. PAL Sum/3
Debs and the builders. NER12/28/1
Donald Evans. DIA 4/2
A dragon fly. FRE 5/3/2
Ebenezer. FOR 9/4
The eternal Helen. FUG 2/4
A Fisher-Shape. NER 5/21/4
Flying-fish. NAT 2/7/3
From a mountain in China. LYR 8/3
The fruits of the earth. POE 8/3
Fruits. FRE10/18/2
A goodbye from the ship. NAT10/11/2
Grass-tops. POE 3/0
"The great iron cat." FUG 12/2
The hill by the lake. NER 9/19/3
The Holy Ghost. OUT11/22/2
I should like to be. BUC 12/4
Imperialists. NAT 2/7/3
Into space. CEN 2/3
Leave some apples to a novelis. FUG 12/2
Lincoln. FRE10/18/2
Lorenzo. CEN 11/3
A modern game. BOO 3/4
Monsters. NES10/11/4
Morning. MAC 6/4
New Mecico magic. NER 1/9/4
The new whistle. BOO 4/2
O hunted huntress. NAT 3/22/2
Oats. NER 2/7/3
The old men and the young men. NER 9/3/4
On Mokamshan. CEN 2/3
On a Mexican lake. NER 7/3
On a bench by the river. NES 1/6/3
One of these days. STM 12/4
Out of Peking. CEN 2/3
Pittsburgh. NER 1/21/0
Premonition. NAT 2/7/3
Pueblo dances. NER12/26/3
Rain. NAT 5/22/0
Remembering Jack London. COV 2/0
Rhythm. NER 8/8/3
The sand-piper. POE 3/0
Sante Fe. NER 12/5/3
Secret cellars. PAL 7/3
Six poems from the Chinese. OUT 6/30/0
A song of the winds. FRE 4/19/2
Spring in the zoo. MEA 5/2
A spring summons. NER 5/7/4
Starry weather. NER 5/28/4
Temples. NER12/27/2
This wave. NAT 2/7/3
Though you would follow me. NER 6/25/4
Through the bamboo. CEN 2/3
To A.E. Housman. NER 7/24
To Henry Ford. FOR 7/4
To a Chinese scholar. FRE 4/26/2
To an inquirer. NER10/25/2
A truant. NAT 2/7/3
The unknown soldier. FRE10/18/2
The wanderer. NAT 1/12/1
When you told me of an eagle. DIA 4/0
Wise men. COV 2/0
Wistaria. NER 6/13/3
A word to the wise. NER 8/29/3
Words. VOI10-11/3
A young satirist. NES10/20/3

Byrne, M. St.Clare
The common things. MAC 5/2

C.,G.H.
Renaissance. AMJ 7/3

C.,L.E.
Saplings. COV 12/4
Spirit wings. COV 12/4
Wood ways. COV 12/4

C.,M.P.
Through the Cajon pass. LYW 7-8/2

C.,T.
The thunderers. COM11/26/4

Cabell, James Branch
The sceond way. REW 10/4

Cades, Hazel Rawson
Feel of brambles. POE 1/1

Cahill, Alice M.
Cannas. LAL 9/4
Necromancy. LAL 5/4

Cahn, Pauline
These two. MEA 1/2
Cain, Camille
Shadows. AMP 8-9/3
Cain, Charles
Street picture. MIL 10/2
Cain, Mildred Palmer
Beauty. AMP 1-2/4
Dead trees. AMP 6-7/3
For those in darkness. AMP 12/3
Caldwell, Clyde B.
At night. SCR 9/4
Autumn decline. SCR 11/4
Itinerant fowl. SCR 8/4
Years of long ago. SCR 11/4
Yesterday. SCR 9/4
Caldwell, Elizabeth
Own own Hawaii Nei. CIV 9-10/4
Swimming song. CIV 9-10/4
Caldwell, Evantha
Challenge. SCR 12/4
Calhoun, Laura
Tropic treasure. AMP 5-6/4
Calkins, Marion Clinch
Song in spring. BOO 5/4
Winter night. SVG 6/3
Calkins, Thomas V.
The sand devil. LYW 10/1
Call, Jessie
Wasted years. LYW 11/4
Call, Oliver
La terre. POE 2/4
The raconteur. POE 2/4
The sugar-maker. POE 2/4
Callaghan, Gertrude
Awakening. STJ 4/4
Cedars. NET 9/10/3
Conspiracy. NEW12/30/4
Easter. NET 4/19/4
Ice maiden. NET12/29/3
A low brow at a symposium. MIN 1/4
May morning. NET 5/22/4
The necklace. NET 12/3/3
Old wives hands. MEA 10/4
Peace offering. NEU 8/3
Protest. STM 12/4
Sea ghosts. NET 8/28/3
A song and a tear. NET 6/21/4
Spring song. NET 6/3/4
Suppliant. MEA 10/4
Tea. NET 2/8/4
To Pierrot. COM11/26/4
What shall I say? AIN 12/4
Wisdom. NET 5/1/4
Calland, Annice
Desert lure. PEG 3/3
The desert rat. LAR 4/4
Genre. LYR 4/4
The ghost sea. OVM 3/4
Lady in green. A<P 2-3/3
My debt to you. LYW 2/4
An old trail. OVM 2/4
On the Pecos. LYW 2/3
Songs of the desert: desert wo. LRW 9/3
When April goes. LYR 4/3
Calpins, Thomas V.
A southwestern day cycle. LYW 9/3
Cameron, Ian
King. STE 2/4
A wood aster. COV 8/0
Cameron, Roy
Dead. COV 6/1
Campbell, Constance
The song of rain and the homes. CEN 3/1
Campbell, Doris
Anguish. POE 12/2
Campbell, Floy
The dunes. POE 8/4
Campbell, Helen M.
The old canals of England. GRA 10/1
Campbell, Joseph
Chiaroscuro. MEA 7/1
The crows. FRE 3/23/1
The curfew. FRE 1/26/1
"Into the gathered cornfields.. DOU 6/2
"The moon rose up." DOU 6/2
New Year's, 1913. NER 1/2/4
Campbell, Margaret T.
California mocking bird. LAR 6/3
The lesson-sermons. CIJ 10/4
Sharing. CIJ 8/4
Campbell, Marion Susan
The guest chamber. CIJ 8/3
Praise. CIJ 8/3
Campbell, Nancy
Innocent sleep. POE 8/1
The mother. POE 3/0
Campbell, Robert L.
Gratitude. SCR 1/4
Campbell, Susan F.
Ruth. CIJ 11/4
Canaday, Elizabeth Barbara
Earth's breast. FOR 8/4
Canfield, Lillian Caroline
From an alien strand. SCR 10/4
From his window. CIV11-12/4
Hours. INT 4-6/4
The last rodeo. INT 7-9/4
The painted desert. INT10-12/4
The saraband. INT 4-6/4
Today's child. CIV 7-8/4
Canfield, Mary Cass
Hyacinth. VOI 5-6/4

Lovely ladies. VOI 5-6/4
Outward. VOI 5-6/4
The poet outside. POE 4/4
Rose. POE 4/4
Tomb epitaph. POE 4/4

Cannon, Rose Leibbrand
Star and song. LAR 4/4

Canon, Ralph
Buzzards. CTY Spr/4
It's too deng cold. CTY Win/3
Life. CTY Spr/2
Milkin'. CTY Spr/4
The old home place. CTY Win/4
Old man winters. CTY Spr/4
Papa horse. CTY Sum/3
The rain predictor. CTY W/2
Spring calls. CTY Spr/3
Sunday hills. CTY Win/4
The thresher. CTY S-A/4
Wods. CTY Aum/2

Carew, Harold D.
Compensation. BOT 8/5/2
Reconsecration. BOT11/19/1
To a rose. BOT 4/12/2
When Bill went west. BOP 3/21/2

Carey, Charles Josef
You can't forget. OVM 7/4

Carey, Neita
Blots. AMP10-11/3

Carleton, Eliza L.
Apple tree. AMP 8/2

Carlin, Francis
Alice Meynell. COM 12/3/4
And was made wise. CAW 1/1
At Christ's mass. AME12/24/1
The cardinal's hat. CAW 5/1
A child's grace. MEA 12/1
Confessional prayer. CAW 2/2
Counsel. COM11/19/4
The golden nickel. MEA 11/2
The good shepherdess. AME12/15/0
Goosling Brook. MEA 12/1
Intimacy. CAW 8/2
The lamb. CAW 2/0
Pax. CAW 6/2
The philomath speaks. NES11/10/3
The shambles. MEA 12/1
The shepherd's return. NES 3/19/1
The six wounds. CAW 3/1
The symbolists. NER 1/14/0
Were you to be out. CAW 6/0

Carman, Bliss
The good priest of Gourin. COM12/24/4
Vestigia. HAM 9/1
Where is heaven? CIC 4/26/3

Carman, Miriam Crittenden
To Slyvia-forever still. EVM 8/1

Carmer, Carl L.
Brunehilde. NOM Spr/4
Evening breeze. NOM Spr/4

Carneal, George
Bluebirds. SMA 1/3

Carnevali, Emanuel
A lady. BRO 3/3
The return. POE 5/4

Carney, Ralph J.
Love all over. CIJ 11/3

Carpenter (tr.), Rhys
Selected odes of Pindar. COV 9/3

Carpenter, Rhys
Curtain-up in the great playho. COV 1/4
The dream of the ropemaker's s. VOI Aut/2

Carr, Laura Garland
A bit of color. GRA 10/2
The hermit thrush. GRA 10/2
Indian summer. GRA 11/2

Carr, Mary Jane
As men grow old. LAR 12/3

Carrell, Ordath Estelyn
To my mother. LAR 8/3

Carrere, Angele
The Cluny Museum (Paris). PAG10-11/1
Correction. PAG10-11/1
Discord. PAG 12/1
Marketing. PAG10-11/1
Morning in Antwerp. PAG 12/1
Salutation. VOI 12/2
Still-life. PAG 12/1
To a jewel box. VOI 12/2

Carrington, James B.
My little house of dreams. SCM 7/1

Carrington, Mary Coles
Homeward bound. LYR 6/2
The lost comrade. DOU 11/1
Orchids. STE 3/3
The vase. LYW 3/3

Carroll, Ellen M.
Dusk-dream. AMP 4-5/3
Escape. AMP 1-2/4
Evensong. SCR 9/3
Faith. SCR 8/4
The gateway. LAR 12/3
Holy communion. SCR 4/4
In mid-ocean. SCR 11/4
Just before night. CIV 7-8/4
Middle age. LAL 5/4
My wish. SCR 10/3
Portrait. LAL 9/4
Sin. SCR 8/4
Southland mirrorings. LAR 3/4

Surrender? AMP11-12/4
Talisman. SCR 8/4
To a dead rose. AMP 12/2
With the first-born. SCR 11/4
Wreckage. BUC 10/4

Carroll, Eva M.
Sunset. SCR 10/3
Wind songs. SCR 10/3

Carroll, Mary Tarver
The poet. AMP Aut/1
The wander-lure. AMP 6/2

Carron, Lionel V.
Commencement. MAG 6/2

Cartach, Sn.
Dreams. NER 3/10/0

Carter, A. Pearle
The alien. PER 7/4
Distance. SCR 6/4
Gray dusk. LYR 8/2
"Night gathers the little sorr. NOM Win/2
Old songs. PEG 3/3
The soothsayer. LYR 4/3

Carter, David Gillis
Dusk. YAR 12/3
Over the city. YAR 1/4
Snapshot. YAR 2/4
Song. YAR 11/3
To one bereaved. YAR 10/3
Wyoming. YAR 3/4

Carth, Jean E.
The revealing. CIJ 10/3

Cartier, Celia Chessman
Lies. LAL 9/4
Recompense. LAL 9/4
To a dead love. LAL 9/4

Cartwright, Dorothy Hawley
Dumbness. STM 12/4
Grey song. LAR 4/4
I am weary of the city. OVM 11/4
In secret places. LYW 2/4
Nocturne. OVM 8/4
The passing. LYW 11/4
To a young idealist. LYW 2/4

Caruducci, Giouse
Sunlight and love. FRE 9/19/3

Caruso, Dorothy
Green garden. SCM 12/3

Caruthers, Mazie V.
Birthday. LAD 2/4
The first Christmas. NEW12/23/4
White nights. BUC 10/4

Carver, Gertrude Nason
Absolution. REW 4/4
Boomerang. COV 2/3
Daphe. COV 10/3
Morning. COV 2/3
October fragments. REW 10/4
Oh! when I love. COV 1/4
Once again, burn ashes. COV 10/3
Paris. COV 5/4
Pax. COV 2/3
Pieta. COV 1/4
Professional. WRM 9/4
The sculptor. COV 10/3
Solitude. COV 2/3
Song of a truant soul. AMP 6-7/3
To Rodin. COV 1/4
To learn to yield. COV 1/4
Weather. COV 2/3

Cary, Robert
Poesy and pense. NEN 3/1

Case, Mildred Spring
The upward flight. CIJ 8/4

Caskey, J. Homer
Bethesda of love. PAL Sum/3

Cassedy, Stephana P.
Christmas glory. CTY Win/3
Doubt dissipated. CTY Spr/4
A mother's thoughts. CTY Win/4
Mystery. CTY S-A/4
One waiting at the gate. CTY Aut/2
She looked beautiful. CTY Win/4

Cassel, Miriam
Autumn haze. SCR 9/2
Gem-lighted temples. SCR 7-8/2
Lament of the garbage man. SCR 9/2
Slag. MID 1/1

Castle, Clara Bushnell
The lute. LAR 5/3

Castle, Horace
The closing year. SCR 12/4
The deserted house. AMP10-11/3
The wonders of nature. SCR 4/4

Catel, Jean
Images vaines. POE 3/0

Cather, Willa
Autumn melody. LAR 10/3

Cattell, Hetty
The north woods. PAG 8-9/1

Cattrell, Frances J.
A lullaby. AMP 3-4/4

Caughey, Mary Lapsley
Theocritus. NOA 6/1

Cautela, Guiseppe
Good-bye. MEA 11/3
Nun. MEA 11/4

Ch'en Tzu-ang
On a gate tower. DIA 12/2

Chain, Julia
There is something. WOW 3/0

Challis, James Courtney
Rain in the country. INT10-12/4
Vision. INT 7-9/4
Wind. INT 7-9/4

Chalmers, G. K.
Picket guard. CAS 1/3
Walking down the hill. CAS 3/3
Chamberlain, J. D.
On the virtue of sobriety. ALS 1/2
Chamberlain, John R.
Advice. YAR 4/4
Lines. YAR 10/3
People. YAR 11/3
Chamberlain, Will
The old blind gardener. SVG 4/3
Chambers, Whittaker
Quag-hole. NAT12/31/4
Chandler, Josephine Craven
Cockaigne. STE 3/2
Lines to a haughty gander. STE 10/3
Chang Chi
A night mooring by the bridge. DOU 3-4/3
Thinking of a friend in the fo. DOU 3-4/3
Virtuous wife ode. MEA 6/2
Chang Chiu-Ling
Fruits of circumstance. DOU 6/2
Looking at the moon and thinki. DOU 3-4/3
Chang Hu
At Chin-ling ferry. OUT 8/30/2
An old song. OUT 8/30/2
On the terrace of assembled an. OUT 8/30/2
Chang Yo-hus
Flowers and moon at night. LYW 2/4
Spring night. LYW 2/4
Chapin, Anna Alice
Fuel. AIN 4/0
Chapin, Henry
Migratory moon. NES 10/8/1
Chaplin, Ralph
Freedom. LIB 3/2
The living dead. LIB 3/2
A Sioux dies in prison. LIB 9/2
Taps. LIB 3/2
To my little son. LIB 12/1
Wesley Everest. LIB 3/2
Chapman, Harry Grafton
Sonnets. POR 1-2/4
Chapman, John Jay
Books and reading. YAR 10/1
Clouds. SCM 8/0
Early spring. IND 6/4
The grandfather. SCM 5/2
Summer's adieu. SCM 10/1
Chappell, Jeanette
What need to fear. TEM 6/1
Chappell, Mrs. H. C.
Beauty. LAR 9/3
Immortelle. LAR 12/3
Charles, Lester
Green stockings. WAV 6/2
Chase, Amanda M.
I love my day. CTY Win/4
Chase, Chilton
Enshrined. NOM Spr/2
Fulfillment. NOM Spr/2
Chase, Polly
Bliss. POE 10/4
Firelight. POE 10/4
Hands on a card-table. POE 10/4
Little things. POE 10/4
Stillborn. POE 10/4
Chastain, Mary Lee
Afterward. GOH 6/2
Chattopadhyaya, Harindranath
Divine dark. WRE 12/4
Noon. WRE 12/4
Chavigny, Mireille
Dawn in the Camargue. MOD Aut/2
Cheatham, Elizabeth
Mood. SOV 1923
Cheesman, Celia
Wisdom. LAL 5/4
Chency, Elias H.
His little flock are we. GRA 9/2
Cheney, Elias H.
What would I more? GRA 2/2
Cheney, Harvey D.
The sweet smell of lumber. LYW 4/4
Cheney-Nichols, Beth
Confession. TEM Aut/1
Spring. CEN 4/1
Strong hands. LYR 9/2
Cheng Hao
The sudden coming of spring. POE 8/2
Cherry, Marjorie Loomis
Coming home. LYW 7-8/3
A ride. LYW 6/3
Chesterman, Hugh
Knowledge. NES11/15/4
Chew, Samuel C.
Homage to Thomas Hardy. NER 6/2/0
Cheyne, Elizabeth Gibson
Labours. CIC 12/7/2
Cheyney, E. Ralph
He begs for dreams. NOM Aug/3
Cheyney, Ralph
Crucifixion. PAG 12/1
Emancipation. PAG10-11/1
Nocturne. NOM Spr/2
Surf. PAG10-11/1
Child, Mary
Seesaw. STM 12/4
Childe, Wilfred

Cor cordium. COV 3/4
Sarras. COV 3/4
Childs, Dorothea M.
Awakened love. LYW 2/2
Deferred. LYW 11/1
One russet-brown tree. LYW 5/4
Sonnet. POA 9/1
Chittenden, Gerald
Gossip at Bow Mills. IND 12/6/4
Chocano, Jose Santos
Archaeology. WRE 11/4
Chodorov, Edward
Phantoum of a triple symbol. CAS 1/3
Choyce, A. Newberry
I can bear so many things. SMA 4/2
Wanderer. SMA 1/3
Christian, Margaret Anne
Lady of property. WAN 4/4
Madrigal. WAN 10/4
Christoph, Charles de Guire
Herons. POE 1/1
Improvisation. POE 1/1
Mood for pianiste. DIA 2/3
Neighbor moon. POE 1/1
Old places. POE 1/1
Profile. POE 1/1
Thought of women. POE 1/1
Chrysler, Josephine Lee
The house on the hill. AMP 6-7/3
Chubb, L. Joan
The wind. MAG 8/3
Chubb, Thomas Caldecot
The grey wolf to the dogs. BOO 2/4
Legend. BOO 6/4
Longshore. SCM 2/4
Portrait of God. REW 1/3
The romancer. SCM 4/3
Chun Yu Seng
The wild geese. COV 4/1
Church, B. B.
Maybe. CUU 4/3
Church, Richard
The purification. NES 2/2/4
Waiting. POE 12/4
Cinneidig, Robert Emmet Ua
Transfiguration. DOU 10/1
Ciolkowska, Muriel
Backwater. POE 5/1
Presence. POE 5/1
Snow. POE 5/1
Clancy, Helen A.
The harbor. LAR 11/3
Clancy, Holling Allison
Joke. BRO 1/3
Clapp, Mary Brennan
A discovery. LYW 11/2
Honey 3300 years old (Tutankha. LYW 6/3
Clarage, Eleanor
Undine. COV 6/4
Clark (Jr.), B. Preston
Twilight. EVM 6/1
Youth. OUT 9/1/0
Clark (Jr.), Charles B.
The old camp coffee-pot. OUT 6/9/0
Clark, Al
Desert thanks. LAR 8/3
Clark, Allen
I am your lover. LYW 5/2
Clark, Badger
In the hills. SCM 3/0
Clark, Caroline
Crumbs of manana. PAR #3/3
Clark, Fannie Hunter
The cycled path. SCR 5/4
An evening flight. OVM 9/4
The last butterfly of autumn. CTY S-A/4
My other self. CTY S-A/4
The silent wood. SCR 11/3
The sunset hour. SCR 2/4
There is no past. SCR 11/3
Through mists. SCR 4/4
Unframed picture. SCR 7/4
Universal search. SCR 5/4
Winter. CTY Win/4
Clark, Imogen
Remembering. SCM 12/3
Clark, J. B.
Autumn. LAR 10/3
Clark, Marguerite Dixon
Afterwards. LAR 3/4
Epitaph for a poet. VOI 12/4
Wind free. MEA 11/4
Clark, Martha Haskell
Beach trails. MAC 4/2
Child's Christmas. SCM 12/2
The children. OUT 12/1/0
From famine fields. OUT 3/22/2
In Irish rain. SCM 5/1
Little house of Christmas. SCM12/20/0
New goods. SCM 2/3
The price. MAC 5/2
The purchasers. SCM 1/4
The specialist. HAM 12/1
Trails. SCM 1/2
Wicket gates. GOH 6/2
Clark, Preston
Beauty. YAR 7/4
Embarkation. YAR 7/4
Clark, Thomas Curtis
After reading a volume of mode. CHE10/30/2
America sings of the dawn.

CIC11/10/1
America to her poets. CIC 8/4/1
Apocalypse. CIC11/23/3
April. CIC 4/12/3
At Gentryville. CIC 2/9/2
At Mount Vernon. CHE 2/22/2
At a crowded shrine. CIC 11/9/2
At evening time. CIC 11/2/2
At half-mast. CIC12/11/4
At the day's beginning. CIC 8/10/2
August. CIC 8/16/3
Autumn. CIC 11/2/2
An awakening America sings. CIC 4/6/2
Blind guides. CIC 9/21/2
Blind. CIC11/22/3
Book magic. CHE 1/1/3
Book magic. CIC12/13/3
Byron. CHE 3/10/2
Caesar and Christ. CIC 9/29/1
Caesar and Christ. CIC12/25/4
The call. CIC11/22/3
Chicago work song. CHT 9/25/1
The Christian. BOT 2/5/1
The Christian. CIC 2/9/2
Corn. CIC12/15/1
Courage. CIC10/16/4
The crusader. CON 2/21/4
The day breaks. CIC 1/12/2
Dead kingdoms. CIC12/21/2
The death of summer. CIC 9/21/2
Deathless (Horati Carmina...). CHT 8/21/1
Destiny. CIC 2/8/3
The dream. CHE 4/22/2
The dreamer. CIC 2/9/2
The enduring. CHT 9/26/1
Escape. CIC10/30/4
Events. CIC 9/25/4
Evidence. CIC 1/18/3
Evidences. CIC11/17/1
Evolution. CHE 1/19/3
Explorers. CHE 1/25/2
Faith and love. CIC 9/25/4
Faith and science. CIC 3/1/3
Foolish and wise. CIC 3/22/3
For those who paid the price. CHE 5/30/3
Fundamentals. CHE 1/12/3
Fundamentals. CIC 1/11/3
Gifts. CIC11/17/1
The glory of Lincoln. CIC 2/9/2
God rules the seas. CIC11/17/1
God's dreams. CIC 11/8/3
God's victors. CIC11/17/1
God. CIC 8/7/4
The golden age. CIC 9/22/1
Greatheart. CHT 2/12/3
The hand of Lincoln. CIC 6/8/2
The hand that wrought. BOT 2/5/1
The heart's country. CIC 10/6/1
Heroes. CIC 9/11/4
Humdrum. MNJ 8/10/1
If winter comes. INI 10/2
"If winter comes." CIC10/12/2
In Shakespeare's town. CIC10/26/2
In Shakespeare's town. CHE10/10/2
In an age of science. CHE10/21/2
In blossom time. CIC 5/17/3
In the age of science. CIC 9/14/2
Influence. CIC 3/30/2
Irony. CIC 1/17/4
July. CIC 7/19/3
A June millionaire. CIC 6/28/3
The king comes. CIC 2/8/3
King of an acre. CHT 9/20/1
Kings. CIC 3/9/2
Life is a feast. CIC12/21/2
Lincoln. CIC 2/15/3
Lincoln. CIC 2/7/4
Lincoln. LIW 2/11/2
Lost Eden. CIC 9/13/3
Lyric. INI 10/2
March yearning. CHE 4/22/2
March. CHT 3/15/2
The Master. CIC 2/9/2
May. CIC 5/3/3
The melting pot. CHT 9/11/1
The miracle. CIC 2/9/2
My America. CIC 10/4/3
The new song. CIC 10/1
Nocturne. CIC 8/2/3
October. CHT10/30/1
On rereading Keats. CHT 8/15/1
The optimism of faith. CIC11/17/1
"Paradise enow." CHE 1/17/2
Pilots. CHT 8/5/1
Poet to cynic. CHT 7/21/1
The poet's call. CHE 2/9/2
The poet's call. CIC 12/7/2
Poets. CHT 8/7/1
The procession. SAF10/10/1
The pursuit. CIC 5/10/3
Rebirth. CIC 1/25/3
Release. CIC 1/25/3
Reveille. CHE 4/13/3
Revelation. BOT 2/5/1
Revelation. CIC10/19/2
Revelation. CIC11/17/1
Revolt. CIC 4/5/3
Roosevelt. CIC 1/3/4
The saint. CIC 1/24/4
The search. CIC 11/9/2

Seekers. CHE 4/12/2
The seer. CIC10/26/2
Shackelton. CHE 2/16/2
Shakespeare. INI 4/2
Sisyphus. CIC10/16/4
Song (Horati Carmina, Lib. I,. CHT 12/8/1
A song for morning. INI 10/2
Song. CHT 11/9/1
Specters. CIC11/23/3
Spectres. CHE11/18/2
Spring song. CIC 4/17/3
Theodore Roosevelt, prophet. CHT10/27/1
Theodore Roosevelt... CIC10/27/1
Time. CHE 3/23/2
To Carl Sandburg. CIC 6/22/2
To Carl Sandburg. CHN 4/12/2
To Charles Granger Blanden. CHE 10/9/2
To Homer - poet eternal. CHT 11/7/1
To John Burroughs. UNI 2/2
To John Keats. CHT 8/15/1
To Mark Twain... CHE10/18/2
To Quintus Horatius Flaccus. CHE 2/20/2
To Robert Burns. MNJ 8/2/1
To Robert Burns. CIC12/13/3
To Thoreau. CHE 1/6/2
To Walt Whitman. INI 4/2
To Wordsworth. INI 4/2
To a celebrity. CHT 8/24/1
To a thousand year old elm. CHE11/13/2
To poetry. CIC 9/1
To the author of Spoon River. CHE 3/22/2
To the poet. CIC 10/2/4
To the poets. CIC10/26/2
To the singer. CIC10/21/1
The tragedy. CIC 2/8/3
Trust and the great artist. CIC 7/7/2
The universal cult. LIW 4/13/2
Upon reading a volume..Chinese. CHE 3/31/2
Utopia. CIC 9/27/3
WHo will sing your songs, Amer. CIC 5/31/3
The wandering Christ. CIC 3/8/3
War. CIC 12/4/4
When nations walk in darkness. CIC 7/19/3
When summer dies. CHT10/23/1
Who made war. CIC12/18/4
Who will build the world anew. CIC 8/21/4
Winter harvest. CIC12/21/2
With gratitude-"Leaves of Gras. CIC 3/9/2
Witnesses. BOT 1/14/2
Witnesses. CIC12/21/2
World builders. CHT 8/25/1
The world's verdict. CIC 2/8/3

Clark, William Russell
The nun's child. GYP #2/4
Romany. GYP #2/4

Clarke, Dorothy Harrison
A song of thanksgiving. CIJ 7/4

Clarke, Harlow
I complain in passing. POE 2/2
An old woman. POE 2/2

Clarke, Helen Archibald
The blase play-goer. AMP 8/2

Clarke, Lucretia
To a rose. SCR 6/4

Clarkin, Lucy Gertrude
A prayer. CAW 10/0

Clarkson, Lillian Jennings
An idle hour. LAR 11/3
The moon and I. LAR 12/3
A place to share. LAR 10/3

Clatworthy, Kate M.
The fairy tree. AMP10-11/3

Clayton, Beatrice
Forgiveness. CIJ 12/4
No enemies. CIJ 9/4

Cleghorn, Sarah N.
If I forget thee. HAM 1/0
Mountains. NAT 6/7/2
On reading many histories of t. WRE 5/3
Precedence. LYR 11/2
The socialist's marriage. POE 2/1
St. Clair hears St. Francis. WRE 12/4
Three great ladies. SCM ?/2
"Vanity Fair." NES 12/9/2
The Vermonter departing. EVM 9/1

Clements, Colin Campbell
From seven plays of old Japan. AMP 4-5/3
If I should die tonight. AMP Aut/1

Clevenger, Herbert Logan
Le commencement. AMP 6-7/3

Clifford, Isobel Gray
The circuit rider. LAR 4/4

Clifford, R.
You. AMP 4-5/3

Cline, Leonard Lanson
Crepuscule. DEU12/19/0
Memorial. DEU 6/13/0
Sonnet (To an unknown lady...). DEU 9/26/0
Sunset (Onekama, Michigan). DEU

9/5/0
Testament. DEU 12/5/0
Wakefulness. DEU 1/30/1
Wounded. DEU 7/4/0

Cloud, Virginia Woodward
Autumn leaf. LYR 10/3
Leaves. COV 10/0
Possession. LYR 4/4
Things. STM 12/4

Clough, Wilson O.
Ballad of the Scotty mine. LYW 11/4

Cluny, James B.
Address to the artisans. DOU 5/3

Coakley, Thomas F.
Perfect condition. AMP 6-7/3

Coates, Archie Austin
Ballade of a secondhand book s. BOO 2/0
Ballade of ladies of the print. BOO 1/0
Ballade of the printed page. BOO 1/0
Trois morts. COV 2/0

Coates, Florence Earle
The violin. SCM 2/1

Coates, Grace Stone
The intruder. POE 4/1

Coatsworth, Elizabeth J.
All goats. POE 2/4
Andalusia. COV 8/2
The apostate gypsy. COV 1/0
The arena. DOU 1/4
At Versailles. POE 6/2
Bear River. MEA 11/4
Broadway. POE 6/2
The centaurs. DOU 5/2
Coast cattle. YAR 7/4
The coming. POE 2/4
Confessional. COV 8/2
The cows. POE 6/2
Crepuscule. DOU 1/4
The crows of Bayeux. LYW 10/4
The dance. LYW 9/3
Daniel Webster's horses. CEN 7/4
Dedicated to Her Highness. DIA 5/4
Demeter. POE 2/4
Desert moon. DIA 8/3
Dolores dances. COV 8/2
Evening. DIA 9/2
Five inconsequential charms. DOU 4/2
Fly low, vermilion dragon. COV 1/2
For butterflies and moths. POE 8/4
For driving away rain. POE 8/4
For new shoes. POE 8/4
For ships. POE 8/4
For the fields. POE 8/4
Hortense. COV 7/4
The hunters. FOR 11/4
I believe. DOU 11/3
I want to see a man...earrings. VOI 9-10/4
In Provence. CEN 12/4
Indifference. VOI 9-10/4
Interregnum. SMA 1/3
Into the sunset. DOU 10/2
The invasion of Holland. DOU 2-3/4
The knight-errant. FRE 4/18/3
Le tour des Francs. DIA 2/4
The madman. DOU 2-3/4
Majesty walks in the garden: S. DIA 12/3
The mystic. LYW 6/3
Nantucket. CEN 11/3
The Nile. COV 3/3
Nirvana. COV 1/2
November. COV 11/4
The old houses. DIA 2/4
The old mare. DIA 2/4
Old trees. NER 2/18/0
On buying a Maine farm. YAR 7/4
Over Carthage. COV 3/3
Park gnomes. NER 6/23/0
Posthumous respectability. DIA 10/4
The princess. DIA 2/4
The proud dead ladies. COV 8/2
Quintessential. DOU 2-3/4
Rain pageant. NER 2/18/0
Rain: St. Augustine. DIA 11/3
The ravens. LYW 10/2
Reflection. DIA 10/1
Retired. VOI 9-10/4
Sails. DIA 10/2
Saint John. RHY 6-7/3
Samson. DIA 2/4
The second crusade. COV 7/4
The ship. POE 6/2
The Sicilian expedition. DIA 5/4
The song. COV 1/2
Songs from travel. VOI 12-1/4
Spanish fashion. MEA 2/3
Stream. POE 6/2
Subjunctive. YAR 7/4
Syracuse. RHY 6-7/3
The three Misses Barker. BOO 6/4
The three gifts. LYW 12/3
To a Negress on Sixth Avenue. VOI 12-1/4
To think! COV 1/3
Traceries. COV 7/4

Transparency for a spring wind. MEA 5/4
The ultimate gift. COV 3/3
Wizardry. COV 1/2

Cobb, Ann
The black sunbonnet. OUT 5/12/0
Hospitality. OUT 5/19/0
Kivers. OUT 2/25/0
The widow-man. OUT 1/14/0

Cobb, William
Interior of a soul. BOO 3/4

Coblentz, Catherine Cate
Love. VER 12/4

Coblentz, Stanton A.
After life. LYW 9/2
As though. COV 12/2
City-weary. CAP 5/3
The commander. WAN 5/4
Diverse gods. AMP 10/2
Eagles and snails. BOO 9/4
Evanescence. LYR 4/4
The exile. LYR 11/4
Frailty. CAP 5/3
The genius. COV 12/4
In paradise. WAN 7/4
Memory and dream. LYW 2/4
Phantom. LYR 10/3

Cochran, Dorothy C.
Strength. POE 3/3

Cockcroft, Julia Walcott
I liken thee unto a pool. CIV 7-8/4
Petition. SCR 12/4

Code, Grant H.
The black beast. PAG 8-9/1
Departed travelers. TEM 6/1
Ecstasy. VOI Win/2
Fancy a garden. TEM 6/1
Grenlin-a biography. COV 2/1
Rhodis. TEM Aut/1
Sea quatrains. POE 10/1
The songs of heaven. VOI Win/2
The sons of the waterfall. VOI Win/2
When you are married. AMP Aut/1

Code, Grant Hyde
Waves on a beach. AMP 8/2

Cody, Alexander J.
April. MAG 4/2
Fears. MAG 10/4
The house of May. MAG 5/2
The mother of a priest. MAG 6/2
Our lady courtesy. MAG 7/2
Pampeulna. MAG 10/3
Shadows. MAG 2/2
To R.M.C.(died Holy Innocents). MAG 12/1

Coffin, Robert P. Tristram
Crecy. FOR 8/4
Dew and bronze. NAT 9/17/4
Dream farm. EVM 11/0
The plowman. SVG 4/3
The ship o' bed. FRE12/13/2
Singing Cotswold towns. FRE10/25/2
Sundown. FRE 3/2/1

Cogdell, Josephine
My sorrow song. MES 12/4

Colahan, Ellwood
Hand on a harp. POE 4/0
Pilgrimage. POE 4/0

Colbert, Nelle J.
"In Flanders Fields." AMP 9-10/4

Colby, M. E.
Under the southern cross. OVM 4/4

Cole, M.R.
The immortal spark. GRA 6/1

Cole, Vera Heathman
An offering. LYW 6/3

Coleman, Ethel M.
To my muse - a confession. POA 9/1
Vicarious life. OVM 11/4

Coleman, Patrick
The burning bush. CAW 5/2
Emparadised. CAW 11/0
Enshrined. CAW 11/1

Coll, Aloysius
Today's task. MUN 7/2

Collier, Elizabeth Fleming
Siskiyou flowers. AMP 2-3/3

Collins, Dorothy E.
After absence. COV 10/2
Come, I have done with thought. COV 1/3
Foreshadowing. CAP11-12/2
Gone. COV 6/4
In a mountain garden. COV 7/3
Motherless. LYW 12/2
Night song. LYW 7-8/2
On a young thing. MEA 12/2
Proportions. COV 6/24
The rainy day. COV 6/4
Spring storm. LYW 3/3
Spring sunrise. VOI Spr/3
The stealer of trash. COV 6/4
To the lover of any girl. LYW 9/3

Collins, Jeannette M.
On the arrival of Mary. LYW 3/3

Colson, Ethel M.
Fusion. LYW 12/3

Colter, Elizabeth
Choice. LYW 4/4

Colum, Padraic
Autumn. DIA 6/1
The bird of Jesus. NER12/14/1
The deer. NER11/10/0

Fuchsia hedges in Connacht. COM11/12/4
The humming bird. NER11/23/1
In a far land. DIA 11/1
In the Carolina woods. MEA 3/2
An Indian showing feats. NER10/13/0
John Butler Yeats. NES 2/11/2
Laburnums. NAT 5/4/1
Lament. NER 2/1/2
Legend. DIA 10/0
Men on islands. NER11/10/0
Odysseus. NER10/24/3
Old soldier. NER 2/1/2
The old toy-booth. MEA 5/1
Plovers. MEA 1/4
The poet. NER 2/1/2
Reminiscence. YAR 4/1
The sister's lullaby. DIA 10/0
Swift's pastoral. POE 1/1
Three Hawaiian poems. DIA 4/4
The wild ass. MEA 3/1

Colvert, Leathe
Drones. MES 7/4
Night. MES 12/4
Weary. MES 7/4

Colvin-Salls, Rupert
Bricks without straw. GUL 5/3
Threnody. GUL 6/3

Colwell, Alberta Wing
The Pacific. SCR 10/4
Through northern woods. SCR 11/4
Wisting. AMP 12/3

Colwell, Jane L.
Sublimated. AMP 10/2

Commins, Ruth
Picture poster. NOM Aut/3

Conant, Isabel Fiske
Across town. CIM 7/3
Answer. COV 12/3
Casements. CAS 1/3
Children. VOI 6-7/3
Chimes. VOI 6-7/3
East of Broadway. NET 7/26/3
Eleonora Duse. POE 8/4
Frail flame. POE 11/4
Heroes. LYR 6/3
Hound of song. OUT 7/11/3
In the Sun. NET 5/3
In time of need. LYR 3/4
A legend of the Christ-child. POE 12/3
Lodging. CIM 7/3
Lonely farm. POE 11/4
Mary of the city. POE 11/4
Morning exercise. PEA 7/3
Mother to child. IND 12/6/4
Mourner for Pan. VOI 12-1/4
O earth, too lovely! AMP Aut/1
Old aunt. POE 11/4
Old men. VOI 12-1/4
Old stone-worker. LYR 11/4
A queen's lament. VOI 6-7/3
Rain. VOI 12/4
Secret. IND 12/6/4
Tangible. BUC 11/4
This is your birthday. BOT10/23/3
To M.D.C. who carries jonquils. NES 4/10/3
Trail. VOI 12/4
Trails in Manhattan. CIM 7/5/3
The unknown soldier. POE 3/25/4
Urn-bearer. PAR #3/3
Verity. MEA 11/4
Willow. VOI 7-8/3

Confucius
Epitaph to a warrior. FRE 4/5/2

Conkle, W.
Lullaby. CTY Win/2

Conkling, Grace Hazard
Are you afraid? YAR 1/2
Box of coral. COV 10/0
Carib canone under sail. NAT12/31/4
Design of the white lilacs. NER 6/4/4
Detail for music. YAR 1/2
Diary written on peony petals. POE 9/0
The different day. NAT 2/16/1
Dominica. CEN 9/4
First crocus. AIN 4/2
The fountain. COV 11/0
Harebells. COV 10/0
The hermit thrush. COV 11/0
In the Maytime pear orchard. BOO 5/2
"Isn't it time?" MEA 3/1
Keepsake. COV 10/0
Love song. HAM 1/0
Martinique. CEN 9/4
Mt. Tom sunsets. COV 10/0
Nevis. CEN 9/4
Nocturne. EVM 3/1
Occasional mist. POE 9/4
Primaveral. POE 6/1
Quicksilver. MEA 10/1
Ranch of the fan. NER 6/18/4
Rough sea. POE 9/4
Spring day. COV 10/0
Squalls of rain. POE 9/4
Strong breeze. POE 9/4
To Hilda of her roses. COV 11/0
Variations on a theme. POM 1923
"What are you thinking?" COV 10/0

Conkling, Hilda
Cloudy-pansy. POE 8/2

Elsa. POE 8/2
Field-mouse. POE 8/2
Flowers faded and gone. POE 8/3
Gorgeous blue mountain. COV 5/20
Happiness. COV 5/20
Hay cook. COV 5/20
Hill-roads. NES 2/19/1
Humming-bird. COV 5/20
I was thinking. NAT10/18/2
"I wondered and wondered." POE 8/2
Little green Bermuda poem. POE 8/2
Lonely song. BOO 8/2
The lonesome apple tree. COV 5/0
Message for a sick friend. OUT 7/5/2
The milky way. NES11/12/1
Night is forgotten. NAT 2/16/1
Only morning-glory that flower. COV 5/0
Poems by a child. POE 7/0
Sea-gull. COV 5/0
Shiny brook. COV 5/0
Snow morning. POE 8/2
Song nets. POE 8/2
Tree toad. COV 5/0
Volcano. MEA 10/1
What I said. POE 8/2
When moonlight falls. POE 8/2
"Why do you love me?" NES 2/19/1

Conner, Adeline M.
Dawn and the lilies. AMP 5-6/4
The hut on the 'Winding Way.'. AMP11-12/4
Waiting. AMP 5-6/4

Conner, Ruth Irving
"And His the glory." PER 7/3
The fulness thereof. LYR 4/4
Imagery. MIN 7-8/4
A lesson. STE 11/4
The passing. LYR 6/2
Set to my hand. LYR 7/3
A thistle sings to the bee. STE 10/3
Wealth. STE 7/4
Winds that brace. AMP 1-2/4
You. LYR 3/4

Conner, Sabra
The breeze. LYW 3/4

Connor, Torrey
Companionship. OVM 2/4
Poinsettias. LYW 10/2
Spanish serenade. OVM 10/4
A tribute to Charles Keeler. OVM 9/4
A tribute to Ina Coolbrith. OVM 6/4
Twilight at Dolores. LYW 2/2
Words. OVM 6/4

Conrad, Harrison
The romancer. LYW 3/3

Conroe, Grace Sherburne
Hope. AMP11-12/4

Cook, Alice Carter
Sonnet. GRI 6/1
Storm. GRI 6/1
The willow in a storm. GRI 6/1

Cook, Harold
Love will return. COV 4/0
Lyrics. POE 1/1
Never did I dream. POE 12/2
Nocturne. COV 6/1
On reading your play. COV 4/0
Standards. POE 12/2

Cook, Harold Lewis
Circles. LYR 8/4
The market place, Cambridge, E. MEA 2/3
Tension. MEA 7/3

Cooke, Edmund Vance
Cain. NAT 8/20/4
David. NAT 8/20/4
Moses. NAT 8/20/4
Ruth. NAT 8/20/4
The serpent. NAT 8/20/4

Cooke, Ida Aleen
Disappointment. AMP 4-5/3

Cooke, Le Baron
After a quarrel. TOV 2/4
Answer. SHA 8/3
April hopes. TOV 2/4
At parting. TOV 5/4
At passing. TOV 3/3
Buddha speaks. COV 8/4
A certain man. COV 11/4
A conceit. BAU 12/3
A confession. SHA 8/3
Existence. BRI 5/3
Fantasy. COV 1/2
Fantasy. TEM 6/1
Futility. SHA 5/3
Group of poems. SHA 1/3
Humoresque. TOV 12/2
Intoxication. TOV 2/4
Laughter and tears. COV 12/0
Masquerader. COV 1/2
New England road. BRI 7/3
Nocturne. TOV 3/4
One asks. TOV 3/3
Retrospect. SHA 9/3
To an idealist. TOV 3/4
The visit. STM 11/4
The wheel of unimportant thing. SHA 8/2
Woodrow Wilson passes. COV 8/4

Cooke, Mattie O.

Evening. NEP 4-5/2
Cooksley, S. Bert
Celia. WAN 9/4
Dernateau. WAN 11/4
Plaint. WAN 11/4
Scheherazade. WAN 5/4
Serenade. WAN 7/4
Tryst. WAN 11/4
Coolbrith, Ina
Stanza. LYW 11/2
Cooley, Winifred Harper
Trivial. AMP Aut/1
Coolidge, Edwin
The strong west. LAR 7/3
Coombs, Edith I.
Brief magic. AIN 7/2
Coon, Marion
Charm against the city. AMP 8-9/3
Cooper, Belle
The quest. LYW 7-8/2
Sonnet, to Rudyard Kipling. LYW 4/1
Sonnet: a deserted city. LYW 1/2
Cooper, Frances L.
The blue places. LYW 2/4
Inarticulation. MEA 9/2
Manana. WRM 1/3
Motor cars at night. LYW 11/2
Cooper, Henri Celestina
Gray ashes. SMA 1/3
Cooper, M. Truesdell
Resignation. AMP10-11/3
Coote, Albert
Hymn to Attila. YAR 3/4
Sonnet. YAR 3/4
Cope, Helen Tyler
"Old Virginny lullaby." CTY S-A/1
Cope, Thomas Pym
Retarius. GUL 6/3
Corbin, Alice
Another spring. POE 9/4
The ballad of Macario Romero. POE 8/0
Bird song and wire. DIA 12/0
Call it stream or bird. HAM 12/4
Christ is born in Bethlehem. POE 8/0
Chula la Manana. POE 8/0
Coplas. POE 8/0
Cundiyo. POE 8/0
El coyotito. POE 8/0
Epitaph. POE 4/0
Excavation at Pecos. HAM 5/2
Flame. POE 9/4
Go touch the silent strings. POE 4/0
Horoscope. POE 9/4
I saw the world go by. POE 4/0
Loss. POE 9/4
Madre Maria. POE 8/0
Manzanita. POE 8/0
New Mexico folk songs. POE 8/0
Old age. NAT 3/2/0
Petrolino's complaint. POE 8/0
The road. NER 3/2/1
Song. POE 4/0
The storm bird. POE 4/0
Summer night. DOU 3-4/3
Summons. POE 4/0
Trees and horses. DIA 12/0
Two ways of love. YAR 7/1
The wood. POE 9/4
Corcoran, Frederick
Immortality. COM12/31/4
Corder, Raymond
The skyscraper. LIB 10/1
Corley, Donald
The dream house in the wood. RHY 2/3
The homecoming of astrology. RHY 2/3
In the tower of ivory. RHY 2/3
The lost chateau. RHY 2/3
Cornelius, Henry H.
Sunshine. NOW 2/3
Cornelius, Mary Chase
Ships that pass. POA 9/1
Cornell, Agnes
Acceptance. PER 1/4
The desert mocking-bird. WAN 5/4
The desert moon before...storm. OVM 8/4
Night fall after the wind. NER 1/14/0
Questioning. PER 4/3
Songs in the desert. WAN 12/4
Corning, Howard McKinley
Autumn twilight. VOI 12/4
Banners in the sun. LAR 5/3
Bondage. BUC 10/4
Dark alleys. PEG 7/3
Dawn in the woods. PEG 5/3
Demise. WAN 11/4
Derision. BUC 10/4
The dreamer. BUC 9/4
Empty streets. PEG 7/3
Epitaph. PAL Sum/3
Futility. AMP 8-9/3
Imminence. VOI 12/4
In asbence. WAN 7/4
"Listen, they speak." PAL Sum/3
Memories. SCR 5/4

Mirage arc lights. PEG 7/3
Oasis. PAL Sum/3
October dayfall. BUC 10/4
A paradise tree. LAR 5/3
The phantom rider. OVM 10/4
Plowmen. CIC 9/18/4
A portfolio of the city at nig. PEG 7/3
Prayers. INT10-12/4
Sea call. LAN 2/4
Sea walkers. WAN 5/4
Segments. PEG 7/3
Spring magical. LAR 5/3
Termination. MEA 2/4
Tide land. LAR 5/3
Tide. VOI 12-1/4
Tragedies. PAL Sum/3
Transformation. LYW 4/4
Undreamed. OVM 5/4
Unframed. PEG 5/3
What wisdom? LAR 5/3
White burial. LYW 2/4

Corwin, John Howard
Caprice. CTY Spr/2
The country burial ground. CTY Win/3
Delft. CTY Sum/3
Four candles. CTY Win/4
Ichabod of Honolulu. CTY Win/4
Katydids. CTY Aut/2
Plowing under. CTY Win/2
The poet in the tall grass. CTY S-A/4
A sunbeam in the barn. CTY Spr/3
To a youth. CTY Spr/3
A wet summer. CTY S-A/1

Costa, Florio
Sicilian love. MUN 5/2

Cowan, Lura M.
Experience. WAN 9/4
Neurotic. WAN 5/4
The pendulum swings. WAN 11/4
Then and now. WAN 7/4
A wish. WAN 5/4

Cowan, Sada
An Egyptian love song. LYW 2/2
The tiger. LWY 7-8/1
To a bit of jade. LYW 7-8/1

Cowdin, Jasper Barnett
Achievement. MID 11/0
Captive feet. COV 3/3
Flesh and spirit. COV 3/3
The home nest. LYW 1/2
Moods. LYW 5/4
When I am dead. COV 3/3
Words. CIV 9-10/4

Cowley(see R.Levinson),Malcolm

Cowley, Malcolm
About seven o'clock. NES 1/22/1
Against nightingales. DIA 5/0
The fishes. DIA 5/3
For a new hymnal. NES 1/20/3
From a young wife. PAG 4-5/0
History. DOU 2/3
Interment. POE 2/3
Mortuary. BRO 2/3
Mountain farm. BRO 5/2
Mountain valley. DIA 12/1
Nocturnal landscape. POE 2/3
Poem for two voices. POE 2/3
Prophetic. POE 2/3
Starlings. DIA 5/3
Sudden encounters. POE 2/3
Three hills. POE 2/3
The town was stretched. GAR 1-2/2
Valuta. BRO 11/2

Cox, Alice
The happy wife. BOO 10/4

Cox, Eleanor Rogers
The assumption. CAW 8/0
Moon cup. COM11/12/4
Music. AME10/15/1
Raphael's "Virgin Enthroned.." SIG ?/4
Viaticum and extreme unction. ROS ?/4

Cox, Lytton
Heritage. LYR 8/4

Cox, Margaret
Glad river. LAR 8/3
The key. LAR 9/3
Mist thoughts. LAR 2/4

Coyle, Delphine Harris
A solar myth. AMP10-11/3

Crafton, Allen
Cycle. COV 1/1
France: the towns. STE 3/3
God unrevealed. COV 10/2
God's song. COV 10/2
Late afternoon. LYR 7/3
October. EVM 10/0
On summer hills. COV 6/2
Resignation. COV 10/2
Retrospect and vision. LYR 12/2
The round of God. COV 3/3
What dawn beat at..hidden door. COV 1/1

Cramp, Winifred
Mary. CIC 4/24/4

Crandall (Jr.), Myron E.
Autumn. LAR 11/3

Crane (tr.), Hart
Locutions des pierrots. DOU 5/2

Crane, Hart
Black tambourine. DOU 6/1
My grandmother's love letters. DIA 4/0

Pastorale. DIA 10/1
A persuasion. MEA 10/1
Porphyro in Akron. DOU 8-9/1
Possessions. LIR Spr/4
Praise for an urn. DIA 6/2
Recitative. LIR Spr/4
The springs of guilty song. BRO 1/3

Crane, Nathalia
Destiny. BOO 12/4
The law. BOO 12/4
The vestal. NES 4/26/4

Crank, Gertrude
Greasewood. LYW 11/1

Cranmer, Catherine
Afterward. ALS 2/2
Favor. COV 8/0
Sisters. MID 8/1
Unmindful. MID 3/1

Crapsey, Adelaide
Blue hyacinths. DIA 7/2

Crawford, Helen Way
Dead gods. LAR 5/3
Songs and splashes from Alder. LAR 12/3
Summer is over. LAR 10/3

Crawford, John
Affinities. BRO 3/3
Brackish well. POE 9/1
Circe. GUL 5/3
Citizens. PAR #2/3
Dirge for Griselda. POE 4/3
Endymion. POE 9/1
Fox-fire. POE 4/3
Gifts. GUL 5/3
Ishmael. POE 4/3
Marah: snow maiden. MOR 1-4/4
Nadir. POE 9/1
Pianissimo. NOM Sum/3
Pilgrim. POE 4/3
Portraits. POE 4/3
Prosperine. MOR 1-4/4
Purr. POE 6/4
Sinbad. BRO 10/2
Sumach. POE 9/1
Tantala. MOR 4/3
The young Bacchus. POE 4/3

Crawford, Nelson Antrim
A. Leon Skipwith takes his soul. WAV 6/3
Around you music. COV 6/1
Branches. POE 10/1
Companionship. POE 10/1
Creed. MEA 9/1
Impotence. POE 10/1
Lake. POE 10/1
Music. PAG 4-5/0
On Main street. MEA 9/1
Song. POE 10/1
The sweeper. MEA 9/1

Crenshaw (Jr.), R. P.
Lady of the sea. YAR 10/3
Milord. YAR 2/4

Cresson, Abigail W.
All-Hallow's Eve. VOI Aut/2
Challenge. POE 12/3
Distance. LYW 7-8/3
Echo. COV 3/3
First show. VOI 12/2
Heights. TEM Aut/1
Hepatica. COV 3/2
How far away is April? SMA 4/2
The king. COV 12/2
Leaf song. VOI Aut/2
Love o' the wind. LAR 12/3
Message. COV 3/2
My field. LYW 7-8/3
November. VOI Aut/2

Crever, Anna Rozilla
The century plant. LYW 10/2
God's fool. CIC 8/30/3
Holy fear. CIC 5/24/3
Mount Hamilton. LYW 11/1

Crew, Alice H.
Embers. LAR 2/4
Genius. LAR 3/4
Night. LAR 10/3
Salinas Valley. LAR 3/4
When he made you. LAR 11/3

Crew, Helen Coale
A grace before meat on Christmas. STE 10/3
In a low rocking chair. STE 10/3
Irish song. POE 1/2
Non sine floribus. SCM 7/4

Crighton, Elizabeth
At sunset. SCR 4/3
Bohemia. SCR 5/3
Candles. SCR 5/3
Messengers. SCR 4/3
Wanderlust. AMP 8-9/3

Crisler, Ben
The masquerade. COV 1/3

Crocker, "Patsy" F. S.
Spring. AMP 6-7/3

Crocker, Bosworth
Wishes. BOO 4/0

Crocker, Helen Cowles
Design. AMP 6-7/3

Croker, Maria Briscoe
At evening. CIV 3/4
The cool springs of Charlotte. CIV 1/4
Immortality. CIV 5-6/4
In the days of Herod the King. CIV11-12/4
Sea lure. SCR 1/4
Song flowers. LAL 10/4
Water lilies. SCR 1/4

Crool, Peter
The almond tree. AMP 5-6/4
Road songs. AMP 8-9/3
Crosby, Ermina Morris
To a violin. AMP 10/2
Cross, Banbury
On the tomb of a noted wit. DOU 2-3/4
To an honest cutthroat. DOU 2-3/4
To the fastidious. DOU 2-3/4
Cross, John
Beauty. YAR 4/2
Cross, Margaret Virginia
Absence. AMP 12/3
Christmas candles. AMP11-12/4
"Couch o' dreams." AMP 2/2
"Garden of dreams." AMP 10/2
A Yuletide gift. COV 12/1
Crosser, Nora Badger
Children of the wood. LAL 10/4
Confirmation. CIV 5-6/4
The medley. CIV11-12/4
Crothers, Janet E.
Renunciation. CAP 5/3
Crowell, Grace Noll
Attitudes. COV 3/4
The canyon torrent. LYW 3/4
Fathers. LYW 3/4
The pines. BUC 12/4
Repetition. BUC 10/4
Silver poplars. SCM 4/3
Sunset on the peaks. LYW 3/4
Symbols. BUC 12/4
There are certain days. BUC 9/4
White fire. BUC 9/4
Youth. COV 6/0
Cullen, Countee
Bread and wine. CUU 6/3
Brown boy to brown girl. OPP 9/4
Dad. CUU 11/2
For a cynic. HAM 12/4
For a lovely lady. HAM 12/4
For a poet. HAM 12/4
For a singer. HAM 12/4
For a virgin lady. POE 5/4
For my grandmother. POE 5/4
For myself. HAM 12/4
Fruit of the flower. HAM 11/4
A lady I know. POE 5/4
Pagan prayer. MES 3/4
Road song. CUU 2/3
Saturday's child. CEN 9/4
Simon the Cyrenian speaks. POE 5/4
A song in praise. OPP 9/4
To a brown boy. BOO 11/3
The touch. CUU 5/3
The wise. NAT11/12/4
Yet do I marvel. CEN 11/4
Youth sings a song of rosebuds. BOO 11/4
Culnan, Ralph
Antiques. BUC 11/4
A garden idyl. AMP11-12/4
Cummings, Edward Estlin
Five Americans. BRO 10/3
Five poems. DIA 4/2
Five poems. DIA 5/0
Four poems. DIA 1/4
Poem, or beauty hurts Mr. Vina. S4N 12/2
Poem. DIA 10/1
Seven poems. DIA 1/0
Seven poems. DIA 1/3
Three United States sonnets. BRO 5/2
Cummings, Franklin
Amid April showers. LAR 4/4
At sunset. LAR 10/3
My mother. LAR 12/3
To Yosemite. LAR 10/3
To a disfigured soldier. LAR 4/4
Cummings, Marion
Here on the cliff's green edge. COM12/31/4
Shuttle song. COM12/17/4
Cunard, Nancy
From afar. BOO 11/4
Cunningham, Margaret Louise
Privileges. MAG 9/4
Rabonni. MAG 8/4
Cunningham, Minna Jarrett
Indian summer. AMP Aut/1
Cunningham, Nora B.
Alma. COV 3/3
Bafflement. COV 2/2
The bloom of pain. COV 2/2
The captive fantasy. COV 2/2
The captive. LYW 2/2
The coming of joy. COV 2/2
Contrast. LYR 5/2
Descent. LYW 12/2
Discretion. COV 3/3
Earth's sweetness. LYW 7-8/3
February. POE 2/4
Friends. COV 10/4
The genius. COV 10/3
Giving. POE 12/2
In praise of restraint. MEA 5/4
On reading Hardy's "Return of. COV 3/3
Perhaps. COV 10/4
The prophet. COV 2/2
Retort. COV 10/4
Surely I may come back. LYW 7-8/2
There's a wide sky. LYW 3/2

A voice. LYW 9/2
When petals fall. COV 5/4
Wild fowl. COV 2/2
The wind. LYW 10/3
Wisdom. COV 10/4

Curley, Lillian Mary
Apple blossoms. AMP 5-6/4

Curran, Edwin
The lions. POE 11/1

Curran, Lucy A.
The seeding. LYW 3/4

Curran, Pauline Garner
A lighthouse. LYW 6/3
Neisau. LYW 6/3
Shadows. LYW 6/3

Currier, Francis
Old man Edwards. FOR 12/4

Currier, Raymond P.
Burma. AMP 8-9/3

Curry, Walter Clyde
Idle questionings. AMP Aut/1
In a garden. AMP 5-6/4
Magic. FUG 6-7/3
Red roses in November. FUG 2/4
Rediscovered. FUG 12/3
Tomorrow. AMP 5-6/4

Curtin, Leonora F.
The first visit. LYW 10/3
A pastel. LYW 10/3

Curtis, A. B.
Mount Shusta. LAR 9/3

Curtis, Christine Turner
After tears. NES 8/9/4
November in New England. GRA 11/1
Penitent. MEA 1/4
Quenched. POE 12/4

Cushing, Edward
The old man. POE 2/4

Cushman, Harriette E.
Now acacias bloom. LAR 2/4

Cushman, Sylvia
A castle o'er the sea. SCR 11/3
The city of Honk Kong. SCR 10/3
In a Dutch garden. SCR 8/3
They call me the cat that walk. SCR 10/3

Cutajar, Mary Wright
Alchemy. CTY Spr/4
The poet. CTY S-A/4
Sea calm. INT10-12/4
Song of..red earth-New Jersey. CTY Win/4
The terrace. CTY Win/4

Cutting, Mary Stewart
The dawning. LAD 2/4

D'Angelo, Pascal
Accident in the coal dump. BOO 11/4
Dawn. BOO 6/4
The last shore. BOO 9/4
Life in life. BOO 8/4
Monte Maiella. NAT10/11/2
Night scene. LIB 7/2
Song of light. BOO 5/2
Song of night. CEN 3/3
Sudden gold. BOO 10/2
To a warrior. LIB 7/2
To some modern poets. CEN 6/2
Whispers. NES 5/20/2

D'Armes, Dominic
Ballad inventory. DOU 2/2

d'Autremont, Hattie H.
Found, not lost. POA 1/2
A portrait of a child. POA 1/2

D'Emo, Leon
The middle ages. CEN 2/1

D'Orge, Jeanne
A child much loved of poets. MEA 5/3
Interiors. MEA 5/3
Point Lobos, California. SCM 12/3
The sink. MEA 5/3

D'Vaughn, Amos M.
Love. AMP 6/2

D.,D.D.
Memoriae aeternae, David Masso. EME 2/3

D.,H. See Doolittle, Hilda

D.,L.
Rosamund, on her portait... ALS 6/1

D.,Z.G.
The road. GRA 10/1

Dabbs, James McBride
To a Lombardy poplar. AMP 8-9/3

Dabney, Julia P.
Stradivarius. COV 1/2
The wind bloweth where is list. LYW 11/2

Daca, David
Or? BOO 7/3

Daily, Alpha B.
Little white ribbon of gold. CTY Aut/2

Daingerfield, Francis Lee
At the year's end. REW 12/1
November day. REW 11/1

Daley, James
Day of doom. WAV 3/4
On a hill. WAV 3/4
Summer. WAV 3/4

Dalton, Power
Bound. COV 9/2

Daly, Elizabeth
Breath of honeysuckle. LYW 11/4
Changeling. VOI Aut/1
Circle. LYW 4/4
Circumstance. VOI 12-1/4
Conviction. VOI Spr/3
Dream child. LYR 8/4
Dreamers. VOI 8-9/3
Finite. LYW 4/4
Flail. POE 11/3
Flame. LYR 6/2
Flame. VOI 8-9/3
Go from me. NET 9/1
Grass daisies. VOI Sum/2
Gulls. POE 11/3
Heart beat. VOI Win/2
I will be still. LYW 9/3
Impulse. POE 11/3
It was a wind. LYW 3/4
L'inevitable. LYW 12/4
My own. MOT 8/1
My thoughts. LWY 11/1
My torch. NEN 3/28/1
Nadir. VOI Spr/3
Noblesse oblige. VOI Spr/3
Omnipotence. TEM Aut/1
Question. COV 5/2
Relativity. S4N 12/2
Request. SNA11/15/1
Sequence. VOI Win/2
Then. TEL 10/1
Time, that is long in coming. COV 1/4
Tree. VOI Aut/2
Triumph. LYW 6/2
Twilight. LWY 11/1
Undertow. COV 9/2
Urns of light. VOI 12-1/4
White hour. VOI 9-10/4
White stairs. COV 10/4
White stairs. VOI 8-9/3
Words. VOI Win/2
Worlds may darken. MEA 12/3
Zenith. VOI Win/2

Daly, Elizabeth
To the ladies. SCM 8/4

Daly, James J.
The beggar-knight. CAW 5/0
Carnival. PRA 1-2/3
Crematorium. BRO 11/2
Friends. CAW 3/0
In Coventry. BOO 11/2
Macabre. BRO 11/2
Midnight. COV 8/2
Storm. COV 8/2
To one afraid. COV 8/2
Words of the old cremator. WAV #4/2

Dalzell, Hugh
The little grey street. PEG 3/3
Longing. LYR 8/1

Damon, S. Foster
Burning bush. POE 4/4
Conversations. BRO 6/2
Epilogue. BOO 1/2
Fete. NER 1/24/3
The holy gilde. DIA 2/2
In the third person. POE 4/4
Kiri no meijiyama, a noh drama. DIA 2/0
A thought after taps. NOA 10/0
Voyage. BRO 6/2

Dancer, Ruth
Mystery. AMP 4-5/3

Dancer, Ruth S.
Bittersweet. AMP Aut/1
In a garden. AMP 3-4/4

Daniels, Earl
Beneath a flowering tree. COV 4/1
Birth. POE 5/4
Candles at dinner. COV 2/2
Comprehension. LIB 8/1
Death. POE 5/4
For Amy Lowell. COV 4/1
In time of great drougth. VOI 9-10/4
Incorrigible. COV 8/4
Lyrical balance sheet. COV 8/4
Protest against realism. DOU 11/3
Renunciation. FRE 2/13/4
Solitude. PAG 8-9/1
Specked apples. BOO 11/4

Danner, Bessie May
The song of the meadow lark. LAR 4/4

Dargan, Olive Tilford
Far bugles. FUG 8/4
Francesca (1904-1917). SCM 8/0
In doubt. FUG 12/4
In the black country. SCM 9/1
The inquisitor. NES10/14/2
The master. COV 7/3
Retarded. COV 7/3
To William Blake. COV 7/3
To a lady sitting in starlight. BOO 12/2

Darling, Esther Birdsall
Life. OVM 3/4

Dashiell, Landon Randolph
The scarecrow man. LOS10/13/3

Datesman, Mrs. M. Laughlin
The postman. AMP 6-7/3

David, Jonathan
Bethel. FUG 6/2
The quiet hour. FUG 6/2
Upon a time. FUG 6/2

Davidson, Anna E.
My prayer. CIJ 5/4

Davidson, Donald

Davies, William Henry
Strange flowers. SMI 6/1
The swimmer. BOT10/10/2
Those who pray seldom sing. VOI10-11/3
To a suitor. DOU 8-9/4
To an outgoing tenant. LIB 5/2
To other Marys. COV 4/0
Two-medicine lake. BOO 4/1
We two and marriage. CEN 9/0
The weapon of laughter. NEN 4/6/1
A week-end dance. LYW 7-8/3
When I no longer care. BUC 12/4
The wise lovers. POE 6/3
Your words. FOR 5/4

Davies, William Henry
The fates. HAM 2/3
The happy man. NER 1/4/2
The hour of magic. HAM 3/2
How many buds. HAM 3/2
Impudence. HAM 3/2
Leaves. HAM 12/2
Love the jealous. YAR 10/4
Love's payment. HAM 12/2
Love, like a drop of dew. HAM 12/2
The snowflake. NER 7/25/3
Strong moments. NER11/10/0
Telling fortunes. HAM 3/2
The two heavens. NER 7/25/3
The two stars. NER11/21/3
Two women. HAM 3/2
Where she is now. NER 6/15/1
The woods and the banks. NER 1/4/2

Davis, Allan
A song. LYR 9/4
Song. MEA 2/4

Davis, Christine Kerr
The ould fiddler. COV 2/1
The stay at home. SCM 1/1

Davis, Clifford E.
How it happened. AMP 10/1

Davis, Harold Lenoir
Baking bread. POE 6/0
Dog-fennel. POE 10/2
From a vinyard. POE 6/0
In this wet orchard. POE 6/0
The market-gardeners. POE 6/0
October: "The old eyes" POE 6/0
Open hands. POE 10/2
The rain-crow. POE 6/0
Stalks of wild hay. POE 6/0
The threshing-floor. POE 6/0
To the river beach. POE 6/0

Davis, Hassoldt
The futurist section. WAN 6/4
Harbour twilight. WAN 6/4

Davis, Helen Bayley
Buttercups. LAL 10/4
The dancer. CIV11-12/4
Late October. LAL 10/4
A spring song. CIV 5-6/4

Davis, Julia Johnson
Antipodes. LYR 6/4
Blackberry wine. LYR 5/3
Dante. LYR 8/1
Dante. PER 4/4
De gospel train. LYR 10/4
The dryad. LYR 4/1
"I love all quiet things" LYR 6/1
Loss. LYR 9/2
Marionette. COV 9/4
My books. LYR 12/1
"Red wine is beautiful." LYR 8/2
She sews fine linen. LYR 4/3
Songs of a little boy. LYW 9/3
To a little boy. LYR 3/2
To my little son. LYR 3/4
Treasure. LYR 5/1

Davis, Leland
The ballad of Adam's first. NAT 8/9/2
The ballad of a judge in Israe. DOU 3-4/3
A ballad of jealousy. LIB 8/1
A ballad of the queen's maying. DOU 1/3
The carol of the cockroaches. DOU 11/3
A ghetto catch. POE 4/3
In old Trinity churchyard. NES 6/3/2
The peril of happiness. POE 4/3

Davis, Leslie G.
The moonlight on the wave. CTY Win/4

Davis, Martha
Magic. LYW 11/4
A mining town. AMP 2-3/3

Davis, Philip Richard
Legacy. WAV 6/3
Purple plectron. WAV 6/3

Davison, Edward
The blind. NES 3/15/4
A grave. OUT 7/6/1
The sunken city. OUT11/10/0
The swan. NES ?/1
The vigil. NES 1/12/4

Davisson, Oscar
Laus Stellarum. BOO 10/1

Dawne, Homer
Three sights. LAR 9/3
Wistaria. LAR 9/3

Dawson, Isabel
Coal. CIV 7-8/4

Dawson, Lulu Brunt

To-day he is twenty-one. CTY S-A/4

Dawson, Mitchell
And no man. LIR Spr/4
Any night. POE 1/4
Baba Va Levala. DOU 10/4
Chicago. DOU 10/4
Contrarywise. WAV 1/2
Dining alone. DOU 6/1
Dry ochre. POE 1/4
Gulls' eyes are cold. POE 1/4
Knowise. WAV 1/2
Kraals. DOU 10/4
Morning songs. DOU 10/4
New days. POE 1/4
Nigger. DOU 10/4
No and yes. POE 1/4
This then is holiness. LIR Spr/4
Tula-bud girls. DOU 10/4

Dawson, Thomas
Impasse. MEA 10/2
Lost. MEA 10/2
O turn your eyes. MEA 10/2

Day, Albert E.
Regret. CIC 5/1/4

Day, Cora S.
Dilemma. GRA 6/2
Dreamers. GRA 8/2
Homesick. GRA 8/2
New houses. GRA 4/2

De Acosta, Mercedes
Lumbermen. POE 1/1
Soiled hands. POE 1/1
To Vouletti. POE 1/1
Unreality. POE 1/1

De Bainville, Theodore
The ballad of the hung. STM 12/4

De Banville, Theodore
To Adolphe Gaiffe. FRE10/10/3

de Ford, Miriam Allen
Agrippina. STM 11/4
At night. LWY 10/1
A city at night. LYW 11/2
Forest love. OVM 3/4
Lady of the morning. LYW 9/3
Man and woman. TOM 9/4
A parting. OVM 7/4
A peasant girl. LYW 11/3
Period. OVM 12/4
Ronsard, 9/11/1524-12/27/1587. POE 9/4
Running water. LIB 10/2
Santa Cruz. LYW 1/2
Shadow canyon. POE 10/1
A sonnet to Shelley. LYW 11/2
Summum Bonum. LYW 2/4
Themes. POE 10/1
Thistle bloom. STE 5/4
The torch. MES 8/2
Traveler's ditty. POE 6/3
Wheatland - 1921. LIB 9/1
Will it be like this? POE 10/1

De Fossett, Theresa
Night in old Vermont. VER 1923

De La Mare, Walter
Ad infinitum. MEA 5/1
Break of morning. YAR 4/2
Captive. NER 3/14/3
Comfort. BRO 12/1
The corner stone. NER 5/25/1
The double. HAM 9/1
The dreamer. MEA 5/1
Epitaph. DIA 6/4
The gigantic image. VOI Sum/2
In the dock. BRO 11/1
Karma. NER 5/25/1
A lullaby. LYR 1/2
Martins: September. NES12/17/1
The monologue. NER11/23/1
Not that way. BRO 12/1
The spectre. NER 5/25/1
The stranger. CEN 12/1
Summer dawn. NER 5/25/1
Sunk Lyonesse. CEN 10/1
Titmouse. NES 9/24/1
The truth of things. NER 5/25/1
The voice. NES 1/15/1
Who? NER 5/25/1
The widow. NER10/18/2

De Laughter, Margaret
A certain one sings of his lad. STE 4/3
Harlequin is overheard weeping. STE 12/2
Invocation. POE 8/1
Knowledge. POE 6/3
A pantoun. POE 6/3
Pierrot and Columbine. POE 8/1
The poet. LAR 3/3
Qui ante nos fererunt. STE 7/4
Refuge. STE 5/4
Renunciation. STE 8/4
Requiem. POE 8/1
Toward evening. POE 8/1

De Lestry, Edmond L.
By the river. LAR 10/3

De Lubicz-Milosz, O. W.
Strophes. DIA 11/1

De Nevers, Lucile
I am yours. AMP 6-7/3

De Pinna, Constance Vivian
Gold. CAP 1-2/3
My freedom. CAP 1-2/3
Song of man to woman. CAP 1-2/3

De Richey, Tina Mondotti
Plenipotentiary. DIA 5/3

De Rubio, Dolores
A Isabel. CAP11-12/2

Straying feet. CAP11-12/2

De Spain, Jay Roderic
The unforgiven fool. OVM 5/4

De Ventadour, Arnault
Beata Beatrice. MEA 5/3
Cleopatra as Mary Garden. MEA 5/3
The cyndus. MEA 5/3
Dames of the old waggery. MEA 5/3
Dona Ana at the judgment. MEA 5/3
Phaedra Pasiphaeia. MEA 5/3

De Witt, S. A.
Surrender. NOM Win/2
To the other woman. NOM Win/2

De Wolf, Richard C.
To a black topaz. MIN 5-6/4

de l'Abrie-Richey, Roubaix
Streetscape. LYW 1/2

DeLancey, Susan
Simple sounds. AMP 6-7/3

DeRan, Edna Smith
Dinner times. CTY Win/4
Let me be a pine. CTY S-A/4

Deacon, Anne
The traveller. POE 11/0

Dean, Agnes Louise
Look nook. LYW 7-8/3

Dean, Eloise Earl
Lullaby. AMP 4-5/3
Sally Lou. AMP 4-5/3
The screech owl. AMP 4-5/3

Dean, Mary
Forecast. MEA 12/1
Incomprehensible. MEA 2/2

Dearmer, Geoffrey
A legend of the desert. COV 6/2

Decker, Frances Macy
My love. LAL 5/4

Deir, David
The frost. EME 12/2

Dell, Floyd
The young wife, waking. BOO 6/4

Dendric
To a fetish. FUG 6/2

Dennen, Grace Atherton
The awakening. LYW 7-8/1
Childhood and memories. LYR 3/2
The coming of dawn. AMP 2-3/3
The end of the feud. LYW 1/3
From a workshop window. AMP 2-3/3
From the workroom window. LYR 9/2
The frost. LYW 1/2
I hope that I remember. LYW 1/3
Magic. LYW 4/2
Pastels. LYW 10/1
The riding of the peaceful Hen. LYW 7-8/3
A song of three harbors. LYW 4/1
Winding the clock. LYW 7-8/1

Dennis, Alberta Johnston
San Marino ranch. LYW 7-8/2

Dennis, E. Mildred
Rondeau. INT 4-6/4

Denny, Eleanor M.
The book of the white birch. LYW 4/2
The destroyer. LYW 6/2
The geyser at Calistoga. LYW 6/2

Derby, Jeannette
Land breeze. NER 2/18/0
A mulberry tree. PAG 8-9/1
Ship song. NER 4/21/0

Derry, Selma
Heritage. VOI 9-10/4
Paphian prayer. VOI 9-10/4

Derwood, Gene
Older ecstasy. RHY 1/3

Desmond, William
Time of beads. MAG 10/4

Detzer, Karl W.
Glory. OUT 5/16/3

Deutsch (tr.), Babette
Evening. POE 12/2
Homer. POE 12/2
A song, by Ivan A. Bunin. FRE 8/17/1
Suffering. BRO 12/2

Deutsch, Babette
And again to Po Chu-i. DIA 9/1
Apocrypha. NEW 3/21/3
Archaeology. BOO 12/4
At Asahi. DOU 12/1
Avatars. DIA 8/2
Capriccio. RHY 2/3
Chess. LYW 3/2
Christmas: Moscow. NER 8/13/4
Colloque metaphysique. MEA 1/3
Dark gates. MEA 7/2
Day laborers. BOO 11/2
Ditch-diggers. NER 6/13/3
Fall fantasia. NES11/19/1
Festival. COV 6/1
Forbidden. POE 2/4
Forgotten. POE 2/4
Fourth dimension. POE 7/1
Fugitive. CEN 6/1
Heirloom. BOO 9/3
Hibernal. DIA 9/2
The hound. NER 8/6/4
In April. LYR 4/3
In August. BOO 8/2
In durance. NER 5/7/4
Infancy. NER 8/8/3
Knowledge. POE 7/1

Leningrad. NAT 8/27/4
Marriage. NAT 3/22/2
The master. DOU 11/1
Maternity. YAR 4/4
Measure. DOU 11/1
"Now speak of love no more." LYW 1/2
Octave. NER 2/28/3
Of beauty and love. MEA 2/2
Of riches. NER 4/12/2
Old women. NAT 8/27/4
Or not to be. NES 8/26/2
Overtones. POE 7/1
Penreb's tomb. NER ?/1
Pity. NES 4/8/2
The pledge of Benjamin. YAR 4/4
Poet. BOO 4/4
Prevision. BOO 10/4
Pungence. REW 11/1
Reflections. POE 7/1
Return. NER 2/8/2
Strange flower. NER 8/27/4
Sustenance. NAT12/10/4
Tak for sidst. POE 2/2
This little body. NES 7/12/4
To a silent man. NER 1/3/3
Ways of love. COV 7/1
Where no thief draweth near. NER 7/23/4
Woods and waters. NER 11/2/1
Words. NER12/31/4
The younn remembers. POE 2/4

Devlin, Jane
Adios amor. SCR 8/3
Bonfire. SCR 1/4
The city's lesson. SCR 1/4
The Far East. SCR 9/3
San Francisco. SCR 3/4
The weed. SCR 9/3

Dewey, Annette Barrett
Your prospects. NEP 4-5/2

Dewey, Edward
Gloria Regis. COV 10/4

Dewey, Marion R.
Flotsam. WAN 6/3
In a public square. WAN 5/4
To those who die in high place. WAN 10/3

Dewing, Andrew
Kwannon. LYW 5/2

Dexter, E. G.
Summer shower. LYW 9/3

Dexter, Ernest
Early morning at Suisun. LYW 7-8/1
Late evening at Suisun. LYW 7-8/2
Sidney Lanier. LYW 12/1
Waved a blade. LWY 9/1

Dickie, Augusta
Spring at the perfume stand. AMP 4-5/3

Dickinson, Charles Henry
The divine presence. CIC 7/26/3
Forecasting. CIC 11/8/3

Dickinson, Emily
A rose. LYR 6/1

Dickson, Margarette Ball
A modern miracle. SCR 12/4

Diehnel, Ellie Tatum
My window box. AMP 12/3

Dier, Caroline Lawrence
Contentment. AMP10-11/3

Dier, Caroline L.
The pioneer. LAR 6/3

Dier, Caroline Lawrence
Flute music. CIM 7/12/4

Diew, Caroline Lawrence
First snow. AMF 12/4

Dill, Mabel
Love. COV 3/0

Diller, Henry Corneau
Summer love and winter love. STE 12/2

Dillerville, Humphrey
Seventeenth Century. CEN 7/3

Dilley, Millicent Davis
Christmas rose. SPT12/21/4
A Christmas wreath. AMP11-12/4
Evening in the green hills. VER 11/5/3
Evening in the Green Hills. VER #5/4
To a humming-bird. VER #9/4
To urbane. DEP 12/4
Trailing Arbutus. SPT12/14/4

Dillon, George H.
A fellow and a girl. MEA 11/4
The humble horse. MEA 11/4

Dismorr, Blanche
Charlotte Bronte. POE 5/1

Ditmanham, Jane Louisa
After the wedding. SCR 10/2
In mercy. SCR 9/2
My heart a plaything. SCR 1/3
Peace. SCR 9/2

Divine, Charles
A beggar. SMA 12/0
Conflicting emotions. SMA 6/3
A cottage in the Catskills. MEA 1/4
I'd make a necklace for your... TEL 5/1
In praise of a house on a hill. MUN 6/2
A mood of a certain color. REW 7/4
A mood of certain color. REW 4/3
My heart. SHA 12/2

A neglected church in Spain. LES 3/19/1
Never will you hold me. NES 6/23/3
O, you belong upon the sea. MUN 4/3
Paris: the Seine at night. COV 2/1
A pleasant trade in spring. COV 4/1
Sea gulls. MEA 1/4
The summer walks in many ways. MUN 8/2
Tonight the gypsies wait for y. MEA 9/2
Tonight you came to me. TEL 4/1
A village far from cities. MUN 10/2

Dix, Fred Keller
A seashell. AMP 5-6/4
Who finds a sonnet. AMP 12/2

Doane, Gilbert Harry
To a Roman tear-bottle, found. LYW 9/3

Dobbs, James McBride
Just beyond. SOU 7/3

Dobby, William P.
Red. MAG 6/3

Dobell, Sidney
The ballad of Keith of Ravelst. GRA 9/3

Dobson, Austin
To a lyric poet. CEN 10/0

Dockham, R. E.
Hang on. CTY Win/2
His question. CTY S-A/1
Just a friend. CTY Spr/2
We three. CTY S-A/1

Dodd, Lee Wilson
Age and youth. POE 4/1
Animula, vagula. YAR 4/3
As the senator puts it. FRE 1/25/2
The flower. CEN 2/4
Riddle. POE 4/1
Son of Adam. BOO 10/2
Vacuum. POE 12/3

Dodge, Anne Atwood
The band concert. MEA 9/2

Dodge, Louis
Derelict. SCR 12/2
Discovery. SCM 3/1
Evening. SCM 5/0
The prison. SCM 5/4

Dodge, Margaret
The mother. CIC 7/6/2

Doell, Frederic
Silver rhapsodies. RHY 2/3

Dolloff, Amy J.
The messenger. GRA 1/1

Dolson, Cora A. Matson
The play. POA 9/1
Violets. SUN 7/3

Dombey
Unitas. COV 1/1

Don, Anita E.
The gray goose calls. SOV 1923
Piping. FUG 6-7/3

Donald, Gene
The old man. REW 2/2

Dondo, Mathurin
The beggar. OVM 7/4

Donohue, Edward F.
Her home. MAG 7/2
Omniscience. MAG 2/2

Donovan, Lois
Credo. MAG 6/3
In hospital. MAG 3/2
November. MAG 11/4
October. MAG 10/3
Today, if ye hear his voice. MAG 6/3

Doolittle, Hilda
At Baia. POE 10/1
At Eleusis. DOU 11/3
Cassandra. RHY 6-7/3
Centaur song. DOU 11/3
Helen. BOO 5/3
Helios. DIA 11/0
Hesperides - Fragment XXXVI. POE 10/1
Hippolytus temporizes. BOO 10/1
The islands. NOA 1/0
Phaedra rebukes Hippolta. DIA 11/0
Phedra remembers Crete. DIA 11/0
Simaetha. COT ?/1
Song. POE 10/1
Thetis. POE 6/3

Doran, Louise A.
The captives. UNV 10/4
Horizon pictures. LAR 11/3
Mist magic. OVM 7/4
Winter. LAR 11/3

Dorrance, Gordon
French darkness. AMP 6-7/3

Dorris, Frances
The organ. NEN 4/1

Dorset, Edmund
At betrothal. CEN 7/4
The boss. COV 8/4
The builders. HAM 11/1
The chauffeur. COV 2/4
A comforter. POE 7/4
An ex-voto. COV 8/4
In the village. POE 7/4
Loyalty. HAM 2/1
McIntyre and Fate. COV 2/4
Mother. CEN 7/4

A non-conformist. COV 8/4
On failure. POE 7/4
Politics. COV 8/4
To a lady. POE 7/4
To another. POE 7/4
The turn in the road. HAM 10/1
Two dead men. COV 8/4
The wind-up. COV 12/3
A wood-carver at Wieringen. COV 2/4

Dorsey, Sallie Webster
Constancy. LAL 10/4

Dos Passos, John
Jardin des Tuileries. DIA 6/1
Of poetic composition. DIA 6/1
Quai de la Tourelle. BOO 3/2
Quias: Rive Gauche. MEA 7/2
Vermilion towers. BOO 11/1

Doughty (tr.), Leonard
The beginning of the fast. TER 7/3
Brides of heaven. TER 7/3
By the fireside. TER 7/3
Cessation. TER 7/3
Comradeship. TER 4/2
Flowers of fable. TER 7/3
He and she. TER 4/2
The home coming. TER 4/2
Horns of Efland. TER 4/2
I dreamed a false sweet dream. TER 7/3
Ich liebe sie. TER 4/2
An interlude. TER 7/3
Lorelei. TER 4/2
The lyre. TER 4/2
The mattress-grave. TER 4/2
The message. TER 4/2
Moon-magic. TER 4/2
Once upon a time. TER 4/2
Palm and pine. TER 4/2
Poet laureate. TER 4/2
Queen Mary. TER 4/2
Sentimentality. TER 4/2
The shepherd lad. TER 4/2
The suicide's grave. TER 4/2
To a child. TER 4/2
To one unborn. TER 4/2
A verse for youth. TER 7/3
Why? TER 7/3

Doughty, Leonard
Childe Roland to..dark tower... ALS 4/1
John of Belgrade. DIA 3/4

Douglas, James Lee
The father of creation. GRI 1/1
The gorilla man. GRI 1/1
The mother of the plains. GRI 3/1

Douglas, Marjory S.
Inarticulate. NOM Win/2

Douglas, William
The duke. MEA 5/1

Douthitt, Harold M.
My star. AMP Aut/1

Dow, Dorothy
Cabaret. POE 5/4
Covenant. POE 6/3
Field-magic. CEN 8/4
Heimweh. POE 5/4
I shall love lightly. BOO 3/3
I shall not bend. VOI Spr/3
In Winchester. PAG 8-9/1
Man of all work. SCM 9/4
Separation. VOI 12-1/4
Spring picture. POE 5/4
There are mouths to kiss. PAG10-11/1
Threads of sorror. VOI Aut/2
To Atalanta. BOO 5/2
To a mirror. PAG 12/1
Two at tea. POE 5/4

Dowe, Jennie E. T.
Idyll. LAL 3/4
Say Shelah ye'll have me. LAL 1/4

Dowell, Ida M.
Retrospect. PEG 5/3

Dowell, Ivan T.
August ninth. PEG 3/3
Grist. DOU 3/2
Poem. DOU 12/2
Words. DOU 3/2

Dowing, Eleanor Therese
The valley. CAW 11/2

Doyle, William V.
Golgotha. MAG 3/2

Drachman, Julian M.
The fighter prays. OUT 4/7/0
Gargoyles. NAT 4/24/0
A hundred villages. COV 1/3
New lamps for old. COV 10/2
You too? AMH10/27/2

Drake (tr.), William A.
The cracked bell. FUG 6/6/3
The former life. FUG 6/6/3
Ill luck. FUG 6/20/3
Invocation. NOM Win/2
Man conversing with his soul. NOM Win/2
Qui regan amore. NOM Win/2
Spleen. FUG 6/20/3

Drake, Sidney
Now that he sleeps. LYW 5/4

Drake, William A.
Armenian love song. COV 4/4
Renunciation. NAT 6/18/4
Tristesse. MEA 6/4
You are to me. MEA 6/4

Dransfield, Jane
Matins. COV 9/1

Mists. COV 9/1
Moonlight. COV 11/0
Morning sunshine. COV 9/1
The mountain. COV 9/1
Raveling. COV 11/4
Searchlight. COV 11/0
Tides. COV 9/1
Wind. COV 9/1
The young poplar tree. COV 9/1

Draper, Jane
Even in thought. VOI 12/2
I look into the stars. VOI 12/2
Other springs. VOI 12/2
Premonition. VOI 12/2
The return. VOI 12/2
Spoken words. VOI 12/2

Dreiser, Theodore
The hidden god. NES12/20/4
In a country graveyard. NES12/20/4
The new day. NES12/20/4
The poet. NES12/20/4
Tall towers. NES12/20/4

Drennan, Marie
Adopted. AMP 12/3
The Leesburg milliner. OVM 12/4
The suppliant. OVM 10/4
Values. OVM 8/4

Dresbach, Glenn Ward
Appleblossoms near the desert. MEA 5/2
Arroyo twilight. STE 1/4
The better ship, Panama. LYW 11/3
The brook under ice. MEA 12/3
A burro-load of cider. OVM 3/4
Cactus bloom. ALS 10/1
Calm near the desert. DOU 10/1
Cattle before the storm. LYR 5/3
Cedar and stone. COV 11/4
Cedar river. VOI 6-7/3
A cock crowns near the desert. LYW 12/3
The colonel's lady. COV 12/0
Contradiction. DOU 10/1
The crow's nest. EVM 11/0
The defeated. ALS 11/1
Desert burial. BUC 9/4
Desert legend. MEA 2/4
Desert morning. LYW 3/4
Desert rain. POE 3/4
Desert shadow songs. MEA 5/1
Dirge for a sailing ship. WAN 9/4
Empty corral. MEA 2/4
The enchanted mesa. MEA 1/2
The game - Panama. LYW 7-8/2
Goodnight song. COV 11/0
Ground. ALS 8-9/2
In western mountains. POE 5/2
The last ship. COV 6/2
The lizzard on the ledge. LYW 7-8/2
Mardi Gras night - Panama. DOU 7/2
Meadow brook. MID 4/1
Mountain pasture. LYW 3/2
Mountain water song. LYW 11/1
Not to a temple dancer. DOU 8/2
O thrush, in what deep grades. WAN 4/4
The old sailor. CEN 3/2
Orchard tragedy. ALS10-11/2
The painted desert. LYW 10/2
The patio. COV 6/2
A place in the sun. ALS 9/1
The pool near the sky. COV 6/2
A rainbow over the desert. DOU 10/2
Recall. ALS 7/3
Renewal. COV 6/2
River songs. MID 7/1
The road. LYW 1/2
A row of willows. ALS 1/2
Ruts in the thaw. VOI 5-6/4
Sailing ship. COV 3/4
Song in autumn. ALS 2/2
Song. BOO 6/2
Song. DOU 1/3
Song. DOU 4/2
Song. VOI Sum/2
Songs in the desert. COV 11/0
Songs of the plains. POE 1/2
Songs while..prairie whispers. MID 10/0
Songs. ALS 5/2
Songs. POE 6/0
Sorcerer's wood. LYR 9/3
Spider web songs. ALS 6/2
Spinning. CIM 6/11/4
Storm-rain songs. LYW 9/3
Sun through glass. NES 6/14/4
The sunken island. BUC 9/4
The Syrian peddler. POE 3/4
Things that were a shelter. VOI 5-6/4
To a road runner. DOU 9/2
To one beloved. POE 10/0
To the desert. COV 1/3
The trapped rabbit. COV 9/1
Victor Watson- the rancher. LYW 6/2
While the appleblossoms fall. COV 5/0
White sails against... DOU 11/1
Wild geese over the desert. DOU 1/2
The wind in the maples. DOU 3-4/3

Witches' song. ALS 8/1
Yucca in the moonlight. VOI Sum/2

Drewry, Guy Carleton
Afterglow. SCR 7/4
Autumn mood. VOI 12/4
The dreamer. INT10-12/4
The immortals. WAN 11/4
Life. DIA 12/4
Penetralia. WAN 7/4
Thoughts. SCR 5/4
To a woman. SCR 7/4
Twilight thoughts. SCR 6/4
Woodland pool. LAL 9/4

Drinkwater, John
Absence. YAR 4/1
Against treason. NAT12/29/0
Condition. NES10/18/4
Decision. MAC 4/2
Dying philosopher to...fiddle. CEN 1/1
Fairford nightingales. SCM 3/1
Hereafter. YAR 4/1
A lesson to my ghost. NOA 11/0
The maid of Naaman's wife. MEA 5/2
The pledge. YAR 4/0
Portia's housekeeping. DIA 1/1
Thrift. YAR 4/0
To and fro about the city. NER 3/31/0
The toll-gate house. SCM 5/1
Union. POE 12/0
Vocation. SCM 3/1
When sleep delays. BUC 11/4
The witch-ball. LYR 7/4

Driscoll, Louise
Bargain. POE 7/4
Cedars at night. LYR 4/4
The conqueror. COV 12/2
The desert has one god. SON 12/0
Folly song. COV 12/2
Fruit trees. TEM 6/1
Futility. COV 9/4
Futility. LYR 3/4
The good hour. VOI 3-4/4
The heir. FRE 3/5/4
The heretic. COV 4/0
Honey. HAM 3/2
I go but my heart stays. COV 4/0
The idol. VOI10-11/3
Immortality. COV 11/0
Keep my hand. POE 10/1
Late autummn. COV 11/0
Lot's wife. FRE10/31/3
The lover. COV 8/2
Moon gift. TEM 6/1
Mountain stream. POE 7/4
The owl. POE 6/3
Petrograd. VOI Spr/3
Portrait. VOI 3-4/4
Premonition. POE 3/0
The solitary. COV 9/4
Speech. VOI10-11/3
The spinet. COV 11/0
Spring market. COV 5/4
Spring thoughts. COV 4/0
Three poems: luck. COV 6/1
Transition. COV 9/4
Two old men. COV 5/2

Driscoll, Marjorie Charles
In Babylon. LYW 5/2
Unrepentant. ALS 7/3

Dromgoole, Will Allen
Mysteries. LAR 12/3
A sonnet of forgetting. SOU 7/3

Drury, John
After a night. CAP 10/2
Aside. NOM Spr/3
Autumn in the city. CAP 10/2
Awakening. WAV 6/3
City streets. CAP11-12/2
Dead sea weed. CAP 10/2
Dusk questions. CAP 10/2
Evening in the west. LYW 7-8/2
Fantasy. MOR Aut/2
Hurried. LYW 7-8/2
I have loved. NOM Spr/3
Incident. TEM Win/3
Morning-glories. STA #1/3
Night lamps. PAR #2/3
Snow-piece. PEG 3/3
Spell of granite. LYW 11/2
Street-lamps. WAV 6/3
Sunlight. CAP 10/2
Three love poems. CAP 5/3
Traffic. S4N 1-2/3

Dryden, Charlotte
Milky way. AMP 9-10/4

Dryden, Cyrus P.
Autumn. AMP 9-10/4

Du Bois, Graham
Haunted. LYR 11/2
The silent dining room. LYW 9/3

Du Gros, Leslie Leigh
Homecoming. LYW 4/4

Du Maurier, Eugenie
Amico de misere. SCR 8/4
At the grave of Poe. SCR 11/3
Autumn has come. CIV 9-10/4
By the sea. CIV 3/4
Clotilde at the organ. SCR 7-8/2
Consummation. SCR 8/3
Dreams. SCR 5/3
Egypt's mystic lotus. SCR 5/3
The first Easter. SCR 3/3
Goldenrod. SCR 8/3

A hundred years from now. SCR 9/3
Icecreamland. SCR 7-8/2
Icicles. CIV11-12/4
In the rain. SCR 11/3
Josephine. INT 1-3/4
The king's quest. SCR 10/3
Lady golden rod. LAL 10/4
Longing. SCR 8/4
A lullaby. SCR 7-8/2
The maid of twilight. LAL 5/4
Morning. SCR 5/4
A nocturne. SCR 5/4
The old man' story. SCR 5/3
Poetry. SCR 8/4
The sea fairies' song. LAL 9/4
Siesta. SCR 7/4
The snowfall. CIV 1/4
Spring has come. CIV 5-6/4
Sunset hour at old St. Paul's,. SCR 3/3
To M.B.C.. LAL 10/4
To a child. SCR 5/3
To her. SCR 9/4
To my sister. SCR 7-8/2

DuBridge, Elizabeth B.
Books. CTY S-A/4
The Christmas tree. CTY Win/4

DuVal, Jeanne
The blind boy. CIV 3/4
Violets. INT 4-6/4

Dudley, Dorothy
Branch. POE 5/3
Fandangle. POE 5/3
Interlude. POE 5/3
Under-current. POE 5/3

Dudley, Helen
Against the sun. POE 5/0
Cootham Lane. POE 5/0

Duer, Caroline
As reported. SCM 11/3

Duff, Donald
Four poems. CAP 5/3
Verses. CAP11-12/2

Duff, Naomi
A memory. INT 7-9/4
My mother. INT 4-6/4
The song of the poet. INT 4-6/4

Duffy, P. J. O'Connor
Holy women. MAG 6/3
Magdalen. MAG 6/3
Mother. MAG 6/3
A shawled peasant. MAG 6/3

Dugan, Mildred B.
Legend. AMP 12/3

Dumont, Henry
Sestina. POE 12/2

Dunaway, M. E.
An acrostic. SCR 7-8/2
At the end. SCR 9/2
City of roses. SCR 2/3
Dreaming. SCR 7-8/2
Enchantment. SCR 9/2
Gone. SCR 9/2
The maid of the mountains. SCR 7-8/2
Mission of gladness. SCR 9/2
Motive. SCR 9/2

Dunbar, Aldis
Forever and ever. LYW 7-8/3

Duncan, Ida Crocker
A homesteader. CIM 3/25/4
Little leafy lane. CIM 6/6/4

Duncan, Mabel S.
Lines on Arthur Rackam's pictu. GUL 9/3

Dungan, Myra Bell
The answer. CTY Spr/3
Choice of occupations. CTY Win/4
Fun in a willow tree. CTY Spr/4

Dunlap, Rachel Thayer
Rebel. OVM 10/4

Dunn, Emmett
Rain forest. S4N 12/2

Dunn, Rhoda Hero
The magic touch. SCM 9/1

Dunning, Ralph Cheever
April. POE 7/4
On a passing funeral. POE 7/4
Sentimental. POE 7/4

Dunsany, Edward J., Lord
In New Hampshire. NES 4/22/2
An interrupted song... DOU 12/1
Omar's song. DOU 12/1

Durham, Frances R.
Presentiment. NOM Spr/4

Durham, Malcolm
La belle vie. POM 1922

Duvall, Bianca
The pines. CIV 9-10/4
"Water of Marah." CIV11-12/4

Duvall, Idello V.
Les miserables. CIV 7-8/4

Duvall, Jeanne
The fairest flower. CIV 9-10/4
If thou hast known. LAL 10/4
Woods. CIV11-12/4

Dwight, H. G.
Codicil. SCM 1/4

Dye, John Homer
Heritage. FUG 12/4
November. CTY S-A/4
Query. CTY Spr/4
Tuesdays. CTY Spr/4

The gift of shamrocks. CAW 3/1
Eagan, Alice Livingston
Alone. SCR 10/4
The awakening. SCR 9/3
Heart of gold. SCR 6/4
I am waiting. SCR 12/4
I see thee ever. SCR 2/4
Night and memory. SCR 11/3
The past is dead. SCR 8/3
To fairyland. SCR 11/3
The world that was. SCR 4/4
Earle, Alice Livingston
Absent. SCR 5/3
Earle, Betty
In the temples of the twilight. AMP 12/2
Paths. AMP11-12/4
Prayer. LYR 6/2
Spirit. TEM 6/1
Earls, Michael
A man at Arachat. COM11/19/4
On a birthday. CAW 9/2
Earnest, Edna L.
Loving-kindness. CIJ 8/3
Eason, Mrs. F. D.
Glacial undine. POA 9/1
Easter, Arthur Miller
Love's acme. CIV11-12/4
The song. CIV 1/4
Woman. CIV 3/4
Eastman, Max
The battle-fields. LIB 10/2
The Missouri. LIB 10/1
A question. LIB 11/1
A telegram. LIB 1/2
To Lisa in summer. NAT12/10/4
To a dancing partner. LIB 2/2
Easton, Emma Watt
The meadow lark. INT 7-9/4
Eaton, Evelyn
The poet. MAC 6/4
Eberhart, Nelle Richmond
Her hands. MUN 5/2
Love reincarnate. MUN 4/2
Twilight. MUN 10/2
Eberle, Irmengrade
Conception. COV 2/1
Eberstein, Myrtle
Song for shredding bark. POE 5/0
Song of mocking...an old woman. POE 5/0
Woman with twins. POE 5/0
Eble, Jessie G.
Renunciation. SCR 7/4
Eddy, Lucy
Rider of sun fire. POE 8/0
Eddy, Rosamond Weston
At dawn. SCR 5/3
At evening. LYW 11/1
Christmas Eve. LYW 12/4
Evening. SCR 2/3
Fog. VOI Spr/2
Regret. LYW 11/1
Thy name. LYW 11/1
Tree music. SCR 2/3
Twilight wonder. LYW 4/3
You. SCR 2/3
Eddy, Ruth Bassett
The dance. OVM ?/1
Desire. PAG 12/1
Her bow. JUD ?/1
Impressions. BRY ?/1
In the country. GRA 7/1
Judge me not harshly. AMP Aut/1
Love athirst. PAG 4-5/0
On the fence. JUD ?/1
Out of college. TOW ?/1
Unsatisfied. GRA 2/1
Eden, Helen Parry
A dialogue of devotion. CAW 9/2
The star. NES 1/8/1
"When Israel out of Egypt came. CAW 7/2
Winter is come. NES12/24/1
Edgar, Charles Tyson
Sonnet to a flower. AMP11-12/4
Edge, Mary Allen
Beginnings. POE 6/3
Edgerton, Gladys
Love's passing. POE 8/1
My sepulchre. POE 8/1
Edgerton, Grace Paddock
Beauty. LAR 2/3
Edholm, Charlton L.
City windows. EVM 11/0
Edman, Irwin
Acquiescence. NAT12/10/4
Portrait of a connoisseur. HAM 12/4
They do not live. HAM 1/3
Edward, Zaida Packard
Absence vs. presence. AMP 6/2
Edwards, Charles
"About it and about." COV 9/1
Le jeune poete du Baudelaire. COV 9/1
Edwards, Jennette
Resurgam. WAN 1/4
Sonnets of silence. WAN 5/4
There is no change. WAN 11/3
Edwards, Zaida Packard
Autumn glory. SCR 11/3
Coin of the realm. AMP 4-5/3
One theme: one song. AMP 12/3
Egan, Maurice Francis
Democracy. CAW 10/2
To John Augustine Zahm. CAW 4/2
To a poet in...summer of life. SCM 11/1

Eggleston, Amy W.
Dreams. MAG 6/2
Fantasy. MAG 6/3
Love's young dream. MAG 6/2
Wrinkles. MAG 9/3
Ehrenstein, Albert
Homer. POE 12/2
Suffering. BRO 12/2
Eichorn, L. D.
Dear memory. AMP 2-3/3
Eisenberg, Emanuel
Tout seul. VOI 12/4
Eldridge, Paul
Boa constrictor. ALS 8-9/2
Cat. ALS 9/1
Chou Chang advises... DOU 1/3
Daisy seed. ALS 10/1
Deer. ALS 9/1
Defiance. LYW 10/3
Don Juan. NEN 3/28/1
Egoists. NOM Spr/3
Elephant. ALS 1/2
Emperor T'Ang-Skeptic. LYW 2/3
An epitaph. COV 1/0
Fang To explains..futility... DOU 1/4
Flea. DOU 3/2
Fly. ALS 10/1
Frog. DOU 3/2
Fung Ku Tchi tells how... DOU 8-9/4
Gander. DOU 3/2
Goat. DOU 3/2
Goose. DOU 3/2
Greetings from Confucius. DOU 7/2
Hog. ALS 8/1
I cross the Styx. BRO 2/3
I die. BRO 2/3
I face justice. BRO 2/3
Infallibility. BRO 2/3
Ku Hung refutes his friend. LYW 2/3
Ling Ma answers his friend... DOU 3-4/3
Lion. ALS 12/1
A maiden passes by. NOM Aut/2
The modernist. NOM Aut/2
Monkey. ALS 7/3
The moon and the ocean. COV 9/9
The mountains. MID 10/0
Mouse. ALS 9/1
My years. POE 2/0
O diamond, beautiful and rare. COV 6/0
Ouan Gu finds his efforts... DOU 8-9/4
Owl. ALS 10/1
Peacock. ALS 12/1
Potiphar's wife. DOU 5/2
Re-incarnation. TEM Aut/1
Resurrection. DOU 9/2
Robin. ALS 8/1
The rose. DOU 8-9/1
Ruins. DOU 4/2
The scarecrow. NEN 3/28/1
The scarecrow. TEM Aut/1
Sic transit gloria Christi. BRO 2/3
Since you love beauty. DOU 2/2
Snake. ALS 10/1
Soul. NOM Aut/2
Spider. ALS 11/1
Swan. DOU 3/2
Tchan Su's...masterpiece. DOU 10/4
To Fo bargains with deity. LYW 6/2
To T'ang and others. STM 10/4
Tsi Ouan wishes to believe... LYW 2/3
Tzu Kung makes an error. DOU 5/3
Vain seekers. COV 8/1
Verdict. BRO 2/3
We, the minor poets. NOM Aut/2
Wedding gifts. DOU 1/2
Wisdom. MID 10/0
Worm. ALS 8/1
Yan Yi explains creation. LYW 2/3
You. TEM Win/3
Eldridge, Sylvia
Impotence. NOM Spr/3
Eliot, Ruth F.
At the play. MUN 5/2
Eliot, Ruth Forbes
Reassurance. MUN 10/2
Eliot, Thomas Stearns
The waste land. DIA 11/2
Ellerbe, Cecilia
The celebrity. AMP 10/2
Makers of life. AMP Aut/1
On lonely coasts. BUC 10/4
Elliot, Ellen Coit
The beggar. LYW 4/4
Song of the waiting land. LYW 2/3
Tag! LYW 3/4
Elliot, Rebecca Strutton
Meditation. AMP 2-3/3
Elliot, William Forster
Ars immortalis. LYW 11/1
Beauty. WAN 8/4
Before the Venus of Milo. WAN 2/4
Catechism. FUG 12/3
Defeat. LYW 2/2
Desert dusk. LYW 6/3
Ideal. FRE 9/5/3

In repudiation. WAN 4/4
In your dressing room. LYW 9/2
Inconsequential. WAN 11/4
Pygmalion. WAN 4/4
A song of earth. WAN 2/4
Summit vigil. WAN 11/4
Tea with Sappho. WAN 6/4
To Eleanor from the city. LYW 2/2
To a poet turning mystic. WAN 10/4
Toward the dawn. WAN 4/4

Elliott, Clara H.
Advent of spring at the seaside. LAR 4/3

Elliott, Ellen Coit
The garlanded sword. LYW 10/4
Prima donna of the Negro Jazz. LYW 4/2

Elliott, Rebecca Strutton
Contemplation. AMP 3-4/4

Elliott, William Yandell
Black man. FUG 8/4
Epigrams. FUG 10/2
Mirror hall. FUG 4-5/3
Roundhead and cavalier. FUG 10/2

Elliston, George
Armistice Day. CIU11/11/2
Christ child night. SAX Xmas/4
End of summer. SAX Fall/4
Freedom. SAX Aut/2
Fulfillment. AMP 2/2
"God bless every one of us." CIU12/25/2
The high road. SAX 4/4
New April. SAX 4/4
Valentines. CIU 2/14/3

Ellsworth, Raymond
Songs of a lover. AMP 4/2

Elmendorf, Mary J.
God's dear forget-me-nots. CIJ 10/3
Lullaby. LAR 12/3
No empty place. CIJ 6/4
Wizardry. OVM 11/4

Elsmie, Dorine
Nocturne. LIB 12/2
To a happy poet. LIB 4/2

Eluard, Paul
Donnez-moi de vos nouvelles. LIR A-W/4

Embry, Jacqueline
Unregenerate. NAT 7/5/2
White butterfly. COV 6/0
With pride and affection. CEN 12/4

Emmet, Rosina H.
Waiting. SCM 10/9

Emrich, Kate T.
Inspiration. CIJ 3/4

England, George Allan
"No value" COV 3/1
The old coach. SCM 12/3
Saint and stoker. COV 6/3
Where is the joy...? WRM 9/4

English, Thomas Hopkins
The western window in Proctor. SCM 8/0

Enslow, Constance
Improvisations. POE 4/3

Eriksen, C. Svend
Riverward, dreaming. RHY 6-7/3

Erskine, John
Apparition. HAM 1/0
Dialogue. VOI 9-10/4
The gods in the street. OUT12/24/4
The sleeping beauty. FOR 9/4
Sonata. OUT 2/6/4

Ervine, St. John
To an unknown lady with somber. NER 1/21/0

Erwin, Margaret
Choice. OVM 9/4
Seasons. OVM 7/4

Eshleman, Cyrus H.
Dreams in the night. AMP11-12/4

Eshleman, Cyrus
The years have been prose. AMP 5-6/4

Eskew. Garnett Laidlaw
The daughter of the stars. NES 4/12/1
Ships in Hampton Roads. NES 4/8/1

Esler, Elizabeth Barnett
The holy house. CAW 9/0
Sunlight. COV 5/3
Why gird at fate? COV 6/4

Euwer, Anthony
Little black bull. LAR 9/3

Evans, Abbie Huston
The bird tree. POE 11/3
Breton song. POE 6/3
The burning hill. OUT 8/8/3
The end of the world. MEA 7/2
First concerns. POE 11/3
Hill-born. MEA 2/3
Juniper. MEA 7/2
The light on the rock. MEA 7/3
Love's fool. POE 11/3
Mid-day. POE 11/3
Says life of youth. MEA 10/2
Sea fog. LAR 6/3
Sea fog. MEA 7/2
The servant of the prophet. MEA 10/2
The spread table. MEA 7/3
The tamarack tree. MEA 7/2

Evans, Gladys La Due

The vine. MEA 11/3
"Was this the face..." OUT 3/14/3
Wild apples. MEA 3/2
Winter fare. LYR 2/3

Evans, Gladys La Due
Two things. COV 6/3

Evans, Lucile
The moon is a singer. LAR 8/3
O love that is born of...moon. LYW 5/2
The shell speaks to me. LAR 8/3
Star and song. LAR 12/3
White lilac. LAR 3/4

Evans, Marian MacGown
Forgiveness. COV 10/4

Evans, Pearl Townsend
Baby fingers. AMP10-11/3

Everett, Laura Bell
Faith. CIC 3/2/2
The man of one poem. LYW 11/3
The sonnet. STE 2/4

Everts, Ella Frances
Little Linnet. AMP 2-3/3

Ewer, W. N.
Five souls. CIC 7/26/3

Eyre, Mary B.
The stampede. OVM 6/4

Eyres, D.M.
The quiet house. HAM 4/0

F.,E.H.
A silver jubilee. CAW 2/2

Fagin, N. Bryllion
And none are silent. VOI 6-7/3
Compassion. VOI 12/2
I sometimes gaze. LYW 4/3
A name. LYW 2/4
Pebbles. ALS 2-3/3
Philosophers all. NES 3/12/1
Sung hunger. GUL 6/3
To a glass door-knob. LYW 4/3

Fagnani, Charles P.
Confessio fidei. CIC 3/2

Fahnestock, Elizabeth Bertron
Lullaby. OUT 4/6/1

Fairfield, Wynne
Class poem, 1921. LIC 11/1

Falkner, William
Portrait. DOU 6/2

Faller, Harold
Fragment. SCR 10/4
Plentitudes. SCR 11/4
Scamp o' woods. HEA 10/4

Farge, Ruth
Shadows. OVM 2/4

Farkaschi, Hazel
Alone. LYW 4/3
September nights. LYW 9/1
Waiting. LYW 4/3

Farley, Grace
Stanzas. AMP 2-3/3

Farnsworth, Dorothy McPherson
Rebellion. SCM 5/1

Farnsworth, Maud Young
The coquette. AMP10-11/3

Farran, Don Wilson
Dowry. OVM 10/4
Man-child. WAN 11/4

Farrar, John
Hymn to Luicfer. SCM 10/3
Squaw. CEN 3/4
Two songs for parents. STE 1/4

Farrar, John Chipman
A comparison. COV 5/0
Ego. COV 5/1
Lucile. COV 2/0
Parenthood. COV 5/0
Wish. COV 5/0

Farrington, Harry Webb
The empty cup. BOT12/31/1

Farron, Don W.
Gypsy folk. OVM 2/4
Leaf drifts. WAN 6/24
Panels. WAN 6/24

Farrow, Jack
Felice. WAN 2/4
Of Zagma. WAN 4/4
A ship's hold. WAN 9/4

Farwell, Gertrude Brice
Liberated. LYW 7-8/2
Mother-heart songs. LYW 12/2
Soul of earth. LYW 7-8/2

Fassett, Saimi
The rosary of hours. OVM 10/4

Faunce, Frances Avery
At sunrise. CAW 6/2
Fashion. CIC 2/4

Fauset, Jessie
Dilworth road revisited. CUU 11/2
To a foreign maid. CUU 2/3

Faust, Henri
Astronomers. WAN 3/4
Autumnal. INT10-12/4
Buzzard Bayou. BUC 10/4
Child prodigy. NOM Aut/3
Coquette. LAL 5/4
Coral builders. LYR 6/4
Gourmet. BUC 10/4
Harsher than death. INT10-12/4
Hyacinths. INT10-12/4
The lake. WAN 9/4
The lunar moth. WAN 6/4
Malady. BUC 10/4
Nocturne. BUC 10/4
Nostalgia. WAN 3/4

Old man's lament at spring. CIV 5-6/4
On waking. INT10-12/4
Remembrance. WAN 6/4
Respite. ALS 8-9/2
Rival. INT10-12/4
Shadow music. OVM 8/4
Skeptic's definitions. DOU 10/4
Sonnets for lost divinities. VOI 9-10/4
These autumn fields. NES 11/2/4
This dust. LYR 9/4
"To wade when twilight deepens. VOI 12/2
Vampire. BUC 10/4
Water-lilies. BUC 10/4

Fawcett, James Waldo
Afterward. UNI12/29/1
All fools address the artful w. LIB 9/2
Barter. CUU 9/2
Joseph Plunkett (May 4, 1916). LIB 1/2
Macabre. MUC12/20/1
Nocturne. UNI 8/4/1
Singer departed. CUU 8/2
Vagabonds. UNI 8/18/1

Fay, Alice
America. VOI 12/4

Fay, Alice M.
Before Abraham was, I am. GYP #2/4
Cote d'Azur. PEG 1-2/4
A Hebrew love chant. CAP 1-2/3
Mirage. CAP 1-2/3
Per ardua ad astra. SCR 4/3
Sans fond. TOM 1/4
Shall we love again. SCR 4/3
Spirit is love. PEG #1/4
Voices of the cities. LYW 3/4
Where? AMP 8-9/3

Fearing, Kenneth
Moral (OP. 2.). DOU11-12/4
Moral (OP. I.). DOU11-12/4

Feathertop, Henry
Call on, deep voice. FUG 6/2
Cul-de-sac. FUG 6/2
Farewell to Anactoria (Sappho). FUG 6/2
In secret valley. FUG 6/2
A scholar to his lady. FUG 6/2

Fee, Harry T.
Rejuvenation. LAR 12/3

Fehl, Delert
The lariat. LAR 2/3

Feibleman, James
Dilemma's end. PAR #3/4
Epigram. DOU 2-3/4
Epigram. DOU 2/3
The last night. DOU 2/2
Resignation. DOU 5/2
Sonnet. DOU 8-9/4

Feldman, Jesse Hugo
Madison. AMP 4/2
Morituri agonisti. DOU 3/2
The old quarry. LYW 12/2

Fellows (& T.Y.Leo)<trs>, A.N.
Virtuous wife ode. MEA 6/2

Fellows (tr.), Albert N.
Return-home writing. MEA 6/2

Fellows (tr.), Albion N.
Evening house top: idle glance. MEA 6/2
Inscribed where once some one. MEA 6/2
Looking out on one departing. MEA 6/2
Query and answer in the hills. MEA 6/2
The war chariot. MEA 6/2

Felshin, Leo
Lonely. BOO 3/1

Felshin, Simon
John Reed and Raymond Lefebvre. LIB 12/2

Fennell, Charles
Fighting Mickey Keefe. COV 6/0
Poe. TEM 6/1

Fenner, Beatrice
Five lyrics. LYW 12/4
I'm going to meet the wind. LOS 5/10/4

Fenton, Carroll Lane
"E be than" POE 4/1

Fenton, Edith
The elfin dance. CIV 5-6/4

Ferguson, Blanche Smith
"April princess." CIV11-12/4
My garden. CIV 5-6/4

Ferguson, Mrs. L. W.
Evening. SCR 5/3

Ferguson, William Martin
Endless Dreams. CIV11-12/4
My pilot. LAL 10/4

Ferril, Thomas Hornsby
Rain song at night. AMP 10/3
Space-after supper. COV 8/0
The uncut page. COV 8/0

Fetzer, Herman
Song about death. WAV 3/4

Feuerlight, Ethel
Swallow song. STE 6/3

Ficke, Arthur Davison
The book of Lu T'ang Chu. POE 5/1
Buddha at Nadika. POE 8/3
Don Quixote. NOA 12/0
Epitaph for a certain sculptor. POE 9/3
Her hands. MEA 11/2

Holy writ. POE 5/1
In that dim monument..Tybalt... POE 9/3
Leaf-movement. POE 4/1
Marcia. MEA 11/2
The middle years. NOA 5/1
My princess. SCM 12/2
Old wives' tales. POE 5/1
Perspective of co-ordination. POE 4/1
Portrait of a stranger. MEA 11/2
Ruth. MEA 11/2
Serenade across silence. RHY 3/3
Serenade at noonday. RHY 3/3
Serenade from among the pines. RHY 3/3
Serenade in absence. RHY 3/3
Serenade in firelight. RHY 3/3
Tomb of a Ming poet. SOU 10/2
Wprld beyond world. POE 4/1

Fidler, Ann Garret
A white violet. INT 4-6/4

Fidler, Ann Garrett
Metamorphosis. INT 7-9/4

Field, Ben
Carriso gorge. PEG 7/3
Come back. CAP 5/3
Plazas. LOS 5/10/4
Salton Sea. LYW 4/1
The spirit of the Prado. WAN 10/4
Winged victory. LYW 6/3

Field, Elliot
Pharisee and Sadducee. COV 1/4

Field, Mildred Fowler
Anchorite. WAN 8/4
Blossom time. CHN 5/8/3
Carpenter Christ. CIC10/16/4
Chanson. CHN 8/27/3
Confession. CHN 4/25/3
Content. CHE 6/13/3
Content. OVM 3/4
Crucible. LYR 11/4
Cycle. WAN 5/4
The dreamer. DAV 6/21/3
Ecstasy. CHN 3/14/3
Elemental. CED 3/18/3
Enough. CHE 4/22/3
Experience. SCR 9/3
Flower park. CHN 4/9/3
Garden magic. CHE 5/16/3
Her talisman. CHN 5/22/3
Hope. WAN 12/3
Idle thoughts. DAV 8/15/3
Infinity. OVM 9/3
June myth. CHN 6/20/3
Magic chest. VIO 6/3
Morning worship. CHE 5/8/3
Pansy pollen. WAN 3/4
Parable. CHN 7/20/3
Peonies. CHE 6/22/3
Psychiatrist. OVM 9/4
Quicksilver. WAN 9/3
Reunited. DAV 4/18/3
Scrub-woman. DAV 7/6/3
The sculptor. VOI 12-1/4
Sleeping beauty. CHN 6/2/3
Something. CHE 8/3/3
Super-feature. DAV 6/6/3
Supplication. OVM 7/4
Symphony. AMP 9-10/4
Transmutation. CHN 7/13/3
Were song enough. OVM 11/4
Why. DAV 5/1/3

Field, Sara Bard
Bird of prey. MEA 6/4
Guilty mothers. ALS10-11/3
The riddle. MEA 6/4
Waiting. MEA 6/4

Field, Wright
Ants. PAL Sum/3
Artifice. INT 7-9/4
Death's gift. LYW 12/2
Heart-weariness. Lar 8/3
Impressions. LYW 7-8/2
John Gates' wife. COV 8/4
Lilac time. LYW 7-8/2
The maple sings. LYW 7-8/2
The nature lover. SCR 5/3
Prescience. BUC 10/4
Service denied. INT 7-9/4
The soul of a garden. LYW 4/3
To a high-born lady. LYW 10/3
Yakima Mountains. AMP 1-2/4

Fillery, William Edmund
Old books. LAR 4/4

Finerty, John F.
Love. POE 5/4
May-day at sea. POE 5/4

Finley, John
And to such as play ... SCM 2/0
The blue flower of Marathon. SCM 6/4
First knight of...Holy Cross. SCM 12/0
"The swan of Tuonela." SCM 12/2
To Florence Nightingale. OUT 6/2/0
The white acres in France. NEY 5/29/1

Fischer, Helen Field
A mystic borderland. LAR 8/3

Fischer, Raymond P.
A woman complains of rain... POE 11/4

Fish, Lisbeth G.
The inner room. AMP 5-6/4

Fishburn, Josephine Redmond
Child-poems. AMP 12/2
Fisher, Caroline
In June. CTY Sum/3
The light house light. CTY Aut/2
Fisher, Carroll Loupe
The white tulip. AMP 6-7/3
Fisher, Eleanor
Fancies. AMP 6-7/3
The forest. AMP 6-7/3
The wind. AMP 6-7/3
Fisher, Eulalee Tyrel
The old house speaks. LOS 5/10/4
Fisher, Mahlon Leonard
Blinded. SON 12/0
Boundaries. GAL 4/4
Chief in my heart. SON 3-4/1
Distillation. GAL 4/4
The garden-spider's web. NAT 7/20/1
The hills. NAT 4/10/0
In a cemetery. NAT 3/6/0
In winter. SON 1-2/0
Life. VOI 8-9/3
No weak believer I. SON 3-4/0
The omnipresent. SON 1-2/0
The questioners. SON 12/0
Relentlessness. SON 3-4/0
Two sonnets. GAL 1/4
Fisher, Raymond P.
Granite cliffs. VOI 6-7/3
A tree. VOI 6-7/3
Fisher, Stokley S.
The spirit of the north. COV 2/1
Without faith. CIC 8/9/3
Fitts, Norman
Trinity. S4N 12/2
Fitz, Isabelle H.
My Chester! GRA 10/2
Fitzwilliam, G. William
On recollecting...certain ladi. LYW 9/2
Flaccus
Rigoletto. HAM 11/2
Flanagan, W. L.
The rabbit hunt. MEA 11/3
Flanders, Helen Hartness
Suite from Smiley Manse. AMP 3-4/4
Transitory. AMP 6-7/3
Flanigan, A. H.
Awe. STE 12/2
Flanner, Hildegarde
Allegiance. BOO 3/1
Communion. POE 2/1
Daphne. YAR 7/3
Dumb. LYW 3/4
Moment. LYW 3/4
Philippian. VOI10-11/3
Prelude. MEA 7/1
Singing. LYW 3/4
Sonnets in Quaker language. MEA 6/4
St. Augustine. DOU 2/3
To a dear friend. LYW 3/4
To one of little faith. VOI10-11/3
Tona tree in bloom. LYW 3/4
Trees. LYW 3/4
Flanner, Thedora Gay
The gnome. WAN 5/4
Flansburg, Fonetta
Beauty for ashes. AMP10-11/3
Fletcher, John Gould
The autumn horseman. MEA 7/3
The black rock,to Thomas Hardy. YAR 7/0
Cro-magnon. FUG 2-3/3
"Dixie." DOU 8/2
From Portofino Point. BUC 11/4
The last frontier. FUG 2-3/3
The lovers. LYR 1/4
Middle age. MIL 12/2
The moon's orchestra. POE 10/0
Pauper death. RHY 1/3
Prayers, I-XI. POE 4/3
San Antonio. DOU 8/2
The silence. POE 10/0
The stevedores. POE 10/0
To Columbus. BUC 11/4
The wanderer. NER 9/22/0
Fletcher, Louisa
Mandarin red. HAM 5/1
Fletcher, Myla
Tell us, Charon! MEA 4/3
Treasure. NAT 5/30/3
Turns. MEA 5/3
Flexner, Eleanor
To the Mediterranean. LIC 1/3
Flexner, Hortense
Children's room. NES 1/3
Death mask...unknown soldier. NOA 2/0
For one no longer three years. LYR 8/2
Foreboding. NOA 10/0
French clock. VOI10-11/3
Frost. VOI10-11/3
A funeral. BOO 12/2
Hour glass. DOU 9/2
The hunt. MEA 4/1
Judgment. NER12/20/2
Purchase (letters,L.de Medici). HAM 11/0
Reflected. DOU 8/2
There is no end. VOI Aut/2
Flexner, James

Elysian Fields. LIC 3/3
In the hours of darkness. LIC 6/3
Nocturne. LIC 3/3
Shadows. LIC 6/3

Flynn, A. J.
The canon-cliffs of Creede. AMO10-11/4

Flynn, Jennie M.
In Bethlehem. AMP 12/2

Fohs, Ella
Prelude. LIC 12/4

Foillard, Hugo
Carl Sandburg. LYW 1/3
Conrad. LYW 1/3
Galsworthy. LYW 1/3

Foote, Elvira
Redolence. LYW 6/3

Ford (Hueffer), Ford Madox
A house. POE 3/1
Rhymes for a child. POM 1922
Seven shepherds. POE 6/3

Forest, Jean
Activities of the sccubus... MOR 10//3

Forsyth, Alice Whitecraft
September dusk in the arroyo. LYW 9/1

Fort, Paul
Eternity. POE 9/1
The lament of the soldiers. POE 9/1
The little silent street. POE 9/1
Louis Eleventh, curious man. POE 9/1
The miraculous catch. POE 9/1
The return. POE 9/1

Forte, Alice
The birth of a fool. LYW 12/4

Fortesque, Thalia
A night. LIC 12/1

Forthun, Myrtle
Life to youth. COV 8/2

Fortune, Jan Isabelle
Autumn. GYP #2/4

Fortune, Jan Isbelle
Eternal. BUC 12/4

Fortune, Lloyd
Passion. CAP 1-2/3

Fosbery, Arthur F.
The captive maid. CIJ 8/3

Fosher, Mahlon Leonard
The soul stilled. LYR 1/2

Foss, C. H.
Women. POA 1/2

Foster, George A.
My baby. GRA 6/1

Foster, Jeanne Robert
John Butler Yeats. NEW 2/6/2
A lament. AIN 3/0

Foster, K. K.
Resurrection. MID 3/1

Foster, Kate Quinlan
Joyous. LYW 3/3
Silhouette. UNV 1923

Foulke, Mildred Pluma
The creation to the Creator. POE 4/4

Fowler, Frederick W.
Just dreaming. GRA 11/2

Fowler, George Leonard
The garden of man. WAN 12/3
A legend. WAN 4/4
Yellow hearts. WAN 11/3

Fowler, J. L.
A summer scene. CTY S-A/1

Fox, Moireen
Deidre. POE 1/1
Disillusionment. POE 1/1
Silence. POE 1/1

Fox, Paul Hervey
The captains of the Corsican. AIN 4/0

Frame, Rita Chisholm
Selfishness. GUL 9/3

Francis, Alexander
Nightfall. INT 1-3/4
A radical at the crossroads. INT 4-6/4

Francis, Helen
Chrysalis. WAN 2/4
For a certain philanderer. PAR #4/4
Frugality. WAN 5/4
Rosemary. WAN 12/3
Tiny thoughts at night. WAN 2/4

Francis, Helen W.
Kilmacrenan horsemen. MIN11-12/4

Francis, Martin
The unknown soldier. CAW 1/2

Frank, Florence Kiper
Baby. POE 11/2
Birthday. COV 1/0
Dialogue. POE 11/2
Elf-child. POE 11/0
Interior. POE 11/2
Journey. WAV 6/3
Married. POE 11/2
Mothers of the world. COV 1/0
Sleep the mother. POE 11/0
Soldier. COV 1/0

Frank, James M.
The helmeted Minerva. FUG 4-5/3
To R.H.F.. FUG 12/3

Frank, Waldo
Defeat. TEM Win/3
Plaint. PRA 1-2/3
A song of Rahab. RHY 6-7/3

Frankel, Valerie
Blossoms. LIC 3/3
The vegetable family. LIC 6/3
Franklin, Viola Price
College memories. OVM 5/4
Fraser, Abbott
A picture of indian summer. MEA 12/3
Weeping willow. REW 7/3
Frasier, Scottie McKenzie
The call to the writer. AMP 2/2
Fields at night. AMP 4-5/3
Forgotten. AMP 10/2
Gifts. AMP 10/2
Hills. AMP 8-9/3
I shall wait. AMP Aut/1
Old perfume. NOM Spr/2
The peacock. AMP 6/2
Why I know. AMP11-12/4
Frazee, Betty Dickinson
Doubt is a gray moth. LYW 10/4
From broken things. AMP 12/3
Frazee, Isaac Jenkinsen
Desert suite. LYW 10/2
The desert wolf. AMP 2-3/3
Old men. LOT 4/15/3
What is love? LAR 4/3
Frazee-Bower, Helen
Age. FRE 7/12/2
Alchemy. LYR 10/2
Alien. VOI Spr/3
Amo immortalis. ALS 8-9/2
Andrea Paula. COV 11/4
Autumn. AMP Aut/1
Boys. UNI 6/1/2
Certainties. COV 11/2
Coler-mood. EVM 8/0
Come hither, wind! EVM 3/1
Courage. LYR 2/3
The day. AMP 2-3/3
Departure. COV 6/3
Descent. COV 11/2
A dove at dawn. COV 11/4
Emblematic. LYR 5/3
Flight. COV 11/2
Great thoughts you weary me. COV 3/3
The heights. COV 11/2
Housewife's lament. ALS 3/2
Love songs. AMP 10/2
My gifts. HAM 6/2
My laughter. PAG 4-5/0
New beauty. LYW 3/3
The newsboy. LIB 11/1
Night and sea. LYW 12/1
Night silence. LYW 2/2
Oh if the spring should come! VOI Spr/2
The prima donna. LIB 8/1
Remorse. LIB 9/2
Roads. LIB 8/1
Sea gulls. LYW 7-8/2
Sea lover. LYW 7-8/2
Sea-gulls. LIB 8/1
A song of diligence. COV 5/2
There is a brown leaf floating. CAP 5/3
There is no word. LYW 7-8/2
These things will live. VOI Spr/2
Thoughts. AMP 1-2/4
Three sisters. VOI Spr/2
The tiger city. LYW 3/3
Tone poem, for reeds. 8-9/3
Travelers. LYW 3/3
Treason. GRA 5/2
Trees in the fog. COV 6/3
Ultimate. LYW 12/1
Water lilies. GRA 8/2
Frazier, John
Nocturne. S4N 12/2
Frazier, Sarah Ruth
"Call to duty." AMP 12/2
Fredenall, Laura C.
Mission Valley. AMP 2-3/3
Fredson, Jean Todd
The hill top. LAR 4/4
Freeburg, Victor Oscar
The rubies of Cleopatra. DOU 7/2
Freed, M. Elizabeth
Queries. POA 1/2
Freel, Carrie M.
My Iowa home. AMP 9-10/4
Freel, E. L.
Christmas in France. AMP 12/3
Freeman (Jr.), Mason A.
Epigrams. POE 8/1
From the Vedic. POE 8/1
Once more. POE 8/1
The triple shroud. POE 8/1
The way. POE 8/1
Freeman, John
Be still today. POE 3/3
The centaurs. RHY 3/3
The meadow path. RHY 3/3
Renunciation. POE 3/3
Freeman, Joseph
Affirmations. NEN 4/6/1
The dancers. LIB 4/2
De profundis. LIB 4/2
Don Giovanni. LIB 4/2
Fantasia. LIB 4/2
Friendliness. NEN 4/6/1
Gloria mundi. NAT 3/6/0
I shall love you. LIB ?/1
Isolation. NEN 4/16/1
Jealousies. NEN 4/6/1
Love at dawn. LIB 4/2
Love. LIB 4/2

Nocturne. LIB 4/2
Not only roses. NAT 7/20/1
Pastoral. LIB 4/2
Regression. BOO 10/1
Renunciation. NEN 4/6/1
Revolutionary prelude. LIB 4/2
Songs for a lady. LIB 9/1
A sonnet for poets. LIB 12/1
Sonnet. NAT10/12/1
Treason. NEN 4/6/1
Vita nouva. MEA 5/4
White stars, bright stars. NEN 4/6/1

Freeman, Mary E. Wilkins
The prisoner. COV 7/2
The vase. COV 7/2

Freeman, Robert
Why? CIC 3/16/2

French (tr.), Louise
Sleep. UNV 7/2

Friedlaender, V. H.
Blue. DOU 1/4
Bus ride in a fog. POE 11/2

Frieson, William
Reactions on the October Fugit. FUG 12/2

Frink, Maurice M.
Fear. STE 6/4

Frippe, Etholelle Ione
Gifts. AMP 10/2
September sunshine. AMP Aut/1
Ships. AMP 2/2
Song. AMP 5-6/4

Frost, Robert
The aim was song. MEA 3/1
Blue-butterfly day. NER 3/9/1
A bottle, a fountain,... BOO 10/3
A boundless moment. NER10/24/3
A brook in the city. NER 3/9/1
The census taker. NER 4/6/1
Fire and ice. HAM 12/0
The flower-boat. POE 8/3
For once, then, something. HAM 7/0
Fragmentary blue. HAM 7/0
A hillside thaw. NER 4/6/1
I will sing you one-O. YAR 10/3
Lodged. NER 2/6/4
Maple. YAR 10/1
Misgiving. YAR 1/1
The need of being versed... HAM 12/0
Nothing gold can stay. YAR 10/3
The onset. YAR 1/1
Our singing strength. NEW 5/2/3
Paul's wife. CEN 11/1
The pauper witch of Grafton. NAT 4/13/1
Place for a third. HAM 7/0
Snow dust. YAR 1/1
A star in a stone-boat. YAR 1/1
The star-splitter. CEN 9/3
Stopping by woods on a snowy e. NER 3/7/3
To E.T. (Edward Thomas). YAR 4/0
To earthward. YAR 10/3
The valley's singing day. HAM 12/0
Wild grapes. HAM 12/0
The witch of Coos. POE 1/2

Frumkin, Morris
Proem. GUL 5/3
Resume. GUL 6/3

Frye, Nellie Dodge
Books are friends. SCR 2/4
Homing. CTY S-A/4
Little things. CTY Win/4
Love's hour. SCR 8/4
The mountain brook. SCR 8/4
My home. SCR 2/4
Rebirth. GRA 3/2
Three scenes. SCR 7/4
The winding road. GRA 5/2
Within. SCR 8/4

Fujita, Jun
December moon. POE 6/1
Echo. POE 6/1
A leaf. POE 6/1
May moon. POE 6/1
Michigan Boulevard, Chicagoo. CAP 10/2
November. POE 6/1
Poem. WAV 6/2
Spring. POE 6/1
Storm. POE 6/1
To Elizabeth. POE 6/1

Fujiwara
Autumn reflections. FRE 11/9/1

Fulcher, Paul M.
Sonnet. COV 12/4

Fuller, Ethel Romig
After rain. OVM 10/4
Answers. CIC12/11/4
Blue hydrangeas. BUC 11/4
Chinese beads. LAR 7/3
Come out and walk with me. LAR 12/3
Distinction. LAR 4/4
Golden days. LAR 12/3
In the park. BUC 11/4
Loneliness. LAR 2/4
Love's cycle. LAR 12/3
Remembered things. LYW 4/4
Sea sonnet. LAR 11/3

Fuller, Mabel
Prayer to poesy. LOS 5/10/4

Fuller, Rex George
Back street, by night. COV 7/4

Doloroso. PAL Spr/3
The eternal rebel. COV 1/3
Fog. COV 6/3
The harvester. COV 10/2
The night rain comes. POM 1922
The plowman. COV 10/2
Portrait of an old gentleman. LYR 2/4
Portrait of an old lady. POE 6/4
Surprise. COV 7/4

Funk, Marian Nevin
Conversation at tea. DOU11-12/4
Garret. DOU 10/2
Inscription. DOU 7/4
Madman. DOU 12/2
She gave me water. COV 9/0

Fuson, H. H.
Lockerbie street. PAR #1/4
My song. PAR #4/4

Gaer, Yossef
Refrain to a unwritten song. OVM 4/4
San Diego sketches. FOU 10/3
Twilight. NOM Aut/3

Gaffey, Ernest
Pitti san. CTY Sum/3

Gailey, Eunice
Old and new. LAR 4/4

Gaillard, Peyre
June song. AMP 6/2

Galahad, Joseph Andrew
Absence. VOI 12/2
Argosy. COV 8/1
Challenge. STE 6/2
The commoner reads the poet. COV 4/3
Easter. COV 4/2
Episode. COV 7/2
Fortress. COV 4/3
Gateway. COV 8/3
Inter nos. AMP 2/2
Isolde. LYW 2/2
The knife. NOA 5/0
Light o' love. AMP 10/2
Long white roads. LYW 12/1
Mile two. COV 1/2
A mood. POE 6/2
No roses. LYW 12/1
Pay to the order of -. COV 7/2
The pines of Lebanon. NOA 3/1
A poet thinks. COV 12/2
A poet's creed. COV 7/2
Promise. LYW 1/3
The round. LYW 9/2
Sic passim. POE 10/1
Sonnet to a little shaver. AMP 2/2
To the star of song. LYW 5/2
Toward the end. STE 5/3
Triumph. BOO 12/1
Vanguard. COV 3/1

Gale, Mona
Elements. LAR 4/3

Gale, Zona
Beloved, it is daybreak... LYW 12/1
Come on! AMP 4/2
Half thought. LYW 12/1
Here is the love. STE 6/2
Kilburn road. BOO 10/1
North star. BOO 9/1
The violin. BOO 8/1

Gallagher, Marie
Shadow tree. PAG 8-0/1
Species homo. PAG10-11/1
Suicide. NOM Spr/2
Tristezza. PAG10-11/1
Will to live. PAG 8-9/1

Gallatin, Neal
Astral stones. LYW 2/2
The ballad of a rented house. LAR 5/3
My talisman. TEM Aut/1
The north sky. LYW 11/3
Pipes o' sky. LYW 7-8/3
Tumble-weed ladies. LYW 10/2

Gallivant, Robin
The house of the sun. FUG 6/2
Teach me. FUG 6/2
The tiger woman. FUG 6/2
The valley of the dragon. FUG 6/2
Voice of the dust. FUG 6/2

Galloway, Elizabeth Joan
The theatre. COV 2/0

Galwey, Charles
La rumba Cubana. BRO 3/3
Stadium concert. BRO 1/3

Gammans, Harold W.
Cacti and leaves. LYW 11/3
Mangua of Hokusai light bridge. COV 8/0

Gard, Lillian
Five years old. LAD 2/4

Gard, Wayne
Anglesey. NEU 1/31/4
Dreamer to dreamer. AMP Aut/1
Life. CIC 5/24/3
Mindon min. NEU 10/3
Shwe dagon. AMP 5-6/4
Songs of a prairie lover. AMP 4-5/3

Garesche, Edward
Niagara in winter. CAW 1/0

Garman, A. D.

Une nuit. PAG 12/1
Garman, A.D.
Yawp. PAG 4-5/0
Garnett, Louise Ayres
Ah's marching on to doomsday. OUT 6/2/0
Ain't got time ter tarry. COV 6/2
The bargain. POE 2/3
Black and white. NER 2/18/0
The captive. COV 9/0
Christmas Eve. STE 12/3
De Lawd am mah shephud. LYR 1/4
De li'l' Jesus-baby. COV 12/3
The door. OUT 3/15/2
Earth-song. OUT12/22/0
Ev'ywhars dat anybody knows. OUT 4/12/2
Fishin'. OUT 2/8/2
Free-song. COV 6/4
Glory hallelu! LYR 5/4
Gwine up ter heab'n. OUT 4/12/2
He ploughs the fields. STE 6/2
How long, Mass Jesus, how long. OUT 5/5/0
Immortal death. POE 2/3
Ivory thumbs. OUT 7/21/0
John Burroughs. COV 12/1
The latchstring. COV 12/1
The little house. LYR 4/3
Mary-of-the-snows. WAV 3/4
Moons. COV 12/1
The mother. EDI 8/1
Myself. BOO 12/2
Nigger heaben. OUT 6/23/0
Night-song. COV 6/2
Norah en de ark. OUT12/15/0
Remembrance. COV 12/1
The rover. POE 6/4
Seekin'. COV 5/3
Silhouette. COV 9/0
The sisters. OUT 8/31/1
Slow en easy. OUT 4/12/2
Soul at play. POE 2/3
Spring song. LYR 4/3
Summer music. COV 9/0
The teacup. POE 2/3
Three-score-and-ten. ALS /2
Three-score-and-ten. ALS 4/2
Tree-dreams. COV 12/1
The tree. COV 6/4
White shadows. COV 9/0
Young loveliness. POE 2/3
Garrett, Clara Maude
Renewal. AIN 3/0
Garrison, Theodosia
The barred way. SCM 12/2
The grandchild. EVM 11/0
A host in Gallilee. LYR 3/2
New Year's Eve. EVM 1/2
November. EVM 11/0
The penitent. LYR 8/1
Prophets. NOM Sum/2
Seventy and twenty. STE 6/2
The star. LYR 12/2
Garrison, W. E.
Hatred. CIC 1/11/3
Garrison, Winfred Ernest
Adventure. CIC 9/6/3
A book. CIC 10/2/3
For an hour. CIC11/29/3
The quest. CIC 6/19/4
Gary, Louise M.
Field song. REW 6/2
Gatens, Mina M.
The fall of Bacchus. LAR 4/3
The lady of deceit. LAR 7/3
Gates, Allene
Concerning a love of clothes. LYW 3/3
The valedictorian. LYW 6/2
Gauss, H. C
Poem. MIN 7-8/4
Gautier, Theophile
The doves. NOM Aut/3
Gavin (jt auth), Mary
The curtains. POE 4/0
Gavin, Helena
Disciples. CIC 5/3/3
Gavin, John H.
Creeds. POE 5/2
Immortality. POE 5/2
Gaw, Ethelean Tyson
A barnegat love-song. SCM 8/0
The desert. LYW 10/3
The minor poet. SCM 12/2
Whence cometh my help. LAR 8/3
Gaylord, Myrtle Levy
I would be silent. LYW 12/3
The lady. VOI Spr/3
Geddes, Virgil
Before rising. CAP 1-2/3
The commentator commentates to. PRA 1-2/3
Denouement. POE 3/3
Excruciation. POE 3/3
Faith. PAG 8-9/1
Fragment for a woman. VOI 12-1/4
An hour at dawn. CAP 1-2/3
In memoriam. TEM 6/1
The leaf. VOI 12-1/4
Liaison in the dead of summer. MOD 10/3
Living through this life. VOI 12-1/4
Old man. CAP 1-2/3
Old theme. CAP 1-2/3
Old woman. NOM Sum/2
Paul Gauguin to his wife. VOI

Aut/1
Persuasion. VOI 12-1/4
Prairie fires. LYW 10/2
Prelude for darkness. POE 3/3
Quarry workmen. LYW 2/4
Rodin's Thinker. TEM 6/1
Singers of song. LYW 9/3
Sparrows. PAG 8-9/1
Summer movement. LYW 7-8/2
Surf beat. CAP 10/2
To F. C.. TEM 6/1
To a Chinese laundryman. PAG10-11/1
To a fountain. PAG 12/1
Valley of slew grass. LYW 3/2
Winds. LYW 1/2

Genn, Lillian G.
The debutante. AMP 10/2
Moods. AMP 12/2
To my mother. AMP 12/3

George, Legare
Breakers. DIA 10/0
Petite chanson discrete pour c. DIA 6/3

Gerahty, Laura
Waiting. CIJ 9/3

Gerbaulet, Joy and Claire
To a secret lover. FUG 12/3

German, Francis H.
Defiance. SCR 6/4
Drifting. SCR 5/4
The fear. SCR 5/4
Shadows. SCR 4/4
A terza rima. CIV 7-8/4

Gershon, Gladys
Climax. LIB 8/1
Interval. LIB 8/1

Gessler, Clifford Franklin
Blue drums. NEN 3/28/1
Chicago. GRI 2/1
Curriculum. NOM Sum/3
Exorcism. MID 4/1
Eyes. NEN 3/28/1
Interlude. MID 1/1
Kapu. STE 3/4
Loop morning. GRI 12/0
Nevertheless. POE 6/1
Oahu shore. NOM Sum/3
Petals of darkness. POE 4/4
Portrait. WAN 2/4
Prayer. POE 6/1
Sholto Street. GRI 12/0
Slants. POE 4/4
Sonnet. WAN 12/3
Spring longings. GRI 8/0
Star-dancers. POE 4/4
"These cities, too..." WAN 5/4
Three minute stop. NOM Sum/3
Two sonnets of memories. GRI 1/1
Van Buren street car. GRI 12/0
The villager sings. SVG 5/2
Your horses. POE 6/1

Gessler, Gertrude Enid
Triolet. AMP 4/2

Ghent, Kate Downing
Faith. SOU 8/3

Gia Dao
Seeing the hermit in vain. POE 8/2

Gibbs, Agnes K.
The hawk. LYW 11/3

Gibson, Charles Hammond
Only the spirit lives. AMP 8/2

Gibson, Frank H.
The home of the soul. LIH 6/3

Gibson, Lydia
The beggar. MEA 12/1
The golden children. LIB 10/1
Never enslaved. LIB 4/2
Not with bright poppies. MEA 12/1
Plunder. MEA 12/1
Poems. LIB 2/2
Sonnet. LIB 3/2
Tahitian holiday. LIB 5/2
Trees in winter. LIB 2/2
Wisdom. LIB 7/2

Gibson, Wilfrid
An epilogue. HAM 8/2
Jocelyn. HAM 8/2
A northern homestead. HAM 8/2

Gidlow, Elsa
Before sleep. VOI Aut/1
Conquest. VOI 8-9/3
Declaration. LIB 8/1
The poet. VOI Spr/2
Retribution. CIV 7-8/4
The solitary. MOR 1/3
Youth criticizes a legacy. EME 5/4

Gifford, Fannie Stearns
Apology. POE 3/1
Death in the sun. POE 3/1
The pupil to his master. NES 3/12/1
Song. CAS 3/3

Gifford, Franklin Kent
Exploitation. LIB 10/1

Gilbert, Ellen Frances
Question. OUT 3/8/2

Gilbert, Morris
About time. LIB 8/1
The boulghar dagh. POE 6/1
Prediction. POE 7/2

Gilbert, Warren
Barren ladies. PAL Sum/3
Editorial. PAL Sum/3
Five poems. PAL Sum/3
The girl with the bright hair.

PAL Sum/3
A girl's mind. PAL Sum/3
Gods. PAL Sum/3
In articula mortis. PAL Sum/3

Gilchrist, Helen Ives
Homesteaders. SCM 12/1

Gilchrist, Marie Emilie
After music. MID 9/0
Answers. MEA 12/3
Beatitude. LYW 11/3
Dawn wind. LYW 4/2
En route-the New Eng. express. NAT 3/13/0
Experienced woman wants... COV 5/4
For immediate sale:...house. COV 5/4
For immediate sale: sewing... COV 5/4
For rent: well-equipped..farm. COV 5/4
Formula. MEA 12/3
Housekeeper wanted... COV 5/4
The illusionist. MEA 12/3
Influence. MEA 12/3
Old window panes. MEA 3/2
She's dying..he..not let me go. COV 5/4
A stolen march. MEA 3/2
To the burrowing kind. LYW 4/2
Weather report. LYW 10/2

Gildersleeve, Basil L.
South Carolina. POM 1922

Gile, Blanche F.
Little things. TOD 5/1

Gill, Ottie
Not these. GYP #2/4

Gilmore, Louis
Agatha. DOU 10/1
Chocolate melody. LIR Spr/4
Colloquy of familiar things. AMH 5/9/4
Doors. AMH 3/4
Florizel in love. DOU 7/4
For the memory. PAR #4/4
Hero. NOM Spr/3
The high hat. BRO 1/3
Idyl. LIR Spr/4
Improvisation. S4N 12/2
In the patio. DOU 2/2
Intermezzo. WAV 2/2
Lines (for Charles H. Whitman). COV 3/4
Nocturne. DOU 4/2
Occidentale. WAV 2/2
A quiet street after rain. NES 5/10/4
Rock. MIN 5-6/4
Sanguine. LIR Spr/4
The shower bath. DOU 1/4
Southern melody. LIR Spr/4
Spiritual photograph. LIR Spr/4
Spring-song in blue. COV 4/4
To John Keats. NES 11/3/3
To a fly. DOU 1/3
To a goldfish. DOU 1/4
To an ant. DOU 2-3/4

Gilmore, Marion Forster
Moonlight motifs. AMP10-11/3

Giltinan, Caroline
Alone in spring. COV ?/0
Annunziata. CAW 3/4
The ball. CAW ?/0
The beggar. LYR 12/2
Bubbles. AMP ?/0
The builder. COV 10/2
The call. CAW 5/1
Consecration. COV 5/3
Dies dominicae passionis. ALE 4/14/2
Enough. AMP ?/0
Escape. COV 5/3
From the ward window. LYR 9/3
The garden. LYR 12/2
The interlude. COV 12/2
Interpreted. BOT ?/1
The invader. LYR 4/4
Magdalen. CAW 3/1
The magician. CAW 7/3
The ocean. CAW 12/3
Reception. COV 9/0
Respite. LYR 9/3
Spring. LYR 5/2
Triumph. COV 9/0
Triumph. COV ?/0
The visitor. CAW 8/0

Giltner, Leigh Gordon
Bride roses. LAR 7/3

Ginsberg, Louis
April. ARG 4/3/0
Curves. LIB 5/3
Evening rush hour. FOR 7/4
For sale. NEZ 12/9/1
Frost. MIN 1-2/4
Heaven on fire. AMH 12/1/2
Nocturne. COV 8/0
Old houses. NEW 1/9/0
Sing a song of houses. PAR #4/4
To a girl weeping. LIB 6/3
To fire. PEA 1/2
To my mother. LIB 9/2
Treasures. ARG 5/15/0
A vision. AMH 12/1/2
Waterfalls of stone. LIB 6/3

Giovanni, Sister Mary
Communion. MAG 8/3
She hath not ceased to kiss... MAG 9/3

Gitlow, Ben
Stone. LIB 3/2

Glaenzer, Richard Butler
After a storm. WAN 6/4
Between the brackets. POE 4/4
Catalina days. LYW 3/3
The Chinese coat. BOO 4/0
The guest. LYR 6/2
Indelible. LYW 3/3
It. MEA 9/2
Nasturtium. AIN 1/0
Older than China's Wall. LYR 11/3
The real pachydern. MID 11/0
Simplicia metella. NES 2/9/4
Solfeggio. NES 2/9/4
Tertium, quid. MIN11-12/3
Trees. RED 10/0
When the east quivers. WAN 6/4

Glaezner, Richard Butler
In an ear of the sea. WAN 9/3
Moon-magic. WAN 9/3

Glascock, K. Irene
Daylight. POE 5/3

Glasgow, Julia
Esther. AMH 3/18/1

Glines, Ellen
Borinquen. POE 4/4
R.I.P. Amor. POE 4/4
Today. POE 4/4
Tropic dawn. LYR 3/4

Glynn, Thomas J.
The woman with the golden tong. AMP 6-7/3

Goff, Harold
Reincarnation. LAR 11/3

Going, Charles Buxton
The figurehead. EVM 10/0
Magic of the moon. MUN 4/2
Spring-song of a shut-in. EVM 3/1
Taken ship. SCM 12/2

Gold, Michael
End of the week. LIB 4/2

Goldbeck, Cecil Hamilton
Release. PAG10-11/1

Goldburt, A.
The night of kid and kiddo. PAR #3/4

Golding, Louis
Beauty a ghost. POE 7/4
A chaffinch, a poplar, a star. LYR 7/4
Full of laughter. POE 7/2
Numbers. POE 7/1
The passer-by. POE 7/4

Goldsborough, Laird Shields
The great Buddha of Kwang Ki. YAR 12/3
The Pope (Innocent IV). YAR 1/4
Prayer to the muses. SCR 9/3
Two in the dawn. SCR 9/3

Goll, Ralph F.
Kokomo arraigned. LIB 6/2

Gondier, Violet Bailey
Old trails. LAR 9/3
Payin' back. LAR 3/3
To Rosemary, a November child. LAR 12/3

Goodenough, Arthur Henry
The golden apple. LAL 1/4

Goodfellow, Peter
Sadie. CTY S-A/1
When wet days of November come. CTY Win/3

Goodman, Blanche
From the journal of Cho-Shi-Ch. COV 2/1
Threnody. FRE 5/3/2

Goodman, Charles
Autumn rain. LYW 9/1
The dancer. LYW 11/2
Forget-me-nots. LYW 9/1

Goodner, Carlton Curtis
These two. LAR 12/3

Goodrich, Constance
Of this last night. MEA 12/1

Gordon, Armistead G.
"We return no more." LYR 10/1

Gordon, David
A spring rondel. HAM 4/0
To a Greenwich Village aesthet. DOU 3-4/3

Gordon, Elizabeth Hope
Pipes of Pan. GRA 6/1

Gordon, Gertrude Mills
The candle's end. CIC 9/13/3

Gordon, Ronald
The forsaker. SCR 10/3

Gordon, William Stewart
Junior's eyes. LAR 9/3

Gordon-Roby, Maude
Eternith hath no age. GRA 3/1
A song of spring. GRA 5/1

Gore, Russell
Where music steals upon you. DEU 6/5/1

Gorman, Herbert S.
Anthony. VOI 3-4/4
Blind time. FRE 8/22/3
The cabin the wood. NET 2/15/0
Conqueror. NER 8/22/3
I cannot put you away. NET 1/18/0
The last fire. OUT 7/12/2
Lese-majeste. OUT 8/16/2
Lilith, Lilith. NET 2/1/0
Madame De Vaudraucourt. NES 2/23/4
The meadow. FRE11/28/3
On a drunken painter... NER 5/21/4

Sylvanus orientalis. FUG 8/23/2
Tea hour. POE 10/3
Trance. FUG 3/7/3
Warning to a blase lady. NAT 1/3/4

Gould, Wallace
Diversion. POE 11/0
The game. DIA 5/2
The last tableau. POE 11/0
Matin. DIA 5/2
The pilgrimage. POE 11/0
Postlude. POE 11/0
Two Greek heads. DIA 3/2

Gower, Jean Milne
Children of the loom. AMP10-11/3

Grace, Richard Joseph
Homesteader's song. LAR 10/3

Graham, Gladys Wilmot
Autumnal rapture. AMP 10/2
Candles. LYW 7-8/2
A city. LAR 6/3
Come, rain! LYW 2/3
False tears. LAR 7/3
March wind. WAN 10/3
Reliquary. WAN 12/3
Sophisms. WAN 6/3
Wait, heart! NOM Aut/2
Winter-bound. AMP 12/2

Graham, Ottie
Futility. MES 7/4

Granich, Irwin
Surrender. POE 6/0

Grannis, Anita
A fillet of thorn. POE 11/1
Lovers of earth. VOI 12/2
The poet. VOI 12/2

Grant-Avery, Bertha
Birches. LAL 1/4

Graves, L. M.
The call of the prairie. COV 11/3
The plainsman. COV 11/3

Graves, Robert
Children of darkness. NER11/29/2
Christmas Eve. NER12/18/1
A dewdrop. HAM 3/3
An English wood. NER 11/1/2
The Lord Chamberlain tells..me. POE 2/3
Mirror, mirror. BOO 12/2
Misgivings... LYR 7/3
On the poet's birth. FUG 12/2
The philosophers. HAM 5/2
The red ribbon dream. NER 3/8/2
The return. BOO 12/2

Gray, Agnes Kendrick
After Whistler. MEA 6/1
At April's end. STE 3/3
A ballad of Shawn the rhymer. COV 6/1
The hill that is almost a moun. BOT 5/19/3
Youth. LYR 6/3

Gray, Eunice T.
The agitator. LYW 12/1
A college dance. LYW 6/2

Gray, Kate Joy
The poets' cove. AMP 2-3/3

Gray, Philip
Adventure's end. LYR 1/4
Autumn. AMP 10/2
Before we part. SCR 1/4
Cargo. STE 2/4
Celebration. SCR 1/4
Circles. CIV 5-6/4
In the hospital. LYW 10/2
June scherzo. LYW 6/2
Language. STE 9/3
Mockery. S4N 12/2
Music. MIN 5-6/4
Narrative in three poems. AMP 12/3
Victory. LYW 10/2
We two. VOI 5-6/4
While strangers walked and tal. AMP 4-5/3

Gray, Whitley
Valley of the Columbia..spring. LAR 2/4
Western moon. LAR 3/4

Grayce, La Pearl
Tenderness. CTY Spr/4

Graydon, Alice
Unknown. MAG 6/3

Graydon, Alice A.
June. MAG 6/2

Grebanier, Bernard D.
A Chopin etude. PAG 12/1
Movement from a Tschaikowsky... PAG 12/1

Green, Emma
Annie in her garden. CTY Win/3
Autumn fields. GUI 10/2
The birds of spring. GUI 10/2
Gray days-cold days. CTY Aut/3
It may be that some one... LIW 4/22/2
A Lake Michigan gull. MII 9/26/2
My garden. GUI 10/2
My muslin curtains blow about. OCO 5/24/3
Peace. LIW 9/2/2
Snow storm near Lake Michigan. AMP 4/2
They are burning over old mead. AMP 4/2
Time to thin your troubles out.

GUI 4/2
When a darting red bird... CTY Spr/4
Where is solitude? AMP 8-9/3
Willow, bending over me. AMP 3-4/4

Green, Jacquelyn
The little breeze. AMP 6-7/3

Green, Julia Boynton
A divine blunder. LAR 4/3
The rose peony. AMP 8-9/3
Song craft. LYW 11/3

Green, Mary Walter
Gilded bars. SCR 2/4
Work. SCR 2/4

Green, Thomas Claiborne
To a poet. CIV 3/4

Green-Leach, L. N.
June. CIV 5-6/4
Keats to Severn. CIV 3/4
A New Year's resolution. CIV 1/4
A rondeau of 1613 Bolton St.. CIV 7-8/4
A village May-queen. LAL 5/4

Greenhood, David
Andante. PAL Spr/3
A belt of bronze tablets. PAL Spr/3
Chocolate and figs. PAL Spr/3
The harvest of heliotrope. PAL Spr/3
The hungry. POE 11/3
Impeachment. POE 11/3
Landscape. MEA 1/2
My flippant mistress. PAL Sum/3
Old refrains. PAL Sum/3
Prayer before receiving honors. PAL Spr/3
A psalm for Cathleen Hoolihan. POE 5/2
Something bad. S4N 12/2
Sonnet. VOI 12/2
Thanks for a season. POE 12/0
Thus. MEA 7/4
Today. POE 11/3
The worker. POE 12/0

Greenwood, Florence
Oh, gladsome day. AMP 8-9/3

Greenwood, R. R.
Casco Bay fish-houses. PAR #1/4
Departure. MIN 3-4/4
The poet. COV 6/4
The threshold. COV 6/4
Two days. COV 6/4

Gregory, Augusta
The old woman remembers. NER 2/20/4

Gregory, Odin
"1917." ALS 1/2
The apostle. ALS 12/1
The feast. ALS 3/2
Femina. ALS 4/2
Ia Nikolai. ALS 2-3/3
Spindrift. ALS 11/1
The thing. ALS10-11/2
The wilding. ALS 2/2

Gregory, Susan Myra
October moons. AIN 10/2

Grey, Robert Malory
The birth of a flower. AMP 6-7/3

Griffin, Clare
A song at leave-taking. SCM 1/1

Griffith, Allison
Painting. AMP 5-6/4

Griffith, Herman J.
Metamorphosis. WAV 12/2

Griffith, William
Adrift. ALS 2/2
Amytis. LYR 4/4
Circe. PEG 7/3
The garret of dreams. DOU 2/29
Ideal. LYW 6/3
Novitiate. LYR 11/1
On using the sun and moon. ALS 2/1
Origins. DOU 6/1
Resurgam. LYW 11/2
Sacrifice. PEG 7/3
A song of Pierrot. AIN 2/0
Sonnet. ALS 2/2
Tidings. STE 1/4
Toll and goal. STE 2/3
Train lost. DOU 8-9/1
Vale. ALS 2-3/3
Vestigia. LYR 3/4
View - Halloo. ALS 10/1

Grissom, Irene Welch
Breaking the prairie. LAR 9/3
A prophecy. LAR 3/4
Vanished days. LAR 10/3

Grisson, Irene Welch
The prospector. LAR 6/3

Griswold, Isabel Winslow
Chicago's municipal pier. EDI 8/1

Grokowsky, David N.
Douglas Park, Chicago. FOU 10/3
Emptiness. LYW 11/1
Spring. PEG 5/3

Gronberg, Fred
Bombast. PEG 1/3
First love. PEG 1/3

Gross, Frances Wetmore
Bits of sand. LYW 7-8/2

Gross, Kathleen Cotter
The courtesan. SOU 1/3

Gross, Ray H.
Retrospection. AMP 8-9/3

The river. AMP 6-7/3
Two Christmas celebrations. COV 12/2

Grossman, Henrietta Mayer
Acknowledgment. CIJ 10/3

Grossman, Jean Schick
The gulf between. SVG 10/2

Grudin, Louis
"All roads lead to Rome." POE 9/2
Dostoyevski. BRO 12/2
Jest. POE 9/2
Man in the street. RHY 3/3
Solitaire. RHY 1/3
To a charlatan. CAP11-12/2
Ulysses. CAP11-12/2

Grudsky, Leo
Family portrait. POE 11/0
In the mirror. POE 11/0
Melodrama. POE 11/0

Gubbins, Florence Irene
Simplicity. CIJ 4/4

Gue, Belle Wiley
The ocean wind. AMP 2-3/3

Guerney, Bernard Guilbert
Prayer for the lonely night. MIN 7-8/3

Guiterman, Arthur
As to poets. BOO 2/4
Barcarole. HAM 5/3
Epitaph. NAT 6/4/4
How lyrics are born. BOO 5/0
The Nordics. NAT 6/18/4
The pioneer. OUT 9/27/2
A plea to poets. NES11/18/2
Pure envy. NES 6/28/4
Sex. NAT 5/4/1
Thanksgiving. SCM 5/3
The young intelligentsia. HAM 2/3

Gummere, Richard Mott
Youth resilient. COV 2/1

Gusling, Kalfus Kurtz
A kiss in the rain. LYW 3/3
You. LYW 11/3

Guthrie, Ramon
La perle de l'Egee. PAS 1/2

Gutterson, Edith
Yellow acacia. LYW 6/3

Guyol, Louise Patterson
"Chart showing rain, winds..." FUG 6-7/3
The color of happiness. GRA 10/2
Opportunity. GRA 12/3
Star-flowers. GRA 2/1

Gwathmey, Margaret Cabell
Living. LYR 7/1
My heart and I. LYR 4/1
Omission. LYR 6/1
The opium poppy. LYR 8/3
The ruby-throated humming bird. LYR 4/4

H.,M.D.
Promise. PAG 8-9/1
Relief. PAG 8-9/1

Haardt, Sara
On reading minor poems. REW 1/4
White violets. BOO 1/2

Hackett, Catherine Isabel
I would not grow old. SCM 5/2

Haddox, Dorothy
Japanese tiger lily. STE 11/3
To a kimono. LYW 10/3
Wistaria. LYW 7-8/2

Hadley, Florence Jones
Bubbles. MAG 7/2
Building a home. MAG 6/2
The day is done. MAG 5/2
God's peace. MAG 7/2
Going a piece. MAG 7/3
Just be glad. MAG 7/2
The little house in the hollow. MAG 8/3
Make-believes. MAG 4/2
My neighbor's house and mine. MAG 9/3
Song of the wayfarer. MAG 7/3
Tomorrow. MAG 2/2
Trusting. MAG 7/2
We go this way but once. MAG 3/2

Hagedorn, Hermann
The argonauts. OUT 9/7/1
The bad lands. OUT 9/7/1
The bad winter. OUT 9/7/1
The "busted" town. OUT 9/7/1
The chicken. NER 11/9/1
Dawn. OUT 9/7/1
Diana. OUT10/10/3
Digby. OUT12/14/1
The ex-cowpuncher. OUT 9/7/1
The eyes of God. OUT10/10/3
The man who sang. OUT 4/12/1
The philosopher. OUT 7/4/3
The quarrel. OUT 9/7/1
Roosevelt. OUT10/25/2
Solomon. OUT10/24/3
Summer dusk. OUT10/10/3
The Texas cowboy. OUT 9/7/1
The visionary. OUT 9/7/1

Hager, Alice Rogers
Cyclamen (Hachiojo). LYW 10/1
Remembered. LYR 7-8/3
Shadows. LYW 10/1
A shrine in Ueno. LYW 10/1

Ume no ki (the plum tree). LYW 10/1

Haigh, Josuf
Pelicans. PAG 12/1

Haines, Paul
The masquerade. GUL 9/3

Halbrook, Nellie R.
Toll. COV 5/0

Hall, Amanda Benjamin
Alas! VOI Aut/2
Alleluia! VOI 5-6/4
The buds have blossomed. COV 5/2
The canary. COV 10/0
A dancer dies. VOI Win/2
The dancer in the shrine. COV 4/0
The dish-washer. POE 3/0
Dolce far niente. VOI Spr/2
Entr'acte. BOO 11/2
Epitaph. BOO 3/3
"Go tell the baker selling bun. VOI Win/2
Growth. COV 5/2
Growth. VOI Spr/2
The haunted well. POE 4/3
Idyl. COV 10/0
Joe Tinker. COV 10/1
Johnny Dick. NES 4/29/2
Kingsborough. SMA 1/3
A lady. PAR #1/4
Mary. COV 9/2
Nocturne. COV 10/0
O singer! O singer! POE 3/0
Overture. VOI Aut/2
Romance. COV 12/0
Silence. COV 9/2
Storm. COV 7/0
Sven. VOI 5-6/4
"These are the gifts." VOI Aut/2
Thief. NES 4/5/4
To a wayfarer. COV 7/1
"To be sung with simplicity." SMA 4/2
To one who passed (H. I. L.). COV 10/0
Too many songs. BOO 5/3
"Too soon the lightest feet." NES 2/10/3
Tramp. VOI 8-9/3
Valse triste. VOI Spr/3
Values. COV 7/0
Waif. COV 1/0
A woman of words. COV 5/3

Hall, Bolton
Doubt. ALS 9/1
In the museum. ALS 8-9/2

Hall, Carolyn
Faith. MEA 8/2
Fritz Kreisler. MEA 6/1
Grey moth. COV 6/0
Husbandry. MEA 9/1
In an empty church. MEA 6/3
Luz de mi corazon. MEA 11/3
New roses. BOO 6/1
The penalty. FOR 11/3
Presage. MID 10/0
Rain-sounds. NES 5/14/1
The singing hands. MEA 11/3
Young Simon Peter. MEA 2/2

Hall, Eliza Calvert
The prayer of prayers. STE 4/4

Hall, Flora
Relations. SOV 1923

Hall, Fred
My ship and I. LIC 2/2

Hall, Grace E.
Beyond. LAR 5/3
Days. LAR 7/3
Except for you. LAR 4/4
Finality. OVM 5/4
Homespun poems. LAR 12/3
Kindness. LAR 6/3
Lone gray gull. LAR 7/3
Love's inspiration. LAR 10/3
Memories. LYW 2/4
My natal day. LAR 7/3
Repetition. LAR 9/3
Silence. LAR 3/4
To a humming bird. OVM 6/4

Hall, Hazel
Ahead of him. LYW 11/2
And either way. VOI Sum/2
Any woman. NER 10/3/3
Apathy. NER 8/23/2
Arraigned. VOI Spr/3
As she passes. OUT 9/13/2
At the corner. LIB 3/2
Audience to a poet. NES 1/5/4
Before quiet. POE 7/4
A boy went by. CEN 10/0
Bracken. REW 7/2
Breath. NER12/19/3
Cooling song. BOO 7/4
Cowardice. POE 5/1
Cross stitch. NEN 4/6/1
Crossed heart. NER 4/16/4
Crowds. LIB 2/2
Death defied. POE 7/4
Destinations. BOO 2/3
Disputed tread. NAT 1/25/2
Echoes of her. LYW 6/2
Eleventh month. NER11/28/3
Ephemera. MEA 8/2
Epitaph for a neighbor. VOI Spr/3
Estranged. CEN 12/3
Experienced griever. POE 7/4
Filet crochet. NEN 3/28/1

Flash. POE 5/1
Flight. NER 8/29/3
Footfalls. POE 1/3
For a broken needle. VOI 3-4/4
The gray veil. COV 1/1
He ran past. VOI Sum/2
He walked on. VOI Spr/3
He walks with his chin... NER 3/29/2
He went by. LYW 11/2
Hearsay. POE 7/4
Heavy treads. NEN 3/28/1
Here comes the thief. NER 7/25/3
The hippity-hopper. LYW 3/3
His eyes are on the ground. VOI Spr/3
Hunger. POE 1/3
The hurrier. POE 1/3
Incantation. VOI 3-4/4
Incidental. NER 6/21/2
Inheritance. VOI 3-4/4
Inland. LYW 2/4
Instruction. POE 5/1
Interim. OUT 7/16/4
A late passer. LYW 6/2
Late sewing. NEN 3/28/1
Light sleep. NAT 4/16/4
Locked out. AIN 3/0
Loneliness. COV 1/1
Maker of songs. NER 5/30/3
A man goes by. NER 11/9/1
The many. COV 5/3
Masks. NAT 2/28/0
Maturity. NER 3/8/2
Middle-aged. LYW 11/2
More than sound. MEA 8/2
Moving show. COV 12/2
My song that was a sword. GRA 2/2
Needlework. POE 4/0
New spring. LYR 6/2
October window. COV 10/2
An old man's walk. DOU 10/2
On the street. LYW 6/2
A passer. NER 3/8/2
Passers - the patrician. VOI Sum/2
Pedestrian. POE 1/3
The pity of it. VOI Spr/3
Pleasantry. POE 7/4
Profit. LYW 3/3
Protest. POE 7/4
Pursuit. LYW 3/3
The ravelling tune. LYW 4/4
The relinquisher. POE 7/4
Riddle. NER 6/11/4
Ripping. NEN 4/6/1
Running stitches. NEN 4/6/1
Sands. MEA 3/1
Sanity. LYW 11/2
The scarf. VOI 3-4/4
The sea. NER 6/20/3
Self inquisition. COV 5/3
Shawled. POE 1/3
The singing. LYR 2/3
Sleep charm. POE 7/4
Slow death. NER 6/18/4
Song to be known before death. POE 7/4
Song to be said while walking. NER 10/4/2
Stairways. COV 1/1
Stranger. LYW 3/3
Submergence. POE 7/4
Summary. NES 2/17/3
Sunlight through a window. COV 1/1
They pass. COV 5/3
They who walk in moonlight. POE 1/3
They will come. NER 1/24/3
The thin door. NER11/22/2
Three girls. CEN ?/0
Three poems. POE 7/1
Three songs for sewing. POE 5/1
Through the rain. BOO 2/3
To a door. COV 1/1
To all quiet persons. COV 5/4
To an indolent woman. NER 4/18/3
To an unpleased passer. COV 5/3
To one coming in sight. COV 5/3
Today. LYW 11/2
The unuttered. NER 5/28/4
Walkers at dusk. STE 3/2
Walking. COV 5/2
The way she walks. LYW 3/3
Weeper in the dark. VOI 3-4/4
Where others walk. COV 5/3
A whistler in the night. POE 1/3
White birches. BOO 11/1
Winter rest. VOI 3-4/4
Woman death. MEA 5/4
A woman ponders. POE 7/4
Words for weeping. NER 3/21/3
Your audience. MEA 2/2
Your camisole. NEN 4/6/1
Youth. DIA 9/0

Hall, Henry Clay

A bachelor's lament. INT 1-3/4
A dreamer's kyrielle. INT 4-6/4
A lover's fancy. INT 1-3/4
Who does not love true poetry? INT 4-6/4

Hall, Ina E.

The key. CTY Sum/3
A thousand thousand years ago. CTY Win/4

Hall, Lena
Six sonnets. VOI 8-9/3
Value. VOI Spr/3
A wood path in autumn. COV 10/2
Hall, Norman
The winter feast. HAM 3/3
Hall, R. Merton
A requiem. MUN 2/2
Hallam, Robert
Guides. GRA 6/1
Haller, Malleville
A boy's tent. NAT 4/9/4
In the subway. SCM 6/0
Old Mr. So-and-So. NAT 5/17/2
Haltiwanger, Caroline B.
Whimseys. AMP 12/2
Worship. AMP 8-9/3
Haman, Coralie Howard
Memories. CIV 7-8/4
The preacher's message. CIC 2/21/4
The tall gods. CIV 3/4
The tramp. INT 4-6/4
Hamilton, Ann
Billers. NAT10/17/3
Brother Rugino. NAT 12/6/2
Chanson d'or. DOU 10/2
Chanson noir. DOU 5/3
The flower-vendor. NAT 8/15/3
Harlequin to Columbine. NAT 12/6/2
Inscription. NAT 12/6/2
Loneliness. NAT 7/5/2
Nymph. NAT10/11/2
Pause. NAT 4/5/2
Peter. NAT 2/15/2
Song overheard on the highway. NAT 8/29/3
Song overheard on the shore. NAT 12/6/2
Sonnet. NAT11/30/1
Susie. NAT 12/7/1
Youth. NAT 5/23/3
Hamilton, David Osborne
Beauty in Fourth street. POE 8/1
The circle. POE 8/1
Creation. POE 4/3
Entreaty. MEA 12/1
The idiot. POE 8/1
The last night. MEA 8/2
Once more the moon. POE 4/3
Our time. POE 8/1
Te deum. POE 8/1
Hamilton, Flora Brent
Life. AMP 1-2/4
Vespers. AMP 10/2
Hamilton, Marion Ethel
The alien. LYW 4/4
Phyllis. LYW 7-8/3
Hamilton, Mary Glenn
Remembrance. DEP 3/4
Hamlin, Amy Whittlesey
No labor after death. OVM 1/4
Hammond (tr.), Louise
Chinese poems. POE 8/2
Hammond, Eleanor
Beggar. COV 5/0
The bond. COV 2/2
Chronometers. COV 5/0
Etchings. LAR 3/3
Fever. SCR 3/3
From a street corner. LYW 11/2
Home. SCR 3/3
Kisses. COV 5/0
Lady moon. COV 6/3
Loneliness. POE 3/4
Love song. COV 6/3
Moribund. COV 5/0
The mountain book. COV 5/0
An old Italian aria. LYW 11/1
The opal. COV 2/2
Phantoms. LYW 11/1
Sky scape. LYW 11/1
Snowfall. COV 1/4
Sometimes. COV 2/2
Transition. POE 6/0
Unfulfilled. COV 5/0
White water. COV 5/0
Winds, blow her here! COV 7/4
Winter woods. COV 1/0
You said. POE 3/4
You, too. COV 7/4
Young roads. CIM 6/11/4
Hammond, Josephine
The parapet. PER 1/2
Hammond, Laura
The marginal way. SOU 8/3
Hammond, Louise S.
The holy child. STE 12/3
Hammond, Maria Johns
Lost at sea. CIV 5-6/4
A mother. CIV 1/4
Han Hung
An autumn evening. FRE 8/15/3
Inscribed in the temple... FRE 8/15/3
Hancock, La Touche
Moods and seasons. LES 11/5/1
So would you. AMP Aut/1
Hanley, Elizabeth
Conversion. BOO 4/0
Hanline, Maurice A.
Drinks. COV 1/0
The symphony of the moon. COV 11/2
Hanline, Maurice
Harlequin plays the ghost... PAL Sum/3
Hannigan, D. F.

The dead boy. LYR 11/2
Hansen, J. C.
Change. PEG 3/3
On a lonely shore. CAP11-12/2
Your love and mine. CAP11-12/2
Hansen, Mabel Evelyn
Your neighbor's heart. AMP 4/2
Hanson, Joseph Mills
Lilacs. STE 5/4
Hardin, Charlotte
The double taking. DEU 7/24/1
The Gordian knot. LIB 8/1
Ragpicker. DEU 2/20/1
Riders in the dust. DOU 8-9/1
The rustling forest. DEU 2/27/1
Harding, Maude Burbank
Low tide. COV 8/1
Hardy, Arthur S.
To Daphne, knitting. SCB 12/2
Hardy, Evelyn
A star. SCM 4/0
The trust. SCM 6/4
Hardy, George E.
Despair moments. SCR 5/4
Harvest. SCR 5/4
Hardy, Thomas
An ancient to ancients. CEN 5/2
The haunting fingers. NER12/21/1
The two houses. DIA 8/1
Hare, Amory
April victorious. COV 2/3
The Olympians. COV 2/4
The theft. COV 2/3
To A.T.B.M.. COV 2/4
To a garden overgrown. COV 2/3
The unseen. COV 2/3
Harkness, Samuel D.
Lives are like books. CIC 4/10/4
Told on Easter, A.D. 33. CIC 3/15/3
Harman, Henry E.
Civic consciousness. SVG 7/3
Like messenger silent and stil. SOU 7/3
My beautiful sun. SVG 7/3
On the road to Enoree. SOU 8/3
Harness, Alden
Nature. LAR 6/3
Vacation time. LAR 6/3
Harpel, O. R.
The lone wolf's prayer. CAP 1-2/3
Harper, Isabel Westcott
"To every man a penny." SCM 2/2
Harrier, Jessie Vaughn
The campers. LYW 7-8/3
"I wonder..a cocker spaniel.." LYW 2/4
Harrild, Elizabeth
Lady fair. LAR 10/3
Harriman, Alice
The waterfront. OVM 2/4
Harris, Florence
Silence. VOI Win/2
Harris, Hazel Harper
Caruso. AMP 2/2
Sunset. AMP 8-9/3
Harris, Hazel V.
The light of victory. CIJ 8/3
Harrison, Freeman
Golden mystery. AIN 6/2
Harrison, M. Clifford
Sacrifice. AMP 4-5/3
Harrold, Fred
Milady's feet. AMP 4-5/3
Triolets. AMP 3-4/4
Hart, Pearl Barker
June days. OVM 6/4
Hartley, Lillian
Ideals. LYW 9/2
Hartley, Marsden
The asses' out-house. POE 5/0
Canticle for October. COT 4/1
The crucifixing of Noel. DIA 4/1
Espanol. POE 5/0
The festival of corn. POE 5/0
Girl with the camelia smile. POE 5/0
Saturday. POE 5/0
To C-. POE 5/0
The topaz of the sixties. POE 5/0
Hartmann, Jo
A night from an alcove. LAR 8/3
Hartsock, Ernest
April sadness. CIV 7-8/4
Beauty's wine. SCR 7/4
Transmigration. SCR 7/4
Vanitas vanitatum. SCR 7/4
Hartung, A. C.
What? CAS 1/3
Haruko Saigo
No reservation. FRE 12/7/1
A splendid sin. FRE 12/7/1
Harvey, Margaret
Disillusionment. AMP10-11/3
Harvey, Shirley
Camilla sings. GRA 3/1
Harwood, Ruth
Allegro. LYW 10/3
Always and always. POE 3/2
Making little clothes. POE 3/2
Mustard bloom. AMPO 10/2
The shoe factory. POE 3/2
Spring dirge. VOI Spr/3
Supremacy. LYW 12/1

Haste, Gwendolen
Aileen. POE 2/2
Barricades. CAP 1-2/3
The barrier. LYW 2/4
Biography. LYW 9/2
Deliverance. NAT10/18/2
The deserted ranch. LYW 2/4
The drylander's daughter. LYW 3/2
Epitaph. LYW 4/3
For a lonely grave. CEN 11/3
The guardians. POE 2/2
The haunted ring. LYW 7-8/3
Hollyhocks. LYW 3/2
Horizons. LYW 3/2
In Montana. POE 1/4
In a new land. COV 6/4
"Knowest thou the land?" NOM Spr/3
The little theatre. SCM 11/2
Moonrise. CAP 1-2/3
The mourner. LYW 2/4
Names. MID 1/1
Nostalgia. CAP 1-2/3
Nostalgia. SCM 10/3
Portrait. PAG 7-8/1
Prayer of the homesteader. MEA 12/2
The revenant. LYW 4/3
Sloth. PAR #1/4
The stoic. LYW 10/1
Time. COV 6/4
Told at sunset. NOM Spr/3
Hastings, Cristel
Aurora. LAR 5/3
Blind. LAR 4/3
Echoes. LAR 7/3
Falling stars. LAR 8/3
Freedom. LAR 6/3
Hunger. LAR 12/3
I wonder. LAR 6/3
If I were the wind. LAR 3/4
Sirens. LAR 8/3
Thirst. OVM 2/4
Hatton, Annie S.
New Hampshire. GRA 7/1
Hawkins, Heloise M. Burough
Anniversary. AMP10-11/3
Crown jewels. AMP10-11/3
Hawkins, Mrs. E. N.
Aeroplane. POA 9/1
Hawkridge, Emma
Hopi sun-christening. POE 1/0
Hawthorne, Hildegarde
Interpreter. SCM 12/2
The years, like torches, flare. STE 6/2
Hay, Lena H.
Neighbors. NOM Sum/3
Hay, Lena Jamison
The river. NOM Win/2
Hayes, Anna Hansen
The road in the sage. AMP10-11/3
Hayes, William Edward
The fall. AMP 10/1
Hayne, William Hamilton
April. SCM 5/0
The giant tree. MAC 3/2
The great game. MUN 1/2
Leaves. AIN 1/0
My lady's eyes. MUN 6/2
The old arm chair. MUN 4/2
Retrospect. SCM 1/3
Haynes, Carol
Binkie. HAM 12/2
Grandma. HAM 2/3
Haysradt, J. M.
Summer festival. YAR 6/4
Hayward, H. Richard
Love in Ulster. TEM Win/3
Haywood, H. L.
Red rose song. PEG 3/3
Hazeltine, Burton
Poem. STE 11/1
Hazzard, Lowell B.
Mysticism. CIC 11/8/3
Head, Cloyd
The curtains. POE 4/0
Head, Jerome
"That I do love you" MEA 4/1
Heartt-Dryfus, Estelle
Acacia branches. LYW 9/1
Gratitude. LYW 9/1
Heath, Winifred M.
Debussy. PEG 3/3
Kinship. LYW 4/3
Life. LYW 11/1
Point Loma. AMP 2-3/3
The voice. LYW 7-8/1
Heideman, Miriam
After death. DEU 5/16/0
Now that my heart. VOI Aut/2
Poplars in silhouette. VOI Aut/2
Prayer. VOI Aut/2
When you think I have died. AMP 10/2
Heine, Heinrich
Comradeship. TER 4/2
He and she. TER 4/2
The home coming. TER 4/2
Horns of Efland. TER 4/2
Ich liebe sie. TER 4/2
Lorelei. TER 4/2
The lyre. TER 4/2
The mattress-grave. TER 4/2
The message. TER 4/2
Moon-magic. TER 4/2
Once upon a time. TER 4/2

Palm and pine. TER 4/2
Poems. TER 7/3
Poet laureate. TER 4/2
Queen Mary. TER 4/2
Sentimentality. TER 4/2
The shepherd lad. TER 4/2
The suicide's grave. TER 4/2
To a child. TER 4/2
To one unborn. TER 4/2

Heller, Helen West
Bees. MEA 9/1
First and last. AMP Aut/1
Inhibition. MID 8/1
Tomorrows. MID 8/1
The two of them don't make... PAG 12/1
Wednesday week. MID 8/1
Words. PAG10-11/1

Heller, Samuel
After harvest. STE 1/3
Autumnal. STE 1/3
From Offenbach. AMP 6/2
May passes. AMP 4-5/3
A robin. LYR 4/1
Roman poppies. NOM Sum/3
The stars will remember. LYW 4/3

Hellman, Rhoda
Puddle. MEA 5/3

Helman, Rebecca
At dawn. CTY Sum/2
At the bookshop. STE 12/2
Change. SCR 5/3
The comforter. CTY S-A/1
The day. SCR 4/3
Dream-fancy. AMP 6-7/3
The fool. CTY Aut/2
The harp. SCR 4/3
Inapt. CTY Spr/3
Kyrielle. CTY Spr/2
Once on a time. CTY Win/3
One library. STE 7/2
The roving heart. SCR 5/3
Spirit. SCR 5/3
When mother sings. CTY W/2

Helton, Roy
August morning. COV 2/3
May Jones takes the air. NAT 2/9/1
Three poems about ghosts. COV 2/3

Hemingway, Ernest
Champs d'honneur. POE 1/3
Chapter heading. POE 1/3
Mitraillliatrice. POE 1/3
Oily weather. POE 1/3
Riparto D'Assalto. POE 1/3
Roosevelt. POE 1/3
Ultimately. DOU 6/2

Henckell, Karl
Songs of the road mender. NAT 3/14/3

Henderson, Anne
The hope-chest. NAT 3/22/2

Henderson, Daniel
Dalliance. COV 12/0
Friendship. POE 6/2
Melting brook. NES 3/31/3
Night picture. BOO 2/1
Pilgrim mothers. OUT 9/15/0
Repentance. BOO 3/1
The sculptor. CIV 12/0
Snow fantasy. BOO 3/2
Snow trails. NES 1/28/2
Songs from Genesis: II. Jubal. COV 7/1
Songs from Genesis: I. Jacob... COV 7/1
The stranger. MAC 5/3
Sunset through an office windo. COV 1/3
Tenement children. BOO 6/3
A test for poets. COV 8/0
A trainman. COV 8/0
Trees in February. MAC 2/3

Henderson, Jessie
Heigh-ho, romance. AIN 3/2
When Broadway was a little... AIN 2/2

Henderson, Rose
The dream. COV 6/1
In the park. LYW 6/2
Lynched. COV 3/3
Nests. COV 6/1
A song of death. FUG 6-7/3
The sun god. EVM 6/1
Tewa corn dance. MID 12/0
Trees. IND 5/13/2

Henry, Edna G.
The dispensary doctor. LYW 11/2
Finis. AMP 6/2
Gone. AMP Aut/1
Hesperoyucca. LYW 7-8/3
One day. LIC 12/1
Trees walking. LYW 3/2

Henry, Thomas Millard
Ode to Paul Laurence Dunbar. NEG 1/1/1

Hensel, Gladys
The shepherd. Poe 6/0

Hepburn, E. MacAlister
The dancer. LYW 5/2
One kiss. NEN 3/28/1

Hepburn, Elizabeth
A priestess of Apollo. AIN 1/0

Herald, Leon
Beauty. POE 9/2
In your eyes. POE 9/2
My wedding. POE 9/2

Heredia, Jose-Maria de

The siesta. COV 11/0
Herendeen, Anne
Capri. NAT 9/27/2
Comrade Levy. LIB 9/1
Madame La Guerre. LIB 9/1
The observant captive. NAT 9/27/2
Reunion. NAT 9/27/2
Revolution. LIB 9/1
Revolution. NAT 9/27/2
Shop-talk. LIB 2/2
The stranger. LIB 2/2
They-. LIB 12/1
Troth. NAT 9/27/2
A true poem. LIB 9/2
A wife. LIB 10/1
Herold, Leon
Melancholy and joy. DEU 3/28/0
Youlia. DEU 3/21/0
Herron, Edna
Patience. POA 1/2
Herron, Vennette
The game. AIN 4/0
Herschdorfer, Helen
All, all are atoms. GUL 6/3
Loves. GUL 6/3
Hersey, Marie Louise
Contrasts. COV 4/0
To Robinson Crusoe. SMI 6/1
The weaker sex. BOT 5/7/1
Hersh, Helen
Retrospect. WAV 12/2
Herzog (Jr.), Paul
The hermit. LIC 4/3
Hess, Maud Hogue
The cabin. LYW 5/2
Hesse, Hermann
Night. NAT 3/14/3
Heyward, DuBose
The autumn. EVM 11/1
Charleston poems. POE 4/2
Dusk. POE 4/2
Edgar Allen Poe. POE 4/2
Gamesters all. COV 4/1
Matins. POE 4/2
The mountain girl. POE 4/2
The mountain graveyard. POE 8/2
The mountain woman. POE 7/0
Heyward, Janie Screven
Autumn leaves. STE 6/2
Daffodils. COV 4/0
Star-dreams. STE 5/2
To my beloved. STE 5/2
Hibbard, Addison
To a Chinese student..America. REW 7/4
Hibbel, Bertha C.
You. PAG10-11/1
Hickey, Agnes M.
Autumn evening. SPT10/14/2
The balloon man. PIT 9/23/2
Fairy flag painters. PAL 5/2
Fairy flag painters. PIT10/20/2
Frank Bacon. NEV12/26/2
Little leaves. NET10/19/1
So comes the snow. SPT 1/14/3
Transient. PIT 8/25/2
Hickey, Alice M.
At Christmas time. NEW12/11/3
Echoes. NET 9/3
Gypsy urge. NET 5/4
If you are there. NET 3/4
Hickey, Emily
At eventide. CAW 11/2
Behold your king. CAW 4/2
Immacculta, ora pro nobis. CAW 1/1
Hickey, Florence Mayne
Sequins. LAR 7/3
Higgins, Annie
The acquired art. VOI Aut/2
All night. LYW 3/3
As the clock strikes. VOI Spr/3
Confession. CAP 5/3
Early spring. NER 4/25/3
Futility. WAV 12/2
I remember. LYW 3/3
In regard to rings. BOO 5/4
Indecision. WAV 12/2
Jewelry. MEA 2/4
A matter of words. VOI Spr/3
Midnight. MEA 2/4
My hands. MEA 2/4
Nausea. MEA 12/2
The next day. WAV 12/2
On growing things. NER 4/25/3
Pillow confidence. CAP 5/3
Postponement. LYW 9/2
Repose. WAV 12/2
Riddance. MEA 12/2
Something to do. VOI Spr/3
Song against art. LYW 9/2
Three crows. MEA 12/2
Higgins, J. Lee
Old channels and wharves. PAG10-11/1
Hill, Dana
Earth and air. MEA 5/4
The tree. BOO 7/4
Hill, Esther Clark
The fog. LYW 4/2
The fog. MAC 7/2
Hill, Florence H.
Compensation. MAG 7/2
Hill, Frank Ernest
The abiding moment. MEA 3/1
Borasan. MEA 6/1
Clouds. MEA 6/2
The earth will stay the same. NAT 6/29/1

Farm-circle. NER 8/29/3
The flyers. NAT 1/10/0
Formation. NAT 4/11/3
Her house. MEA 10/2
High mountains. MEA 10/1
Lundy. MER 1/3
Midnight tenement. MEA 5/3
Mirage. NAT 11/1/2
Moonlight, vermillion valley. LYW 2/3
The pass. LYW 6/3
Snow water. NER 1/18/2
So passes the glory. NER 5/21/4
They who are what they are. NER11/22/2
Upper air. NER10/10/0
Words for gardening. NER 6/11/4

Hill, Lucie Haskell
To till the ground. CIJ 4/4

Hill, Marvin Luther
The doubter. LYW 12/3
Lowlands. VOI 12-1/4
March storm. LYW 3/3
To Madeleine. LYW 9/3

Hilliard, John Northern
Gifts. LYW 12/3
Romance. LYW 6/3

Hillman, Carolyn
A portrait. POE 10/3
Wild geese. VOI Sum/2

Hillman, Gordon Malherbe
African harbor. SHA 5/2
The first command. OPE 9/1
The first command. OPE 2/1
The fish patrol. CIM 3/26/1
Fog. CIM 5/21/1
Garlands. SHA 8/1
Gypsies. MUN 11/1
Harlequinade. TEL 3/4
If winter comes. GRA 10/1
Lucile. LYW 6/3
Memphis. COV 4/1
Montreal. MOT 5/1
A Morayshire lilt. MOT 3/2
Night fall. LYW 11/2
Northern blood. CIM12/15/1
Persian Gulf. CIM10/14/1
Poets. SMA 10/1
Rio de Janeiro. CIM11/12/1
San Francisco. COV 4/1
Sea lure. ADV 2/18/0
Sea roads. CIM 1/10/2
Sea turn. CIM 6/7/1
Sea winds. LYW 7-8/2
The ship turns home. ADV 4/3/1
The siren. CIM 6/26/0
The tankers. ADV 2/18/0
Tea ships. ADV 9/32/0
The tramp. OPE 10/0
Typhoon. ADV 3/3/1
Variety show. VOI Aut/2
The wild geese (Chun Yu Seng). COV 4/1
Yellowhead pass. CIM 1/13/1

Hills, Gertrude
Christmas tree. VOI 12/2
To a stranger. VOI Sum/2
Worship. VOI 12/2

Hillyer (tr.), Robert Silliman
Evening. AMS 3/2
"The plants stand silent..." AMS 2/2

Hillyer, Robert Silliman
And now at sunset. NER10/25/2
Ballade. DIA 3/0
The blue forest. VOI Spr/3
The coming forth by day. FUG 3/21/2
Disillusion. MEA 4/1
Egyptian suite. VOI 7-8/3
Elegy on a dead mermaid washed. NER 4/5/2
Entomology. OUT10/11/2
Epitaph. LYR 4/3
Ethics. LIF 8/5/1
Flower-market, Copenhagen. OUT 2/22/1
For Maister Geoffrey Chaucer. OUT 7/19/2
Free will. BOO 4/3
"Her own shall bless her." BOT 1/28/2
The hills give promise. LYR 2/2
Interlude. COV 2/1
Interval. HAM 10/2
Interval. LYR 1/4
Interval. LYR 8/1
Intimacy. AIN 5/2
Invocation. AIN 4/2
Largo. AIN 9/1
A letter. HAM 6/1
Mentis trist. NER 1/30/4
Moo. NER10/31/3
Nocturne. DIA 3/4
Portrait. LYR 9/3
Scherzo. OUT 5/9/3
Sonnet. REW 4/4
St. Sylvius. OUT 5/23/3
Suspense. NER 1/18/2
Threnody. BOO 11/1
The treadmill. LIF 12/1
The treadmill. LYR 9/2
The two twilights. AIN 8/1
Yesterday. OUT 1/17/3

Hirsch, Sidney M.
Nebrismus. FUG 12/2
Quodlibet. FUG 3-4/3
To a dead lady. FUG 10/2

Ho Chih-chang
Return-home writing. MEA 6/2

Hoard, Prescott
Carnival. MEA 8/2
Cobwebbed trapese performer. MEA 6/3
Episode. MEA 6/4
Interruption. MEA 12/2
Model. MEA 6/4
Saturday barnyard. MEA 7/4
Sky line. MEA 12/2
Woodcraft. MEA 12/2
Hofer, E.
What shall I write? LAR 2/3
Hoffman, C. Gouverneur
Clouds. SCM 6/1
Hoffman, Ella
The echo. S4N 12/2
Hoffman, Harold
To Thomas Hardy, dark poet. MEA 1/3
Two winter poems. POE 1/4
Hoffman, Phoebe
Dreams. AMP 6-7/3
The foolish virgin. NES 2/3/3
The old man. COV 12/2
The old pilot speaks. COV 8/2
The poet finds himself. COV 1/0
Hoffmansthal, Hugo von
Two of them. PAG10-11/1
Two. NAT 3/14/3
Hogan, Mamie Lahey
The old Seth Thomas. POA 9/1
Hoisington, May Folwell
Ad interim. CIV 3/4
Buried treasure. CTY Win/4
The children's flowers. CTY Sum/3
Dissociation. COV 12/3
El Dia de Reyes. COV 12/3
Gods of the corn. SCR 5/4
The gypsy child. INT 4-6/4
The lass of Ilfracombe. LAL 5/4
"Queen Anne's dead." CTY Spr/3
The smiling ghost of Blaith. COV 5/4
The song of Bahram. CIV 7-8/4
Thora and the Nykkur-horses. SCR 6/4
The word of Solon. SCR 5/4
Holbrook, Weare
The belle of the ball. LYW 10/3
The drifter's wife. LYW 2/2
Ergo tam doctae. LYW 9/1
In which a poet slips the blue. WRM 4/1
The middle years. MID 4/0
Minor poets. COV 8/0
Pacis amor deus. LYW 1/2
Risus eram positis. LYW 9/1
To flat-face. WAV 3/4
Holden, Ella
Dream poem. MEA 11/2
Holden, Floyd T.
Mnemosyne. CIV 7-8/4
Holden, Raymond
After the circus. YAR 10/2
Escape. MEA 6/3
Firewood. NAT 8/16/2
A glance toward middle age. MEA 2/3
Night above the tree line. POE 6/2
Spring building. MEA 7/2
Sugaring. POE 7/0
Thompson Street. MID 1/0
Though almost anything. MEA 6/3
To nine who vanished long ago. MEA 6/3
To the dead, New Year's Eve. MID 1/0
To the urbane. NES10/21/2
Two worlds. MID 1/0
Wild honey. MEA 2/3
Holladay, Helen H.
Vanity. LYW 4/2
Holladay, Paula
Memory. AIN 3/0
Holland, Laura Grant
Summer. CTY S-A/1
Holley, Horace
The fool. POE 2/1
Holliday, Carl
Dream ships. GRA 12/3
Old "Prof." Dickerson dies. SCM 9/3
A preface for any book. GRA 7/3
Hollis, Barbara
Destiny. GRA 7/1
Home builders. GRA 7/1
In appreciation of tea. AIN 4/2
The test. HAM 3/3
To a little ship. HAM 3/2
Vagabond. OVM 4/4
Hollister, Hilary
For a fan. MEA 5/3
Holloway, John Wesley
Dar's gwine to be a weddin'. CTY Sum/3
Holloway, Robert
Sorrow. POE 3/4
Holme, Jamie Sexton
Love in autumn I do not weep. SCR 6/4
Holmes, Calvin Russell
Madonna. POE 8/3
Holmes, Charles Nevers
After the snow storm. GRA 2/1
Holmes, John Haynes
Good men. NAT10/26/1
Holstein, Ludwig
Father, where do the wild swan.

POE 11/2
Holt, Elizabeth Kendrick
Broken nights. GUL 6/3
Holt, Florence Taber
Flowers. DIA 2/0
To Pan. DIA 2/0
The wind of love. DIA 2/0
Holt, Guy
And I did eat. REW 4/3
She for whom the leopard... REW 12/1
Holway, Edith Boyder
The onlooker. LYW 9/3
Holz, Arno
From phantasus. POE 12/2
Hood, Evelyn
When night is darkest. COV 1/31/4
Hood, Joseph R.
Arcadia. AMP10-11/3
The wayfarer. AMP 4-5/3
Hope, Ethel
At parting. AMP 10/2
Masquerade. LYW 10/3
Two songs of summer. AMP 8-9/3
Hopkins, Frances Case
When I am dead. AMP 2/2
Hoppe, Theresa L.
A crushed flower. LAR 3/4
Songs my mother sang. LAR 4/4
Horgan, Joseph Lee
Grey symphony. AMP10-11/3
Horgan, Paul
Litany. POE 6/4
The temples and the gongs. POE 6/4
Winter night. POE 6/4
Horn, Frederica L.
My temple. AMP 8-9/3
Serenade. AMP 12/2
A song for you. AMP 4-5/3
Horst, John H.
The rebel poet. INT 1-3/4
Horton, Dabney
The winged soul. SCM 10/0
Horton, Edith
My kitchen. SEW10-12/1
Hoskins, Ruth Corley
The early morning crowd. LYW 10/3
Hosmer, Charles
Fledgling. VOI 7-8/3
Houdlette, Florence
The bugle call. CIJ 1/4
Hough, Mary E.
April. GRA 4/1
Day-time. GRA 6/1
A degenerate of the pink famil. GRA 10/2
The Hampshires. GRA 8/2
On the road from Cormicy. GRA 9/2
Houghtelin, Guy R.
Obedience to God's call. CIJ 11/3
Houghton (Jr.), Walter Edwards
Benediction: recall. YAR 10/3
Chimes. YAR 1/4
The eager years. YAR 11/3
Just today. YAR 10/3
Houk, Gertrude Deane
The way. CIJ 6/4
House, Roy Temple
Tankas from the Japanese. LYW 2/4
Housman, Laurence
Death of day. HAM 7/2
To a rider drwoned at sea. NER 5/26/0
Houston, G. d'A.
Hidden. PAG 8-9/1
Houston, Margaret Belle
Memory. POE 8/1
Hovorka, Emily S.
The mute. SCR 2/3
Howard, J. Frederick
Meditation..old deserted house. AMP10-11/3
Howard, Katharine
By San Diego. LYW 3/4
Howard, Katherine
Coast range. LYW 7-8/3
A sonnet to the dawn. PEG 1/3
Howat, Helen
Challenge. LYW 9/1
Howe, Mark Antony De Wolfe
The music garden. SCM 10/0
Howe, Nancy Lee
Blue-bird time. LYW 4/2
Howe, Susanne
Absence. MEA 11/2
Immortality. MEA 11/2
The sanitorium. CPV 2/0
To M.A.S.. MEA 2/2
Tumble-weed. MEA 2/2
Howell, Editha
The return. LYW 10/1
Howell, Lucile Topping
Little mother with snow-white. WOW 5/0
Howells, Mildred
Sleep well. SCM 2/4
To an amiable little boy. SCM 7/4
Howes, Grace Clementine
The desert flock. NET 10/3/1
Faith. WOW 1/2
From the desert. LES 11/5/1
Indian starlight. NET 8/25/1
Mid-winter. NET 1/14/2

The mountains. LYW 7-8/3
The mountains. LYW 2/4
An old man of the trails. LYW 4/4
Rosemary and Rue. FOT 4/24/2
The runaways. NET11/22/1
The sailor's child. SAB 9/1
Sea lover. MAC 6/4
The stairway. LYW 7-8/2
The summons. NET12/23/1
The trail. NET 8/25/1
The tree. AMF 10/1
Western autumn. NET10/19/1
Winter dawn. WOW 1/2

Hoy, Arthur Dwight
A day dream. WAN 7/4

Hoyt, Helen
At the edge of the pier. VOI 5-6/4
The bride and the matron. POE 10/3
Chant of rejoicing. POE 10/3
Control. NES 5/22/4
Day's end. POE 10/3
Flower and flame. POE 10/3
Fragment. COV 5/4
Gravid. POE 10/3
I have known. COV 5/4
I must turn myself...sorrow. PAR #3/4
Let me keep your hand. COV 5/4
Now I will unknit my life away. MOR 1-4/4
O white, white. COV 5/4
October letter. POE 10/3
Recession. COV 5/4
Recompense. POE 10/3
Sleep, sleep on. COV 5/4
The stone. POE 10/3
The trees are troubled... VOI 5-6/4
Tulip bed. PAL Sum/3
What I dreamed..be so strange. COV 5/4
The white leopard. VOI 5-6/4
Your words. POE 10/3

Hoyt, Helen Underwood
Automobiles on Sunday. POE 3/0
By the lake. POE 3/0
Chicago. POE 3/0
Creator. POE 3/0
The cynic. DOU 9/2
Detachment. COV 11/2
Encounter. POE 3/0
The first time I loved. AIN 2/0
Headstone. POE 3/0
How can I keep my hands? VOI 6-7/3
I must turn my face from your. AMP 4-5/3
More lovely that a mountainsid. MEA 7/3
Mountain-morning. COV 12/0
Mummy. DOU 8-9/1
Muse of astronomy. GRA 11/2
My own song. PIR 3/2
Night. POE 3/0
O do not fear for your life. PAL Spr/3
On the breakwater. VOI 6-7/3
Our favorite selves. PIR 8/2
Place. VOI Sum/2
Red ribbon. BOO 3/2
Scars in air. COV 1/3
The stone-age sea. POE 3/0
Then first it was. DOU 4/2
There was a time. POE 3/0
To "A Stropshire Lad" MEA 6/1
Trying to think by the water. VOI 6-7/3
An unprejudiced mind. MEA 7/3
Urania. GRA 11/2
Vita nuova. LYR 10/2
We never left our love unsaid. NER 1/18/2
When we are asleep. POE 3/0

Hoyt, Henry Martyn
The ballad monger. OUT 7/7/0

Hoyt, Morton
Sex lebris. NES 3/12/1

Hsu Hun
Early autumn. FUG 7/4/3
Inscribed in the inn at T'ung-. DOU 5/3

Hubbard, Ernest
The ghost. DOU 7/4

Hubbard, George Henry
A Christmas wish. GRA 12/1

Hubbell, Lindley Williams
Sonnet. MEA 2/4

Hubbell, Martha M. F.
Mother thoughts. OUT 5/10/2

Huckfield, Leyland
Birch artistry. COV 8/3
Ceramics. COV 2/1
The land of plums. COV 4/1
Last road home. MID 3/1
Oil of man. MID 3/1
Riding west. MID 1/1
Spell of the river. MID 1/1
To a parakeet. MID 2/1
The tramp girl. COV 9/2
A winter gale. COV 2/0

Huddleston, Mabel Barker
The roof-garden. POE 5/0

Hudnut, William Herbert
The call denied. CIC 4/5/3

Hudson, Addie Cropsey
Loneliness. AMP10-11/3
The silent feller. COV 11/3

The singing trail. LYW 6/3
Hudson, Hoyt H.
In the city. GRI 6/1
Hudspeth, William Herbert
A wakened memory. AMP 12/2
Hueffer (see Ford M. Ford), F.

Huelsenbeck, R.
Chorus sanctus. LIR Spr/4
Hughes, Adelaide Manola
Cuivre dore. BOO 8/2
Hughes, Glenn
Arizona night. LAR 6/3
In the city. LAR 6/3
Revelation. AIN 5/0
Hughes, Langston
After many springs. CUU 8/2
Beggar boy. CUU 9/2
Danse Africaine. CUU 8/2
Dreams. WRE 5/3
Gods. MES 3/4
Grant Park. MES 3/4
Monotony. CUU 5/3
Mother to son. CUU 12/2
Our land. WRE 5/3
Poem for the portrait of an Af. WRE 5/3
Prayer for a winter night. MES 7/4
Song for a banjo dance. CUU 10/2
When Sue wears red. CUU 2/3
Hughes, Mary
Rain. COV 6/2
Hughes, May
Jasmine. COV 5/3
Laughter. COV 5/3
Magic. COV 5/3
Hughes, Richard
Dirge. POE 8/1
The horse trough. BOO 7/2
The moonlit journey. NES 11/5/1
The singing furies. DIA 6/1
Hughes, Robert M.
Alone! I am alone! LAR 10/3
Below the Rio. POE 1-2/4
Chiquita. COV 11/3
The country girl. LYR 1/4
The coyote hide. COV 11/3
The misfit. LYR 1/4
A sapphir fragment. LYR 9/3
The star roper. POE 1-2/4
Yellow flowers. AMP 8-9/3
Hughes, Russell Merriwether
Autumn. AMP 10/2
In the mawnin'. TEM Win/3
The return. TEM Aut/1
Huguenot, Stephen
Possession. WAV 1/2
Huiginn, E. J. V.
Jean. SAD11/30/1
Life. SAD12/23/1
Little Lassie. SAD 1/24/2
The mistletoe. SAD12/30/1
The rose. SAD 11/3/1
Santa's visit. SAD12/24/1
The vase and the rose. SAD 5/2
Hume, Isabel
The curious eyes. NOA 2/1
Hummel, Edna Logan
Arbutus! GRA 5/2
My wife's roses. AMP 6/2
Humphreys, Rena Lloyd
What you are like to me. CIV 5-6/4
Humphreys, Rolfe
Companion piece. WAN 1/4
Dreams. NAT 7/2/4
Eagle. NER 7/2/4
Eloi, eloi. MEA 2/4
Europa. MEA 7/4
Hard-wood woman. VOI 3-4/4
Imminent. VOI10-11/3
In your own words. WAN 9/3
Mistress death. MEA 2/4
Night rider. NAT 5/21/4
On leaving. STE 4/4
Parting shot. WAN 4/4
To the greatest city... CEN 6/4
Whence cometh my help. LYW 4/4
Humphries, Rolfe
Drowning. MEA 11/2
Eternal recurrence. LIB 1/2
Evening on Tahoe. LYW 7-8/2
February. LYW 2/2
Grey sunset. AMP 2-3/3
Inadequate. WAN 6/3
Indiffferent. PEG 3/3
A sad little lyric for vacatio. LYW 7-8/2
Solitary. LYW 7-8/3
Hunt, Leigh
The Nile. GRA 9/3
Hunt, Robert Booker
Puzzle. LYR 1/4
Hunter (tr.), Grave
My prayer. STE 2/4
Hunter, Isabel Robins
The attack on the harem. NEW 5/9/0
Hunter, Rex
And tomorrow comes. CAP 10/2
Instructions for entering...ro. CAP11-12/2
Sinclair at the theatre. WAV 3/4
Huntington, Julia Weld
Off the highway. POE 5/1
Hussey, Jennie E.
The harbinger of Spring. GRA

4/1

Hutchins, M. Doris
Finis. LYW 9/3
To the soul of a dancer. LYW 4/4
Your room. LYW 3/3
The Yucca. LYW 7-8/2

Hutchinson, Hazel Collister
Adoration. COV 10/0
Autumn arabesque. ALS 3/2
Caesura. DOU 6/2
Dawn in Eagle street. ALS 12/1
Inheritance. POE 11/3
Paris impression. POE 11/3
Paris. DOU 12/2
Reims. POE 11/3

Hutchinson, Mary K.
Lights and shadows. POA 9/1

Hyatt (Jr.), Jack
The beggar. LYW 4/2
Blindness. LYW 3/3
Ching Loo dreams. LYW 9/2
Prayer. LYW 12/3
Sidewalk spectres. TEM 6/1
Similia. LYW 3/3
Steps on the stair. LYW 7-8/3

Hyatt, Lucy
On Flanders field. CTY Spr/2

Hyde, Edna
Jealousy. LAL 1/4
Kin. LAL 3/4

Hyer, Helen von Kolnitz
Beaches. POM 1922

I.,M.
Lines on Watt's 'Hope'... CAW 1/1
Sea-queen. CAW 5/2

Imam, Syed Mehdi
Harp of my hand that tuneless.. LYR 1/3

Ingemann, Bernhard Severin
Evening. AMS 3/2

Inman, Arthur Crew
As thru a veil. COV 1/3
At the coming of spring. COV 4/3
The captive. COV 1/3
Columbine dances. VOI Aut/1
Could I express. AMP 3-4/4
The derelict. COV 1/3
Desert. COV 7/3
The deserted barn. REW 4/3
The fakir. COV 6/4
From an abandoned pier. LYW 6/3
The generation that is. SOU 7/3
Georgian memory. SOU 7/3
Grey (1865). COV 6/4
In a sunken garden. SOU 8/3
Lee, retreating...Gettysburg. COV 6/4
Mood. VOI Aut/2
The ocean. LYW 2/4
Paths across the sea. FRE 7/12/2
River song. COV 7/2
Solitude. COV 1/3
The spring house. REW 7/4
To Columbine. LYW 2/4
The tryst. TEM Aut/1
The watcher at the bow. COV 7/2

Irving, Minna
An Othello of the sea. MUN 5/2

Isenbeck, Dorothy C.
Spring snows. AMP 8/2

Ishikawa Kin-ichi
After a long night. VOI 6-7/3
Barefoot twilight. VOI 6-7/3

Ives, Mabel Lorenz
Four famous Chinese poems. SCR 4/4

J.,S.V.
L'Englise a collioure.. STC 1/10/0

Jackson, Jessica
Days. PAL Sum/3
Lines written by the sea. COV 6/3
Peas. PAL Sum/3
Shelling peas. PAL Sum/3
Song. POE 8/3

Jackson, Lou
At twilight. AMP 2-3/3

Jackson, Phyllis
Prairie mother. POE 7/4

Jackson, Sarah
Day dreams. GRA 7/2

Jackson, Winifred Virginia
Baby bluebird. BRW 7/1
Bobby's wishes. BRW 12/0
The bonnet. NAU 3/1
Brown leaves. CUU 7/0
The cobbler in the moon. COS 6/1
A deafness. COS 6/1
Dora of Aurora. BOP12/12/0
Driftwood and fire. NAU 2/1
Dust song. EME 6/3
Ellsworth to great pond. BRO 10/3
Eyes. COS 6/1
Finality. COS 6/1
Hoofin' it. COS 6/1

Not for publication. NER 7/2/4
On some modern poets. BOO 11/3
On the line. NER 7/9/4
Phoenix. NAT 11/9/1
The puppet booth. NAT 3/6/0
Recreant. LYR 8/3
Rejected. OUT 8/8/3
Salute! W. M. R.. ALS 6/1
Solstice. OUT11/29/2
Sophistry. NER 10/4/2
Stranger. CEN 10/3
Sustenance. BOO 11/2
This dust of dreams. NAT 2/21/0
Threshold. NER 9/19/3
Tide line. NER 5/21/4
Travesty. NAT 9/20/2
Trumpets at Jericho. OUT 8/2/2
We are not forward. NER 11/9/2
We come from Babel. NER11/23/1

Jennings, Viola
O, ship! My ship! LAR 10/3
Spring dreams. LAR 5/3

Jenny, Florence G.
To April. COV 3/2
To spring. COV 3/2

Jesson, Frederick Shea
The archer. POE 9/0
A certain girl. POE 9/0
Earth-song. POE 9/0
North Ohio village. POE 11/2

Jessup, Frederika Peterson
Chaldean song. FRE 2/15/2
The child to the ghost of Karl. SCM 1/0

Jewell, Hugh
My old home. NEP 4-5/2

Jewell, Lucy
Adam walking. AMP10-11/3

Jewett, Eleanore Myers
Ballade. CAW 10/1
Before you came. WOW 3/0
Sorrow's house. CAW 4/2

Jewett, John Brown
Arbiters of fate. ARG 6/21/4

Johansen, Dorothy O.
Seaside echoes. LAR 12/3

John, Cecil
Disillusion. POE 4/4
The exile. POE 4/4
The first-born. POE 4/4
Gone under. POE 10/2
Ha! POE 4/4
In Africa. POE 4/4
The old-timer. POE 4/4
Tanganyika. POE 4/4
To Africa. POE 4/4
The toss. POE 10/2
Unforgotten. POE 4/4

John, Hildegarde H.
Trail's end. SCM 12/2

Johns, Orrick
Treasure. DOU 5/3

Johnson, Arthur
The antique shop. SCM 3/2

Johnson, Charles Bertram
Easter. CUU 4/3
Mocking bird. CUU 5/3
Old things. CUU 3/3

Johnson, Delphene
Freedom. LAR 10/3
The orchestra. LAR 2/4

Johnson, Georgia Douglas
Armor. MIN 7-8/4
Measure. CUU 6/2
Motherhood. CUU 10/2
Paradox. MES 7/4
Your voice keeps ringing... MES 7/4

Johnson, Ida Judith
Fire. COV 10/2
The swamp. COV 3/3

Johnson, J. Rebe
Messages. AMP 4-5/3

Johnson, James Weldon
The creation (a Negro sermon). FRE 12/1/0
My city. CEN 9/3

Johnson, Josephine
Betrayal. CUV 11/3
Black, black the night. LYR 7/1
Clay. LYR 4/3
Consolation. GYP #2/4
Courage. COV 7/4
The fear of death. COV 10/3
Fool's paradise. LYR 11/3
Grey day. LYR 5/3
Her garden. LYR 7/1
"It's hard to waken mornings." COV 7/4
The level way. LYR 7/2
Life. LYR 5/1
October apple blossoms. COV 10/3
On the bridge. LYR 11/1
Presence. LYR 1/2
Quo Vadis. LYR 10/3
Renunciation. LYR 10/1
Scents. NOM Sum/3
Silence and solitude. LYR 4/2
Song in absence. COV 7/4
Song. LYR 1/4
Song. SMA 7/3
Two questions. LYR 3/4
The unwilling gypsy. LYR 11/2

Johnson, Lamont
The signal light. LAR 3/4

Johnson, Reba
My life. MAC 7/4

Johnson, Robert Underwood
The great adventure. SCM 11/2

Johnson, Roy Ivan
Moon song. POE 6/3
Johnson, Saimi
Bewilderment: I love them both. LAR 12/3
Johnson, Siddie Joe
The carpenter. LYW 12/3
Johnson, Stanley
Earth. FUG 6-7/3
A false prophet. FUG 2-3/3
Fiat. FUG 10/2
I would not give one beauty up. FUG 4-5/3
The pagan. VOI 3-4/4
Pier. FUG 10/2
Ships. FUG 4-5/3
Sonnets of the yellow leaf. FUG 12/3
Theological. FUG 6-7/3
To a certain man. FUG 12/2
Two at sea. FUG 12/2
The wasted hour. FUG 4-5/3
Your harvest. VOI 3-4/4
Johnson, Vlyn
Friends. COV 6/0
Johnson, Willard
The horseman of Poo-Poo. NES11/18/2
The living root. PAL Sum/3
Mountain fire. PAL Sum/3
Purple medicine: Zuni. PAL Sum/3
Purple medicine. PAL Sum/3
Sixth song of...holy young men. OVM 7/4
Zuni. PAL Sum/3
Johnsten, Louise Stalm
Other gardens. AMP 6-7/3
Johnston, Mary
The River James. REW 4/3
Virginiana. REW 2/2
Johnston, William
Fantasy. MID 12/0
Sketch. MID 5/0
Johnston, Winifred
One weds. PAL Spr/3
Songs to a little sister. PAL Spr/3
"These your flowers and wisely. PAL Spr/3
Johnstone, Julian E.
Jehovah! CAW 12/0
Jolas, Eugene
The peasant. LIB 4/2
Vagabond. PAG 4-5/0
Jonas, Rosalie M.
Their secret. HAM 11/1
Jones (Jr.), Thomas S.
Jerusalem. BOT 3/26/1
Night in the garden. BOT 4/2/1
The revelation. BOT 2/4/2
Saint Oran. BOT 2/2/2
The vigil:Louise Imogen Guiney. BOT 3/12/1
Jones, Alo W.
Forest love song. LAR 8/3
Golden sunset. LAR 8/3
Happiness. LAR 4/4
Indian lament. LAR 8/3
Tired. LAR 3/4
Winter. LAR 12/3
A wish. LAR 12/3
Wyoming rancher to his bride. LAR 8/3
Jones, Archer G.
Deity. REW 3/2
Jones, Bonnie B.
Green peace. CIC 8/30/3
Jones, Byron B.
Jest her way. ARG 6/21/4
Jones, Charlotte Wells
In a garden. AMP 1-2/4
Jones, E. Clement
Interlude in the antique mode. YAR 7/2
The interpreter. YAR 4/4
New England burying-ground. YAR 1/2
Jones, Elizabeth Warren
After rain. COV 5/3
One woman. COV 3/4
The pool. POM 1922
Jones, Howard Mumford
Artemis. FRE 2/9/1
Fisherman. FRE 2/7/3
Ideal. AMP 12/3
Imperfect tribute. COV 9/0
The last ride of Don Quixote. UNV 7/2
Metaphysics. COV 9/0
Poem. ALS 8-9/2
The poet of the Mississippi... AMP 4/2
Romance. FRE 4/6/1
Solitary. ALS 5/1
They that dwell in shadow. MID 2-4/0
To a jazz singer. ALS 8/1
Jones, Leah Durand
The winds of March. CIC 6/15/2
Jones, Louise
When love is gone. POE 4/2
Jones, Ralph Mortimer
Mary. CIC 3/9/2
Prayer. CIC 6/15/2
A prayer. COV 5/0
Jones, Ruth Lambert
Because we love each other... BOO 5/4
The chameleon. LIF 8/31/2

The cycle. COV 1/3
In various veins... NES11/24/3
Inviolate. BOO 1/0
Measure. EVM 8/0
The pipe of Pan's devising. COV 6/4
Poems for..Thanksgiving season. NES11/24/3
The prodigal. SCM 1/0
River boats. LIF 8/24/2
Skepticism. COV 12/3
Smoke. LAD 8/1
To one absent, journeying. COV 6/4
Vision. COV 1/3

Jones, W. K.
To Thomas Gray. LYW 2/4

Jonsrud, Eunice
Exquisites: your love... LAR 12/3
Incense. LAR 12/3
Some day. LAR 12/3

Jordan, David Starr
There was a man. CIC 3/15/3

Jorgensen, Johannes
"The plants stand silent..." AMS 2/2

Josephson, Matthew
Four etudes. BRO 5/2
The last lady. POE 10/0
Pursuit. BRO 1/3

Joslen, H. A.
Helen of Troy. GYP #2/4
Pity. GYP #2/4

Joslin, William W.
The life of a rose. AMP 8/2
A sailor's haven. AMP 8-9/3

Joy, Carry
The memory of a day. AMP 8/2

Junkin, Charles Irvin
An old-fashioned wedding hymn. WOW 6/0

Juvenal, Yvonne
Dagmar. DOU 12/2

K.,J.
Ave Maria, gratia plenis. PAG 8-9/1
Choice. PAG 12/1
Quasi adagio. PAG10-11/1
Salut. PAG 12/1

Kalar, Joseph A.
In a graveyard at night. GYP #2/4
Smiles. GYP #2/4

Kantor, MacKinley
The bed of poppies. CHD 7/5/4

Kao Shih
To my friends vice-prefects Li. WAV #4/2
The Yeh song. WAV #4/2

Kapstein, Israel
Discus. CAS 3/3

Karfunkle, Anna
So fair a sorrow. MEA 2/4

Karn, Esther Nelson
In winter day. AMP 12/3

Kassack, Louis
No. 19. BRO 12/2

Katz, Adaline
Three slender things. DOU 10/2

Kauffman, Reginald Wright
Americans. SVG 11/1/2
For the critics. OUT 8/10/1
On the scales. OUT 8/23/2
The price. AIN 2/2

Kaufman, Leah
I sat on top of the moon. GUL 6/3

Kaufman, Regina
Grand Canyon. UNV 7/4
Symbols. LAR 11/3

Kawada, Jun
Fate. FRE 11/9/1
Is't possible. FRE 11/9/1
Memory. FRE 11/9/1
Threatened. FRE 11/9/1
Transmuted. FRE 11/9/1

Kean, Lillian Logan
To you. ARG 6/21/4

Keech, Lilian Sue
Dreams. GRA 9/2

Keeley, Dorothy
On the wings. POE 1/2

Keene, Erwin F.
Constantinople. GRA 11/1
The haven of lost ships. GRA 9/2
South of Mogador. GRA 10/2

Keene, Meta Fuller
Comradeship. CTY Spr/2
Immortality. CTY Win/3
My garden. CTY Spr/2
Recompense. CTY S-A/1
Winter revery. CTY Win/2

Keiyt, Henrietta Jewett
The old poet's protest. BOO 4/4

Kellerman, Stella V.
Song. AMP 2-3/3

Kelley, Florence Finch
Bloom of May. NEW 8/19/3

Kelley, John Edward
I looked on man. AMP 10/2

Kelley, Katherine Hearne
The queen's gift. MAG 7/2

Kelley, Leone
Snow. POE 1/0

Kells, Marion C.
My crown. LYW 6/3
Kelly, Henry
My old Fairmont. NOW 2/3
Kelly, Sarah Hammond
Fog. LYW 1/2
Kathleen. LIB 9/1
Kemp, Adelaide R.
Spring's promise. LAL 5/4
Kemp, Harry
Autumn colors. MUN 10/2
Beethoven, deaf. MUN 5/2
Catallus consoles. NES 9/2/2
Cities of the world. MUN 7/2
Disparity. AIN 5/0
The dunes. NES 2/16/4
Each day's perfectness. MUN 3/2
The fiddler. CEN 9/0
Fishermen. BOO 2/3
Homeric retrospect. BOO 8/2
I know that flowers fade. AIN 4/0
In a quiet heart. MUN 4/2
Joses, the brother of Jesus. CIC 6/15/2
Quicksand. NER 6/4/4
There is one ill. AIN 10/2
To a new poet. MUN 1/2
The Venus de Milo. LAR 3/4
You talk of this and that. OUT 1/28/0
Kemper, S. H.
The convalescent. HAM 9/0
Kempson, John Whitman
The river leaf. COV 7/0
Kendrick, Lucile
Beauty shall bind. COV 12/2
The captive. COV 6/2
Iconoclast. COV 12/1
Lad's love. STE 11/2
The lonely child. COV 12/1
Madrina. COV 6/2
Parting ways. AMP 6/2
Peonage. POM 1922
Prison song. STE 3/2
Spendthrift. COV 12/3
While it is day. COV 12/3
Kennedy, Charles W.
I've worked for a shilling. SCM 11/3
Love walked with me. SCM 10/1
The poet. SCM 11/3
Kennedy, F. U.
Windows. BOO 6/4
Kennedy, J. H.
At passing. SCR 7/4
Sometimes. SCR 7/4
Kennedy, James H.
Two made one. MUN 7/2
Kennedy, Mary H.
As oil poured out. MAG 12/1
Invocation. MAG 5/2
Kennedy, Thomas
Incipit vita nova. AMP 6-7/3
The lake. WAV 6/3
The little wild girl. BOO 7/4
Night dancers. BOO 7/4
An old street. WAV 1/2
Pleasure. STE 12/2
Riddle. WAV 1/2
The rug. WAV 1/2
White glory. WAV 1/2
Kennison, Edgar
Alluring Arizona. Lar 2/3
Kenyon, Bernice Lesbia
After music. OUT 5/30/3
Alter ego. COV 5/2
Ancestry. LIB 12/1
Answer to a timid lover. OUT 10/5/1
The answering heights. LYR 3/2
Art. MUN 3/1
Autumn. SCM 2/4
Autumn. SON 9-10/0
Awakening. CIM 5/4/1
The cheat. COV 10/1
City rain. SCM 12/2
Death will not frighten me. VOI Aut/1
Defiance to false gods. BOO 10/2
Earth-bound. SON 3-4/0
The enduring. NAT 7/5/2
Experience. LYR 11/2
Futility. LIB 4/2
Green twilight. CIM 3/31/1
Heroics. VOI 8-9/3
Homecoming in a storm. NAT 9/21/1
"If on the morrow." VOI Sum/2
Impregnable. OUT12/20/2
In a Greek garden. SCM 2/3
In a conservatory. NER 3/2/1
In winter. LIB 10/1
Life. SCM 2/4
Lissa in the garden. OUT 4/23/4
The love song. SCM 12/1
May Sunday. COV 5/2
Memory. SCM 2/4
Mountain pool. LIB 12/2
New raiment. COV 5/21/1
Night of rain. SCM 6/3
Night sailing. OUT 7/20/1
Nocturne. OUT 7/26/2
November night. COV 11/2
October. COV 10/1
Palimpsest. OUT 5/17/2
Portrait. OUT11/23/1
Potentialities. OUT12/20/2
Premonition. OUT 1/25/2

The shore, sunrise. VOI Aut/2
Sleepless night. MEA 6/4
Smiling woman. OUT12/20/2
Snow-trail. GRA 1/1
A song in September. GRA 1/1
"There is no quiet." LYW 2/3
To a violinist. VOI 8-9/3
To one who walks the highroad. OUT12/20/2
Unrest. LIB 10/1
White throat. LYR 6/2
A woman life a shell. OUT 11/7/3

Kenyon, Doris
Before dawn. LYR 2/4
The birth of the firefly. AIN 1/0
The two birds. GOH 6/2

Kenyon, James B.
My love lies in..gates of sand. LYR 11/3

Kenyon, Theda
A gargoyle in Flanders. NOA 9/0
The haunted house. MUN 5/2
Moonlight in a museum. SCM 3/4

Key, Robert Ellis
Investment. CIJ 6/4
The way. CIJ 4/4

Keyes, Frances Parkinson
Roses. GRA 10/1

Keyting, Margaret Lee
Wedded. STE 3/3

Khasimir, Randaulfe
The flying leaf. CAP11-12/2
Winter winds. CAP11-12/2

Kiang Kang-Hu. See Bynner,W.tr .

Kidd, Walter Evans
Blue morning. LYW 9/3
White beauty. LYW 11/3

Kilbourne, Fannie
Faithfulness. AIN 2/0

Kilmer, Aline
Atonement. OUT 5/19/0
Charmian's song. POE 5/1
Diagonals. POE 10/2
Dispersal. OUT 4/18/3
Escape. POE 10/2
Every sea is the sea. BOO 7/3
Favete linguis. OUT 4/18/3
For all ladies of Shallott. POE 5/1
The garden. BOO 3/0
The gift. OUT 6/22/1
A guest speaks. OUT 4/19/2
The heart knoweth... POE 5/1
Ignis fatuus. POE 10/2
Light lover. BOO 10/1
The poor king's daughter. OUT11/28/3
Release. POE 10/2
Song. LYR 3/4
The stirrup cup. LYR 7/1
To Sappho, about her apple. LYR 6/1
Tribute. SCM 3/1
Week-end. POE 10/2
When those who have loved us a. OUT 9/20/2
You asked me not to die. HAM 8/2

Kilpatrick, Luella
The way to win. CTY Sum/3

King (Jr.), James Gore
The Harvard 1920 class poem. OUT 8/4/0

King, Eleanor Lyne
Fish. LYR 1/4
Intercession. LYR 5/3

King, Ethel
The calendar. CTY Spr/4
Courage. CTY Win/4
Pottery. CAW 9/2
Repentance. LAR 3/4

King, Gertrude
The moon. LIB 10/1

King, Sterling P.
Daddie is coming. CTY Spr/3
A song for mother's day. CTY Spr/4
The valley of the shadow. CTY Sum/3

King, Vernon
Epitaphs. PAL Spr/3

Kingston, Irene McFadden
The land of afternoon. POA 1/2

Kinsolving, Sally Bruce
Adventure. REW 1/2
Anguish. POE 9/2
Ariadne on Naxon. BAA 1/17/3
Daffodils. BAA 4/1/2
Hampton. REW 1/3
Prelude. BAA 3/2/2
Spring voices. BAA 5/5/2
Stript. LYR 2/4
To the statue..Edgar Allen Poe. BAA 5/11/2

Kinzer, Gordon Neale
The Spanish sinks. LAR 8/3

Kipling, Rudyard
A ballade of photographs. WAV 6/2
The gods of the copybook maxim. HAM 1/0
To W.C.W.M.D.. POE 2/0

Kirk, James
The stone cutter. DOU 7/4

Kirk, Richard
The alien. DOU 11/3
Appreciation. DOU 7/2

The blinded. DOU 2-3/4
Conundrum. STE 7/2
"Fear death?" COV 9/1
Fellow creature. DOU 12/2
Hamley. DOU 10/2
His later manner. COV 9/1
I'll keep my grief. DOU 11/3
Ironic invention. DOU 5/3
Jane Horner. DOU 7/2
Life in a song. DOU 2-3/4
Little dust. COV 9/1
The memorial. DOU 2-3/4
The monotonous year. COV 9/1
On wedding. COV 9/1
Prudence. DOU 3-4/3
"River dusk," by Miss Gray. STE 12/3
The stone cutter. DOU 11/3
A stone is the quietest thing. DOU 3-4/3
The talking stream. DOU 2-3/4
Things for granted. DOU 9/2
The words spoken above him. DOU 3-4/3
Yes, you must be happy. DOU 11/3
You'll say. DOU 8/2

Kirwan, Marie
Patterns in snow. VOI 12-1/4

Kiser, S. E.
The life of the party. CSA 4/3
What people call success. CSA 5/3

Kleinman, Bertha A.
Each passing hour. SCR 8/3
Friendship. SCR 11/3
The mountain bee. SCR 9/3
The prodigal father. SCR 11/3
The song of the world. SCR 9/3

Klemm, Wilhelm
Night. POE 12/2
Petals. BRO 5/2

Kling, Joseph
Dream. NOM Aut/2
Macabre. VOI Win/2
Quasi adagio. TEM 6/1
Wish. VOI Win/2

Kloss, Phillips
From the cliff. WAN 12/3
A Mexican village. WAN 3/4
The nightingale sparrow. WAN 1/4

Klotz, Beth O'Neil
My lady of the gingham gown. AMP10-11/3

Knapp, Ethel Marjorie
A golden day. CIM 7/28/4
Hollyhocks. CIM 7/8/4
I've a hundred deaths. LYW 4/4
In cedarlane way. CIM 6/26/4
Love. LAR 7/3
The mother-heart. LYW 4/4
My brain. SAB 4/4
Return. NEW 7/25/4
The shower. CIM 8/11/4
Though tomorrow she die. NEW 1/6/4
To the lady on the dime. SPT 2/17/4

Knight, Gladys
Western gold. SCR 1/4

Knipe, Bertha McE.
The almond blossoms. LYW 3/3
Mary. LYR 6/2
The walls of St. Francis. LYW 12/1

Knister, Raymond
Boy remembers in the field. VOI 5-6/4
The hawk. POE 4/4

Knox, Florence Clay
Apology. COV 2/2
Pity. COV 2/2

Koenig, Myra Manning
In the desert. AMP 6/2

Kohnfelder, E. J.
A dream. AMP 6-7/3

Konecky, Eugene
George Sterling. STE 2/4

Kopeloff, Nicholas
First spring. MEA 6/3
Gold. LIC 3/3

Kopp, Lillian
Love's dwelling. GUL 6/3

Korns, Andre
Asperities of..lady at sunrise. MOR 10/3

Kosmak, Katherine L.
By the sea. LIC 11/1
Sunrise. LIC 4/2

Kowaleski, E. A.
Dawn in the hills. PAR #3/4

Krainin, Blanche
Triumph. PAG 4-5/0

Kramer, Arthur J.
After an evening. WAV 2/2
Dust. WAV 3/4
Moment. POE 9/3
Shadows. POE 9/3

Kramer, Edgar Daniel
Crucifixion. COV 1/3
Dream street. CIV 1/4
Enlightened. COV 4/4
Los muertos. FRE 2/13/4
Marble. CIV 1/4
Sculptor. COV 1/3
Souls. COV 8/3

Kresensky, Raymond
Swan and crow. WAN 6/4
A window. PAR #4/4

Kreymborg (tr.), Alfred
Chilono. BRO 12/1
Rio Bo. BRO 12/1
Kreymborg, Alfred
Advertisement. NER 3/14/3
And she said and I said--. NER 8/8/3
And white the white invokes. POE 9/3
Another grieving forest. POE 9/3
Bloom. DIA 5/2
Boomerang. NAT 2/16/1
But what will they remember. HAM 3/3
City chap. DIA 11/3
Cradle. POE 2/0
Crocus. DIA 9/3
Dorothy. DIA 3/0
A drop of any sea. POE 9/3
Festoons of fishes. DIA 6/3
A finger or a whisper. NER 12/5/3
G. string. NER 9/26/3
Her voice. NER 5/3/2
Hermit thrush. DIA 11/3
The huddled one's behold. POE 9/3
Indian sky. POE 1/0
Italian stream. POE 6/3
The kingdom of the air. POE 9/3
The likeness of his yesterdays. POE 9/3
The lines of her wary body. DIA 7/3
Little ego. MEA 3/1
Madonna di Campagna. POE 9/3
A man besmitten so. HAM 3/3
A man whom men deplore. NES 2/9/4
Melodious the morning. RHY 1/3
Miss Sal's monologue. COV 2/0
Monocles. DIA 6/1
The mountains stoop to hills. HAM 3/3
Neighbors. DIA 11/3
People read books. BOO 2/1
Pianissimo. POE 7/2
Rain enters Maggiore. NAT 6/13/3
A ribbon two yards wide. POE 9/3
Robin. DIA 11/3
Savanarola burning. PRA 1-2/3
Song sparrow. DIA 11/3
Spirit. POE 2/0
Swallows. DIA 11/3
Turtles. BOO 6/1
When they require gardens. POE 9/3
The while they cradle clothes. RHY 1/3
Krikorian, Alice Sargent
An August picture. GRA 9/2
The black rock of Nantasket. GRA 11/2
A dream of Mt. Kearsage. GRA 2/2
Opulence. GRA 8/2
When summer days have fled. GRA 10/2
The white flower. GRA 7/2
Krussell, A. H.
The clue. CIC 4/5/3
Kuck, Clara Elizabeth
Truth's messenger. CIJ 5/4
Kuder, Blanche Bane
God loved a garden. OUT 8/11/0
Kuhns, Grace Taylor
Alice. CTY Spr/2
Consolation. CTY Spr/3
A day's journey. CTY S-A/1
Fidelity. CTY Win/2
A friend: a song. CTY Win/4
A gift of my youth. CTY Spr/2
Jewels. CTY Win/2
Our friend. CTY S-A/1
Playing well his part. CTY Win/2
Rastus Brown. CTY Spr/3
The red haw tree. CTY Sum/2
"Roseunworthy." CTY Win/2
Spring showers. CTY Spr/4
This is June. CTY Sum/3
"Unhidden." CTY Win/2
The wild orioles. CTY Spr/3
Kuskulis, Elizabeth Fairley
The fog-girl. COV 8/3
Ghosts. COV 8/3
Hope. AMP10-11/3
On the altar. COV 8/3
Kyle, Patricia Murray
Earth's fair corners. AMP 2-3/3

L'Anson, Alice
Wa-wea-tah. OVM 2/4
L.,D.K.
Vachel Lindsay. DEU 1/23/1
L.,E.U.F.
Dornroschen. LIB 1/29
Passion death. LIB 11/1
L.,M.
The story of Jacopone Da Todi. CAW 3/2
L.,R.G.
A confession. GUL 5/3
La Dow, Elizabeth

Language. LYW 9/3
La Viere, Hesse Cooper
Brain children. SOU 7/3
Hands. SOU 7/3
Labaree, Mary Fleming
Blind clay. NAT 5/24/2
Lackey, Alexander M.
Lightless Susan. COV 9/2
Sleep. COV 9/2
Ladd, Virginia B.
A February afternoon. GRA 2/1
Laedlein, Laura Landis
Time. POE 12/3
Laforgue, Jules
Locutions des pierrots. DOU 5/2
Lahey, Thomas A.
The harp that once thru Tara's. CAW 2/1
Laik, Regna
Little Jean. LIB 9/1
To my husband. LIB 8/1
Laird, William
Backgrounds. COV 4/0
The eldest born. COV 1/3
A list of lyrics. COV 12/0
New love. COV 12/0
Oh, when I die. COV 12/0
Lake, Stuart N.
Dad an' me. OUT 6/9/0
Lal, Gobind Behari
Child and sea. WAN 11/3
Cinquains:flagellation of clay. WAN 8/3
Headlong sinners. WAN 6/3
Machiavellian night. WAN 8/3
Pagan folly. WAN 8/3
Plum-tree. WAN 8/3
Reformation of clay. WAN 8/3
Technique. WAN 4/4
Lamb, Charles W.
The bone yard...Sturgeon Bay. AMP 4/2
The Indian face...limestone... AMP 4/2
Lamb, Esther Hill
To Piereth-gone. ALS 4/2
Lambert, Mildred E.
Shadows. STE 5/4
Lampson, Fredick Locker
Some unpublished sketches... SCM 4/1
Lanahan, Hortense M.
The sailor. AMP 6-7/3
Landels, Thomas D.
A song of the sea. OVM 2/4
Landrum, Grace Warren
A Georgia roadside. LAL 5/4
Lane, Carroll
Interlude. COV 6/3
Lane, Edwin Renold
Cancion a Manuelita. AMP 2-3/3
The sun goes down. PEG 1/3
Lang, Ellen Irene
A toast to the Lariat. LAR 10/3
Langbridge, Rosamond
The gentle housewife. POE 7/2
The winter moth. POE 7/2
Langebek, May Wyon
Comforters. MID 1-3/0
Langley, Allan Lincoln
New worlds. LIB 10/1
Lappin, Charles F.
Where the woodland stream... INT 4-6/4
Laprade, M.
The bandicoot. HAM 3/0
The rime of the last Bolshevis. HAM 2/0
Larabee, Mary Fleming
Drowned fires. CIC10/18/3
Laramore, Vivian Yeiser
Autumn. COV 12/1
Folly. COV 3/4
Hidden. LYR 5/4
Incognito. COV 11/2
June joy. COV 6/0
Little leaves. COV 3/1
Love's gifts. WOW 1/0
My mother was a dancer. LYR 1/4
On Easter long ago. COV 5/4
On Mother's Day. WOW 5/0
On parting. COV 3/4
Preference. DOU 12/1
Preparation. REW 1/2
She laughs somewhere. COV 3/4
Talk to me tenderly. COV 11/2
Larkin, Margaret
For the guitar... DOU 1/4
Good-bye - to my mother. KAN ?/1
Nikral. ORE Spr/2
Nikral. POE 6/4
The returning. ORE Spr/2
A snake poem. POE 6/4
Larson, Ernest S.
Song. DEU 3/2/0
Larsson, R. Ellsworth
An arragement..inquiring oboe.. DIA 4/4
At dawn. VOI Win/2
Brink. CAP 10/2
Chamber music. LYW 12/2
Communion. TEM 6/1
Coversation at twilight. VOI 5-6/4
Interior. VOI 7-8/3
Old woman. TEM Win/3
Processional. VOI 7-8/3
Swan song...for two pianos. DIA 5/4

Lataday, A.
A pastoral. NOM Sum/2
Lathrop, Louise
Small town courtesies. SOU 7/3
Lauder, E. Louise
Sweet Elysium. MES 3/4
Laughlin, E. O.
Isolation. STE 2/4
The Lincoln circuit. LAD 2/4
Laurie, B. L.
The end of a great city. NEP 4-5/2
Law, R. H.
Bridge and moonlight. ALS 9/1
Lawless, Margaret H.
Asleep in the Argonne Forest. AMP Aut/1
Awakenings. SAC 11/1
Barriers. ROS 12/2
The bride of the year. AMP 6/2
A dream in the dusk. ROS 3/4
A dream of Pilate's wife. CAW 3/4
Faith's offering. MAG 6/1
An ideal. TRU 3/2
In the catacombs: a picture. AMP 9/3
The journey's end. SAC 10/1
Late roses. ROS 11/0
Mary's month of birth. SAC 5/3
The mighty ruler. SAC 10/0
Opportunity. CLC 7/0
The other nine. SAC 10/0
Our dead. CLC 11/0
The plaint of Haman. MAG 7/2
Sanctuary. SAC 1/3
Song of the frost. SAC 1/1
Three sacred words. SAC 1/3
Tidal waves. MAG 6/3
Lawrence, David Herbert
The apostolic beasts. DIA 4/1
Bare almond trees. NAT10/10/3
The evening land. POE 11/2
Humming bird. NAT10/10/3
The mosquito. BOO 7/1
Nostalgia. PAL Sum/3
Peace. NAT10/10/3
Pomegranite. DIA 3/1
Saint Matthew. POE 4/3
Tropic. NAT10/10/3
Lawrence, Gordon
Grasshoppers. DOU 1/4
Lawrence, Harriet Paine
Stars in the sea. POE 11/3
Lawrence, Lucas
Nature. MES 7/4
Lawrence, Seabury
Love of the night. HAM 8/2
Poor harlequin. HAM 4/2
Lawrence, Will
An idly idyll. CTY S-A/1
The leaves. CTY Win/2
Lines to a violet. CTY Spr/2
Mis' summah! CTY S-A/1
Song of the road. CTY Win/3
Song. CTY Sum/2
Lawson, Eleanor Eversfield
Taps. INT 4-6/4
Lawson, Evelyn
John Constable goes sketching. SCM 5/3
Lawton, Grace
Perplexity. LAL 5/4
Laynor, Florence M.
Cloud pictures. INT 4-6/4
The mother. INT 1-3/4
Le Cron, Helen Cowles
The bride goes marketing. COV 9/1
The department store window. COV 1/3
Experience. COV 9/1
Familiar. COV 4/0
The home-keepers. COV 9/1
Lost magic. COV 1/3
Marriage. COV 9/1
Prayer in Spring. COV 4/0
Things. COV 8/0
Le Gallienne, Hesper
Cottages in England. HAM 12/2
Improvident. HAM 2/4
Matinal. HAM 8/0
Return. HAM 6/2
Le Gallienne, Richard
Anima mundi. HAM 3/1
Ballade of his lady's wardrobe. AIN 1/0
A ballade of pessimists. HAM 2/0
Ballade of the unchanging... AIN 4/0
A ballade of water lilies. HAM 7/2
Catalogue of lovely things. HAM 2/0
Cosmic friends. MUN 4/2
Country largesse. HAM 8/2
Far away and long ago. MUN 2/2
The fortunate voyage. MUN 3/2
Gaudemus. HAM 9/1
The immortal gods. MUN 5/2
Love's arithmetic. HAM 2/1
Love's birthday. MUN 10/2
Love's blessings. MUN 7/2
A lover's warning. HAM 6/1
The magic flower. HAM 3/2
Of making many books. BOO 10/2
On re-reading "Le Morte D'A.." BOO 1/0
Pax Americana. MUN 3/2

River music. MUN 1/2
To his lady, with country flow. MUN 6/2
A walking song. HAM 4/0
Whene'er I sing of you. AIN 2/0

Le Noir, Phil
Down on the ol' Bar-G. POE 8/0
Ol' Dynamite. POE 8/0
The puncher poet. POE 8/0

Le Padre, Ruth
Lady with hair of tangled gold. LAR 9/3

Le Suer, Meridel
Nests. POE 5/4

Leach, Bert
Nostalgia. AMP Aut/1

Leamy, Edmund
Daisy fields. EVM 6/1
The dream destroyed. EVM 4/1
The ticket agent. HAM 1/3

Lear, Althine Scholess
Opportunity. GRA 6/1

Lear, Althine Sholes
When the birds fly north. GRA 3/2

Lechlitner, Ruth
Dream fear. MEA 12/3
Presence. MEA 12/3
To the wild rose. COV 11/1

Lee (Jr.), Lawrence
Old man. NOM Spr/3

Lee, Agnes
The ancient sleeper. POE 6/0
The blunted age. POE 11/1
The ilex tree. POE 6/0
The jilt. POE 11/1
Mrs. Malooly. POE 6/0
Old Lizette on poetry. POE 6/0

Lee, Borghild Lundberg
"The awakening." AMP 10/2
Silver birches. AMP 5-6/4

Lee, G. D.
My sweetheart California. CTY Spr/4

Lee, Harry
April. AIN 4/2
Bagdad. EVM 10/1
Bermuda-lilies. STE 5/4
A city street. OUT 5/31/2
The first Easter. OUT 4/12/2
For remembrance. OUT 6/2/0
Gossip. AIN 6/2
The letter-carrier. OUT 6/1/1
The letter-carrier. OUT 6/16/0
Lights of Blackwells. CAW 7/2
Lilacs. OUT 11/1
Lilacs. OUT 8/23/2
Makers of flowers. OUT 5/21/4
Martyrdom. CAW 11/0
Mary McGindry. OUT 7/26/2
The "penny-a-ride." OUT 4/11/3
The shrine. CAW 5/1
The source. CAW 8/0
To the supreme. CAW 3/0
Winds from heaven. OUT 3/16/1
Wintery winds. CAW 3/2
Withered wreaths. OUT11/15/2

Lee, Lawrence
April night. NOM Spr/4
Little songs of Lois. NOM Spr/4
Portrait of a lady. LYR 1/4
To a young girl. NOM Sum/3

Lee, Linda
Cycle. OVM 7/4
The mesa dwellers. OVM 3/4
The symbol. OVM 4/4
What matter! OVM 2/4

Lee, Margery
Misunderstanding. PAG 12/1
To a man in a bank. PAG10-11/1

Lee, Muna
Barranquitas. VOI 8-9/3
The flame-trees. MEA 6/2
Mushroom town. AMM 4/4
San Cristobal. DOU 7/2
Song in autumn meadows. SMA 1/3
Songs. POE 6/3
The sonnet. POE 8/2
Things that do not change. AIN 3/0

Leete, Rebecca M.
The disturbers. AMP 1-2/4

Lefroy, Edward Cracroft
A palaestral study. GRA 6/3

Lehmer, D. N.
The stroller. LYW 7-8/3

Lehmer, Eunice Mitchell
Driftwood. OVM 2/4
My cove. OVM 7/4
The narcissus flower. LAR 4/4

Leigh, A. B.
Invitation. SCR 1/4
Joan of Arc. LAR 4/4

Leigh, Alice
Kinship. SCM 10/3
A moth in a subway train. VOI Spr/2
Possession. COV 7/3
Sails. GRA 10/2

Leigh, Frances
Ecstasy. AMP 8-9/3

Leigh, Richard
Ballade of the unchanging... MUN 2/2
The dream and the stream. MUN 4/2
In the moonlit woods. MUN 6/2
Marketing in the moon. MUN 3/2
Now that she is gone. MUN 5/2
The poet's lot. MUN 1/2

The vain fear. MUN 10/2
The whole duty of a man. MUN 7/2

Leitch, Mary Sinton
By flesh estranged. SOU 8/3
The child of the childless. LYW 12/2
The dead thrush. PER 10/2
Dusty triumphant. LYR 2/4
Expectancy. COV 5/3
Fanny Brawne. COV 5/3
The flower. LYR 9/2
The forgotten grave. LYR 6/1
How can I find and reach you? LYR 2/4
Idolaters. COV 9/2
In a railway station. LYW 3/4
The kiss. AMP 4-5/3
Losting hearing. LYR 12/1
The modern god. LYR 8/2
Moods. LYW 7-8/2
Moon-lit mist. LYR 6/3
Now I shall march. LYW 7-8/3
The old men. LYW 7-8/2
On being told that my child... LYR 5/2
One rose. NOM Sum/2
Out of my griefs. LYR 10/3
Perspective. COV 5/3
Perspective. LYR 10/1
Point of view. BOT 11/2
The post. BOT 11/2
Remembrance. LYR 4/1
Roses and bread. LYR 6/3
Sea burial. ALS 7/3
The secret. LYW 6/3
Ship of the years. BOT 5/16/3
Silence. LYW 5/2
Snowfall in the wood. PAR #1/4
The summit. LYR 11/2
To Barbara. LYW 12/3
To Thomas Hardy. REW 4/4
To a flying-fish. LYR 10/2
To a hermit thrush. STE 10/2
To a holly tree. AMP 10/2
To my mother. LYR 3/2
To one who is dead. CUV 11/3
To the earth. PER 10/2
To the yellow jasmine. COV 5/4
Two gardens. NOA 7/3
Waiting. LYR 7/1
Why must all beauty...? PER 1/4
The winter woods. COV 12/2

Lemon, Don
Resurrection. AMP 3-4/4
Sing me a ballad. AMP 2-3/3

Lemont (tr.), Jessie
Charles XII of Sweden rides in. POE 9/1

Lemont, Jessie
My faun. VOI10-11/3
Notre Dame Chapelle. CAW 6/1
Sport of the gods. MEA 7/1

Lench, W. H.
Any day in the street. AMP 2-3/3
Desire. LYW 2/2
The fishing fleet. PEG 1/3
Gladness. LYW 11/19
Humming birds. CAP11-12/2
A lighthouse. PEG 1/3
Loneliness. LYW 11/19
Purity. LYW 11/19
Result. LYW 5/4
San Miguel. CAP11-12/2
Song of my native land. FOU 10/3
Spider web island. PEG 5/3
Symphony. PEG 5/3
We are like gold fish. LYW 5/4
The windmill. CAP11-12/2

Leonard, Clair T.
Finis. GRA 1/1
Memories. GRA 3/1

Leonard, Dorothy
The proof. OUT 5/12/0
"You think me cold" HAM 2/0

Leonard, O. H.
The thunder storm. COV 8/0

Leonard, Orville
Afterthought: I never knew. POE 1/4
Because I've learned. POE 1/4
Forest triumphant. AMF 12/3
The song of the pine. AMF 10/1
The visitor. POE 1/4

Leonard, William Ellery
Another statue. AMP 2/2
The beggar. NAT 8/24/1
Ex ponto. TEM 6/1
A group of poems. AMP 5-6/4
The lynching bee. NAT12/29/0
Saecla ferarum. NAT 6/6/3
The visitor. POE 1/4

Leroi, Ralph
In a Virginia garden. NER 1/18/0

Lesemann, Maurice
After a lost friend's calumny. MEA 10/2
Apparitions. DOU 10/2
Appointment. POE 4/0
The crying cranes. POE 4/0
Dark rain: New Mexico. POE 8/3
No poem. POE 4/0
Storm gathering. POE 8/3
To himself in Autumn. POE 4/0
Tramps. POE 4/0
The withered ones. MEA 10/2

Lesesne, Jeanne
So many worlds. AMP 4/2
Lesier, Joseph
Sambatyon. TAL 10/2
Leslie, Shane
Ireland: 1922. CAW 11/2
Lett-Haines
Kabyle songs. GAR 1-2/2
Letts, W. M.
The children's ghosts. YAR 10/0
Letts, Winifred M.
Hallowe'en. SEW10-12/1
No night in heaven. YAR 1/2
Leui, Jeannie Orr
Winter fields. AMP 2/2
Levinson (& M. Cowley), Ronald
Wells' springs of history. NES 3/19/1
Levy, Newman
The path of glory. HAM 1/3
Lewis, Benjamin Harrison
City streets. LAR 11/3
Clogged pools. LAR 4/3
Memories. LAR 3/3
Open spaces. LAR 9/3
Peace at dusk. LAR 8/3
Reticence. AMP 4-5/3
Your kisses. LAR 8/3
Lewis, Bertha
The ancient potter of Isin. AMP 12/2
Bird songs. CTY Spr/3
A color rhapsody. AMP 1-2/4
The spinner. CTY Spr/4
A summer evening. CTY Sum/3
The tired hired hand. CTY Win/4
Lewis, Carolyn M.
The trysting place. AMP 1-2/4
Lewis, Charlton M.
Methusaleh. YAR 4/0
Pygmalion. YAR 7/1
Lewis, Frank C.
Fall. LYR 12/2
Fool's gold. LYR 3/2
Two days. LYR 5/2
Weakness. LYR 9/2
Lewis, George Warburton
Fetish. AMP 12/2
Unlovely gods. AMP 10/2
Lewis, Janet
A gull-following song. POE 1/3
In the woods. POE 1/3
A song for the grandmother. POE 1/3
A song for the wife of Maniboz. POE 1/3
The wild crab-apple tree. LYW 5/2
Lewis, Janet Loxley
Austerity. POE 6/0
The end of the age. POE 6/0
Fossil. POE 6/0
Geology. POE 6/0
Lewis, Jay
Eyes. LYR 11/1
Lewis, May
Onlookers. MEA 1/4
Sonnet to a young man. CIV 7-8/4
Lewis, Mildred A.
Travel. LYR 2/4
Lewis, Ray
Destiny. INT 4-6/4
Satin slippers. INT 4-6/4
Lewisohn (tr.), Ludwig
Two. NAT 3/14/3
Lewisohn, Ludwig
Together. NES 5/24/4
Lexenm, Fesmar J.
The ballad of a philosopher's. LIC 1/3
Li Po
A bitter poem. MOR 10/3
Bringing in the wine. FUG 5/9/3
Cries of the raven. FRE 4/5/2
A farewell to a friend. PAR #4/4
Hard traveling in Shu'. NAT 5/3/2
Hard traveling. FUG 5/23/3
In the night. MOR 10/3
The lonely wife. BOO 9/1
Ode to Nanking. FRE 7/12/2
On climbing to Phoenix Terrace. PRA 1-2/3
Query and answer in the hills. MEA 6/2
The retreat of Hssieh Kung. DIA 10/1
Sailing down to Chiang-ling. PAR #1/4
The silk spinner. YAR 5/4
The terraced road... ASI 10/1
A valediction. YAR 6/4
Li Shang-yin
Poems of the court. PAL Spr/3
Li T'ai-Po. See Li Po

Li-Tai-pe. See Li Po

Lieberman, Elias
Ballade of lost illusions. AIN 2/0
Lieberman, Frank B.
Cabins. SCM 8/1
Luck. SCM 8/1
The old canoe. SCM 8/1
The old frontier. SCM 8/1
The trout pool. SCM 8/1
Lincoln, Elliot C.

Evening. LYW 3/4
Gray butte. COV 6/0
Loss. LYW 10/3

Linderman, Fannie B.
The snow baby. AMP 4-5/4

Lindsay, Donald
Arcady revisited. PAG 8-9/1

Lindsay, Vachel
Doctor Mohawk. NER 12/5/3
How a little girl sang. POE 8/3
In praise of Johnny Appleseed. CEN 8/1
Litany of heroes. NES 2/24/3

Lindsey, Therese
The answer. SCR 5/3
Earth. POM 1922
Lost. MEA 1/4
The mountain cat. NER 12/6/2

Linerbarger, Iva B.
Prayer. CIJ 9/3

Ling, Barbara
Bordeaux. REW 6/2

Linnell, John
Old friends. FUG 4-5/3

Lipp, Frances Mullarney
October. AMP Aut/1

Lippmann, L. Blackledge
Twilight. HAM 2/0

Lister, Queene B.
To an old friend. LAR 9/3

Litsey, E. C.
Pantheism. ALS 1/29

Little, Robert D.
The hurdy-gurdy. AMP 4-5/3

Little, Ronald Erl
A song of spring. SCR 7/4

Liu Chiang-Ch'ing
While visiting...Priest Ch'ang. PAR #1/4

Liu Shen-hsu
A quiet gate. FUG 2/4

Liu Yu-Hsi
The city of stones. DIA 10/1

Livesay, Florence Randal
Two Ukrainian folk songs. POE 10/3

Livezey, Herman
Nocturne, Key West, Florida. WAN 3/4

Llanelly, Elra
Epitaph. GUL 9/3

Lloyd, Anne
My iris army. LYW 7-8/3

Lloyd, Jeannette Hortense
Over that sea. AMP 6-7/3

Lobel, Paul A.
Cacophony. GUL 7-8/3

Locher, Harriet Hawley
Kindred. MIN 9-10/3

Lockwood, Harriette I.
Arguing with Pegasus. WRM 3/1

Lockwood, Marion
The place of truth. LAR 10/3

Loftus, J. B.
The sea. PAG 12/1

Loftus, John
The house summit-set. MEA 9/2

Logan, Marian Russell
Diary. NOM Spr/3
The poet. LYR 10/3

Long (Jr.), Frank Belknap
Exotic quest. LAL 3/4

Long, Haniel
After reading Bynner's transla. PAL Sum/3
Butterflies. PAL Sum/3
Girl-athletes. POE 10/3
The masker. COV 1/1
The new moon. TEM 6/1
Pittsburgh: a clear day. TEM 6/1
Proud cities. TEM 6/1
To a boy dancing with six girl. NOM Sum/3
Unimportant dialogue. WAV 1/2

Long, Peter Edward
The luck of Placer Jim. LAR 5/3

Long, Rose Baskerville
Grass. LYR 8/2

Long, Vivian Aten
Nastrutiums. LYW 4/2

Longfellow, Herbert H.
Allons. COV 1/4
The fishers. COV 7/4
Habit. COV 10/3
Harvest. COV 4/4
I am a little boy traveling. COV 4/2
The king's horses. COV 10/3
Mirrors. COV 4/2
My hands. COV 4/4
A prayer. COV 4/2
Resurgat. COV 4/3

Longley, Snow
April illusions. LYW 4/2
The dying favorite speaks. LYW 1/3
In spring. LYW 4/1
Mid-Atlantic. LYW 4/1

Longstreth, T. Morris
After hearing the Tschaikovsky. COV 6/2
Carte blanche. FOR 4/4

Looker, Samuel E.
Ventnor memories. CTY S-A/1

Looker, Samuel J.
Beauty, I've loved thee. CTY Win/2
Friendship. CTY Sum/2
Morn. CTY Spr/2

Loomis, Cassius M.
Sympathy. CIJ 9/3
Loomis, Edith
A little nun. NAT 3/28/3
Loucks, Allan P.
In the city of...silver lotus. DEU 9/19/0
Loupe, Carroll
To one absent. PAR #2/3
Louthan, Hattie Horner
Delusion. AMP10-11/3
Delusion. LAR 5/3
Love, Adelaide
December midnight. AMP 12/2
Motif. AMP 8-9/3
Undercurrent. AMP 8-9/3
Love, Jane Groome
The rain. PIR 4/2
Winter evening. COV 2/2
Loveman, Robert
Death. CIC 9/6/3
Loveman, Samuel
In Pierrot's garden. LAL 1/4
Interlude. LAL 3/4
Loving (tr.), Pierre
Two of them. PAG10-11/1
Loving, Pierre
Churning. MEA 9/1
Crucifixion. DOU 7/4
Daughter of Herodias. S4N 3-4/3
Dust in the wind. MEA 7/2
If I went back. NAT 3/1/2
Loss. DIA 9/1
Marine. WAV 3/4
Mountain hunger. LYW 10/3
Nocturne. WAV 3/4
Star market. LIB 8/2
Low, Benjamin R. C.
After a trip from Albany... SCM 8/0
Spring, riding. COV 4/2
The too high. HAM 6/1
Yellow leaves. HAM 9/1
Lowe, K. Elmo
The sieve. WAV 6/2
Lowell (tr.), Amy
The city of stones. DIA 10/1
The lonely wife. BOO 9/1
The retreat of Hssieh Kung. DIA 10/1
The terraced road... ASI 10/1
Lowell, Amy
Acquatint framed in gold. NAT 6/7/2
Alternatives. NER 1/16/4
And so I think, Diogenes. YAR 1/3
Basket dance. DIA 9/0
The book of stones and lilies. SCM 11/1
Charleston, South Carolina. POE 12/2
Chill. REW 10/2
The day that was that day. POE 11/0
Decoration Day. DIA 10/2
A dimension. BOO 4/1
Dissonance. RHY 1/3
A Dracula of the hills. CEN 6/3
Easel picture. DIA 10/2
Eleonora Duse. POE 8/3
Evelyn Ray. POE 12/3
Exercise in logic. NER 12/5/3
Fact. SCM 3/3
Footing up a total. DIA 8/1
Fugitive. NER 12/5/3
Gavotte in D minor. DIA 6/0
The green parrakeet. POE 12/3
Grievance. HAM 11/2
Heraldic. PRA 1-2/3
The house in Main street. CEN 2/2
The humming-birds. BOO 5/4
The immortals. CEN 9/2
In excelsis. CEN 9/2
Katydids, ...Lake Michigan. DIA 1/2
A legend of porcelain. NOA 3/0
Lilacs. BRO 11/1
Magnolia gardens, Charleston,. POE 12/2
Many swans, sun myth...America. NOA 8/0
Merely statement. BOO 5/0
The Middleton place, Charlesto. POE 12/2
Miniature. CEN 8/1
Morning song, with drums. NER 10/6/0
A New Year's card. CEN 1/2
Nuit blanche. DOU 2/3
Orientation. DIA 10/2
The paper in the gate-legged... CEN 5/4
Paradox. TEM Aut/1
The "Plum Blossom" concubine... REW 1/4
Portrait. HAM 11/2
Prayer for lightning. DIA 9/0
Purple crackles. BOO 7/2
The red knight. DIA 10/2
The revenge. NER 7/12/2
The sand altar. BOO 5/4
A shower. CEN 4/0
Silhouette with sepia backgrou. POM 1922
Song for a viola d'amore. HAM 11/2
A South Carolina forest. POE 12/2

FUG 2/4
Mabie, Mary Louise
A song of children. MUN 6/2
Two beacons. MUN 1/2
MacAlpine, James
To an Irish blackbird. NES 3/8/4
MacDonald, Anna Singleton
My undine. CIV 3/4
MacDonald, Jessie
A prayer. POE 3/1
MacDonald, Susanne Rike
At the hospital. LYW 2/3
MacDonald, Wilson
The maker of dreams. COV 4/3
A vagabond's song. COV 8/3
MacDougall, Allan Ross
Bouncing Belinda. NES 1/22/1
MacDougall, Dugald
Hope triumphant! CTY Win/2
Reveries. CTY Spr/2
Worker's song. CTY S-A/1
MacGill, Caroline Elizabeth
The singer in silence. MAG 7/2
MacIntosh, Mavis
To an elder. BOO 6/4
MacIntyre, Carlyle Ferren
Elf music. AIN 4/0
The informing spirit. NAT 4/27/1
MacLeish, Archibald
Captured. YAR 1/4
Corporate entity. NER 7/4
High road. NER 5/16/3
Impulse. NER 8/29/3
MacMahan, Anne D.
A what not. WRM 2/1
MacMillan, Eleanor
The back door. LAR 11/3
Desertion. LAR 11/3
Dreams. LAR 11/3
Fellowship. LAR 11/3
Growth. LAR 3/4
Horizons and skylines. LAR 11/3
Intensity. LAR 11/3
The loom. LAR 11/3
Love's season. LAR 11/3
The new west. LAR 9/3
Propinquity. LAR 11/3
Recognition. LAR 11/3
Reincarnation. LAR 11/3
MacTowner, Earl
The ads. LAR 3/4
Mackall, Virginia Woods
Artisan. NAT 3/15/2
Education. NAT 8/9/2
Many waters. MES 6/3
Mackenzie, Jean Kenyon
The little path. MAC 10/2
The warning. MAC 3/2
The wild heart. MAC 11/2
The young trader. MAC 7/2
Macready, M. A. K.
A pine tree in evening. COV 8/1
Macy, John
Cosmic scandal. MEA 4/3
Couplets in criticism. MEA 5/3
Numbers. MEA 4/3
Passage. MEA 4/3
The poet. MEA 4/3
Vigil. MEA 4/3
Well? MEA 4/3
Maddock, Frances
Forgetting. MAG 7/2
Waste. CAW 2/2
Madeleva, Sister M.
David. AMP 12/3
Swaddling clothes. AMP 12/3
Mage, Doris
Not alone. PAR #3/4
Magruder, Mary Lanier
At joyous gard. MAC 2/3
The mocking bird. STE 10/2
Mahon, Elizabeth Adams
Comparisons. INT 4-6/4
Interlude. INT 1-3/4
Monotony. INT 4-6/4
Moon's progress. INT 1-3/4
Maisch, Lilah Esther
Sense impressions. AMP 2/2
Maisel-Goldstein
Twilight canvas. NOM Spr/4
Major, Montgomery
My words neglect the beauty... VOI 7-8/3
Mala, Yenomdrah
Ambition. CAP 5/3
At the great threshold. CAP 5/3
The novel reader. CAP 5/3
Malloch, Douglas
Just walking and talking. REB 5/3
Malloy, Mary J.
Assumpta es Maria. MAG 8/3
Mary and May. MAG 5/2
Maltby, Ian
The half moon smiles. CTY S-A/1
Manchester, Genevieve
Night moth. PEG 5/3
Manchester, Leslie Clare
Bitter-sweet. AMP 3-4/4
Down at the spring. STE 2/4
Dream-land. AMP 4-5/3
Mother's growing old. AMP 8/2
Mann, Fred B.
A memory. POA 9/1
Mann, Stella Lucia
Laudations to Andy. COV 8/0
Manning, Oliver
The "snowy peaks" unveiled. LYW

9/1
Mansfield, Katherine
Winter bird. NER 4/30/4
Manship, Albert A.
A wish. SCR 5/3
March, J. M.
Autumn prophecy. POE 9/0
Marconnier, Byrne
Ghosts. NAT12/19/3
Marin, Luis Munoz
Counsel. MEA 7/2
Finis. MEA 7/2
He makes a picture of his love. MEA 7/2
Moods. MEA 7/2
Maring, Helen Emma
Dreams. AMP 8-9/3
Marino, Josephine
To Dante. FOR-Dan#/1
Maris, Faith
Sand lily. LYW 10/2
Markham, Anna Catharine
Keeping faith. STE 10/2
Markham, Edwin
Again the mood of Eden. STE 6/2
Everlasting. MAC 6/2
In High Sierras. LYR 1/2
Love's dream. LAD 2/4
Man's great task. AMP 5-6/4
The perished pool. MAC 6/2
The pool. MAC 6/2
The Rajah of Mysore. MAC 6/2
Sappho's song. MAC 6/2
A song to a tree. BOO 7/1
Youth and you. MAC 5/2
Markham, Lucia Clark
"Beauty for ashes." COV 5/1
A brich tree singing. LYW 3/3
"I went away." COV 8/2
"A little golden memory." LYR 2/3
The new house. COV 12/2
Night and I. COV 8/2
November night. LYW 11/2
Rain in the night. LYW 3/3
Recurrence. COV 7/3
Songs for a little girl... COV 5/1
To Geraldine Farrar... COV 5/0
Marks, Jeannette
Again? NOA 4/1
Blind sleep. COV 8/1
Clear pools. LYR 9/1
Cobwebs. BOO 12/1
Dragon. BOO 5/1
Dust and dreams. NOA 2/1
Even as here. NAT 6/5/0
God's acre. BOO 4/4
Green golden door. NER 3/3/0
Hate. BOO 6/3
Indian summer. LYR 10/1
Journey's end. AIN 3/0
Many sorrows. OUT 5/26/0
Rosy Miller. POE 3/0
Salt of sorrow. BOO 10/3
Sea-gulls. POE 3/0
Markus, Elizabeth
Butterflies. LAR 5/3
Marlatt, Earl
The return. AMP 4/2
Marlow, James
The heart breaker. GUL 9/3
Marpha
Grieve not. FUG 6/2
To a curious, modest lady. FUG 6/2
Marple, Charles F.
Woman. HAM 1/0
Marquis, Neeta
The alien. LYW 1/2
April dusk. LYW 9/3
Awakening. MUN 7/2
March song. LYW 4/1
An old garden by the sea. LYW 7-8/2
On Christmas Eve. LYW 12/1
On the desert. CAP 5/3
A redwood forest in winter. LYW 12/1
To the south. LYW 4/1
Twilight song. LYW 4/3
Marr, J. N.
Mary, a memory. LYR 8/3
Voice of the violin. LYR 2/3
Marsh, Charles Howard
Candlelight. PEG 7/3
Color music. AMP 3-4/3
The urn. PEG 5/3
Marshall, A. G.
Desecration. AMP 2/2
Marta of Sillen. See Sillen

Martin, A. E.
As we journey along. POA 9/1
The star nest. POA 9/1
Martin, Alice L.
Old home flowers. GRA 8/2
Martin, Frances Watson
A California sunshine. LAR 11/3
Sunset at Santa Monica. LAR 8/3
Martin, Herman Ford
Afterward. AMP Aut/1
The annointed. FUG 4-5/3
Apotheosis. LYR 3/4
City streets are cold. AMP 2/2
Flame. COV 4/4
Home. FUG 2-3/3
Hunger. MIN 7-8/4
Jetsam. AMP 3-4/4
The juggler. AMP 10/2

Sea foam. MIN 3-4/4
The wandering minstrel. SCR 10/3
Whom the sea calls. AMP 12/2

Martin, Janette
First love. LAR 9/3
Still hours. LAR 8/3

Martin, John
Kitty. STE 1/4
Tiger-tiger. STE 1/4

Martin, Portia
Aspens. LYW 4/2
A Chippewa lullabye. AMP 2/2
In the moon-of-red-blooming... LYW 4/2
A letter. AMP 2-3/3
Love wakens in the heart... LYW 2/3
Plover-wing sings in the fog. LYW 11/3
Rain. AMP 2-3/3
Song of Chief Soaring-Gull... LYW 2/3
Song of the Woman-of-the-Rifte. LYW 2/3
The swing. LYW 5/4

Martin, R. Helen
Failure. LYW 6/3

Martin, Winona
The ego. POA 9/1

Martines, Pura E.
Dimple cheek. AMP 2/2

Martyn, Wyndham
Autre temps. AIN 4/0

Marvin, Frederick Rowland
Upto the end. BOT 3/17/3

Marvin, Reignold Kent
Celia Thaxter. GRA 8/2

Maryngoff, Anatoly
October. BRO 5/2

Masa-Ko Chino
Overcome by confession. FRE 11/9/2

Masefield, John
Four sonnets. COV 4/0
In a theatre. MEA 6/3
Lyric. YAR 1/0
The passing strange. YAR 4/0

Mason, Francis C.
Cultivation. CUV 11/3
Disillusioned. NOM Aut/3
Inopportune. NOM Aut/3
Magister linguisticus. LYR 6/4
Prayer. LYR 9/3
Treasure. LYR 8/3

Mason, Gibbs
You'll say farewell. AMP 12/3

Mason, Harrison D.
The thrush is calling. AMP 6-7/3

Massey, R.
Last pilgrimage. HEA 6/4
Omega. HEA 5/4

Masters, Edgar Lee
Balfour Tozer. MAC 3/2
Douglas Strong. MAC 3/2
Golden fox. BRO 4/2
Keats to Fanny Brawne. POE 1/1
Lithographs and life. NES 5/3/3
The Mason County hills. NES 2/24/3
Mind flying afar. POE 2/4
O you young eagles! NAT12/12/3
Ode to autumn. POE 8/3
Reason Robb. MAC 3/2
The return. POE 9/3
Wallace Hardy. MAC 3/2
Worlds. POE 10/2

Masters, Hardin Wallace
Chicago. CAP 10/2
Quest eternal. NOM Aut/2

Mastin, Florence Ripley
From the telephone. POE 8/2
Your hands. POE 8/2

Mathers (tr.), E. Powys
Chinese poems. BRO 11/1

Mathers (trans.), E. Powys
Five Afghan love songs. DIA 10/0

Mathewson, Mary M.
Shifting winds. POE 4/3

Mathis, Florence S.
Moon over the prairie. LAR 2/4
Sunset. LAR 2/4

Matson, Mabel Cornelia
Christmas wreaths. GRA 12/0
Oh, come and walk with me. GRA 5/2
There is a house upon a hill. GRA 2/1
To an acorn. AMP 8/2
What grief? POE 5/0

Mattes, L.
Autumn. AMP10-11/3

Matthews, Emily W.
My little love. GRA 1/1
Nature. GRA 4/1

Matthias, Blanche Coates
Dawn's night. ALS 12/1
The wish to sing. ALS 10/1

Mavity, Nancy Barr
A fragment from Sappho. COV 5/1
The home-maker. CEN 4/1
In the garden. COV 5/1
"In whose service is perfect." COV 5/1
Lost language. COV 5/1
Modern love. NES11/25/2

Maxon, Berle Deane
"Father, forgive them, they kn.

AMP 10/2

Maxwell, Ellen Benton
Clynmalira. CIV 3/4
Fame. CIV 5-6/4
The rhythm of silence. CIV 3/4

Maxwell, George
A typewriter. LYW 11/3

May, Beulah
By way of warning. WAN 5/4
The canyon trail. LYW 9/3
Homesickness. OVM 4/4
March. CTY Win/4
Memory. OVM 3/4
Mojave. LIB 8/2
Mojave. WAN 2/4
Music. LYW 11/1
Night on canyon. WAN 11/3
Peter's canyon. CTY Spr/4
Redondo Beach. LYW 5/2
Saint Anne's wind. LYW 2/3
The sheepherder. LIB 9/2
Ulysses. WAN 12/3
The wanderer. LIB 9/2
"The white soul of a sculptor" WAN 7/4
Wind at night. WAN 12/3
The wind of Han. WAN 4/4
Winds from the sea. LYW 2/3

Mayfield, A. U.
The church of my childhood. LAR 11/3

Maynard, Theodore
Autumn mist. YAR 1/4
The denial. OUT 7/14/0
A gray day in California. NER 1/18/2
Inscription to my mother. HAM 2/1
Memory. YAR 4/3
Ode in time of doubt. CAW 10/2
Peace and justice. OUT 5/18/1
Sonnet. OUT 11/3/0
To Dame Paula, O.S.B.. CAW 1/1

Mayo, Thomas
Bess. COV 12/3

McAlmon, Robert
Away. BOO 7/4
The blackbird. BOO 2/2
Form destructionist: sculptor. POE 12/0
Surf of the Dead Sea. COT ?/1
Today's music. POE 12/0
White males. POE 12/0

McBlair, Robert
Man. LYR 8/1

McCaigue, Philip
Gratitude. MAG 8/3
Hail, full of grace. MAG 3/2

McCarn, Corneille
Ghosts. FUG 4-5/3

McCarthy, Dixie
Hills. LYW 6/2

McCarthy, John Russell
Are they deriding? NES 1/19/4
Ask the Bacillus. WAN 9/3
At the Grand Canyon. PER 1/3
Beside a river. LOT12/17/2
Between the stars. LOY 9/10/2
The bright steel wall. LOT12/18/2
But song shall rise. LYR 7/3
City dwellers. PEA 10/2
Described and deeded. LYW 9/2
Every golden face. COV 4/4
Evidence. COV 4/4
Friends. LYW 4/3
From nowhere. LYW 4/3
The gift of beauty. LYW 11/1
Girl with the grey bonnet. LOT 6/25/2
A grey day. LYW 7-8/3
Hills. COV 9/2
A hobo faring. LOT 6/23/2
The holiday. LOY 9/10/2
I shall return. CAP 5/3
Just as old as you. LOY 9/10/2
Lament in southland. COV 4/4
Lizard. WAN 5/4
Machines. PEA 5/3
A man walking. COV 8/0
March. COV 3/1
The new clerk. LYW 9/2
No answer. WAN 1/4
Now I who saw. LOT 10/1/2
On miracles. SMA 8/2
Only yesterday. LOT 9/17/2
Our friends. COV 3/0
Over the waters. BRI 1/3
Peering water. BOO 6/2
The presence. LOY 9/10/2
Priests. LYW 1/2
The real estate broker. TEM Aut/1
Rue Anemone. LYW 1/2
Shadows. LOT11/25/2
She walked in rags. BAU 11/3
So fair the rose. COV 9/2
So has God made the world. PEA 8/2
Spark out of heaven. LYW 2/4
Still waters. SMA 4/3
Talk. CAP 5/3
Themselves. COV 12/3
These also. WAN 9/3
This life the last? LYW 11/3
A titlark ditty. SAB 4/3
Today I shall make friends. COV 9/2
Trillium. PAG 8-9/1
Under the stars. LYW 4/3

Wave your magic rod. LYR 3/4
We are not lost. COV 12/3
Who are we...? SMA 12/2
Who has forgotten. WAN 11/3
The winter winds. PEA 11/2

McCarthy, Kathleen L.
The king's Ushabti. GUL 7-8/3

McCarthy, Thomas F.
A gypsy's song. DEV11/16/1

McCarty, Dixie
At a flower stand. LYW 11/2
The ride. LYW 6/3

McClellan, Walter
Arrangement in black and gold. DOU 8-9/1
Gayoso girls are golden. DOU 12/2
Je suis belle, O mortals... FUG 2/4
An old man dreams. DOU 5/2
Unquiet. DOU 12/1
A woman of the blue grass. FUG 2/4

McClennan, Walter
The eel-spearer. COV 8/0
Tolstoi's good-bye. POE 10/0

McClure, John
Duet. DOU 1/4
Golden era. BOO 1/4
Jazz. DOU 10/1
Laughter. WAV 6/2
Le boune chanson. CEN 8/0
Love is such a mischief. DOU 2/2
No charms have bound me. DOU 2-3/4
Owl-blasted. POE 6/2
Sorrow! Sorrow! NES11/18/2
Then while alive we be. NAT 8/16/2
Thomas A-Maying. DOU 7/4
Time forgets us as we go. VOI Aut/1
The winter of his discontent. DOU 7/4
With all their vessels. DOU 6/1
Wizard's lament. VOI Aut/1
The word. LYR 4/2
You and I are gay now. DOU 1/4

McCluskey, Katherine Wisner
The bird and the brook. COV 12/0
Darkness. COV 6/0
Envyings. POE 7/0
A follower. COV 7/1
"Fowl that may fly above..." COV 7/1
A heat wave. POE 7/0
Home-coming. COV 12/0
A jester. COV 3/0
A parable. POE 8/2
A secret. COV 7/1
The spree. POE 8/2
Transit. POE 8/2
Wholly happy. POE 8/2

McComb, Dorothy Shepard
We quarrel. LAL 5/4

McComb, Dorothy Shepardly
The bride speaks. MUN 6/2

McCord, David
Oregon rain. VOI10-11/3
Trees and lonely things. VOI 12/2
The winds of morning came. VOI 12/2

McCormick, Anne O'Hare
No one sees beauty. NER 8/16/2
Song of praise for not being... NER 5/3/2

McCormick, Nadine
Ten just in Barfar. GUL 7-8/3

McCormick, Virginia Taylor
Attainment. BOT 11/8/2
August. LYR 8/1
Awakening garden. LYW 4/3
The basket maker. AMP 10/1
A Baudelaire. LYR 7/1
Bryon. STE 4/4
Dandelions. LYR 12/1
Dante, 1321-1921. VOI Aut/1
The dark. SMA 11/1
Days of happiness. LYR 5/1
Dresden China. MIN 7-8/3
Explained. GYP #2/4
Faces in the fire. TEM Aut/1
The faithful. BOT 4/7/3
The far country. NOM Spr/2
Flags. AMP 6/2
Flower of quince. PAR #1/4
For beauty does not die. LYR 7/1
The fugitive. LYR 4/2
Hepzibah of the cent shop. LYW 5/3
I go to meet my beloved. LYR 1/2
I remember. LYW 4/3
Indian summer. LYR 11/1
Instrospection. SMA 7/2
La petit fiancee. LYW 3/4
Lilies. LYR 6/4
Mackerel sky. SMA 6/3
Mammy. LYR 7/2
Meadows at night. LYR 5/1
Melusina at Lusignan. REW 10/2
Memories. NOM Sum/2
Meredith, prophet of joy. PER 7/4
Mountains. LYW 1/2
Noel. LYR 12/1

Old songs. NOM Spr/2
Pain. LYW 10/3
Perfection. LYR 4/1
Pierrette. MUN 6/2
The pine tree. PER 1/2
Poems. LYW 10/1
The pretty lady reading. CLS 2/2
The price. SMA 5/3
Remembering. COV 11/3
"A sea unfathomed." LYR 8/1
Shelley. STE 7/2
Sorrow. LYW 10/1
Spending the day. BOT 6/23/3
Sunset after storm. PAG 12/1
Thought. LYW 1/2
The thousand dollar Nigger. BOT 4/21/3
To Nausikaa. LYR 12/2
To one away. NOM Win/2
Traffic. LYW 9/3
Troy, and after. CUV 11/3
Twilight. TEL 2/2
Unknown. CLS 8/1
Unsatisfied. BOT11/11/2
Wherein I find my god. LYR 2/2
Willow branches. NOM Spr/3
The Yorktown road. PER 7/3
Young Stephen. LAR 10/3
Youth's sorrow. LYR 4/2

McCourt, Edna Wahlert
Query. POE 5/0
Strangers. POE 5/0
You and I. POE 5/0

McCourtie, William B.
A New England spinster. NES12/10/1

McCracken, Georgia Burns
To a song. LAR 3/4

McCrea, Marion
Earth talk. PAG 12/1

McCreary, Frederick R.
Alone on the hill. POE 2/2
Before winter. VOI10-11/3
Buds. POE 5/4
Buttons. POE 5/4
The foreman. COV 8/0
Hill orchards. VOI Aut/2
Judges. POE 2/2
Memories. VOI Aut/1
Moon mark. VOI 7-8/3
A naked maple. POE 2/2
Noontime. POE 2/2
Old age. COV 8/0
Sand-memory. POE 5/4
Snow walk. VOI 7-8/3
The sowing. VOI 6-7/3
Winter rain. POE 2/2
A word from the east... NAT 6/21/2

McCreary, W. H.
Butterflies. COV 10/3
The fairy set the stage. COV 4/4
To a caterpillar. COV 10/3
To a spider mending her web. COV 4/4

McDonald, Jane
At the Grand Canyon. CAP 1-2/3

McDonald, Lawrence S.
Off brigantine. AMP 6-7/3

McDougal, Mary C.
Boiler makers. COV 10/3
Burned poems. NEU 2/7/3
The cloud. COV 7/2
Cover your faces. NEW 8/26/2
The floods of the moon. COV 7/3
In Battery Park. COV 7/3
The joke. COV 1/0
The liar. NEW 2/17/2
Mocking birds. NEU 2/23/3
The plains of silence. NEW 11/4/1
Silences. COV 10/3
The subway accident. NEs 7/12/2
Three men. COV 7/2
To an ancient man at 47. COV 1/0
To something indomitable. COV 1/0
The waves. NEW 5/25/2
The wire stringer. NEU 7/6/2
A woman's song. LYW 7-8/3
A woman's song. NEU 7/4/2

McDougal, Violet
The call of the sea. NEW 3/18/2
Chameleons - Manhattan roof. NEU 7/23/2
Chinatown. ARG 8/2
The fire-eater. NEW 1/25/2
Heredity. NEW 1/10/2
The knife thrower. NEW10/14/1
The phantom round-up. KAN 3/6/3
Romulus and Remus. NEW 7/14/2
The very old. NEW 12/2/1
White wolves. NEW 4/11/2
The wonder river. ARG 7/8/2

McFadden, Athena
Your words. POE 6/2

McFadden, J.
Ole's brevity. NOW 7/3

McFarland, Helen
A wish. HAM 4/0

McFarland, Stewart C.
When I am gone. AMP 6-7/3

McFee, William
To a child. BOO 5/3

McGaffey, Ernest
Ballade of Mary,Queen of Scots. LYW 4/1

McGowan, Clelia P.
Ballade of the Maya maiden. LYW 7-8/2
Molly by the shore. LYW 4/1
McGowan, Clelia P.
The swamp. POM 1922
McGowen, Elizabeth K.
"And I remember." CTY Sum/2
The barrier. LYW 11/2
Barter. CTY Aut/2
Bitter-sweet. CTY S-A/1
The clover wind. CTY Spr/3
The deserted house. LYW 1/3
Evening. STE 3/4
Heartbreak. CTY Win/4
Hidden gold. CTY Aut/2
Home, sweet home. CTY Spr/3
Hunting season. CTY Win/3
Idols. CTY S-A/1
Illusion. CTY Sum/2
Merciless time. CTY Spr/2
"Narcissus." CTY Spr/2
Outshining deeds. CTY Spr/2
The prisoner. CTY Sum/3
Prophecy. STE 3/4
Repentance. CTY Spr/2
To baby Patricia. CTY S-A/1
The treasure. CTY Win/4
"Water lilies." CTY Win/2
Westfield water. CTY Spr/3
Winter comes. CTY Win/3
Wood fires. LYW 11/3
McGregor, Smith
Indian summer. CTY S-A/1
McGroaty, John S.
In the San Joaquin. AMP 2-3/3
McGurrin, Buckley
Ephemera. POE 4/3
Love on a spring night. POE 4/3
Sayonara. POE 4/3
McHugh, Margaret
Disillusionment. LAR 4/4
McIntyre, Carlyle F.
The brimming cup. POE 5/0
Compensations. POE 5/0
The green door. POE 5/0
The house of laurels. POE 5/0
Lady of autumn. POE 5/0
The mourners. POE 5/0
Promenading. POE 5/2
The scissor-grinder. POE 5/2
The untamed. POE 5/0
The visit. POE 5/2
McKay, Claude
Africa. LIB 8/1
Alone. LIB 5/2
Baptism. LIB 10/1
Flirtation. LIB 8/1
French leave. LIB 4/2
Futility. LIB 1/2
Honeymoon. MIL 10/2
In bondage. LIB 8/1
Jasmines. LIB 8/1
La Paloma in London. LON 1/2
A memory of June. LIB 8/1
Morning joy. LIB 8/1
Negro spiritual. LIB 5/2
The new forces. LIB 7/2
The night fire. LIB 5/2
On the road. LIB 3/2
Subway wind. LIB 8/1
Thirst. LIB 12/1
Through agony. LIB 12/1
To one coming north. LIB 8/1
To the intrenched classes. LIB 5/2
Voices of night. MIL 10/2
The white city. LIB 10/1
The white house. LIB 5/2
McKay, Margaret Curtis
Protest. GUL 7-8/3
McKee, Ruth E.
Mind. LYW 11/2
Spring sadness. LYW 5/4
A study in pastels. LYW 5/4
McKenny, Margaret
Arctic summer. COV 6/1
Artic memory. COV 2/1
Autumn lily blooming... COV 10/1
Emotions. COV 10/2
"From the unconscious..." COV 6/4
Ice. COV 2/1
The meadow. COV 7/0
Summer. COV 7/0
Sweetpeas. POE 7/0
Veneer. COV 10/2
McKenzie, William P.
Revelator. CIJ 12/3
Spring o' the year. CIJ 4/4
McKie, Mae
In his own way. AMP 2-3/3
McKinney, Kate Slaughter
Autumn's flight. SCR 1/4
A castle in Spain. SCR 10/3
Christmas memories. SCR 1/4
Conversation. SCR 4/4
Easter. SCR 4/4
Four cinquains. SCR 5/4
Immortelles. SCR 7/4
On the trail. SCR 10/3
Only a fern leaf. SCR 3/4
Peace and unrest. SCR 5/4
Two cinquain. SCR 3/4
McLane (Jr.), J. L.
First snow. BOO 1/3
McLauchlan, Kate Lewis
Travail. CIV 7-8/4
McLean, Daniel
Hopes. MEA 6/2

McLeod, Frances
A tale of terrific traffic. NOW 2/3
McLeod, Irene Rutherford
April. NER 5/0
Free will. CEN 6/0
McLuckie, Harriet Smith
Prayer. CIC 2/21/4
McMullen, Dysart
John Keats. LYR 8/1
McMullen, Mary F.
A quince tree in bloom. LYR 5/1
McNeal (Jr.), Thomas H.
Confession. TER 7/3
Finis. TER 7/3
For pardon. TER 7/3
Rebellion. TER 7/3
The sympathetic one. TER 7/3
The throne of God. TER 7/3
The un-godly. TER 7/3
McNish, Alvin G.
L'amateur. MOR 7/4
McPartlin, Catharine
At the shrine..Lady of Grace. MAG 9/3
February. MAG 2/2
Saint Joseph. MAG 3/2
Sunset in the south. MAG 10/3
McVickar, Dorothy
Heaphy herself. POE 5/1
Thought's white night. COV 11/1
Mead, Ida A.
Woman. AMP10-11/3
Meade, Merrill C.
"In the smoke of a cigarette." POA 9/1
Tears. POA 1/2
Meader, Mattie Bennett
Sunset on Lake Winnepesaukee. GRA 9/2
Meadowcraft, Clara Platt
Prophecy. VOI Spr/3
Meadowcroft, Clara Platt
Ego. LYR 6/4
Meadowcroft, Clara Pratt
Road song. COV 1/0
Meadowcroft, Clara Platt
Upper chambers. OUT10/31/3
Mearns, Hughes
Alien. HUE 7/4
A father in defense of clamor. HUE 7/4
Reprieved. HUE 7/4
Some other world it was. HUE 7/4
Mechem, Kirke
Cobwebs. WAN 4/4
Mechen, Kirke
Deforested. NER 5/2/3
These ageless themes. HAM 11/2
Meehee, Picayune
The first meeting. SCR 9/2
Home again. SCR 1/3
Lonely. SCR 11/2
Rum's curse. SCR 9/2
Tomorrow morn. SCR 1/3
Meeker, Marjorie
Airs for a flute. POE 2/4
And so it never mattered... ALS 11/1
Annette. COV 5/3
Before you came. POE 2/4
But like mad builders, walls. MEA 12/3
By a window. POE 1/2
Color of water. POE 1/2
Comrades. POE 1/2
Dancer. ALS 5/1
Decoration. OUT 2/21/3
The defeated years. OUT 6/27/3
In darkness. POE 1/2
Larkspur. OUT 8/15/3
Lonely sky and sea. POE 1/2
Ode to myself trying to sleep. POE 1/2
An old woman. ALS 11/1
Only the bright derision. MEA 2/4
Portrait by Renoir. ALS 5/1
Sentimental history. MEA 2/4
Song for a May night. POE 1/2
Song in midsummer. COV 5/3
A sonnet for Kate Pennifether. DOU 1/3
Sonnets. POE 2/4
Strangers. COV 5/3
These are the listeners. COV 5/3
Wake-song. POE 6/3
The waters. NOA 4/1
Where my step falters. POE 2/4
Words said in an attic. POE 2/4
Meily, Clarence
The aged lover prays. WAV 2/2
Song of the ghouls. WAV 3/4
Meisinger, Mary M.
Impotence. LYW 11/3
Meisinger, Mary
Fantasy. LYW 2/2
Melbourne, Harold
An old New Yorker. MUN 1/2
Melendez, Engracia
Defense. POE 12/3
In Berkeley. POE 12/3
The ladies of the Fuerte. MEA 6/2
Lontananza. POE 12/3
Mi Marido. POE 12/3
Ruben Dario. POE 12/3
Melton, Wightman Fletcher

Melville, Herman
The call of the hills. SOU 8/3
Melville, Herman
California bound, 1849. LAR 4/3
Menefee, Kate Randle
How they grew. LYW 4/2
Joy and pain. STE 7/4
Meredith, Clyde Robe
A ballad of rue. CIV 5-6/4
Meredith, Floyd
All of a piece. STE 3/3
Heritage. LYW 6/3
Impermanence. LYW 2/2
Sacrifice. LYW 6/3
Shadows. TEM 6/1
Stone flowers. LYW 11/2
Windows. LYW 11/3
Merington, Marguerite
Adam Daulac. NOA 4/0
Merlin, Valentine Karl
A song to the Pecos River. LAR 2/3
Merrell, Lloyd Frank
The infant love. MID 3/1
Merriehaw, Martha Webster
April rain at sunset. VOI 12-1/4
At Point Firmin. CIM 1/4
A bird I remember. CIM 6/3
A crest before the sea. CIM 10/3
Dawn waking in the mountains. WAN 6/4
Dune-daughter. WAN 10/3
Equality. CIM 1/4
Finale. WAN 10/3
The gleaners. CIM 10/3
Hangar chanty. CIM 12/3
Let it be kelp. WAN 10/3
Love at first sight. LOS 5/10/4
Midnight freight train. CIM 3/4
Nasturtiums. CIM 12/3
Vivian Creek. CIM 7/3
A voice in the night. MEA 11/3
Want to go forward. CIM 6/3
Merriman, Faye N.
The haunted house. PIR 1/4
Merry, Marion D.
When mother bobs her hair. LAR 3/4
Merryman, Mildred Plew
Bride and groom. WAV 3/4
Caged owl. STE 11/3
Florida pines. NOM Win/2
Funeral. NOM Aut/3
The housewife. POE 11/2
In the shadow. LYR 6/2
Molds. MEA 1/2
On windy nights. LYW 4/4
Red silk. STE 10/3
Song for a windy evening. NOM Sum/3
That year. MEA 12/3
Thoughts of a bookkeeper. LYW 7-8/2
To Chicago at night. WAV #4/2
To a lamplighter. MEA 6/2
To a pickaninny eating... MEA 2/4
To a public library. NES 6/3/2
Two at a concert. COV 5/0
Whirlwind. WAV 12/2
Merten, H.
Thy love. LAR 3/4
Merten, Jack
Children at play. POE 11/0
Metzger, Elizabeth Stewart
Ambition. MEA 11/3
Violets. COV 5/2
Metzger, Ruth
Moonlight phantasy. GRA 1/1
Mew, Charlotte
Last year. LYW 7/3
The rambling sailor. BOO 6/3
To a child in death. BOO 4/2
Meyer, Josephine A.
Nocturne. AIN 3/2
Meyer, Lucy Rider
W'en ye doan' know what to do. OUT 3/24/0
Meynell, Viola
A girl adoring. NER 8/24/1
Mezquida, Anna Blake
The captive. AMP 1-2/4
O spring! GOH 3/4
The spirit of progress. UNV 7/4
Miall, Agnes M.
To a portrait. LYW 6/3
Michelson, Max
The haunted hat-shop. POE 2/1
Middleton, Lilian
Behind the swinging door. MOR Aut/2
In rein. AMP 8/2
Inconstancy. VOI Aut/2
Wind. NOM Spr/3
Wishing well. VOI 6-7/3
Middleton, Scudder
Answer. POE 11/3
The bag of sin. COV 1/3
The beast. POE 11/3
Conflict. MEA 3/4
Friends. COV 12/3
Jezebel. NAT 2/13/4
Meeting. COV 6/3
Mountains. BOO 12/3
To W.E. Burghardt DuBois. NAT 7/9/4
To a contemporary... COV 12/3
Miehm, Clara
The boys at the movies. VTY

Spr/2
Chubby little fellow. CTY Win/2
Consider the oyster. CTY Aut/2
Harbingers. VTY Spr/2
How loves comes. CTY Spr/2
Little baby dear. CYT Win/4
Little old lady. CTY Sum/3
My friend. CTY Win/2
October days. CTY Aut/2
The opening game. CTY Spr/3
When you came along. CTY Spr/2

Milam, May Thomas
Jenice. POE 4/2
Open a door. POE 4/2

Millay, Edna St. Vincent
Autumn chant. YAR 10/2
The concert. POE 5/3
Doubt no more than Oberon. NAT 4/13/0
Keen. CEN 7/3
Lament. CEN 3/1
Mariposa. AIN 5/0
Memory of Cape Cod. RHY 2/3
Mirage. AIN 3/0
Passer mortiuus est. CEN 3/1
Song for "The Lamp and...Bell" YAR 10/2
Song of a second April. AIN 2/0
Sonnet. AIN 4/0
Sonnet. CEN 3/1
Sonnet. NER 8/24/1
Sonnets from an ungrafted tree. HAM 5/3
To a dying man. VAN ?/3
To a poet that died young. NER ?/1
To love impuissant. DIA 3/0
To the Liberty Bell. LIB 10/2

Miller, A. York
The future. MUN 7/2

Miller, Anna
Moods. CAP 10/2

Miller, Dorothy Fortescue
April's awakening. INT 4-6/4
Earth moods. INT 1-3/4
In my old garden. WAV 3/4
The storm dance. INT 1-3/4

Miller, E. E.
The cropper speaks. NAT 2/22/2
Katharine Sherrill. NAT 9/20/2

Miller, Fuller
Sea's promise. AMP 4-5/3

Miller, J. Corson
Abraham Lincoln. BUF 2/12/1
Always I flung you garlands. VOI Win/2
Amor in excelsis. COV 4/3
Aphrodite. FOR 2/0
Architecture. AVE 4/30/1
Aspiration. CAW 3/1
Autumn storm. MAG 10/3
Ave Maria sanctissima. MAG 7/3
Benedict XV. MAG 2/2
Breton love-song. BOT 2/4/0
A bride of Christ. CAW 10/0
Cathedral bells. AVE 11/3/3
Chimera. VOI10-11/3
Christmas carol. SIG 12/1
Combat. AVE10/14/2
Communion. COV 3/4
Companionship. CIT 3/29/4
Compensation. FON11/15/3
Conquerors: Joseph M. Plunkett. MAG 9/0
Consecration. AVE 10/8/1
"Coup de grace." WAN 7/4
The crucified. AVE 3/19/1
Dagonet makes a song for the k. VOI 12/2
Dissolution. LYR 1/4
Dolorosa. AME 4/12/4
Dusk. EXT 8/2
Dusk. ROS 4/1
The enduring. AVE 7/15/2
Ephemerae. FOR 2/1
Evening over the valley. COV 8/1
Evening. BOT 4/27/1
Ex nocte ad lucem aeternam. AVE 1/14/2
Four Japanese love poems. JAP 6/2
The great trees of California. FOR 10/0
Grotesquerie. PEA 5/2
Guenevere. COV 3/4
The harper. WAN 5/4
Harvest-moon. BOT 1/26/1
Heritage. NET 1/2
The home-lane. SHA 2/1
Humpty-Dumpty. NAT 5/9/3
Ideal street. MAG 6/2
Immolation. AME 1/6/3
Immortality. ROS 9/3
In hoc signo. SIG 10/1
In scarlet and gold they come. MAG 5/4
Inaugural. MAG 5/2
Infinitas infinitatis! COV 9/2
The ironworker. INL 1/3
Jewels. FON 6/1/1
Karinna. BOT 4/7/0
The knight-errant. AME 6/11/1
Lady of jewels and song. AVE 4/5/4
The last judgment. ROS 9/1
Let me be remembered! COV 4/1
The little house of love. TEM Aut/1
The lover speaks. SHA 2/1

Madonna de Notre Dame. AVE 11/3/3
Madonna of the moonlit hours. AVE 5/8/0
Madonna of the roses. MAG 7/2
Madonna-Del-Robbia. MAG 6/3
The magic pool. NOM Win/2
Majesty. AME11/26/1
Mater Dolorosa. MAT 3/2
Mater amata. AVE 2/12/1
Maximilian marvelous. NEW 2/8/0
Metamorphosis. COV 9/2
Moon-mist. VOI 12/2
Nocturne. CIT 1923
Obsequies. NEW11/10/1
The old mother. CIH 12/3/1
On a dead sparrow. LYR 10/3
On the birth of a little son. AME 9/17/1
Our Lady of the Poor. AME 7/14/3
Our lady of song. MAG 4/2
Panorama. BOT 2/9/1
Pilgrimage. AVE 4/1/2
Prairie sunset. NET 5/7/3
Premonition. MOT 3/2
The racing pigeon. RAC 4/1
The rainbow. CAW 7/0
Recompense. FOR 4-5/0
Regeneration. FON 6/2
Regina Coeli. MAG 2/2
Remembered love. FOR 6/2
Rendezvous. WAN 2/4
Renunication. AME 6/16/3
Resurrection. MAG 4/2
Return. MEA 12/2
The sassafras man. NEW 9/19/1
Sepulchre. VOI 3-4/4
Sheltered. ROS 5/4
Sometimes, like distant music. VOI Sum/2
Song for love's coming of age. LYR 2/3
Sonnet. LYW 3/4
Sorrow has borne me beauty. AME 6/24/2
Street-lights. LYW 12/3
A sunset on Olivet. SIG 11/1
The super-philosopher. FON 8/15/2
Testament. SIG 1/2
Theodore Roosevelt. FOR 12/1
To Pavlowa in the Bacchanal. BAU 2/2
Transformations. NEW 1/5/0
Twilight. MAG 8/0
Twilight. NEU 3/
Values. ROS 2/1
The victor. ROS 2/0
Vignette. MIN 9-10/3
A wayside shrine. MAG 6/3
Where beauty lives. AME 1/14/2
Widow's weeds. LYR 3/4
Winter woods. AME 2/16/4
The world. CAW 6/0

Miller, Joaquin
The sermon the mount. LAR 8/3
Shadows of Shasta. LAR 9/3
To be. LAR 10/3

Miller, Mabel Northrup
Dreams. LAR 9/3

Miller, Madeline Sweeney
Christmas in the open. CIC12/21/2
June's basket. CIC 6/15/2
My study desk. CIC 3/2/2
To a community Christmas tree. CIC12/20/3

Miller, Mrs. L. A.
Sing like Saadi. LAR 9/3

Miller, Nellie Burget
At timber-line. AMP 3-4/4
The coming rain. LAR 6/3
Compensation. AMP 6/2
Improvisations. GUL 7-8/3
Improvisations. AMP10-11/3
Joy walks in the morning. LYW 11/2
A pagan in church. LYW 5/2
Prophecy. LYW 11/3
The shower. SCR 3/4
"Sir, we would see Jesus." AMP 12/2
Truancy. MID 10/0
Words. LYW 11/2

Miller, Norma
June midnight. LYW 6/3
The sea is like a nun. LYW 7-8/2
Spring tarries long. LYW 2/4
Street lights. LYW 11/2

Mills, Ellen Morrill
The dream immortal. PEG 3/3
Inland. LYW 3/4
Sea shells. LRW 7-8/2
Spring, the herald. LYW 5/2
"To lovers, lingering." AMP 2-3/3

Milner, Elizabeth
The call of the wasted land. GUL 9/3

Mims, Samuel Stewart
Kuros'ty. SCR 8/3
"Lel-lo, Dad." SCR 5/3
Ole black mammy and lil' honey. SCR 5/3

Miniter, Edith
Bureau. POE 10/3
Caen-wood. LAL 3/4
Flanders Field - today. LYW 6/3

Huckleberries. POE 10/3
The lesson. LAL 5/4
Mirage. LAL 1/4
Purple window glass. LYW 12/3

Mishkin, Olga
A dance. CEN 5/1

Mitchell, Bee
Lake in the woods. LAR 12/3
The reward. LAR 4/4

Mitchell, Cyprus R.
Dear hands of Jesus. CIC 3/2/2

Mitchell, Cyrus R.
Hands. CIC 8/23/3

Mitchell, Ruth Comfort
Gaydiang. LYW 4/1
Old bones. NES 12/2/2
Pullman portraits. SCM 4/2
The travel bureau. CEN 8/1
Voyagers. HAM 1/2

Mitchell, Stewart
A character. DIA 8/0
Lorraine. DIA 8/0
Not mellow sunlight. DIA 8/2
A picture. DIA 8/0
Postscript. DIA 8/0
A shrine. DIA 1/2
Tell me, if I had died. DIA 8/2

Mixter, Florence Kilpatrick
Alchemy. POE 8/1
All Soul's Eve. POE 8/1
The bridge. MID 7/1
Chinese epitaph. POE 8/1
A country funeral. MID 11/0
Lullaby. POE 8/1
The marriage of the spruce. MID 7/1
The older wisdom. MID 7/1
A print by Hokusai. BOO 9/1
September. MID 7/1
To a young girl. MID 7/1
Winter landscape. MID 7/1

Mizen, M. Louise
Pines. LAR 9/3
Wanderlust. LAR 10/3

Mombert, Alfred I.
On the stairs leading to my ma. BRO 12/2

Monica, Sister M.
Gold. CAW 10/1

Monro, Harold
City storm. POE 3/0
Fate. POE 2/2
Introspection. POE 3/0
Officers' mess (1916). POE 2/1
One moment only. BRO 12/1
Unknown country. DIA 3/1

Monroe, Harriet
At O'Neill's point-Grand Canal. AMP 7/2
The difference: 1823-1923. POE 1/3
El Greco. POE 3/4
Fra Angelo's Annunciation. POE 3/4
Furer's portrait of himself. POE 3/4
Goya. POE 3/4
In high places. POE 7/2
In the Yellowstone. POE 7/2
Murillo. POE 3/4
On the train. POE 7/2
Rubens. POE 3/4
A song. POE 6/3
Ten years ago. POE 1/4
Their god. POE 3/4
Titian on Charles V... POE 3/4
Utah. POE 7/2
Velazquez. POE 3/4

Montgomery, Elizabeth Shaw
Alternative. VOI 5-6/4

Montgomery, F. L.
At dusk. MUN 7/2

Montgomery, Louise Moss
The delta. CLA 8/3/1
Easter. CLA 4/15/2
To a mocking bird. CLA 7/25/2

Montgomery, Roselle Mercier
Again Mary and Martha. NET 2/20/3
Archytas. NEW12/21/2
The banquet. MUN 10/2
A child speaks. NEW 5/26/3
The circus. NET 6/20/3
Cleopatra. NEW 2/15/3
De huntin' call. NEW10/24/2
Divided. NET12/13/2
Environment. LAD 9/2
Envying Horace. NEW 4/14/3
Every woman. NEW 5/12/3
Fall model, 1922. NET11/18/2
Fulfillment. MUN 1/3
The funny house. NET 3/1/3
God give me eyes. NEW 2/25/3
God loves New England. NEW10/20/2
Hail and farewell. NET 2/27/3
The happy days. NET12/27/2
The hill woman. NEW 9/18/2
The hostelry. NET 9/12/2
I do not know. COV 7/4
I jes' p'tend. NEW12/17/2
In country graveyards. NEW 7/22/3
In reserve. NET 7/19/3
Insatiate. NEW 1/2/3
Islands. MUN 10/2
A late rose. NEU 3/12/3
Life, I am yours. NEW10/30/2
The lovers of sea and land. ARG12/16/2

The loves of Horace. NEW 1/16/3
My place of dreams. NEU 9/13/2
A newspaper poet to a real poe. NEW12/28/2
The next number. ARG 2/21/3
The novice. ARG 4/14/3
On the ruins of a Greek theatr. NEW 1/29/3
On the simple life. NET 8/18/2
Pansies. NET 7/18/3
The poet's prayer to Apollo. NEW11/24/2
Potentiality. NEW11/14/2
Pro patria mori. NEW 9/20/2
Quality. NEW 7/30/3
Red tape. NET 2/21/3
River song. COV 7/3
Rondeau on a rondeau. NET11/29/2
The secret place. NEW 1/21/3
Seek not to know. NEW 5/6/3
Shining towers. NEW 8/1/2
Shylock. NET12/18/2
A sprig of myrtle. ARG 11/4/2
Sunset at Shippan. NEW 7/15/3
To Albius Tibullus. NEW 1/9/3
To Aristius Fuscus. NEW 12/5/2
To Glycera. NET10/17/2
To Lydia grown old. NET 9/19/2
To Lydia in reproach. NEV 8/29/2
To Maecenas. NEW 10/6/2
To Munatius Plancus. NEW 3/2/3
To Pyrrha. NEW 8/27/2
To Virgil. NEW10/15/2
To an angry sweetheart. NEW 8/13/2
To his lyre. NEW 11/6/2
To one in passing. NET 4/14/3
To one who withdraws. NEW 7/22/3
To the dawn man. NET12/18/2
The torch. NEU12/23/2
The traveler. NEU 8/1/2
Triolet on a triolet. NET 12/8/2
Triolet on free verse. NET12/23/2
Ulysses returns. NEW 6/10/3
Villanelle of roads. MUN 7/3
Villanelle on a villanelle. NET 1/17/3
Villanelle. NET 2/7/3
The visitor. NET 5/15/3
Voices in the night. NET 8/30/2
What does it mean to be an Ame. NEW 3/11/3
When-. NEW 2/7/3
Youth will have its way. MUN 2/3

Montrose, Lois Seyster
To Charmian, unborn. CEN 5/3

Montross, Lois
Galleon dawn. LIB 11/1

Moody, Winfield Scott
A rejoinder. SCM 9/1

Moomaw, Benjamin Cline
The perfect art. PAR #2/3

Moore, A. Teresa
Longing. SCR 11/3
Pirates of peace. SCR 11/3
Secure. SCR 11/3

Moore, Dorothea
Age. BOO 9/2

Moore, Edward Roberts
Jesus. CAW 5/0

Moore, Kathleen
Crupert. S4N 12/2

Moore, Marianne
England. DIA 4/0
The labor of Hercules. DIA 12/1
New York. DIA 12/1
Novices. DIA 2/3
People's surroundings. DIA 6/2
Picking and choosing. DIA 4/0

Moore, Merrill
After death years. FUG 4-5/3
Arabian night. FUG 12/2
Autumn noon rain. FUG 12/2
Charleston nights. FUG 10/2
Cumae. FUG 2/4
Dawn honey. FUG 10/2
December in Arnold Wood. FUG 4-5/3
From a conversation... FUG 2/4
Ivan's dog. FUG 2/4
Mrs. Winnie Broaddus. FUG 12/3
Salty bread. FUG 10/2
Seven flower queen. FUG 10/2
Sonnet of American life. FUG 12/3
Sonnets of a rembered summer. FUG 6-7/3
Sonnets to Lucia. FUG 2/4
Story. FUG 12/2

Moore, Oliver C.
The arrogant poet to his lady. MUN 7/2
A country churchyard. MUN 10/2
The drifting year. MUN 5/2
I shall be there. MUN 6/2
Love's treasure-trove. MUN 4/2
A lovers' quarrel. MUN 3/2

Moore, Ruth
Before darkness. GUL 6/3
The old sailor dies. GUL 5/3

Moquin, Elizabeth Spencer
From a tenement. OVM 7/4

Morand, Paul
Echantillon. DIA 9/0

6/3
Our house. AMP 6-7/3
Parson's pleasure. NES 6/10/2
Preliminary instructions... NES 7/30/1
The tavern of the fools. NES 2/19/1

Morrill, Jane
Bathing beach. VOI10-11/3
City spell. WAN 1/4
Girl pedestrians. WAN 10/3
Goblin day. PAR #2/3
More like moonlight. WAN 7/4
Petal time. WAN 4/4
Silently over the grass. WAN 2/4
They who know the flame. WAN 7/4

Morris, Hilda
The scribe. COV 1/4

Morris, John
O lente, lente, currite noctis. MEA 6/1

Morris, Kenneth
Evening over false bay. COV 6/0
The flowers. COV 6/0
A morning in September. COV 6/0
Noon on the hillside. COV 6/0
Pampas-grass. COV 6/0
The rain. COV 6/0

Morris, Lydia
Springtime. COV 12/3
To sea! COV 8/2
Youth. COV 8/2

Morris, Mary Youngs
Autumn leaves. SCR 6/4
Consecration. AMP 12/3
Contrast. SCR 4/4
Design. AMP 3-4/4
Hope. SCR 4/4
My New Year gifts. CTY Win/4
Nature's sequences. SCR 1/4
The one immortal joy. SCR 11/3
Roses. AMP 3-4/4
Sea-sonnets. SCR 4/4
The sheer, steep heights. SCR 11/3
Singing of you. SCR 11/3
Solace. PAR #1/4
Song of love. CTY Spr/4
The songs we sing. PAR #4/4
Three roses. PAR #4/4
The verities. SCR 1/4
Violets. PAR #4/4
Waiting. SCR 3/4
Where the surging sea uncurls. AMP 3-4/4

Morris, Maurice
Iowa. NEU 7/23/2

Morrison, Frances
Last song. POE 12/2
Promises. POE 6/3

Morrison, Ruth St. Clair
April showers. AMP 3-4/4

Morrison, Theodore
Harvard class ode. BOP 6/20/3

Morrow, Elizabeth
Highroad. VOI 3-4/4

Morse, Beatrice L.
Eucalyptus trees. PEG 3/3

Morse, Vera Frances
Lacquered mandarin moments. LYW 10/3

Morsell, Mary
"Oh flaming sword." COV 6/4
This house. VOI10-11/3
Women who have foregone...love. VOI10-11/3

Morton, David
Acquaintance. NAT 3/30/1
After winter. NAT 7/16/4
After your playing. OUT 3/21/3
Alchemies. NAT 3/6/0
Always when there is music. CEN 7/4
Anonymous. OUT 2/14/3
"Astray." VOI 8-9/3
Attendants. EVM 11/0
A certain oak. AIN 2/0
A certain one who died. AIN 1/0
The convict. POE 2/0
Country gossip. OUT11/14/3
Discovery. MEA 3/1
Exit. BOO 1/4
Fever. COV 11/0
Harbor talk. BOO 8/1
Harvests. VOI10-11/3
Here are griefs. BOO 11/2
How one walked in sorrow. MEA 7/3
In an old street. BOO 5/1
In the cemetery. POE 2/0
In time of long heat. VOI Sum/2
Invasion. NER 12/5/3
Jewels. EVM 10/0
Music. HAM 5/2
New sorrow. BOO 9/2
Of two lovers. FUG 2/4
One day in summer. EVM 6/1
One guest. LYW 7-8/3
One lover. OUT10/17/3
Presence. FUG 12/2
Ruins. COV 11/0
Safe. COV 11/0
Scars. MEA 1/4
The school boy reads his Iliad. COV 11/0
Sonnet: fugitives. CEN 2/1
Sonnet: moons know no time. CEN 2/1

Crudellissimus deus. TEM Aut/1

Murphrey, Florence Noon
China asters in an eastern urn. GUL 7-8/3
Evening dress. GUL 7-8/3

Murphy (tr.), Olive Frances
The poet. EME 4/3

Murphy, Charles R.
Advent. POE 8/1
All things flow. VOI 12-1/4
Autumn in the valley. COV 10/0
By the Wissahickon. IND 9/24/1
The corn-field. POE 10/0
Dante - 1921. BOO 9/1
The desert. VOI Win/2
The divine forest. COV 11/0
Fields in spring. COV 3/3
Fields of thought. VOI 8-9/3
The flag. COV 12/1
The hand of the hunter. VOI Spr/3
Humility. POE 8/1
In the making of a house. COV 7/0
Landscape. VOI Win/2
The last labour. VOI 12/2
Mid-day. POE 8/1
A portrait. COV 6/3
Shadow of flesh. COV 3/2
Song for winter. VOI Win/2
Sown. POE 8/1
Spring. POE 8/1
Threnody. COV 7/0
To earth. POE 8/1
To those who despair bravely. COV 4/1
Waves. VOI Win/2
Winter-bound. COV 2/0
Winter. POE 8/1

Murphy, Francis
As might high ladies. LIB 6/2

Murray, Ada Foster
The shadow in the rain. LYR 10/3
The shadow star. LYR 4/4

Murray, Amy
"Against the mountain" MEA 3/1
Looking east at sunrise. MEA 6/1
"So still, so sorrowful" MEA 3/1

Murray, Thomas J.
Villanelle. GRA 5/1

Murtagh, H. J.
The church. GUL 7-8/3

Murtland, Blanche Nevins
Paths. AMP 4-5/3

Muse, Will D.
Saddle leather. LAR 4/4

Musser, Benjamin Francis
Cloistered. MAG 7/3
"Le bon Dieu, qu'il est bon!" MAG 5/2
Love's prayer. MAG 5/2
Mental player. MAG 4/2
Mystical communion. MAG 5/2
A novice on the Lady Poverty. MAGB 8/3

Myatt, Stella L.
Gratitude. CIJ 6/4
"He hid with Christ in God." CIJ 4/4

Myers, Launah
Apache joy-song. SCR 7/4

N.,A.
Out of the dark. POE 6/0

Nance, Berta Hart
Moods. PAR #4/4

Nathan, Robert
At the symphony. NES 3/18/2
Bells. EVM 12/0
For wisdom. REW 7/3
Joan to her father. REW 10/2
Love hath no physic. NAT 7/5/2
Memory. CEN 12/0
A moral emblem of maturity. REW 11/1
Security. REW 5/2
Since she is dead. REW 1/4
When the last word. REW 7/2

Naumburg, Margaret
Country Sunday. DIA 8/3
In Central Park. DIA 8/3

Neely, Emily L. E.
A spring pastel. SOU 7/3

Neff, May T.
Wireless. AMP 6-7/3

Neilson, Caroline
Dawn. COV 6/0

Nelson, Alzire
A negation. POE 2/4
Sequoias. POE 2/4

Nelson, Ethel Davis
Retrospection. GRA 10/2

Nethercot, Arthur H.
At the football game. PAL Sum/3
In chapel. PAL Sum/3
In study hall. PAL Sum/3
In the class room. PAL Sum/3
On the tennis-court. PAL Sum/3
Quintessence. PAL Spr/3
The skeptic. VOI 6-7/3
Sonnetina: spring song. WAV 3/4
Souvenirs d'une nuit d'Attaque. VOI 6-7/3
To Lorado Taft's Figure...Time.

PAR #3/4
Triad. POE 9/2
Trite observations... PAL Sum/3
Ultimate dictation. MEA 2/3

Nevin, Hardwicke
Soissons. SCM 5/0
Wanderlust. SCM 11/1

Newberry (tr.), John Strong
Eternity. POE 9/1
The lament of the soldiers. POE 9/1
The little silent street. POE 9/1
Louis Eleventh, curious man. POE 9/1
The miraculous catch. POE 9/1
The return. POE 9/1

Newberry, John Strong
Against insects. FUG 9/27/2

Newberry, Mary
Ring. AMP 12/2

Newman, A. Evelyn
Mountains are best..heartbreak. LYW 4/4

Newman, Helen L.
The angel of the hidden place. GRA 7/1

Newman, Wheeler F.
The junk. LYW 3/2

Newman, William
Days. PAG10-11/1
To one I know. VOI Spr/2

Newsome, Agnes Mary
Tapestry. AMP 8/2

Newsome, Effie Lee
The bronze legacy. CUU 10/2
Magnificat. CUU 12/2
Sun disk. CUU 6/3

Newton, Mary Leslie
Sestina of the dead mother. LYR 8/3

Nicholl, Louise Townsend
Amber. CEN 4/4
Apples falling. MEA 9/2
Austerity. MEA 3/1
Beauty. POE 10/0
Brown magic. MEA 12/2
Candles burning. MEA 12/1
Communion: New Year's Eve. STE 1/4
Decision. MEA 6/1
Enclosures. NES 6/10/2
Eve. NES 3/4/2
Group. MEA 11/3
Hymn. POE 6/4
In the street. MID 4/0
Initiate. MEA 2/4
The lost phrase. NER 8/9/2
Madison Square. MEA 11/3
Marigold. VOI 5-6/4
The milkman. MEA 3/2
Mural. MEA 6/2
New world. MEA 8/2
Nobody's loot. NES 6/7/4
The old turntable. MEA 12/1
Sleep song. BOO 7/3
Snow mark. MEA 2/3
Sonnet in B. MEA 12/2
Tenuous. VOI10-11/3
Thin rain. MEA 3/2
This blue. CEN 3/4
Timelessness. POE 8/1
Waves. POE 10/0
Wedgwood. VOI 5-6/4

Nichols, Beth Cheney
Dunes. MIN 1-2/4
The heart of a poet. AMP 3-4/4
I am ashamed. AMP 10/2
Spring budding. LYW 6/3
The torch. LYW 12/3

Nichols, J. T.
A hawk's nest. S4N 12/2

Nichols, Robert
The long road. CEN 6/0
The pilgrim. CEN 6/0
Seventeen. YAR 4/0
Song and soul. CEN 1/0
The sprig of time. YAR 1/0

Nicholson, Lilian
The poet comes. STE 5/3

Nickerson, Paul S.
Awe. MEA 3/2
Beauty. COV 4/3
The betrothal. LYW 12/3
Compensation. LYW 12/2
The cup of water. COV 4/3
Dalliance. DOU 10/2
The difference. TEM Aut/1
Dumb. LYW 2/4
Episode from "Faith." COV 4/4
Fancy. VOI Sum/2
Fisherfolk. COV 4/3
Improvisation. NOM Sum/2
Magic. WAV 6/3
Mystery. WAV 6/3
October. EME 12/2
Paradox. COV 4/3
The peace of evening. COV 4/2
Rumor. NOM Sum/2
Rumor. TEM Sum/2
Song. LYR 5/2
Song. VOI Sum/2
Symbols. LYR 7/3
Tragedy. DOU 9/2
The vase of leaves. COV 10/2
Viewpoint. VOI Sum/2
Waiting. COV 4/2
The watcher. WAV 6/3
The way of love. AMP 8/2
The white sin. LYR 7/3

Yearning. COV 7/4

Nielson, Frank
Evening meditation. SCR 5/4

Nietzsche, Friedrich
Star morals. NAT 3/14/3

Noe, Cotton
To a caged canary. STE 5/4

Noguchi, Yone
The boat of Camellia. ALS10-11/3
Economy. DOU 7/4
A farmer. ALS10-11/3
The independence of existence. ALS10-11/3
A No mask of woman. DOU 11/3
A reward for laughter. ALS10-11/3
The sen. ALS10-11/3
To Meredith. DOU 11/3
To Robert Browning. DOU 11/3

Nolan, Charl
For Clair. WAN 1/4
Moon love. WAN 1/4
Tea. GUL 9/3
To her about to wed. PEG 5/3
White flowers. WAN 10/3

Norcross, Elinor L.
Caprice. SCR 3/4
Destiny. WAN 2/4
Fantasie. OVM 5/4
I used to sing. SCR 10/3
A memory. SCR 3/4
Nostalgia. OVM 7/4
Paints. SCR 3/4
Three quatrains. SCR 2/4
To Sister Mary Margaret. SCR 10/3
Tonality. VOI 12-1/4
When I am dead. SCR 2/4

Norman, Hilda Laura
The blind. GRI 2/1
"La course du flambeau." PAG 8-9/1
An old gate. CAP11-12/2
The untried. GRI 6/1

Norris, Geoffrey
Composition No. XIV. NEN 4/6/1
Composition No. XIX. NEN 3/28/1

Norris, W. A.
After snow. COV 2/0

Norris, William A.
Facts. MEA 2/3
Matthew Arnold. FUG 1/3/3
O changing one. POE 7/1
Texas. NAT 6/11/4

North, Charles J.
My own hymn to greater America. NEP 4-5/2

North, Jessica Nelson
Ambush. MEA 9/1
Boatman. POE 8/2
Bogie. POE 8/2
Bulbs. LYW 4/2
The decision. POE 4/3
Dreams. POE 8/2
Exacting. AIN 4/2
Exchange. MEA 7/2
First autumn. POE 8/2
Herbs. MEA 10/2
Hunger Inn. DOU 12/1
In a dance. DIA 3/4
The late guest. ALS 6/2
Lullaby. MEA 9/1
Noli me tangere. DOU 1/4
An old tale. VOI 6-7/3
Once on a time. DOU 3-4/3
The other wind. POE 4/3
A prayer rug. GRI 9/0
A promise. MEA 10/2
Sand. LYW 10/3
The sleeper. POE 8/2
Sonnet. POE 9/3
Suddenly. POE 8/2
To the man who loves twilight. POE 8/2
The wages of sin. POE 11/1
Wheels and wings. LYW 4/3
A young boy. POE 4/3

Norton, Grace Fallow
Armor. DOU 5/3
The burned house. POE 2/0
Domestic harmony. POE 7/4
The fool. POE 7/4
I cannot hear your music. HUE 6/21/4
I shall remember. POE 1/1
Irish blood. COV 3/1
Iron had I. COV 3/1
The miller's youngest daughter. POE 7/3
Misadventure. POE 7/4
Or did you love death? POE 2/0
Shy perfect flower. POE 1/1
Thoughts about stars. HAM 2/2

Norton, Meredith
The little things. LYW 11/3

Norwood, Robert
Philip to Christ. COV 7/1

Nott, Jane Prothero
The poppy. STE 6/3

Novak, Ruthele
A field of golden rod. COV 8/2
The grove. COV 3/2
In a dining car. COV 1/0
Inarticulate. COV 2/1
Moonrise. COV 3/2
Peach blossoms. COV 3/2

Noyes, Alfred
Mountain laurel. YAR 4/0
Sea distances. HAM 10/0

Noyes, Minna B.
Settin' by. LAL 5/4
Nuhn, Ferner R.
How long? CIC 12/6/3
Nye, Jean Palmer
Love's inning. AMP 6/2
The loving heart. SPO 9/28/1
The lumberjack. LAR 12/3
My place. HAR 10/7/1
On the lonesome road. HAR10/14/1
The penitent. AMP 3-4/4
Nyman, Georgia Currier
And autumn passes. LYW 12/3
Child in the rain. WAN 6/4
A man's appraisement. POA 1/2

O'Brien (tr.), Edward Joseph
The offering of Plebs. BRO 2/2
O'Brien, David
An image. CAP11-12/2
O'Brien, Edward
Exit. CEN 3/1
O'Brien, Justin
Madeleine. WAN 4/4
O'Brien, Mary J.
The holy tree. CAW 3/0
O'Brien-Moore, Ainsworth
Odysseus. SCM 12/1
O'Connell, Martin T.
The blind man. CAW 10/0
O'Connor, Armel
Beauty. CAW 2/0
The coward. MAG 2/2
A great little song. MAG 12/1
Jesus. MAG 7/2
The king's caves. MAG 12/1
Le monent infini. CAW 9/2
Realization. MAG 3/2
A saint's portrait. CAW 4/1
The white queen. MAG 2/2
O'Connor, Norreys Jephson
All Hallows. COV 10/2
At a time of promise. COV 1/1
Bells of Erin. COV 3/0
In memoriam (Alan Seeger). VOI Sum/2
The road. COV 3/0
The song without end. COV 3/0
Songs for the beloved. AIN 8/2
The swordsman. COV 3/3
O'Donnell, Charles L.
The mountain. CAW 8/1
Said Alan Seeper unto R.Brooke. SON 1-2/0
Twilight. BOO 3/0
O'Donoghue, Julia
I thank thee, father. MAG 7/2
O'Flannigan, Ivan
Thou. CIV 3/4
O'Hara, Frank
Voyager. WAN 3/4
O'Hara, Joy
My message. OVM 4/4
O'Neil, George
April (a song from the Greek). LYR 4/3
The bather. BOO 8/1
Circe. COV 3/0
The clarion of spring. COV 3/1
The deserted hour. COV 3/1
Events. MEA 9/2
For the golden pipe. VOI10-11/3
For those inland. MEA 9/2
Illusion. MEA 12/1
In a theatre. MEA 10/1
In the Esplanade Des Invalides. MEA 5/3
Inlander. NER 5/4
Lullaby. NER 7/23/4
The magicians. LYR 10/2
Morning. MEA 7/3
The mother. MEA 10/1
Narrative. LYR 12/2
Night takes the winter forest. MEA 3/1
No son of Adam. NER 4/16/4
Nostalgia. VOI 12/2
O be not silent. MEA 7/3
Parable of the orchard. LYR 3/3
Passers-by. MEA 10/1
Refuge. MEA 5/3
Reminders. BOO 5/1
Research. DOU 11/2
Song of the barren year. MEA 5/3
Song of the wanderlust. CEN 4/0
South wind. MEA 3/1
Symbol. VOI 12/2
Ten songs by the dead singer i. MEA 1/3
Three poems: leave taking. COV 3/1
Tourists' day. VOI10-11/3
Two in the twilight orchard. MEA 7/4
Walking in an inland city. DOU 8/2
Where it is winter. MEA 2/2
The white rooster. NES 4/19/4
Youth in mid-summer. COV 7/0
O'Neil, Sheila
Possession. PAG 12/1
The price. MAG 4/2
Sewing song. MAG 7/3
The test. COV 1/0
To one afar. PAG 4-5/0

O'Neill, Genevieve D.
Despair. COV 6/0
O'Neill, Mary J.
All in all. SON 7-8/0
Cork. SON 3-4/1
Cowardice. SON 3-4/1
Lament. SON 7-8/0
Lovers. SON 7-8/0
Outlasting. SON 9-10/0
Paradox. SON 7-8/0
Sub ferula. SON 3-4/1
O'Neill, Natolia Therese
A Japanese fan. CUV 11/3
John Barrymore. CUV 11/3
O'Riordan, Conal
My little boy's New Yr prayer. ALS 2/1
O'Seasnain, Brian Padraic
Alone. CAW 7/1
Behind the bars. CAW 1/2
Vision. CAW 3/2
O'Shea, Patrick
Enchantment. MAC 6/3
O'Sheel, Shaemas
"Mine eyes are blurred with ga. LYR 3/3
One glorious daughter of the s. LYR 10/2
Oafer, L.
The horses of hell. FUG 6/2
Oakes, Katharine Sawin
Dear echoes. GRA 5/2
October. GRA 10/1
Oaks, Gladys
Compensation. NES 5/10/4
Dance, little demon. BOO 9/2
Interior. LIB 9/2
A rebel grows old. LIB 8/2
Seventeen. LIB 8/2
Six lines about Peter. VOI10-11/3
Stoic. NOM Sum/3
Summary. VOI10-11/3
Your gifts. LIB 10/1
Odhner, Madefrey
Ashes. OVM 2/4
Old, Ida Crawford
Out of the past. AMP10-11/3
Oliver, Jenkins
Gibraltars. BOT 2/13/4
Hill. BOT 2/17/4
A ship comes in. CIM 1/14/4
Oliver, R. Blair
The diurnal trinity. LAR 2/4
Perhaps. LAR 3/4
Oliver, Wade
At the shaking of the dawn. POE 1/3
Black water. POE 1/3
Broken stars. COV 7/0
Dedication. COV 4/2
Dud. PAL Sum/3
Escape. COV 7/3
The geese fly south. COV 10/1
How how shall I know thee? COV 4/2
I have known laughter. COV 4/2
In times of fatness. PAL Sum/3
Kinship. COV 4/2
Lean. MEA 11/3
Moon-wane. PAL Sum/3
The name. COV 7/0
Patter. POE 1/3
Presage. COV 6/1
Requiem. POE 2/1
Solace. COV 10/1
Sons of Adam. POE 1/3
Stone house. COV 7/3
Vigil. POE 2/1
"Wanderer." COV 4/2
What suns? What moons? POE 1/3
When I consider. COV 6/1
Who'll ride with me? POE 1/3
Witch of the wood. COV 6/1
Wood-fire. COV 6/1
Olsen, Charles O.
My lady's hand. LAR 10/3
Rain. LAR 2/4
Olson, Elizabeth T.
April wine. LAR 3/4
Improvidence. LAR 3/4
Invitation. LAR 8/3
On Mount Hood. LAR 3/4
Olson, Ruth Lees
Colorado in October. AMP10-11/3
Olson, Ted
The believer. LYW 10/1
Ephemera. WAN 3/4
Finale. LYW 10/1
For verse makers. COV 6/3
Fountains. LYR 8/3
Futility. COV 8/2
It is not wise. WAN 7/4
Masquerade. WAN 1/4
Pursuit. LYW 12/1
Renegade. WAN 10/3
Symbol. COV 6/0
Onions, Willia, Ellwell
Thwarted. LYW 7-8/2
Onions, William Ellwell
The harpist. LYW 4/4
Wind. LYW 12/3
Oppenheim, Bertha
The hermit thrush. CTY Spr/2
Legend of the mother unconsole. CTY Win/3
March, the promise. CTY Spr/3
Portulaca. CTY Sum/3
Sanctuary. CTY Aut/2
Orcutt, Grace Stuart

I want to sing. GRA 4/1
Ordway, June MacMillan
The lesson. LAR 11/3
Orr, Hugh Robert
As God is to me. CIC 3/15/3
Litany of night. CIC 2/15/3
Song of wonders. CIC 6/28/3
There came a song. CIC 1/11/3
Until today. CIC 1/11/3
Orr, Mabel Guinan
The heavens declare his glory. LYW 7-8/2
Osborn, Elizabeth
Barn dance. CTY Win/3
The dahlia. CTY Sum/3
Dreaming. WAV 12/2
Dusk. CTY Spr/2
Magic. CTY Spr/2
The mower. CTY Spr/3
Old books. AMP 4-5/3
The old cow. CTY Spr/3
Old witch. CTY Win/3
The rose jar. PAG 8-9/1
Sachet. CTY Win/2
Spinsterhood. PAG10-11/1
Surmise. WAV 12/2
Osborne, Edith D.
Fever. CTY Aut/2
The matinee girl. LYW 9/2
A pagan's rosary. LYW 4/4
The scrubwoman. LYW 9/2
Osborne, Elizabeth
From Horace. WAV 3/4
Osborne, Maude Freeman
April. LAR 4/4
Compensatiop. SCR 6/4
The little lights. SCR 3/4
Spring sorrow. SCR 6/4
Winter. SCR 2/4
Osgood, Ernest Earle
The church gates. AMP 10/2
Ostenso, Martha
Before storm. MEA 3/4
Bethrothal. VOI 5-6/4
The farmer's wife. MEA 3/4
First show. NES12/16/2
In the pool. MEA 5/4
King. MEA 5/4
On a stile. COV 8/3
Romance. VOI 5-6/4
So I say. VOI 5-6/4
Solitude. POE 6/4
The unicorn & the hippogrif. MEA 3/4
Waste-land. POE 6/4
"What need have I?" COV 8/3
Otis, Helen Chicester
"The thing called dying." LYR 8/3
Owre, Perl Riley
The tramp. LAR 4/4

Packard, Doris
Disturbed. LYW Spr/2
The intruder. LYW 5/4
Prisoner. VOI Win/2
Thievery. LYW 1/2
The tryst. LYW 7-8/2
Westward crawling trains. VOI 7-8/3
Packard, Marjorie
The homeland. GRA 12/1
Paddock, Paul R.
Steam shovel: Chicago. CAP 1-2/3
Page, Dorothy
Autumn. LYW 9/1
Bewilderment. COV 9/1
The brat. COV 9/2
Chanson triste. COV 9/2
Comedia. COV 5/3
Echo. PEG 5/3
Encounter. PEG 1/3
First rain. COV 10/3
Hill-tides. WAN 9/3
In greeting. COV 5/3
La naive. LYW 4/3
One day. PEG 3/3
Song (for B.). PEG 1/3
Whimsy. LYW 2/2
Page, Jessie Allen
Yellow. AMP 6-7/3
Page, Paula
My call. LOS 5/10/4
Paine, Albert Bigelow
The coming race. HAM 3/3
Thaw. HAM 2/0
Paine, Jean
A worshipper. LYW 6/3
Youth. LYW 9/3
Paisley, Dorothy C.
Rest. CIJ 2/4
Pakter, Paul D.
Mood. PAG 12/1
Palazzeschi, Aldo
Chilono. BRO 12/1
Rio Bo. BRO 12/1
Palmer, Jean
Fugitive. WAN 11/3
Palmer, Lillian Pray
Reflections. AMP 2-3/3
Paradise, Viola
After the season's first ride. FOR 6/4
Pity. DIA 9/1
Parker, Arlita Dodge
Grey dawns. VOI Sum/2

Wayfaring. MOR 1/3
White windows. VOI Spr/3

Parker, Helen Adams
The bird's message. GRA 4/2
Early morning. GRA 11/0
Extinctus amabitur iden. GRA 11/2
March. GRA 3/2
Pine tree song. GRA 9/2
Rain in April. GRA 4/1

Parker, Hetty C.
The adventures of Mollie Cule. PAG 12/1

Parker, Hetty Cattell
Sensorial sketches of women. PAG 4-5/0

Parlett, Ernest E.
To Edgar Allen Poe. CIV 7-8/4

Parmenter, Catherine
The voice of the wilderness. LYW 6/2

Parmeter, Catherine
The first crocus. LYW 3/4

Parrish, Emma Kenyon
Joy. COV 5/0

Parsons, Eugene
The hermit. LYW 5/3
The wider patriotism. AMP10-11/3

Parsons, Mabel Holmes
Andante. STE 3/3
For love of the road. AMP 2/2
Forest love song. COV 10/2

Partridge, Mary E.
Summer time. GRA 7/2
Sunapee Lake. GRA 9/2

Patterson (tr.), Antoinette DC
The siesta. COV 11/0

Patterson, Antoinette De C.
Challenged. LYW 1/2
A dream poem. POE 7/4
Folk song - from the Danish. POE 8/1
A garden by the sea. COV 6/3
In Venice - long ago. LYW 5/2
In a moonlit garden. COV 11/0
In old Siena. LYW 12/3
Judgments of history. LYW 1/2
Lilies of the valley. COV 6/2
Lucrezia Borgia's last letter. POE 8/1
The madician. LYW 1/2
Moonlight in the birch wood. COV 6/0
Notre Dame D'Afrique (Algiers). AMP 6-7/3
On the visit of a...tanager. COV 5/4
Persistent errors. LYW 4/3
The response. COV 6/0
The seeker. POE 10/2
The sunset hills. LYW 9/3

Patterson, Dorothy
Telegraph Hill. LYW 3/2

Patterson, J. L.
The leaves in autumn. COV 12/2
We never can know. LAR 2/3

Patterson, Kathleen
Tumble-weed ladies. LAR 11/3

Patterson, T. C.
Oppression. YAR 3/4
Ships that pass. YAR 6/4

Patterson, T. M.
Joachim Miller. LAR 9/3

Patterson, Vernon
Boon Ruang. PAL Sum/3
Gypsy. MEA 2/4
Road to Romany. OVM 4/4
Songs from Siam. PAL Sum/3
To a lady. PAL Sum/3
Yontaralucksua. PAL Sum/3

Patterson-Guyol, Louise
Goddess-moon. GRA 10/1
The gracious lover. GRA 12/1
Sonnet. GRA 12/1
To a cynic. GRA 11/1

Pava, Malcolm
Beauty triumphant. HEA 5/4
Blodwen. HEA 7/4
Defeat. HEA 2/4
The enchanted. HEA 4/4
Old gods. HEA 6/4

Payne, Dewey
Way out west. LAR 11/3

Peabody, Emily Welles
Christmas trees in the forest. AMP 12/2

Peace, Arthur Wallace
A day from paradise. WOW 1/0

Peach, Arthur Wallace
Answered. MUN 2/2
Fable. CIC 9/27/3

Peacock, Marion
Dull. CTY Spr/2
Now. CTY Spr/3
Part of an autumn letter. CTY Win/3
A study in yellow. CTY Aut/2
The woods are brown. CTY Win/2

Pearsall II, Robert
In the shadows. LAL 5/4

Pearson, Charles C.
Betty. CTY Spr/4

Pearson, Ruth R.
The "barrier." CUU 1/3

Pease, Josephine Van Dolzen
Any time, O Lord. LYW 12/2
A carol of the way. LYW 4/3
The Catskills. CAP 10/2
Convenience. PAR #4/4

Natale. LYW 12/3
Noel. LYW 12/3
Sunsets. LYW 7-8/2
White birches. LYW 4/3

Peattie, Elia W.
Lanier in the valley. SCM 11/2

Peattie, Louise Redfield
Susan Lou. POE 7/4

Peck, Edla Park
Identity. AMP10-11/3
The old house. SCR 11/3
Recognition. SCR 1/4
Spectre. SCR 11/3
Why? SCR 4/4

Peck, Samuel Minturn
Before the mirror at three... BOT 2/13/2

Peel, Maud
Chloe's quest. LYW 11/2

Peet, Jeania
Suppose love waited? OVM 4/4

Pelee, Lillian Sutton
Shirley poppies. LYW 4/2

Pelly, Thomas Minor
Old wounds. AMP 12/3

Pendray, G. Edward
A windy day. LAR 3/4

Penman, Harriet Clay
Old wives. COV 10/0

Penman, Satella Jaques
Bountiful shadow time. AMP 5-6/4
The coming of morning. AMP 3-4/4
The great musician. AMP 2-3/3
Tribute to Dr. H.J. Stewart. AMP 5-6/4

Pennant, Antoinette West
Meed. HAM 3/0

Penny, Henrietta G.
The north wind. LYW 12/3

Percy, William Alexander
Adventure. COV 5/0
Advice in springtime. COV 4/3
After hearing music. COV 6/4
Autumunal. SCM 3/0
Beth Marie. DOU 5/2
A Brittany love song. BOO 5/1
A burnished calm. COV 2/2
Calypso to Ulysses. WAV 3/4
A canticle. SCM 8/2
The clue not found. LYW 2/3
Courage. COV 2/1
Delight. POM 1922
The delta autumn. YAR 10/2
Dirge. DOU 11/3
A ditty. EME 5/4
Exchange. NEN 3/28/1
Fanfare. LYR 3/2
Farmers. COV 5/0
For a word. YAR 7/3
Four Capri impromptus. MEA 2/3
A fragment. LYW 10/3
French blue. COV 4/3
The green bird seeth Iseult. COV 7/2
His peace. COV 7/1
The holy women. COV 7/1
The honey-locusts. STE 10/2
Hyme of the Magdalene. COV 7/1
In the cold, bright wind. COV 7/2
In the delta. NOA 3/1
Insomnia. POR 1-2/4
A mad maid's song. COV 4/3
A memory. COV 2/2
October. COV 10/1
One path. COV 2/2
One way to be popular. DOU 6/1
The pilgrims of the upland... COV 7/2
A prayer answered. DOU 6/1
Rain patter. MEA 12/3
Safe secrets. FUG 12/2
She grieves in the dusk. VOI Sum/2
Sight and sound. LYR 12/1
Siren song. COV 1/4
Song. PAG 6-7/1
Tempermental. DOU 6/1
Three spirituals. COV 7/1
To one dying. SEW10-12/1
A true sport. DOU 6/1
The unloved to his beloved. BOO 6/2
The water oaks. LYW 5/3
Winds of winter. COV 1/3
Youth. LYR 7/2

Peret, Benjamin
Le quart d'une vie. LIR A-W/3

Perham, Shaila
If: to Isobel Luke. AMP 8/2

Perkins, Lucy W.
At twilight. GRA 2/2

Perkins, William T.
The circuit rider. LAR 4/4

Perry, Albertus
Time. SCR 5/3

Perry, H. G.
Friends. SCR 11/3

Perry, Lilla Cabot
The cup. HAM 5/0
Forgive me not! HAM 5/0
How does a woman love? COV 9/1
Impromptu. COV 1/4
The rose. HAM 5/0

Perry, Octavia
Duty. SCR 8/3
September. SCR 10/3

Perryberry, John

Life and love. SCR 5/3
Peter, Lily
Chrysanthemums. AMP Aut/1
Peter, Uno Gwyn
A dream. SCR 11/2
Hither thither. SCR 12/2
My dearest. SCR 3/3
My pen. SCR 12/2
Thy love. SCR 3/3
Peterkin, Julia M.
Advice. POE 11/3
Boy-chillen. POE 11/3
Gifts. POE 11/3
Greed of the ground. POE 11/3
Green Thursday. POE 11/3
Men. POE 11/3
Prayer...lang syne plantation. POE 11/3
Two kinds of love. POE 11/3
Warning. POE 11/3
The wind. POE 11/3
Peters, Donald S.
Beasts. COV 8/0
Peterson, Ames
Autumn. LYW 9/3
Discovery. PAL Spr/3
The last song. LYW 12/2
Old gardens. LYW 2/2
Vancouver barracks. LYW 11/3
Peterson, Flora Rice
Triolet. AMP 2-3/3
Peterson, Frederick
"The House of Coradine." FUG 4/11/3
Three wise men of the east. NAT 6/1/1
The winter garden. NAT 1/17/0
Petgen, Dorothy
Vix matris. POE 6/3
Petri, Lori
Futility. LAR 6/3
Thunder. LAR 6/3
Travail. LAR 2/4
A wife. LAR 2/4
Peyton, John R. C.
Geyser. POE 11/1
The lake and I. COV 2/0
Shooting star. COV 2/0
Three men. COV 6/3
Three riders. COV 3/1
Time. COV 2/0
Wolves. COV 2/0
Peyton, Mary W.
Farmer's wife. AMP 4-5/3
Morning in October. AMP 10/2
Pfeiffer, Edward H.
At a window. COV 11/1
Broadway. LYW 11/2
Caliban aspiring. LYW 10/1
Confesseth the image-breaker. COV 3/2
The idol. NOA 7/2
In a wood. LYW 5/2
July. LYW 7-8/2
Late love. AMP 2/2
Life. NAT 4/4/3
Long days. IND 2/4/2
The mirror. COV 3/2
Ninon d'Enclos. NES 9/10/1
Revelation. COV 3/2
She dreams of autumn. LYW 11/1
The soul speaks. STE 3/4
The sower. MEA 6/2
A woman's memory. COV 3/2
Phares, Earle
Familiarity. COV 8/0
Philbrook, Helen Mowe
The reckoning. GRA 10/1
The turning of the tide. GRA 3/2
Phillips, Cecile
Equality. S4N 12/2
Phillips, Charles
The silver maple. CAW 9/0
Phillips, Harriet Duff
"Baby mine." AMP 2/2
Phillips, Mabel
Cancion. CTY Spr/4
Comrades. LAR 2/4
Nomads. AMP 2-3/3
Perfumes. LOS 5/10/4
Pioneers. LAR 4/4
To a tree. AMP 10/2
Phillips, Marie Tello
Albert to Hortense. AMP Aut/1
Come to Bethlehem. AMP 12/3
The fragrance of a lily. AMP 3-4/4
It was a dream. AMP 6-7/3
A little while. AMP Aut/1
My own. AMP 6-7/3
On the mountain-top alone. AMP 10/2
Soul to soul. AMP 3-4/4
Watch with me. AMP 2/2
The weary workers of the world. AMP 12/2
Phillpots, Eden
The puddle. SCM 9/0
Philora
Fugitive unbound. FUG 6/2
Phinney, Leslie H.
Autumn song. CTY Aut/2
A country idyl. CTY Spr/2
The elfin chorus. CTY Spr/3
Her smile. CTY Win/3
The hired man's spring song. CTY Spr/4
Lilacs. CTY Spr/2
A springtime reverie. CTY Spr/3

Sweet lavender. CTY Sum/3
Work-a-day dreams. CTY Sum/2

Phllips, Mabel W.
Calcutta. LYW 5/2

Pickens, William
Up sons of freedom. MES 1/4

Pickerill, Edward
Sixteen. POE 11/2

Pickthall, Marjorie L. C.
Dedication for a book of verse. CEN 1/3

Pierso, Jane A.
Dissonance. AMP 2/2
Unchanged. AMP Aut/1

Piety, C. R.
My world. CIC 9/20/3

Pike, Mary E.
Wind songs. AMP 8/2

Pillsbury, Dorothy Pinckney
Camp fires. LYW 10/3
Coastwise hills. LYW 3/2
In the High Sierras. LYW 10/3
In the desert. LYW 10/3
On a lonely headland. LYW 10/3
Voices. LYW 7-8/2

Pinch, Esther
In the park. GUL 5/3
November day. GUL 6/3

Pinckney, Josephine
After winter. REW 1/4
Dead poet. REW 7/4
Evening-Whooping Island. COV 7/4
The harbor. COV 5/3
Idealist. REW 7/3
In the barn. POE 7/1
The milk-boat. POM 1922
The outcast. POE 7/1
Spring makes me wonder. POE 4/2
Strange. POE 7/1
Swamp lilies. POE 7/1

Pindar
Odes, sels.. COV 9/3

Pinder, Florence Dickenson
Forgotten. LYR 7/2
His flowers. FOR 4/2
Marsh pools. POE 4/2
Sea marsh. POE 4/2
Shallows. POE 4/2
Sonnets. COV 3/2
Wind of April. POB Spr/2

Pinder, Frances Dickenson
Answer. COV 12/2
As a bird. AMP 12/3
Barter. POM 1922
Checkers. LIF10/19/2
Flotsam. LYR 9/3
Frost. POE 2/3
I am the sea's. COV 6/1
Leaves. AMP 12/3
Lilacs. AMP 12/3
Magic casements. NER 8/11/0
Release. REW 1/3
Sea music. LYR 9/3
The secret. COV 6/1
Storm in the hills. MEA 2/3
To love. NOA 10/2
The voyagers. COV 10/3

Pinifer, Alice
The wind. COV 5/0

Pinney, Delia Delight
Jaquina sings. LAR 3/4

Piper, Edwin Ford
Balm. MEA 10/1
Bindelstiff. POE 1/0
The debt. POE 3/1
Home. POE 3/1
In the potato field. MID 4/1
The line fence. POE 10/2
Low voices. COV 4/3
March wind. POE 3/1
Old man winter. MEA 10/1
Quarryman's joy. MEA 10/1
Sweetgrass range. POE 1/0
Under roof. MEA 10/1
Whispering often. POE 3/1
Whoa, Zebe, whoa. POE 1/0

Piper, Margaret Rebecca
Spring is on her way. COV 5/1

Pippen, Sallie Macon Garland
My heart..always a child-heart. AMP 8-9/3

Platt, Charles D.
Heart of God. CTY Win/2
Must friends be faultless. CTY Sum/3
Phyllis of the highlands. CTY Spr/3
Pig philosophy. CTY S-A/1
A song of New Jersey. CTY Aut/2
We stand. CTY Spr/2
When women think. CTY Sum/2
Winters in New Jersey. CTY Win/3

Plotnik, Eva Helen
Sonnet. UNV 7/2

Po Chu-yi
A song of the palace. FUG 2/4

Poele, Romanie Van De
Dawn in a hospital. LAL 5/4

Poindexter, Fielding L.
Girl at the gate. CIV 5-6/4

Poland, Joseph Franklin
Post office sketches. LYW 11/3

Polen, George P.
Sonnet to-. POA 1/2

Pollitt, Josephine
Jennie. POE 3/4
Off to college. MEA 3/4
President emeritus. POE 1/4

Pollock, Lillian Irvine
Fraternity. AMP10-11/3
Pool, Ethel
Bedtime on a Kentish farm. CTY S-A/1
Poole, Fanny Runnells
At peace beneath blue skies. GRA 7/1
Canoeing on Granite Lake. GRA 10/1
From the trail. GRA 7/1
Lodestars. GRA 7/2
The morning cometh. GRA 12/0
A talisman. STE 4/3
Poole, Louella C.
Beyond the sunset skies. BOT11/30/1
Poole, Peter
Gifts. AMP 6/2
Night riding. AMP Aut/1
Poor, William G.
The daughter of the dawn. CON 5/17/3
Poore, C. G.
Cyriadis. YAR 4/4
The last harbour. YAR 2/4
Quatrains. YAR 10/3
Viaticum: XIV century, Italy. YAR 12/3
Poore, Dudley
Black wind. DIA 9/2
For you, conquerors. DIA 9/2
Marigold pendulum. DIA 4/3
Poem. DIA 7/3
Stunned by the August sun... DIA 9/2
They ride through the olive... DIA 10/0
Three canticles... DIA 9/1
Was it Marouf who found...? DIA 9/2
Who is it waves to you...? DIA 9/2
Pope, Katharine
Wild lilacs in California. LYW 4/3
Porcher, Mary F. Wickham
Afterthought. COV 1/4
Capriole. COV 1/4
Solitude. MAC 5/3
Porcher, Mary F. W.
Song of youth. COV 5/3
Porcher, Mary F. Wickham
Miracle. COV 1/4
Porter, Anna
At the zoo. LYW 7-8/2
Far Niente. LYW 4/1
Haunt. LYW 4/1
Moon shadow. LYW 4/3
On the dunes. LYW 7-8/2
A Sierra juniper. LYW 7-8/2
The voice. LYW 4/1
Porter, Katherine Anne
Fiesta de Santiago. MEA 1/4
In Tepozotlan. MEA 1/4
Two songs from Mexico. MEA 1/4
Porter, Laura Spencer
Magic. HAM 11/1
Show me the gates of morning. HAM 4/2
Porter, Ruth Stephens
"O, what would you do, little. AMP 6-7/3
Potamkin, Harry Alan
Bassoon. WAV 12/2
Malachi. WAV 12/2
Mercutio. DOU 7/2
Potter, Jeanne Oldfield
Alien. AMP 6-7/3
Potter, William Paris
The last reveille. AMP 2/2
Nature's lure. NEP 4-5/2
Potts, John H. Lowden
Molokai. CAW 6/1
Pound (trs.), Ezra
Strophes. DIA 11/1
Pound, Ezra
Eighth canto. DIA 5/2
The fourth canto. DIA 6/0
Ode pour l'election... DIA 9/0
Three cantos. DIA 8/1
Yeux glanques. DIA 9/0
Powell, Frank E.
Sunset in the mountains. AMP 8/2
Powell, Julia
Gifts. LYW 12/3
Wild weather. LYW 12/3
Powers, Charles J.
A prayer upon the sea. CAW 3/0
Powers, Helen
Mary Magdalene. CIC 6/14/3
Powers, Jessica
Dreams of you. AMP 3-4/4
Powers, Lilian Amy
The little winds of April. OVM 6/4
Powys, John Cowper
Lullaby. DIA 5/4
The riddle. POE 6/0
Prall, Dorothea
Reticence. COV 5/0
Pratt, Alice Day
The rider. LAR 11/3
Pratt, Harry Noyes
Beloved. LYW 12/2
A blackbird calling. LYW 4/4
Contentment. UNV 7/4
Dreams. OVM 5/4
The embarcadero. LYW 7-8/2

Enduring. WAN 8/3
Eternity. OVM 6/4
The eucalyptus. OVM 7/4
The gardener. LYW 4/2
The gypsy heart. STE 3/3
Gypsying in Junetime. CTY Sum/2
The helmsman. LYW 3/4
Journey's end. PEG 5/3
Lord of the woods. CTY Win/3
Maya. AMP 5-6/4
Mid-March. OVM 3/4
Old songs for new. AMP 5-6/4
The shadow trail. LYW 7-8/2
The stars. NEN 4/6/1
The summit. OVM 5/3
The wood of Tara. LYW 9/3
Pray, Frances Mary
Alone. GRA 11/0
Preble, Cora M.
The home. POA 1/2
Prendergast, Alice M.
The Easter miracle. MAG 4/2
Night. MAG 2/2
The spirit wind. MAG 12/1
Vision. MAG 12/1
Prescott, Elinor Manning
The swallow. LYW 6/3
When life is done. AMP 5-6/4
Prescott, Elizabeth D.
Grief. SCR 4/4
Her letter. CIV 7-8/4
The odor filled the room. AMP10-11/3
The opal-for October. AMP10-11/3
Trapped. LYW 3/4
Pressfield, Harry
No sea. CIC 11/2/2
Preston, Elizabeth D.
The sky-lark. STE 6/3
Preston, Eugene D.
In the Midi. AMP 2/2
Noel. AMP 12/2
Preston, Harold P.
An old clerk. ALS 3/2
Report. NOM Sum/2
Preston, Jane F.
Frail joys. REW 4/2
Preston, Keith
Dawn: a pastoral. BOO 11/3
Magazine anthology. BOO 1/4
The mesh. STE 1/4
Price, Daisy Conway
A follower. CIC 7/24/4
"O slow of heart." AMP 6/2
Outside. CIC 5/1/4
Worship. CIC12/13/3
Price, Ruth Clay
Butterfly etudes. CAP11-12/2
Cinquains, from a California g. AMP 2-3/3
Elizabeth. ALS 2-3/3
Hokku. LYW 11/3
Interludes. LYW 1/2
Prosartes. PEG 5/3
Revealed. NOM Win/2
Sea-clan. MIN 9-10/3
Sea-spell. AMP 10/2
The wild-cat oil well. PEG 3/3
Wood notes. LYR 4/2
Price, Thomas Evelyn
Leaven of truth. CIJ 10/3
Price, William James
The caged bird. SCR 10/3
The editor writes an interlude. INT 4-6/4
Egyptian flowers. INT 4-6/4
A few figs and thistles. INT 4-6/4
A fisherman's kryielle. INT 4-6/4
The growing of an oak. CTY Win/4
Hark! the voice of angels. CTY Spr/3
In actu. SCR 11/3
John Harlan. STE 9/3
Memory. CTY Aut/2
The quadroon. SCR 10/3
Retribution. LAL 5/4
Shattered cities. AMP 12/2
The song's mission. INT 4-6/4
Spring's awakening. INT 4-6/4
The time for lovers. INT 4-6/4
Via Crucis. INT 4-6/4
Prideaux, Rolla
Point Loma. LYW 3/2
Prideaux, Tom
The cynic. LIC 12/2
Fads. LIC 1/3
From a minaret. LIC 12/1
The opium eater. LIC 1/3
Prim, Roger
Destitution raiseth her voice. FUG 6/2
Epitaph. FUG 6/2
Necrological. FUG 6/2
The sure heart. FUG 6/2
Probst, Leetha Journey
Orientale. LAR 3/4
Proudfoot, Andrea
Imagination and travel. LAR 12/3
The orchard. LAR 9/3
To a departed father. LAR 2/3
Provines, Mary Virginia
The chalice of the gods. LAR 8/3
The silver river. LAR 5/3
Provost, Marie Louise

But not the sea! SCM 8/0
Prudden, Helen Danforth
Dawn. COV 5/4
Happiness. COV 3/3
Herbs. COV 3/3
Spring is a beautiful woman. COV 5/4
Pruesrer, Sara V.
Wild rose hips. AMP 12/2
Pugh, Louise K.
Day-dawn-dusk. GRA 12/1
Pulsifer, Harold Trowbridge
The duel. OUT 6/28/2
Ghosts. SCM 10/3
The harvest of time. NER 2/7/3
Haven. OUT 9/14/1
Home hunger. OUT 10/5/1
"I accept" OUT 6/1/1
Thoughts upon a walk... OUT 11/9/1
The waters of Bethesda. ATM 6/2
Purdy, Charles McMorris
Dreams. BOO 6/1
Purington, D. V.
Yesterday. CAP 10/2
Purnell, Idella
Afternoon song. LYW 5/2
And never look back. AMP 4-5/3
The beauty-circle. LYW 12/2
Biography. POE 8/3
Closed doors. POE 2/4
Eve. POE 2/4
Evening song. LYW 5/2
The horseman. LYR 2/4
Image. LYR 11/3
Imperial Valley. LYW 10/2
In shorthand. VOI Aut/2
Life. POE 2/4
Music. LYW 12/3
Noon song. LYW 6/3
Peace. SCR 3/3
Repenting. LYW 3/4
A song for sorrow. VOI Aut/2
Stenography. VOI 5-6/4
This day. POE 2/4
To a Pittsburgh poet. STE 1/4
Tonala besieged. POE 2/4
Two men. VOI 5-6/4
The wall. POE 2/4
Weather. VOI Aut/2
Winter. NOM Sum/3
Putnam, F. S.
His rendezvous. COV 8/0
Plums. MID 9-10/1
Presage. POE 1/1
To remember. MID 9-10/1
The wild crab-apple tree. MID 9-10/1
Putnam, H. Phelps
A lost world. ATM 6/3
On a college commencement. NER 6/6/3
Putnam, Sam
Architectonics. MOR 1/3
Cock-sure. POE 10/2
The kiss. CAP11-12/2
A sea-piece. CAP11-12/2
Putnam, Samuel
Autumn. PAR #1/4
Sacrilegious exhortation. NOM Aut/3
Two nuns in a city street. NOM Aut/3

Queerman, Joe
About ready to die. CTY Spr/3
For a lawyer. CTY Win/3
Steers. CTY S-A/1
Quesenberry, Dorothy L.
Consequences. INT 1-3//4
His majesty-Lil Ting. INT 1-3//4
Remembrances. INT 4-6/4
Ships that pass. INT 4-6/4
Quick, Dorothy
Ave Maria. PAR #4/4
Balances. PAR #4/4
The combat. PAR #1/4
The dancer. PAR #1/4
O lover of mine. PAR #1/4
Sympathy. PAR #4/4
Quimby, Mary Abbott
The better way. NEP 4-5/2
Innocent magic. NEP 4-5/2
Quinn, John J.
The bluebonnet. SCR 7/4
Quinter, George
Birds. COV 2/2
Late November. GRA 11/2
Vignette. PAG10-11/1
Quirk, Charles J.
Autumnal soliloquy. MAG 12/1
The battlefield. NOM Sum/3
Clouds seen in a summer sky. CAW 8/2
Daybreak in the city. LYW 1/3
The first Christmas carol. CAW 12/0
Grand Coteau Louisiana. LYW 1/3
The graves of Keats and Shelle. PEG 7/3
Inconsequential. LYR 3/2
A little boy questions... CAW 5/2
The lovers. CAW 12/1
My mother. CAW 11/1
Our lady of Oxford. CAW 10/2

Pastel (evening). CAW 8/1
The presentation. CAW 2/1
A promise of spring. MAG 4/2
Shelley. LYW 8/2
The sleeping beauty. CAW 4/1
The Southern Cross. LYW 1/3
Souvenance de Louvain. AMP Aut/1
Unseen! CAW 2/2
Upon discovering a rose... CAW 7/0

R.,T.
Conquest. S4N 12/2
R.,V.R.
Red dahlias. LYR 8/1
Rain, Pixie
Poor pussy-willows. LIC 2/2
Raison, Milton
Baffled. BOO 4/2
The cabin passes. BOO 7/2
The captain and the crew. SCM 8/2
The cheated mate. CEN 4/2
Discipline. CAP 1-2/3
The door closes. CAP 1-2/3
The last word. BOO 6/4
The lookout. CEN 4/2
The night watchman. CEN 4/2
Portrait of a sailor. CEN 4/2
Valparaiso. BOO 2/2
Ralph, Genevieve
Silence. HUE 7/19/4
Ramseur, Frances B.
The whoo-whoo man. GUL 7-8/3
Rankin, Mary Louise
The nun. LYW 4/4
Ranlett, Susanne Alice
Plea of the heart of Jesus. MAG 6/2
Ransom, John Crowe
Agitato ma non troppo. FUG 4-5/3
April treason. FUG 4-5/3
Bells for John Whiteside's... FUG 2/4
Boris of Britain. FUG 10/2
Captain Carpenter. FUG 2/4
Conrad at twilight. FUG 2-3/3
Emily Hardcastle, spinster. NES 11/3/3
First travels of Max. FUG 6-7/3
Here lies a lady. NES 3/24/3
In process of a noble alliance. FUG 12/2
The inland city. FUG 4-5/3
Nocturne. FUG 6-7/3
Number five. FUG 12/3
Old man playing with children. FUG 12/3
On the road to Wockensutter. DOU 10/2
Philomela. FUG 2-3/3
Poets have chanted mortality. FUG 10/2
Prometheus in straits. FUG 2/4
Spectral lovers. FUG 6-7/3
The vagrant. FUG 10/2
Vaunting oak. FUG 12/3
Youngest daughter. FUG 12/2
Ratcliffe, Dorothy Una
Grassington Road. POE 12/3
Saint Bridget's lullaby. POE 12/3
Ravenel, Beatrice
The atheist. COV 3/0
The bigot. LYR 1/4
Coasts. LYR 7/2
The damp garden. LYR 7/3
Dew. POE 4/2
The gypsy. POE 10/0
Harbor water. POE 4/2
In. COV 3/0
The Indian to his tree. COV 12/1
Lill' angels. POE 4/2
Love's humility. MEA 12/2
The old man. MEA 5/1
The only child. POE 4/2
The pirates. COV 3/4
The sailor. LYR 3/3
Spell. COV 12/1
To a poet. COV 3/0
White azaleas..magnolia garden. POE 4/2
The Yemassee lands. POM 1922
Ray, Louise Crenshaw
Garden fancies. NOM Aut/3
Warning. NOM Spr/4
Raymund, Bernard
After plenty. MEA 7/3
All good children. PAR #1/4
And yellow poplar. WAN 1/4
Bewit's store. ALS 8-9/2
Blackbird. MEA 7/1
Cold. MID 8/1
The dark pool. COV 6/1
Drama. MID 3/1
Early start. MID 8/1
Empty. ALS 9/1
Flutes and strings. COV 8/0
Havoc. TEM Aut/1
Is there joy? WAV 6/2
Lake in the hills. MID 8/1
Late spring. ALS10-11/2
Listener. POE 12/0
The lumber shed. COV 3/3

New love. TEM Aut/1
Not beautiful. COV 11/2
On a holiday. LYW 3/2
Over the hill. LYW 6/2
Possession. TEM Aut/1
The quickening. WAV 6/2
The rain. LYW 5/4
River song for a red deer. LIB 12/1
The roundhouse. LYR 5/3
Song at evening. VOI 6-7/3
There is a wood. LIB 2/2
These fields. VOI Win/2
To what still garden. WAN 3/4
The tower. COV 3/1
"Up the North River." COV 3/3
Wanderer. NER 6/29/1
Watergates. NEN 3/28/1
Weather sign. ALS 8/1
White rose. WAN 1/4

Recht, Charles
Sundown in America. LIB 7/2

Reddick, Mary
Sleepin' out-o'-doors. LAR 4/4

Redegar, Herb
Angel guardian. CTY Aut/2
Change of heart. CTY Spr/2
Grind of the woodpecker. CTY Sum/3
Ladybug. CTY Spr/3
A memorial. CTY Win/3
On the piny trail. CTY Win/2
Rejuvenation. CTY Spr/2
To a snowman. CTY Win/4

Redfield, Louise
After fever. POE 4/0
After storm. POE 12/2
A shy child. POE 4/0

Redman, Ben Ray
Abdication. CEN 3/23/3
"Child of a line accurst..." NES11/18/2
Colophon. NAT 2/22/2
Gestation. NAT 3/14/3
In the chess club. NAT10/18/2
In the night. REW 10/3
Magic. HAM 11/0
Men, women and words. DOU 12/2
Post cineres gloria venit. NAT 7/5/2
Seaward. REW 4/2
Sonnet. HAM 6/2
Sonnet. POE 12/2
Visitation. NES 1/13/3

Reed, Anna Nelson
Keats 1821-1921. LIB 2/2

Reed, Edward Bliss
The shepherds' fields. YAR 1/1

Reed, Edwin T.
The cedar tree. LAR 6/3

Reed, Frederick W.
Lasting peace. SCR 11/3

Reed, Marjorie
Autumn reveries. LAR 12/3

Reed, Mary Davis
One year to live. CIV 7-8/4

Reely, Mary Katherine
Resurgence. MID 4/1
The train passes. MID 4/1

Reese, Lizette Woodworth
April weather. LYR 4/1
Brambles and dusk. BOO 8/2
A Celtic maying song. LYR 3/3
Dead men. LYR 3/3
Elaine. LYR 9/2
Emily. POM 1922
A foggy afternoon. LYR 3/3
I weep for him. AIN 3/0
The kiss. NAT 8/9/2
The last testament. BOO 6/4
Loneliness. BOO 8/2
Loveliness. HAM 2/4
Old Eli. COV 7/0
The old path. LYR 3/3
A Puritan lady. LYR 3/3
A rose. LYR 6/1
A rose. PER 7/3
A song of separation. LYR 3/3
To love. AIN 8/2
To time (on a false lover). COV 7/0
Were I to love you less. BOO 6/4
White flags. BOO 8/2
The young beauty. LYR 4/2
The young ghosts. NES 5/27/2

Reeves, Franklin H.
The reconciliation. CIC 3/29/3

Reeves, Franklin Henry
Reveille! CIC 4/24/4

Reid, Betty
Little cattlepillar. LIC 3/2

Reid, Eulalia
Friendship. AMP 12/3

Reid, Phyllis
Life a roseleaf. POE 3/3
Prometheus. POE 3/3

Reigelman, Perry Prescot
The magic carpet. OVM 5/4

Reinstein, Herman
Infinitives. POE 4/4
Lilliputian. POE 4/4

Reister, Philip Benjamin
From a Japanese mountain inn. MIN 3-4/4

Renick, Dorothy
True Thomas. LYW 3/4

Reverdy, Pierre
Naufrage. LIR A-W/3

Revere, Paula

The minuet. LYW 1/3
Reynolds, Eliza Jane
Side streets. AMP 10/2
Reynolds, Harriet
A Christmas legend... INT 1-3/4
The vesper sparrows. INT 4-6/4
Reynolds, Julia R.
To Sappho. POE 1/2
Rhinow, Arthur B.
Credo. CIC 2/22/3
The guide. CIC 9/21/2
The past. CIC11/15/3
Rice, Al
Boy time and girl time. CTY Spr/2
The by-road. CTY Win/3
The educated boy. CTY S-A/1
Home grown proverbs. CTY Spr/3
I'm feeling good. CTY Win/3
The talker. CTY Aut/2
Rice, Cale Young
After much theatregoing in New. BOO 5/3
Alienation. REW 11/1
Cold. DOU 12/1
The great seducer. CEN 12/0
The jungle. HAM 7/2
Rapport. SOU 8/3
A self-server. CEN 6/4
Storm - apparitions. REW 6/2
To a comet. TEM Win/3
Unharvested. LYR 9/3
Victory. ALS 6/2
Rice, Lucile
Embroidery. COV 11/2
On awakening. COV 11/2
Rice, Ruth Mason
Queen Victoria. VOI 7-8/3
Trailing Arbutus. POE 5/1
Rice, Susan
I wash my dishes. CIC 4/27/2
Rich, H. Thompson
Beauty. LYW 9/3
Blind man. AMP 2-3/3
In passing. PEG 5/3
Lamp-glare. CAP11-12/2
Return. CAP11-12/2
Song. POE 4/1
To a mocking bird. FOU 10/3
To earth's great dreamers. LYW 1/3
Richard, Marie E.
Again Fiesole! SCM 2/3
Richards, E. K.
Song of silence. LAL 5/4
Richards, Edward H.
Eventide. GRA 8/2
Richards, Elizabeth Davis
Although we part. AMP 6/2
Changeling. PAR #1/4
Conflict. NOM Sum/2
Night reigns, then day. AMP 10/2
Reality. PAR #1/4
Richards, Helen Mitchell
Kitchens in heaven. STE 3/4
Richardson, Dorothy
Buns for tea. POE 6/4
Waiting. POE 6/4
Richardson, Hester Dorsey
Back to the farm. CIV 7-8/4
Richardson, Inez M.
Exile. MES 7/4
Thoughts of someone. MES 7/4
Richardson, Isla Paschal
A field of goldenrod. AMP Aut/1
A thought. AMP 12/3
Richardson, Mabel K.
The Persian rug. AMP Aut/1
Richardson, Mary
The pilgrim woman. GRA 2/2
Richardson, Willis
The after thought. CUU 6/3
Richmond, Charles A.
Brother Jonathan's opportuniti. OUT 4/19/2
Rickenbacker, M. C.
Portrait of a miner. GUL 7-8/3
Rictus, Jehan
If Christ came back. COV 11/3
Ridge, Lola
After storm. POE 9/0
The ailanthus tree. MEA 4/1
Altitude. POE 9/0
Bees. BOO 6/2
Bolsheviki. NES 9/16/2
Cactus seed. POE 9/0
Canaries. AIN 1/0
Chicago. POE 3/4
Child and wind. BOO 3/1
The dream. POE 9/0
The fifth floor window. POE 3/3
Hospital nights. BRO 11/1
In harness. NER 5/26/0
Incognito (to Padraic Colum). NES 1/22/1
Lainyappe. POE 3/3
Marie. POE 3/3
My care. AIN 3/0
New Orleans. NER 5/12/0
An old workman. NER 5/19/0
Om. NER 7/2/4
Portrait (to Evelyn Scott). NER 12/5/3
Saint's bridge. POE 3/3
South-east wind. NER 7/2/4
The spilling of wine. POE 7/2
Thermopylae. VOI 7-8/3
Veteran. NER 6/11/4
Waste. BRO 6/2

The white bird. POE 7/2
Wild duck, I-II. POE 9/0
Wind in the alleys. NER 5/12/0

Riding, Laura (Gottschalk)
Adjustment. LYW 11/3
The city of cold women. POE 1/4
The floorwalker. COV 6/4
Gardens. POE 1/4
Houses. POE 1/4
Initiation. FUG 2/4
Interludes. POE 1/4
The lightning. STE 12/3
The lovers. POE 1/4
A pair. NOM Aut/3
The quids. FUG 2/4
The sky. POE 1/4
Starved. FUG 2/4
To an unborn child. FUG 2/4
To the sky. COV 6/4
Voices. POE 1/4
The wind. POE 1/4

Riggs, Katharine
Mockery. POE 12/0

Riggs, Lynn
Autumn morning. PAL Sum/3
I have not looked on beauty. COV 12/3
Rhythm of rain. POE 8/3
The singing stars. PAL Sum/3
Spring day. COV 4/4

Riggs, R. Lynn
Autumn morning. PAL Sum/3
I was a king. SMA 4/2
The patrician. REW 10/2
The singing stars. PAL Sum/3
Song. SMA 4/2

Righter, Caroline
Exile. GUL 7-8/3

Rihani, Ameen
A Maya song. STE 6/2
A Syrian song. STE 4/3

Rilke, Rainer Maria
Charles XII of Sweden rides in. POE 9/1
What will you do? POE 12/2

Ringland, Glenneweir
"Thy will be done." CIJ 1/4

Rios, Francesca
Autumn. POE 11/2

Ripley, Sherman
At eventide. ROT 4/2
Crazy Billy. ADV 3/10/2
Incense. ADV 3/30/2
The painter of windows. BOY 3/2
The sign. CON 5/17/3

Ritchey, Gwynnyth J.
Agatha. LYW 1/3

Rittenhouse, Jessie B.
The haunted heart. HAM 10/0
The lad of Flanders. MAC 3/2
The miracle. LYW 11/1
The quest. HAM 5/0
The radiant lass. LYR 7/1
The secret. LYW 11/1
Unsung. LYW 11/1
Vision. BOO 9/1

Ritter, Margaret Tod
December. LYW 12/2
An etching, from memory. LYW 4/3
Faith, I wish I...a leprechaun. PAR #3/4
Following a night of tears. CAP11-12/2
From a nightinale to...beloved. AMP10-11/3
I will hew me a house. COV 9/2
Prelude. COV 1/4
Sculpture. MEA 10/1
Sonata apassionato. COV 1/2
Sonata da chiesa. NAT 10/4/2
Sonata pathetique. LYW 7-8/3
Sonata tragica. FOR 1/4
Sonnet of underfeat. LYW 12/3
Sonnet to a plough-woman... COV 1/1
Travail. LYW 12/2

Rivola, Flora Shufelt
Question. POE 5/2

Robbins, Jacob
From the Russian of Maximilian. LIB 9/1

Robbins, W. Davis
Fate. AMP 5-6/4

Roberts, Edith J.
Wind of the ages. CTY Aut/2

Roberts, Edna J.
Beacon lights. CTY Win/2
Childhood mysteries. CTY Win/3
Garden mysteries. CTY Sum/3
Treasure. CTY Spr/3

Roberts, Elizabeth Madox
August night. POE 8/2
Autumn. POE 8/2
A beautiful lady. POE 8/2
A child asleep. POE 7/1
Cinderella's song. POE 7/4
Cold fear. MIL 12/2
The cornfield. POE 7/1
Crescent moon. POE 7/1
The fox hunt. MIL 10/2
My heart. POE 7/1
Numbers. POE 8/2
Orpheus. POE 7/4
The people. POE 8/2
The pilaster. POE 7/1
The sky. POE 8/2
The star. POE 7/1
Strange tree. POE 7/1
Stranger. BOT 10/6/3

Water noises. POE 7/1
Roberts, Florence Cicilia
The diver. AMP 2/2
Roberts, Lillian Mayfield
The professor's wife. SCM 11/1
Roberts, Mary Eleanor
Life the lion tamer. COV 2/1
Mirage. COV 2/1
Roberts, Walter Adolphe
Ave (Madame Olga Petrova). AIN 4/0
The dreamers. AIN 2/0
Robertson, Clyde
The afterglow. SCR 5/3
The dead years speak. SCR 4/4
Golden dreams. SCR 7/4
I loved you. SCR 6/4
November days. SCR 8/3
The pagan rose. AMP10-11/3
Repression. SCR 1/4
Sufficiency. SCR 1/4
The telegraph pole. SCR 1/4
The thousand years of peace. SCR 1/4
Vachel Lindsay. LAR 2/4
Robeson, H.
The brook. COV 6/2
Robinson, Ann B.
Blue. STE 12/3
Communion. INT 4-6/4
Indian pipes. STE 11/3
A narcissus. COV 6/4
The passing. COV 10/3
Youth departing. INT 1-3/4
Robinson, Anne Mathilde
Across the sea. SCR 3/4
Answer. INT 7/4
The awakening. PAR 3/4
The call of May. SCR 4/4
Cheer. CTY Aut/3
Christmasing. CTY Win/3
Dawn and dusk. SCR 4/4
A day dream. CTY Sum/2
Dust bound. AMP 6/4
Elemental. SCR 7/4
Hidden memories. AMP 6-7/3
I built a wall. LYR 7/3
A March idyl. CTY Spr/4
A May wedding. CTY Spr/4
A portent. STE 5/4
Reminiscences. STE 1/3
Secrets. SCR 2/4
Singing hills. SCR 4/4
Sympathy. CTY Aut/2
Tombs. SCR 3/4
Unto Caesar. INT 7/4
Robinson, Anne B.
Youth departing. INT 1-3/4
Robinson, Anne Mathilde
April comes. CTY Spr/3
Easter bonnets. CTY Spr/3
A lullaby. CTY Sum/3
Noel. CTY Win/3
On the sands. SCR 7/4
Out of the past. INT 4/4
Peggy O'Reilly. CTY Spr/3
Sea born. SCR 7/4
Stitches. CTY Win/3
Twilight. AMP 12/2
Robinson, Corinne Roosevelt
An invocation-Christmas 1923. SCM 12/3
Robinson, E. Jewel
God's day. CIJ 2/4
Robinson, Edwin Arlington
And so it was. BOO 3/4
As it looked then. DIA 2/4
Avenel Gray. POE 10/2
Ben Trovato. NAT 1/26/1
Caput mortuum. YAR 10/1
En passant. NES 7/19/4
The garden of the nations. NER10/31/3
Glass houses. YAR 7/4
Haunted house. CEN 12/3
"If the Lord..make windows..." NER 5/21/4
Inferential. DIA 1/0
Job the rejected. NES 1/22/1
Karma. NER12/26/3
The laggards. YAR 4/4
The long race. NER 9/29/0
Many are called. NER 11/3/0
Maya. NER12/26/3
Modernites. DIA 5/1
Monadnock, through the trees. OUT 1/5/1
New England. NER 12/5/3
Not always. DIA 4/4
Recalled. BOO 4/1
Reunion. NAT 11/7/3
The sheaves. NES12/15/3
Thomas Hood. POE 8/3
The tree in Pamela's garden. NER11/24/0
Vain gritítudes. NER11/24/0
Why he was there. NER 7/2/4
Roche, Loretta
Absence. LYW 2/4
Image. LYW 2/4
Memorandum. STE 5/4
Moment. LYW 4/4
Murmuring. WAN 3/4
Return. LYW 2/4
Rodker, John
Theatre. BRO 4/2
Roe, Robert J.
The albatross. COV 4/1
Apparition. POE 6/2
Apprentice. POE 11/2

Roediger, Janet M.

Artist to a woman. COV 4/3
Barney. POE 6/2
Black waters. VOI10-11/3
The bully. BOO 5/3
The captain's wife. NER 3/17/0
Cattleman's wife. DOU 2/3
Cautious. POE 6/2
Civilized. COV 4/3
Clear eyes. VOI10-11/3
Conservation at twilight. VOI 12/2
Cortege. POE 11/2
Dawn at sea. COV 4/1
Dead calm. VOI Aut/1
Death. POE 11/2
Diet. BOO 5/3
The disillusioned. MEA 12/2
Egoist. COV 8/3
Gangway. COV 1/2
Green logs. BOO 1/2
Hesitant. VOI 12/2
Homesick. BOO 6/3
Humble. COV 1/2
Immortality. COV 9/0
Incubus. COV 9/0
Insight. POE 6/2
Jack. POE 6/2
La hacienda. COV 8/2
Lesson. COV 1/2
The lookout. COV 4/1
Love. NER 2/18/0
Meinself. POE 6/2
Moon. POE 6/2
Moral. COV 1/2
"Much against my heart." VOI10-11/3
Mutation. VOI 7-8/3
Nostalgia. COV 4/3
Oriental love song. COV 8/1
Overcoats and dreams. COV 4/3
Parade. VOI10-11/3
Philosophy. BOO 5/3
Portrait of a girl. DOU 5/3
Portrait of a man. POE 11/2
A reasonable being. COV 4/3
Recuperated. COV 4/1
Restless. BOO 3/3
Sailor. POE 6/2
Sea. POE 6/2
Spinning oakum. COV 8/2
Spring song. COV 4/1
Stars. POE 6/2
Sunrise on Cajon. COV 4/1
Symphonie pathetique. POE 11/2
Thoughts. COV 4/1
Typhoon. POE 6/2
Verlaine. DOU 2/3
A walk at evening in...desert. COV 4/1
Wind. POE 6/2
Wisdom. COV 8/2
Wishes. COV 4/3

Roediger, Janet Marferding

Night light. AMP10-11/3

Roesner, Oscar H.

A thousand years from now. WAN 9/3

Rogers, Harold Herbert

To Fay. LYW 7-8/3
Wind impressions. LYW 12/2
Winter dust. LYW 12/2

Rogers, Helen A.

Bully, the north wind. LAR 6/3
California colors. LAR 6/3
A goldfish. LAR 6/3
When Muriel smiles. LAR 6/3

Rogers, Jessica

Home. EVM 10/0

Rogers, Lillian

The Italian church in Chinatow. LYW 7-8/3

Rohrer, Gertrude Martin

My garden. AMP 6-7/3

Rollins, Leighton

The aviator. GRA 1/1
Be kind to me death. SPT 12/1
The call him Mountain. CAS 1/3
Credo. CAS 1/3
Dark. PAR #1/4
Daughters of my fears. LYR 6/4
He dreamed of beauty. GRA 10/1
His thoughts shall never die. GRA 11/0
Presence. GRA 3/1
Star dream. AMP 8/2
Thoughts on the colors... GRA 5/1
Unborn stars. GRA 7/1
Vigil. HEA 7/4

Romany, Robin

A longing. LYW 9/1

Romig, Edna Davis

Open sesame. AMP10-11/3

Root, E. Merrill

Auntiquity. LIB 7/2
Birth. MEA 3/4
"Co' boss." MEA 3/4
Cranberry marshes. COV 9/0
Dreadnought. LIB 7/2
The farmer. LIB 3/2
Love's sadness. WAN 7/4
Modern man. MEA 3/4
Monkeys. MEA 7/4
The mountain of skeletons. COV 5/0
Night on the river. POE 7/0
The panther soul. WAN 4/4
Pessimists. MEA 3/4
Prisoners. MEA 3/4
A southern holiday. LIB 3/2

Stubborn. MEA 7/4
To a successful hen. MEA 5/4
A visitor. NEN 3/28/1

Rope, H. E. G.
The gift. MAG 6/3
No abiding city. MAG 7/2

Rorty, James
After the drive is over. SVG 5/3
The bell. NAT 5/24/2
A birth. NAT11/14/3
California dissonance. FRE 2/16/1
A change of weather. HUE 7/19/4
The day: July 2. NAT 7/27/1
The four crows. MEA 7/4
High fog. LIB 7/2
The intruders. CEN ?/3
Nocturne. CEN 6/4
Prelude: when we dead awaken. NAT 2/9/1
Quests. DOU 3-4/3
Words. NAT 7/26/2

Roselle, Mercier Montgomery
At the Poetry Society. NEW 6/1/4
At the end of summer. NEW 9/4/3
August days on the Sound. NEW 8/15/3
Back to the old gods. MUN 8/1/3
Before Eve. NEW 6/21/4
A business woman. NET 5/15/4
Dawn at Shippan. NEW 7/14/4
Experience. AIN 1/1/4
The first grandchild. NET 9/11/3
From life. NEW 11/3/3
From out of the air. NEW 8/13/3
Ghost of a rose. NET 9/4/3
His wife...to Atlas. NEW 2/9/4
Horace invokes the muse. NET10/26/3
How will it be..., Manhattan? NEW 9/12/3
I do not know. COV 7/1/4
I journeyed in a valley. NEW 8/6/3
I, too, have dwelt. NET 8/14/3
In St. Paul's churchyard. NEW 2/9/4
Invocation (Horace). MUN 10/1/3
January 19, 1924. NEW 1/19/4
The minstrels pass. MUN 7/1/4
The moderns...and Pan. NEW12/13/3
A mother speaks. NEW 12/9/3
My words are like slow ships. NEW 10/6/3
Night in New York. NEW 1/26/4
The president passes. NEW 5/21/4
The prisoner. MUN 4/1/4
Richesse. NET 9/1/3
The Rosetta Stone. NEV 9/7/3
Savannah River. NEW 8/26/3
Scotty, a character sketch. CIM 3/27/4
A sonnet from the subway. NET 11/9/3
A squall on the Sound. NEW 9/15/3
Taxes. NET 11/6/3
Te morituri salutamus. NEW 2/24/4
Thanksgiving. NEW11/29/3
To a stained glass saint. NEW 7/20/4
To an oriental poppy. NEW 6/25/4
A traveler. NEU 9/10/3
Two words. NET 9/11/3
Upon a night. CIM12/24/3
Winter by the Sound. NEW 1/12/4
The woman I am. NET 9/7/3

Rosenbaum, Benjamin
America...giant. COV 4/4
Broken lines. VOI 8-9/3
Change. POE 11/3
Classic night. COV 4/3
Coversation. COV 4/4
Day piece. POE 11/3
The disappearance. VOI 3-4/4
Envy. VOI 8-9/3
Envy. VOI Son#/3
The etcher. MEA 6/3
Face. MEA 2/3
Fog. VOI Spr/3
Forget me. VOI Spr/3
Glimpses of her. POE 1/1
Gone. POE 1/1
Granite man, a prayer. COV 4/3
He. POE 8/3
Hill hunger. LYR 10/3
Hill souls. LYW 2/4
If you come. POE 8/3
In a public library. MID 7/1
Low hills. STE 3/3
Memento. VOI 3-4/4
My people. TAL 10/2
My purple gown from Tyre. POE 1/1
Niagara. POE 11/3
Night talk. POE 11/3
Oxford. VOI 3-4/4
Point of view. COV 4/4
Prayer. COV 7/3
Prayer. POE 11/3
Precedent. COV 4/4
Psalm. COV 4/4
Rain. VOI Spr/3

Road song. MEA 12/3
Saul. LYW 2/4
Seeking love. POE 1/1
Silent things. DOU 3-4/3
Solace. VOI Spr/3
When I am dust you cannot say.. LYR 9/3
White horse. STE 12/3
Wind fantastio. VOI Spr/3
Withered woman. COV 4/3
You. POE 11/3

Rosenthal, A. A.
Fantasy. POE 10/0
The musicmeister. NOM Sum/3
Piece work. CAP11-12/2
Portrait of an old Jew. PEG 7/3
Records. MOR 4/3
Shade mountain. MOR Aut/2

Rosenthal, Albert A.
Alabama. PAL Sum/3
Asters (D.D.). PAG10-11/1
Aubade. TEM Aut/1
Autumn. VOI Aut/1
Echo. PAG 8-9/1
Oskeola George. NOM Spr/4
Pattern. NOM Spr/4
A poet. PAG10-11/1
Syncrasy. POE 7/2
Tenth Avenue, north. NOM Spr/4
Willard Jo Jackson. NOM Spr/4

Rosenthal, David
Cornbread and eyes. BRO 10/2
The days. NAT 3/2/1
Truant-leaves. NER 8/4/0
Warning. MEA 4/1
Ydoni sings to his people. NER 11/3/0

Ross, Gertrude Robinson
I don't care if you love me or. LAR 2/3
I never looked on Helen's face. NAT 3/7/3
I was made of this and this. NAT 3/14/3
I, who danced my youth away. LAR 2/3
My heart that bragged of gypsy. LAR 2/3
Nativity. CAW 12/1
Prayer to Valentine. LAR 3/4
Song for Barbara Blomberg. OVM 5/4
Star flowers. LAR 2/3
A very young person's song. LAR 4/4
When Pierrot left me yesterday. LAR 2/3

Ross, Kathleen Wheeler
Foregiveness. POA 9/1
His talent. POA 9/1
Holdin' on. POA 9/1
Room at the top. POA 9/1
Worry. POA 9/1

Ross, Margaret Wheeler
The days. MAC 3/4

Rossetti, Christina Georgina
Uphill. GRA 9/3

Rossiter, Ida B.
Life. GRA 1/1
The old man of the mountain. GRA 3/1

Roth, Samuel
Black London. POE 11/2
Yohrz. NAT 5/8/0

Rothrock, Beatrice R.
Query. AMP10-11/3

Rounds, Emma
City trees after snow. LIC 1/3
Princesses. LIC 11/2
The sea king's palace. LIC 12/1
The spoilers. LIC 4/2

Rouveyrol, Aurania
Over again. LYW 12/2

Rouveyroll, Aurania
My heart's a rift of song. LYW 11/3

Rowles, George
Duette. LYW 9/1
Pictures on my Japanese fan. LYW 1/2

Rowles, Georgia
Lilacs. LYW 6/3
Tankas. LYW 6/3

Rubio, Dolores
Pale hands. CAP 5/3

Ruble, Esther Louise
First snow. POE 1/2

Rumry, F. Layton
Fairie pondery. COV 4/2
Reflections. AMP 2/2

Rumry, Florence Layton
Dreams for Frederick. COV 8/2
Ladies in waiting. AMP 12/2
On gossamer wing. COV 8/2

Runbeck, Margie-Lee
Apology. LYR 4/4
Ballet (in a dandelion patch). VOI Aut/1
Cycle. AMP Aut/1
Deep sea sonnet. EME 1/4
Emptiness. POE 4/4
Evanescence. TEM 6/1
Hope. AMP 8/2
Lullabye. AMP 2/2
Nonchalance. GRA 5/1
Records. EME 1/4
Talent. VOI 6-7/3
Tree child. LYR 6/3
Welder of steel. VOI 6-7/3

Runnette, Mabel

To a cardinal. COV 4/0
Rurner, L. Lucile
Song of the young wolves. WAN 3/4
Russ, Penelope
Before passion. POE 8/3
Grass song. VOI10-11/3
Knighthood. DOU 7/4
Two paths. LYW 10/3
Russell, D. K.
The prisoner. YAR 11/3
Spring mood. YAR 3/4
Russell, D. Keith
A fool's prayer. CAS 1/3
On beauty. CAS 1/3
Russell, Edith M.
Vision. POA 9/1
Russell, Frances Theresa
Vignette. UNV 7/4
Russell, Sidney King
Alms. LYW 12/3
Desire. LYW 10/1
The enigma. LYW 5/4
Interim. MEA 9/2
Legend. LYW 5/4
Mists. LYW 5/4
The poet in the city. LYW 11/2
Woodland fear. LYW 10/1
The young David. LYW 5/1
Russell, Winifred
The dogwood. SOU 7/3
Russmann, Helen C.
Fantasy. POE 6/2
Russsell, George William
Michael. DIA 3/0
Ruthenburg, Grace
Poems. DEP 12/3
Ruthraff, Saidee Gerard
My mother was sweet. LYW 12/2
Ruthrauff, Henry Fitzgerald
She wants such simple gifts. LYW 10/3
Ruthrauff, Saidee Gerard
For April. LYW 4/2
There's a sound of singing. LYW 4/4
Wan water. LYW 10/3
Rutledge, Archibald
Arrivals. SOU 8/3
Lee. SOU 7/3
Mt. Pisgah. POM 1922
Radio. SCM 7/2
Rutts, Norman
Sack of Niveveh. GUL 9/3
Ryan, Kathryn White
Atonement: Arlington, 11/11/21. CAW 12/1
Convent. POE 6/2
Day. MEA 7/2
Death. MEA 4/1
Despair. VOI 5-6/4
Disarmament and Arlington. CAW 12/1
Earthen urn. VOI 8-9/3
Empress Eugenie. VOI 7-8/3
Fog. POE 11/1
Ireland: invocation. NAT ?/2
Lake Superior. FOR 11/1
Landscape. BOO 6/3
Mea culpa. VOI 7-8/3
Moon. MEA 7/2
Moonlight. POE 6/2
Needles. BOO 10/3
Peace. VOI 5-6/4
Portraits of unfading women. VOI10-11/3
River. MEA 7/2
The snow-capped mountains see. FOR 12/2
Soldiers. MEA 7/2
Song after travel. POE 4/4
Surrender. VOI 7-8/3
To a child. CAW 5/1
The Washington Monument. SPT10/16/1
Woman of mists, Ireland. CAW 7/1
Woolworth Tower. VOI 5-6/4

Sabel, Marx G.
The abandoned place. MID 8/1
Afternoon on the St. John's. COV 7/0
Amor patitur moras - Seneca. TEM Aut/1
Bats. COV 9/2
The core. POE 4/2
The cynic shamed. DOU 8-9/1
Discovery. NOM Sum/3
Down a hill. COV 3/1
A fable. BOO 2/1
The far end. COV 1/4
Fellow fighter. MID 8/1
The forest. COV 1/4
Ichor. MOR 4/3
If only. REW 3/2
Immortal cause. REW 6/2
Incomparable. VOI Sum/2
Inviolate. COV 2/0
Jeremiad. POE 6/1
Litany. LYR 11/2
The masquerader. VOI Win/2
No good thing. POE 6/1
Off! DOU 3/2
Passing love. COV 2/0
Precipitate. LYR 7/2
The prophecy. COV 2/0

Punishment. LYW 1/3
Query. SMA 1/3
Recordition. POE 4/2
Refutation. COV 2/0
Remembering. LYW 1/3
Romance. NOM Aut/2
The silent dweller. COV 1/4
The snare. NOM Spr/2
Song for the presumptious... COV 2/0
The strange load. POE 6/1
The talker. VOI Sum/2
The thought. COV 1/4
The tryst. LYR 3/2
Unwavering. CAP 5/3
Withdrawal. DOU 6/1

Sachiwo Ito
The consequence. FRE 12/7/1
Love's lesson. FRE 12/7/1

Sackville, Margaret
Adventure. NER 7/26/2
Epitaphs. ALS 4/1
Finis. NER10/18/2

Sadler, Aeldryn
The pensioners of beauty. POE 2/4

Salbador, Ava Fisher
The anesthetic. CTY Spr/4
Atonement. CTY S-A/1
Color magic. CTY Spr/2
If you've felt. CTY Spr/3
In philosophic mood. CTY Win/3
The Italian woman. CTY Spr/2
A memory. CTY Aut/2
Panaeca. CTY Win/4
Seen from a window. CTY S-A/1
The smile of God. CTY S-A/1
So sorry dear. CTY S-A/1
Transmutation. CTY Spr/3
When the world seems blue. CTY Sum/3

Saling, Leah E.
A lull-a-abye. CTY Aut/2

Salinger, David
Rainy season. ALS 8/1

Salley, Ruth E.
Why? ARG 6/21/4

Saltus, Edgar
The feast. WAV 2/2

Samuels, S. H.
Hereafter. GUL 9/3
Rope. GUL 5/3
To a gargoyle. GUL 5/3

Sanborn, Alta C.
Salvation. LAL 5/4

Sanborn, Pitts
After a fool's banquet. MEA 5/1
Jeanne de Bordeaux. MEA 5/1
Tristan of Morbihan. MEA 5/1
Two sonnets. MEA 5/1

Sanborn, Robert Alden
The children and Thomas. LYW 1/3

Sandburg, Carl
Ambassadors of grief. BOO 4/2
And so today. FRE 1/18/2
At the gates of the Tombs. LIB 1/2
Baby song of the four winds. MIL 10/2
Bas-relief. POE 2/0
Bitter summer thoughts. CEN 5/2
Bitter thoughts: No. 3. NAT 6/4/4
Black horizons. NER ?/1
Broken-face gargoyles. DIA 3/0
Bug spots. NAT 6/4/4
Carriers. NER 1/9/4
The dinosaur bones. NER 4/20/1
Evening waterfall. POE 2/0
Feather lights. POE 3/2
Flat waters of the west:Kansas. DIA 7/4
Four preludes on playthings... NER
Frog spring songs. NER 3/12/4
Gypsy mother. POE 3/2
Hats. DIA 3/0
Hemstitches. NER 3/12/4
Hiker at midnight. BOO 3/1
Jailbirds. NER 3/9/1
Jazz fantasia. DIA 3/0
Joke gold. NER 12/5/3
The law says. POE 2/0
The lawyers know too much. DIA 1/0
Let them ask your pardon. NER 12/5/3
Losers. POE 2/0
Man & dog-early winter morning. NAT 6/4/4
March of the hungry mountains. CEN 5/2
Medley. POE 3/2
Moist moon people. NAT 6/4/4
Monkey of stars. NAT 6/4/4
Moon hammock. NER 12/5/3
Moon-riders. POE 3/2
The naked stranger. POE 3/2
Night-movement--New York. POE 2/0
October paint. NER 1/9/4
Peace, night, sleep. NER 4/2/4
Pennsylvania. DIA 3/0
People who must. POE 2/0
Primer lesson. BOO 3/2
Proud of their rags. CEN 5/2
The rakeoff and the getaway. BRO 5/2
Sea-wash. POE 2/0

She opens the barn door... NER 1/9/4
Slabs of the sunburnt west. DIA 3/2
Smoke and steel. POE 2/0
Spring cries. CEN 4/4
St. Joe: the Big Muddy... NER 3/12/4
This - for the moon - yes? BOO 3/2
Three spring notations..bipeds. NAT 5/15/0
Understandings in Bule. NER 1/9/4
Unintentional paint. NER 4/20/1
Washington Monument by night. HAM 6/2
Waters meeting. NER 1/9/4
The windy city. NER 3/22/2
Winter gold. NAT 6/4/4
Without notice beforehand. NER 12/5/3

Sandelin, Charles C.
"Be still, and know." CIJ 1/4

Sanders, Emmy Veronica
Adelaide Crapsey. POE 2/1
Beggars. MEA 5/1
The cow. MEA 10/1
Dai butsu. COV 1/2
The fisherman. DOU 6/1
Hill speech. POE 9/2
Hilltop duet. POE 2/1
Into these things. POE 9/2
Laughter. POE 9/2
Passing. POE 9/2
The pine tree. COV 1/2
Stigma. DOU 4/2
Tea time. MEA 10/1
You are the road. POE 5/3

Sanders, Nettie P.
Eve of All Saints. AMP 6-7/3

Sanders, Ottys
Daggers of white men. SOV 1923

Sanderson, Betty
Caprice. SCR 8/3
Conceived in darkness. SCR 9/3
Sonnet to--. SCR 9/3
That which might have been. SCR 8/3
Wisdom. SCR 8/3
Youth. SCR 8/3

Sandoz, Paul
Attic nights. MOD 1-4/4
Danae. WAN 4/4
Impeceability. MOD 1-4/4
Sunday evening. WAN 7/4

Sangster, Margaret E.
Christmas song. AIN 1/2
Geisha girl. AIN 4/2
Home. SCM 12/2

Santayana, George
A minuet on reaching the age o. CEN 4/3

Santmyer, Helen
For old beliefs. MID 4/1
The prairie town. BOO 12/1
To the Egyptian lady Sennuwy. SCM 11/3

Saphier, William
Idle afternoon. DOU 8-9/1

Sapir, Edward
Barker. PAG10-11/1
The dumb shepherdess. POE 7/0
French-Canadian folk-songs. POE 7/0
A girl. MEA 6/1
God. COV 3/0
The harvest. NAT 6/19/0
Helen of Troy. NER 3/10/0
The house to the incoming tena. NAT 9/7/2
The king of Spain's daughter... POE 7/0
The king of Thule. NAT 7/26/2
Mist and gleam. PAG 12/1
The moon's not always beautifu. DOU 10/1
The old town. POE 5/1
Optimist. DOU 9/2
Overlooked. POE 5/1
The prince of orange. POE 7/0
Promise of summer. DOU 7/4
She sits vacant-eyed. POE 5/1
Sullen silence. PAG 4-5/0
This age. VOI 12-1/4
Upholding the world. DOU 11/1
Vestments. DOU 1/2
A walking poem. POE 9/2
White as snow. POE 7/0

Sarett, Lew
The box of God. POE 4/1
Breakers of bronchos. NES11/11/2
Double-bear dance. LYW 10/1
Drought. COV 11/1
Fisher of stars. LYW 6/2
Ghost-wolf dance. LYW 10/1
God is at the anvil. FAR 2/0
The great divide. ARG 5/24/0
Indian love song. NOA 8/3
Indian sleep song. NOA 1/2
Indian summer. COV 11/1
Iron-wind dances. LYW 10/1
Jumping-river dances. LYW 10/1
Leave me to my own. LIB 11/1
Let me flower as I will. CAP 10/2
Look for me. COV 11/1
The loon. AMF 5/0
Maple-sugar song. BRO 11/1

Mesa-mist. COV 11/1
Number ninety-seven talks. WAV #4/2
October snow. VOI Aut/2
Old oak. VOI Aut/1
The sword. STE 7/2
Teton mountain. COV 11/1
Thunderdrums, a Chippewa war... LYW 10/1
To a dead Pembina warrior. LYW 3/2
To a wild goose over decoys. ATM 9/3
The tribe sings. LYW 10/1
The weaver. COV 8/1
Wind in the pine. COV 11/1
Yellow moon. BOO 2/3

Sargent (Jr.), Samuel M.
Intersection. LYW 11/3
Of Africa. WAN 6/4
The ogress. SCR 2/3
The quest. SCR 10/3

Sargent, Sarah
Bessie. LIC 4/2

Sargent, William D.
The head hunter. LIC 4/3
O wind a-blowing. LIC 3/2

Sassoon, Siegfried
An all-British sonnet. NER 4/28/0
"The case for the miners" NAT 5/11/1
Clavichord recital. NER 7/4/3
Fete galante. NER 7/4/3
Finn fantasia. BOO 6/1
First night: Richard III. NER 3/17/0
Martyrdom. NER 7/4/3
Scientific rapture. NER 4/6/1
Solar eclipse. NER 7/4/3
Vigil. NER 7/4/3

Sater, Elsye Tash
Loneliness. COV 1/4

Satterlee, Anna E.
Birthdays. LYW 7-8/2

Saul, George Brandon
All. COV 8/1
"And will the dawn be sad..." COV 11/1
"As the violets came" COV 5/1
A biography. COV 12/3
By an old window. VOI 12/2
Chorus. NER 5/10/2
The cup of sand. LYW 9/3
Dawn: a dead girl on the beach. COV 9/0
Daybreak. VOI10-11/3
Dialogue. COV 11/1
Doves. COV 4/2
Dust wandering. VOI10-11/3
Elizabeth. COV 4/2
The end. LYR 12/1
Ending. VOI10-11/3
Episode. COV 8/2
Fantasy. VOI 12/2
Figure. NER 6/14/2
For Margaret. COV 8/2
Fragment. COV 7/4
"I know..." COV 2/3
I love the mountains. COV 9/0
"I saw the white Christ like a. COV 11/1
I thought of you at fall of ni. COV 8/1
In a black hour. COV 8/2
In the garden. COV 8/2
Ione. LYR 4/4
"It is night and the wind blow. COV 11/1
Like a forgotten city. LYR 10/3
"Like a strange march of shado. LYR 7/3
Love song. NER 1/30/4
Memory. COV 11/1
Midsummer night's premonition. NES 7/26/4
Night and rain. COV 11/1
"The night-storm lashes at the. COV 12/2
Of an invalid stricken...youth. COV 5/1
Old philosophy. AMP 6-7/3
Over one dying. LYR 3/4
Paean. LYW 2/3
The poet. LYW 2/4
Prayer. VOI Win/2
Question. LYW 9/3
Rain at dusk. COV 8/2
Revisitation. AMP 6-7/3
"Say not..." COV 8/2
Shadow. LYW 9/3
Skeptic. AMP 6-7/3
The song in the night. COV 8/1
Sonnet. COV 4/2
Sonnet. VOI Win/2
Sonnets for Margaret. VOI Sum/2
Strange tale. COV 12/2
The stranger's song. MEA 5/1
There is no need for love. LYR 1/2
The three bells. COV 12/2
"To think of her..." COV 12/2
Vigil. AMP 6-7/3
The vision of death. VOI10-11/3
When dawn is music on the snow. VOI Win/2
Where the nether waves of hell. COV 12/3
A woman watches the sea. LYW 2/3

The years go. VOI Aut/1
Saul, Henry
Feeling. POE 12/3
Sorrow and joy. POE 12/3
Saunders, Lois Fay
The circuit rider. LAR 4/4
Saunders, Whitelaw
Adaigio. STE 2/4
Bondwoman. LYR 10/2
A dead butterfly. WAV 3/4
The dead woman. ALS 11/1
Debussy. PAR #3/4
From the Grieg ballad. STE 2/4
Gargoyles of Notre Dame. WAN 4/4
I love you! NOM Spr/3
In a clearing. STE 2/3
In sepia. STE 2/4
The masquerade. GRI 1/1
The matinee: a rondeau. COV 4/1
An old spinnet. ALS 4/1
Pagan. PAG 12/1
Red tulips. WAN 1/4
Sheep herders' songs. LAR 4/3
Theme for a ballet. LYW 10/2
Vexed love. LYW 10/2
Wild geese sing. LAR 4/3
Winter scenes. COV 1/4
The woman with a fan. TEM Aut/1
A woodcarving. LYW 6/2
Savage, Edgar
Michael. WAV 1/2
Self-slain. WAV 1/2
Savage, Henry
The witch. WAV 2/2
Savage, Mary Stebbins
The patriot. CIC 7/6/2
Saveresy, Marie Montabe
Calling to thee. LAR 11/3
Desire. LAR 12/3
Freedom. LAR 12/3
Why do make of me a wanderer? LAR 3/4
Wyoming dawn and dusk. LAR 12/3
Sawyer, M. White
Ragged mountain. GRA 9/2
Spring promise. GRA 6/2
Scaife, C. M. O.
Dolores in Spain. LYR 7/4
Scanlan, J. A.
St. Catherine. CAW 4/1
Scarborough, Cornelia Meade
The desert passes. LYW 10/2
Scarborough, Dorothy
The pawn shop. EVM 11/0
Scarborough, Duncan
Realism. AMP 8/2
Schack, William
Revery. LIB 10/2
Schaeffer, M. L.
Ghosts. CAS 3/3
Scharr, Barbara A.
Hail to the Rockies. LAR 3/4
Heard in the Rockies. LAR 10/3
Winter. LAR 12/3
Schauffler, Robert Haven
Andante con moto. LYW 11/2
Before the great adventure. LYW 10/3
Divers. OUT 6/9/0
Harvest. COV 10/2
Music in hospital. LYW 10/3
The new continent. EME 3/4
Poet to reader. COV 1/1
Portals of dawn. HAM 11/2
A soul remembers. COV 1/0
Word music. LYR 2/3
Schaukal, Richard
Rococo. POE 12/2
Schayer, Isadore
Advice. SOU 7/3
Intolerance. SOU 7/3
Loneliness. SOU 7/3
The weaver. SOU 8/3
Scheffauer, Ethel Talbot
The tropic screen. DOU 8-9/1
The warners. WAV 3/4
Scheinbaum, Samuel
I men a man beneath a moon. PAR #4/4
Loneliness. PAR #1/4
Schimberg, Albert P.
My mother's picture. MAG 9/3
Schlesinger, Helen
Blue moths in Yosemite. LYW 10/2
Schmidt (Jr.), Fritz L.
Christmas memories. POA 1/2
To the new year-1922. POA 1/2
Washington. POA 9/1
Schneider, Isidor
Advice to Maxwell Bodenheim. NES 1/22/1
The beggar and the vendor. MEA 1/2
Coversation. POE 6/2
Empty lot. MEA 1/2
The gutter. MEA 1/2
The heroes. POE 10/0
History. MOR 1-4/4
The houses. MEA 1/2
A hymn for the lynchers. POE 10/0
The lampposts. MEA 1/2
A memory. POE 10/0
The mist. POE 6/2
Orientale. RHY 1/3
The people. MEA 1/2
Question: history of a convers. MEA 7/3

Sentimental dialog. MOR 4/3
Sunset. MEA 1/2

Schonberger, E. D.
Bethlehem. CIC12/21/2
The prophet. CIC 6/28/3

Schoonmaker, Edwin Davies
On dying young. HUE 6/21/4
The quarrel. HUE 7/19/4
The undertow. HUE 7/5/4
The window. HUE 7/5/4

Schuster, Ad. B.
The old cowboy. SUN 7/3

Schutze, Lenore
Sonnet, to Alfred Tennyson. LYW 7-8/2

Schutze, Lenore C.
May. LOS 5/10/4

Schutze, Martin
May. FRE 5/31/2
Wild geranium. HUE 6/21/4

Schwartz, Ida D.
Autumn. NOM Aut/3
Before dawn. NOM Spr/2
Birmingham. NOM Spr/4
Melody before rain. NOM Spr/4
Thought. NOM Spr/4
Tokens. NOM Spr/4
Violinist. NOM Sum/3
White trash. PAG10-11/1

Sclarf (tr.), Olive
Petals. BRO 5/2

Scollard, Clinton
Christmas canticle. SCM 12/1
The cypresses of Monterey. LYW 11/3
An epistle to Alexander Pope. HAM 5/0
The great event. HAM 1/1
A Greek song. SCM 4/1
I know from dreams. SCM 11/3
In the plaza (Saint Augustine). LYR 5/2
An intimate night. POE 2/1
The journey. MUN 5/2
Mirage. OVM 3/4
Moonlight. MUN 2/2
The numbered hours. AIN 1/2
A Pacific dayfall. LYW 7-8/3
Pastoral. HAM 9/0
Songs of a Syrian lover. BOO 12/2
Tomorrow. MUN 6/2
Vagabond days. HAM 6/2
White sails. LYR 5/1
The white thought. HAM 1/2
The wind of the Sierras. OVM 7/4

Scollard, Elizabeth
The garden. MUN 6/2

Scott, Arlie Wyatt
The secret impetus. POA 9/1

Scott, Carroll De Wilton
The pepper tree. AMP 2-3/3

Scott, Duncan Campbell
The lovers. SCM 5/3

Scott, Evelyn
After youth. DIA 1/0
Air for G strings. DIA 9/0
Ascension: autumn dusk... DIA 9/0
Autumn night. DIA 1/0
The death of the Columbine. DIA 1/0
Devil's cradle. DIA 1/0
Immortality. DIA 1/0
Isolation ward. DIA 1/0
Narrow flowers. DIA 1/0
New moon. DIA 1/0
Night. DIA 1/0
The Red Cross. DIA 1/0
Spring song. DIA 9/0
Touch. RHY 2/3
Tropic moon. DIA 1/0
Winter moon. DIA 1/0

Scott, Harold P.
"Right royal"-a review. DEU 1/9/1

Scott, Jack
Dago love. CAP 5/3
My epitaph. CAP 5/3
Rutherford Pinckney Hamilton. CAP 5/3
Sex songs. CAP 5/3

Scott, John G.
Bastard. CAP 1-2/3
Visioning clean sin. CAP 1-2/3

Scott, Ray Hamlin
Thinking. GUL 7-8/3

Scrimger, Edna Baker
Lilacs. AMP 5-6/4

Scruggs. E. J.
The call. NOM Spr/2

Seabury, David
Gethsemane. HAM 3/2

Seabury, Emma Playter
Pictures. STE 7/2
A toast to Mrs. Seymour. STE 1/3
A tree in winter. STE 2/3

Seal, Lynas Clyde
On recognizing an old handkerc. AMP 4-5/3
Spirit of Christmas. AMP 12/3

Seaman, Helen
L'homme machine. CIC 3/27/4

Searcy, Helene
April dawn. LYW 4/2
Personality. LYW 4/2

Seawell, Ellen
Cana. AMP 6/2

The Crucifix. AMP 2/2
Seawell, Meade
A hermit's song. AMP 8/2
Seccombe, Annmary
White hands. VOI 12/2
Who puts pride. MEA 6/4
Sedgewick, Katherine
Words. BOO 6/4
Sedgwick, W. Ellery
When I am gone. SCM 4/3
Seibel, May
Healing. CIJ 11/3
Seiffert, Marjorie Allen
Affaire cerebrale. POE 6/4
As you are now. POE 7/1
At certain challenges. POE 2/3
The chambermaid. DOU 1/4
Cubist portrait. POE 7/1
Cythaera and the worm. POE 6/0
Cythaera and the leaves. POE 6/0
Cythaera and the song. POE 6/0
The dark hour. POE 2/3
Dark magic. DOU 1/3
Dingy street. POE 7/1
Dream-kiss. POE 7/1
Enigma. VOI Sum/2
Finale. COV 11/2
The giver. COV 1/0
Grey moth. POE 6/4
Grotesque. COV 11/2
If loving me. POE 2/3
Interior. POE 7/1
Kinfolk. DOU 11/3
Lunatic. DOU 10/2
Mecca. COV 3/3
Nocturne. POE 7/1
The ogre. POE 2/3
Portrait of a lady. POE 7/1
Prelude. COV 11/2
Red leaves. POE 6/3
Resurrection. COV 1/0
Riding. POE 6/4
Sarabande. COV 11/2
Sequence. COV 5/2
Shadow. POE 7/1
She once thought love. POE 6/4
The shop. POE 7/1
The singing bowl. POE 6/4
Stranger. POE 2/3
Three sonnets (of) good & evil. POE 9/3
Two women. POE 7/1
Where beauty walks alone. POE 2/3
Winter rendezvous. VOI 12/2
Seitz, Don C.
The lynching. NAT12/27/2
Seitz, Mildred
The wanton. HAM 6/1
Sell, Rose Osborne
The flame. GUL 7-8/3
Selleck, Lilian E.
The Immaculate Conception. CAW 12/0
Selva, Salomon De La
Love in Mexico. PAL Sum/3
Selver, P.
Suburban landscape. BRO 2/2
Semay, Dyoll
Coyote Bill's holiday. LAR 10/3
Light o'love. LAR 11/3
The rough and rugged hills. LAR 11/3
Sesame. LAR 12/3
To the sea. LAR 3/4
Sempel, Jane
Content. SCR 11/3
My prayer. SCR 5/3
Night. SCR 11/3
Seng Dji-Nan
An old man's song of spring. POE 8/2
Serles, Lila
Crossing the Mojave. PEG 1/3
Sessions, Barbara
After slight acquaintance. S4N 12/2
May 5, 1921. S4N 1-2/3
Seton, Harold
Cupid, conjurer. MUN 10/2
The little things of life. MUN 3/2
The players and their plays. MUN 2/2
Puzzles in proverbs. MUN 1/2
Seymour, George Steele
Ballade of any town. STE 2/2
Dedication. STE 4/4
Portrait of Danton. STE 12/2
Rain. STE 1/4
Scaramouche. STE 6/2
Stevenson portraits. COV 2/1
Shallcross, Eleanor C.
Chivalry. CAW 4/1
Shallcross, Eleanor Custis
Rain. CAW 5/2
Shanafelt, Clara
A death. NER 4/7/0
A dynamic personality. NER 4/28/0
Major. NER 2/18/0
Shanks, Edward
Lew is Piaget, Alba: from the. REW 12/1
The rock pool. CEN 11/0
The wind. MEA 3/2
Winter trees. MEA 3/2
Shao Yeh
Looking out on one departing. MEA 6/2

Sharp, Clarence A.
Absolute faith. CTY Spr/2
The apples do it. CTY Win/4
The blue of the snow. CTY Win/4
Boyhood scenes. CTY S-A/1
By the coal heaver. CTY Win/2
Christmas morning. CTY Win/3
Concerning swallows, etc. CTY S-A/1
Eighteen and fifty. CTY Win/2
The enemy. CTY Win/4
Familiars. CTY Sum/3
The farmer to the oak. CTY Win/3
Giving up. CTY Win/2
Her first civic idea. CTY Aut/2
Her rebuke. CTY S-A/1
Impressionism. CTY Win/2
In my autumn garden. CTY S-A/1
Inspiration. CTY Spr/2
Is it you? CTY Win/2
It rains for Molly. CTY Spr/3
A January boy. CTY Win/2
Joseph's kind. CTY Spr/2
Just to be out. CTY S-A/1
Loss the greatest. CTY Spr/3
My lesser songs. CTY S-A/1
My pines. CTY Spr/3
November late. CTY Aut/2
A November song. CTY Win/2
O Chanticleer. CTY Win/2
O I could write. CTY S-A/1
O sing me some song. CTY Spr/2
The plea at Ellis Island. CTY Spr/2
A prayer. CTY S-A/1
Rainy day verses. CTY Win/2
The river. CTY Win/2
Rural advices. CTY Win/2
The smell o' the hay. CTY Win/2
Snowbirds. CTY Win/2
Song of a team-driver. CTY S-A/1
The spirit of poetry. CTY Spr/4
Things of eternity. CTY Sum/3
To Clytie. CTY Spr/2
Too eager. CTY S-A/1
A twilight picture. CTY S-A/1
Waited for. CTY Win/4
The war-sower. CTY Aut/2
The way she's made. CTY Aut/2
When Muther reeds a novl. CTY Spr/3
Work creed of a real man. CTY Spr/2
Your mountain. CTY Aut/2
Sharpman, Maude Ralston
India's roll call. UNI 6/1/2
Shaw, Alice Jacqueline
The mount of vision. CIJ 10/3
Our petition. CIJ 9/3
Shaw, Dorothy Stott
Mountain passion. AMP10-11/3
Shaw, Frances
Autumn road-song. POE 10/3
Contentment. POE 3/3
Good Friday song. POE 3/3
Rain. POE 2/1
Renewal. POE 3/3
Soldier's night. POE 3/3
Tapestry. POE 3/3
Unfailing. POE 2/1
Who loves the rain. LAR 2/3
Shaw, Peryl
Night. TEM Win/3
Shaw, Ralph G.
Wealth. BOT 2/6/4
Shead, Flossie Faith
Sunset. LYW 11/3
To the little Babe in a manger. AMP 12/3
Sheap, Harriet
My au revoir. AMP10-11/3
Shedd, John A.
The living Dante. FOR
Sheehan, Murray
The after-path. ALS 6/1
The wind. ALS 2/1
Shelton, R.V.A.
City rain. NER 6/9/0
Shelton, Thomas Russell
Autumn. AMP 10/2
Crusaders. COV 12/3
Gifts. AMP 12/3
A legend of the star. AMP 12/2
Shenton, Edward
A song for evening. COV 7/3
Shepard, Alice M.
Awakenings. GRA 3/2
The road to Jericho. GRA 4/1
Trees in autumn. GRA 10./0
Shepard, William Gamaliel
Landscape. BRO 2/3
Sheperd, Dombey
Lead on! LYW 11/2
My wish. COV 12/2
Southern breeze. AMP 8/2
Shepherd, Dombey
Concordia. AMP 2/2
Freedom. COV 12/1
Omnipresence. COV 12/1
The outcast. COV 12/1
Reflugence (Joseph Andrew Gala. AMP 6/2
The supreme adventure. AMP 2/2
Sheridan, Annette A.
A reverie. AMP 8/2
Sherman, Ellen Burns
The great imagist. LYW 5/4

Sherman, L. Adelaide
Fantasy. GRA 10/2
In violet time. GRA 4/1
The road. GRA 8/2
Sherry, Laura
Bohemian town. POE 10/0
Grand-dad's bluff. POE 9/2
Howard Bentley. POE 9/2
The hunter. POE 10/0
In mist. POE 9/2
Jean Joseph Rolette. POE 10/0
Late autumn in the hills. POE 9/2
Light magic. POE 9/2
Louis des Chiens. POE 10/0
Morning in the hills. WAV 3/4
My country. POE 9/2
My town. POE 10/0
A native. POE 9/2
Nothin'--somethin'. POE 9/2
On our farm. POE 10/0
A woodsman. POE 10/0
Sherwin, Fred
To a fir tree clinging to a mo. PER 10/2
Sherwood, Margaret
The present hour. SCM 2/2
A sign. SCM 8/2
Shields, Helen
The fat old star... DEP 12/3
Happiness. DEP 12/3
Rain. DEP 12/3
Shipley, Joseph T.
By night. LYW 7-8/3
Can I believe. FUG 6-7/3
Cynic. FUG 12/3
Kit Marlowe to Cabell. DOU 2/3
Wave hollow. VOI 12/2
Shipman, Clare
The figurehead speaks. FRE 10/3/3
In the light of Xmas candles. LYW 12/3
Meadow lark. LYW 10/2
Orange pekoe. LYW 1/2
Recompense. LYW 1/2
Shipp, E. Richard
The abandoned house. LYW 9/3
The abandoned mine. LAR 4/4
As night comes. LAR 11/3
Crossing the desert. OVM 3/4
Dreamland. LYW 5/4
Eighteen-ninety. LAR 7/3
Five thoughts. LAR 7/3
Mariposa. AMP 4-5/3
Midnight thunderstorm. LAR 5/3
The nation mourns its chief. AMP 8-9/3
Prairie-dog town. LAR 7/3
Sunrise to sunset. AMP 10/2
Today the cowboys ride. LAR 11/3
The touch. LAR 7/3
True harmony. LAR 7/3
True harmony. LYW 9/3
Viking. AMP 3-4/4
The west. PEG 7/3
The wise men. AMP 12/2
Sholl, Anna McClure
Our Lady of Good Voyage. CAW 8/2
Ruysbroeck. CAW 1/2
Shreve, Dorothy
Madonna. AMP 2-3/3
Shuler, Esta Brooke
Envy. CIV 3/4
Shumaker, Harriet Hall
Lovers. LYW 12/2
Seen in April. LYW 4/3
Siegrist, Mary
The choice. EVM 11/0
Evening on the hills..Newburgh. NEW 8/3
Gandhi. SUR 4/8/2
Karma. SHA ?/3
Let us have done with words. SVG 7/3
Let youth ride on! ORI 2/3
Main street mumbles on. NEW 1/27/2
Makers of music, in invocation. NEW 7/30/2
My torch. GLE 6/2
The poets. NEW 7/17/2
Rain your rain softly. NEW 4/9/3
Reality. NEU 1/8/2
A sculptor in marble. NEW 12/9/2
Silence. SVG 7/3
The silent singer. NEW 9/18/1
The trees of the silvermine. NEW 9/9/3
Unhailed nativities. GLE 1/3
While song enthralled. MAC 6/4
Whom spring loves best. NEW 3/12/2
Sigmund, Jay G.
Aviators. DER 2/2
Barnacles. SPT10/23/1
The bat. CHE 3/30/2
Bewilderment. PAG 12/1
Birds of prey. AMP Sum/1
Blue-jay. CED12/16/1
A break in the drought. CHE 7/7/2
The builder. CTY Spr/2
Cards. LYW 11/2
The cicada. CED 7/18/2
Circus sideshow portraits. CHE

9/10/2
Corn country paean. CED 1/14/3
Cowslips. CTY Spr/2
Crows. CTY Aut/2
Faded wreath. DAV 12/5/1
The father of waters. ROC10/11/1
Five corn-belt village portrai. DAV12/21/2
Forecast. WAN 12/3
Fossils. DAV 11/7/1
A fur coat. ROC 12/3/1
In the house of the living dea. ROC 4/22/2
John Turner, M.D.. ROC 2/28/2
July. WAN 7/4
June woods. ROC 5/27/2
Just angle-worms. SPR 3/3
The killers. ROC 3/5/2
Kingdom for horses. REW 10/3
Lady's maid. ROC 4/1/2
The letter-carrier. DAV 11/7/1
The lone linden. CAP11-12/2
Marsh road. WAN 8/3
The minister's wife. CTY 12/1
Mississippi River village folk. DAV 7/26/3
Mushrooms. MID 7/2
The mystic river pool. MOR Aut/2
Pageant. CHE 3/31/2
The parrot. CIU10/25/1
A plowman sings. CTY Spr/4
Rabbits. SPR 2/2
A rain song. CED 5/27/2
Sacred ibis. CHE 6/4/2
Squaw winter. CTY Win/4
Storm. ROC 6/4/2
Summer solstice. CED 6/23/3
Tempted. ROC 3/29/2
"They say." CTY Spr/3
Thistle. AMP 6/2
To a corn belt farmer. CHN 6/26/3
To a garden snail. ROC 7/10/2
To a goldfinch. ROC 4/8/2
To a harelipped child. NOM Win/2
To a scissors grinder. CHE 4/24/2
To a toad. LYR 4/3
To a wood duck. CHE12/10/2
To my daughter. CED 5/27/2
Train message. ROC 4/3/2
Two troubadours of Bacchus. CHE10/28/2
We who forget. CTY Spr/2
The white moment. LYR 4/2
The wise man. ROC10/17/1
Years. ROC 11/1/1
The yellow, breasted chat. ROC 7/8/2

Sill, Louise Morgan
Song in spring. HAM 4/0
Tigers. HAM 1/2

Sillen, Marta of
The burden. LYR 4/3

Silvay, Challiss
Book shop impressions. WAN 5/4
Road's end. WAN 10/3
Shadows. WAN 12/3
Words. WAN 12/3

Silvey, Challiss
Inversion. PEG 3/3
To a nearly completed skyscrap. PEG 5/3

Simmons, Laura
Affirmation. CAW 1/0
Apocalpyse. CAW 6/2
Bartimaeus. CIC 7/3/4
Bartimeus. CAW 11/1
The sister of mercy. CAW 10/2

Simmons, Mona Josephine
Sweet peas. STE 5/4
Winged words. CIC 5/17/3

Simons, Hi
A dance theme. MOR Aut/2
Dust in the road. POE 2/2
Eternally. WAV 6/2
Holiday air. CAP 10/2
Moonrise. WAV 6/2
Open window. MIL 10/2
Portrait of an old roue. POE 2/2
Scintillations. WAV 6/2
The star. POE 2/2
Taps. POE 2/2
Tree. WAV 6/2
Two lines. CAP 10/2
Waters. CAP 10/2

Simple, Sam
Concerning paintin'. CTY Win/2

Simpson, Mabel
Vision. DIA 3/4

Simpson, William H.
Bareback. POE 5/2
Burdens. POE 1/0
Burro loads. POE 5/2
Campo Santo. POE 5/2
Country night. POE 5/2
Dance of the dust witches. POE 1/0
De Noche. POE 5/2
Desert night. POE 5/2
Deserted. POE 1/0
The fog ghost. POE 1/0
Ghosts. POE 1/0
Grand Canyon. POE 1/0
Hepi song of the desert. POE 5/2

Homesick song. POE 1/0
Hopi maiden. POE 1/0
Hopi-tuh. POE 1/0
Inarticulate. POE 5/2
Landscape. POE 5/2
Manana. POE 5/2
Navajo. POE 5/2
The new day. POE 1/0
The north woods. POE 1/0
November. POE 1/0
Pity not. POE 1/0
Shadow faces. POE 1/0
So little you are. POE 5/2
Tewa song. POE 5/2
Trees. POE 5/2
Yucca is yellowing. POE 5/2

Sinclair, Van Buren
Reverie. GUL 7-8/3

Siple, Jessie Allen
Jus' right. CTY Spr/4
The picture. CTY Spr/4

Sitwell, Edith
Winter. RHY 3/3

Sitwell, Osbert
Dead man's wood. POE 12/0
Malgre Lin. DIA 12/0
Maxixe. POE 6/2
Mrs. Freudenthal consults... POE 12/0

Siviter, Anna Pierpont
The tree. AMP 6-7/3

Skeen, Ruth Loomis
The archbishop's garden. LYW 7-8/3
The blue bird. LYW 6/2
The hills of Sante Fe. LYW 6/2
In Santa Fe. STE 7/2
In the cathedral at Santa Fe. STE 10/3
March. POE 3/0
A mother's prayer. MAG 2/2
To the little flower. MAG 2/2

Skelton, Virginia
Out yonder. LYW 10/2

Skinner, Constance Lindsay
As the rivers. COV 9/1
Creed. LYW 12/1
Kan-il-lak the singer to Nak-k. LWY 7-8/2
Mandolines under the moon. LYW 5/2
Naku-ku replies. LWY 7-8/2
Sea cliff. LYW 7-8/2
Song of David before Saul. LYW 9/1
Stars. COV 8/0
Swiya's night song. BOO 1/3
Swiya's songs beside running w. LYW 4/3
Swiya's songs... LYW 3/4
Sycamores in winter. LYW 1/3
Winter dawn. POE 2/2

Slater, Eleanor
Foreboding. CAS 3/3

Slater, Mary White
Rain. COV 3/0

Slayton, Elizabeth
Ashes of oak. CAS 1/3
Heart's bitterness. CAS 3/3
Winter's memory of winter. CAS 1/3

Sloan, J. Blanding
Atlas. CEN 4/2

Sloan, J. Vandervoort
Life and sleep. DOU 8-9/1

Slovin, S. L.
The birth of light. INT 1-3/4

Sloyer, Monroe W.
Gems. AMP 6-7/3

Slyke, Berenice Van
The circle. COV 3/0
For a little time. COV 9/0

Slyke, Bernice Van
First snow. POE 12/3
Je viendrai au jardin. POE 12/3

Small, Florence S.
April. COV 1/4
God, the poet. COV 2/3
Mortality. COV 2/3
Words. COV 2/3

Smith, Adeline Holton
In the valley of the mad river. GRA 2/2
Spring and dawn. GRA 4/2
The woodsey trail. GRA 6/2

Smith, Alfred J.
Stroms. POA 9/1

Smith, Amy Sebree
Dawn-sea. PEG 1/3
Night skies. PEG 1/3

Smith, Bess Foster
Dream child. LAR 3/4
Picture of Idaho. LAR 7/3

Smith, Chard Powers
Adirondack evening. COV 10/3
Flying thistles. COV 10/3

Smith, Charles Payne
Come play with me. AMP10-11/3

Smith, Clark Ashton
The absence of the muse. LYW 10/1
Alienage. WAN 11/3
Chant of autumn. LYW 10/2
Don Juan sings. WAN 3/4
The fugitive. WAN 1/4
Haunting. LYW 10/1
In Lemuria. LYW 7-8/2
The infinite quest. LYW 7-8/2
Plum-flowers. LAL 3/4
The refugee of beauty. LAL 5/4

Requiescat in pace. MID 5/0
Rosa mystica. LYW 12/1
The song of Aviol. LYW 3/4
We shall meet. WAN 5/4

Smith, Dorothy W.
Tam o'shanters. GRA 2/1

Smith, Edith Livingston
Love's secret path. ARG 6/21/4

Smith, Freeman Pinckney
The mouse hunt. DOU 8/2

Smith, Hariette G.
The dreamer. LYW 3/4
Little love of mine. SCR 11/3
The mist. LYW 3/4
The siren. LYW 4/4

Smith, Harriet E.
November. PAG 8-9/1

Smith, Harriet
The ghost. AMP 1-2/4

Smith, Hilda W.
Mid orchards. COV 8/0

Smith, John D.
A song of the hoe. SVG 4/3

Smith, John F.
The spirit of music. AMP 8-9/3

Smith, Laurine
Ceremony. POE 10/1
First comer. POE 10/1
Joy. POE 10/1
Swallows brush a pool. POE 10/1
Wind. POE 10/1

Smith, Lewis Worthington
Fires in the urn. COV 9/0
On a woman with a lover. SCM 2/4
Roofs. COV 1/0
A vase from Nippon. COV 1/0

Smith, Marion Couthouy
Arachne. STE 12/2
The city of the dead. SEW10-12/1
Companions. COV 3/2
Death and the flying man. OUT12/27/2
The doorway. COV 3/4
The fantasies. OUT 9/5/3
The Hermes of Praxiteles. LYR 11/3
I shall not mind. OUT 9/28/1
In a cemetery. OUT 2/18/0
Late in the spring. NEW 5/2
The lyrics. OUT 9/5/3
May, the artist. LYW 5/4
The old burying ground. COV 3/2
On silent wings. HAM 7/2
The passing of the song. STE 9/3
A picture. HAM 11/1
A retrospect. OUT 8/9/2
The sea speaks. LYW 12/2
The silence of the pines. LYW 5/4
Song and imagery. COV 5/3
To a friend in the woods. OUT 9/3/0
Valedictory. COV 3/2
Willows. COV 5/3
The years walk gaily. STE 6/2

Smith, Mary E.
Whom? CIV 3/4

Smith, Ninna May
Her son. OUT12/10/3

Smith, Nora Archibald
Death, the sculptor. SCM 7/2
Dusk and solitude. OVM 7/4
Let me in! COV 1/2

Smith, Phoebe
Sumach. STE 5/4

Smith, Roy Churchill
Thrills. LAR 3/4

Smith, Sarah Bixby
Blowing grasses. LYW 3/1
Bypath. LYW 3/4
My coyote. LYW 12/3

Smithson, Edith M.
O tell me. NEP 4-5/2

Snedigar, Robert
Negligee. LIB 12/1

Snow, Charles Wilbert
Olaf. NAT 2/7/0
The paving quarry. NAT10/12/1

Snow, Royall
Cloud-rift. COV 2/2
Portrait in sinister lights. MEA 10/2
The ruined abbey. COV 4/4
The street singer. COV 1/1
Variations on a very old theme. PAG 12/1
Veritas. PAG10-11/1

Snow, Wilbert
Advice to a clam-digger. NAT 2/27/4
Concarneau. FOR 5/4
Country funeral. SCM 3/3
Impressions. NAt12/26/3
Morning world. FOR 5/4
Youth. MEA 3/4
Zeb Kinney on professors. CEN 2/4

Snubbers, Gabriel
Two poem tones. STE 9/3

Solomon, M. Walter
Images Japonaises. PAG 4-5/0

Someple
Lady road. LYR 9/2

Soupault, Philippe
Arthur Cravan. BRO 10/2
Chansons. LIR A-W/4
Francis Picabia. BRO 10/2

Louis Aragon. BRO 10/2
Marie Laurenchin. BRO 10/2
Paul Eluard. BRO 10/2
Theodore Fraenkel. BRO 10/2
Tristan Tzara. BRO 10/2

South, Ira
View-points. EVM 11/0

Southern, Lou
Adventure calls. AMP 8-9/3

Southworth, Victor E.
To the meadowlark. UNI 6/22/2

Spates, Anna Elisabeth
I dream. NET 1/6/1

Spaulding, Edith B.
Thyri of Westra. STE 3/4

Spears, Raymond S.
Opportunity. MUN 1/2

Speight, E. E.
The adventures. HAM 8/0
Danger. HAM 5/0

Spence, Roberta
Bird of happiness. CTY Aut/2

Spencer, Alice B.
Night. COV 8/1

Spencer, Anne
White things. CUU 3/3

Spencer, Evelyn
Across the world. WAN 12/3

Spencer, Henry P.
Song. AMP 8/2

Spencer, Lilian White
Apache wife--Arizona. VOI 7-8/3
Aspen - Colorado. COV 5/2
Aspen moods--Colorado. AMP 10/3
Atonement. LYW 5/4
The cathedral window. PEG 7/3
Continental divide. VOI 7-8/3
De Soto. COV 12/3
Faust. FOR 6/4
Mesa Verde-A.D. 1000. FOR 3/4
The old Pueblo. LYW 11/1
On a broken statue. COV 8/2
Pan. COV 8/2
A rondeau of recompense. SAU 9/2
San Miguel Tlazcaktecos. LYW 2/2
Santo Domingo - Easter. LYW 4/2
To Walt Whitman. LYW 12/3
Wild cat ledge. COV 12/3

Spencer, Nellie Gray
How? CIC10/25/3

Spero, Anna Kalfus
In my dreams. WAN 5/4
The rustle in the house. OVM 7/4

Sperry, Tilla Barbara
The waves lullaby. AMP10-11/3

Speyer, Leonora
Affinity. SMA 1/3
Assault. NAT 1/10/3
At the hospital for the insane. POE 9/2
Bagpipe player. MEA 4/3
Being forbidden. VOI Spr/3
The confidant. COV 7/0
Couplets. POE 9/2
Dawn. POE 7/0
Discovery. COV 5/3
Duet. POE 9/2
Faggi's statue of Eve. COV 7/2
First communion. COV 7/0
Forgetting and forgetting. COV 5/3
A gift. TOU ?/0
Gold-fish. COV 7/0
Herod. MEA 4/3
"I have a rendezvou with death. LYR 9/1
I heard a woman singing. COV 5/3
In praise of Abrigada. POE 2/2
Iron virgin. MEA 4/3
Italian quatrains. FRE 12/5/3
Kind fate. POE 9/2
The kleptomaniac. FOR ?/2
The ladder. REM ?/0
The last morning in...country. NAT ?/0
Little lover. COV 5/3
The locust. POE 7/0
Looking on. POE 9/2
Mary Magdalene. NAT 5/25/1
Measure me, sky! BOO 9/1
Migration. CEN 7/2
Mist over the Dolomites. MEA 1/3
Moon hunter. MEA 4/3
Moon in the morning. VOI Spr/2
New moon. COV 7/0
Opinions. NES10/22/1
Paganini's violins. VOI 3-4/4
Pain. FRE ?/0
The pet. BOO 4/1
Protest in passing. MEA 3/2
Saint in petticoats. MEA 4/3
Sewkhmet the lionhearted. COV 4/0
She says. VOI Spr/3
Sign of the heart inn. NAT 11/9/1
Skyway robbery. COV 7/0
Song overheard. POE 9/2
Spring cowardice. COV 4/0
The squall. POE 7/0
The story as I understand it. CEN 4/4
The stronghold. POE 9/2
Suddenly. CEN 3/0
The tear-bottle. COV 3/1

Tears for sale. NES 7/8/2
Therapy. MEA 7/1
Third floor landing. BOO 3/4
Three Persian tiles. NAT10/12/1
To a little XII century figure. SON 9-10/0
A truth about a lie. POE 9/2
Two on a hill. COV 11/0
Two women meet. COV 7/2
Upon reading a love lyric. COV 8/1
Victory. NAT 3/20/1
Words to sleep upon. BOO 5/2

Spicer, Anne Higginson
The auction. WAV 6/2
The cathedral calls. ALS 2/2
The foggy sabath. AMP 2/2
Three griefs. POE 1/3
The valley unvisited. AMP 6/2

Spiller, Robert E.
The moment. COV 3/0
The road. COV 3/0

Spingarn, Joel Elias
Shrine. NAT 3/22/2

Spire, Andre
Dagmara. DIA 3/1
Midi. DIA 3/1

Spofford, Harriet Prescott
Cadwallader. HAM 1/0

Springer, Nannae Neal
Contrast. LAR 11/3
Page from a diary. LAR 11/3

Squier, Edythe
Thwarted. GUL 9/3

Squire (Solomon Eagle), J. C.
The lover's lute. LYR 7/4

St. Jerome, Mother
The bells of St. Quintin. MAG 12/1

St. John, S. M.
Religious profession. MAG 12/1
A summer idyl. MAG 7/2
Visitation. MAG 6/2

Stafford, Wendell Phillips
Sower and reaper. SCM 12/0

Stahel, Louisa
California nighingale. AMP 2-3/3
The cup. PEG 1/3
The rainbow. PEG 5/3

Stait, Virginia
Appointment. AML 5/1
Before communion. TEM Aut/1
Bequeathed. AJA 8/1
Broken. CEN 5/4
Finalities. AMP 2/2
Ghosts. CEN 10/2
Lotus. AJA 7/2
Miser and spenthrift. LYR 8/2
"Other's bread." POB Sum/3
Residue. DAI 4/2
The return. LYW 9/2
Rhythm. AMP 5-6/4
Roses foresworn. COV 7/3
The secret. AMP 10/2
Time to go. LYR 6/4
To a hyacinth song. LYR 12/2
Unsepulchered. POB Sum/3
The vased rose. LYW 9/2
Weights and measures. COV 3/1

Standish, Marian Eddy
Lullaby. DET 12/8/3

Stanley, Irene
Void. LAR 4/4

Stannard, Everett Earle
And you. LAR 4/4
Riches. LAR 10/3

Starbuck, Victor
Buttflies of Uganda. REW 1/3
Carl Sandburg. STE 4/3
The clock. COV 4/4
The freeholder. POE 9/0
Jane Foster. VOI Spr/3
Paradox. BOO 1/3
Pensee. DOU 10/2
Pippa passes. STE 12/2
Resurrection. HAM 5/0
A rondeau of sonnets. FUG 9/27/2
Song for a youth. COV 4/4
The widower. OUT 6/21/2

Stark, Anne Campbell
To Alice. DEU 5/0

Stark, Dare
Under alders. MEA 4/1

Stark, Elsie M.
Cherry blossoms. SCR 4/4
Sonnet. SCR 2/4

Starrett, Vincent
Crescent moon. DOU 6/2
Cricket. STE 5/2
Dandelions. VOI Sum/2
Death watch. NAT 8/1/3
Dies Irae. STE 6/2
House. ALS 9/1
Ivanhoe. FRE 5/3/2
Kyrie Eleison. MAG 9/3
Palimpsest. ALS 9/1
Picture. BOO 1/2
Rain. ALS 9/1
Return. ALS 9/1
Self portrait. ALS 8/1
Squirrel. STE 5/2
Turtle. STE 5/2
Windows. STE 1/4

Statius, Publius Papinius
Sleep. UNV 7/2

Stefan, George
The lord of the isle. NAT 3/14/3

Steiner, Richard Morrow
Black belt at night. GRI 3/1
Steiss, A. J.
The blind poet. MAG 9/3
Gray sails. MAG 2/2
The poet dying. MAG 10/3
Stephens, James
The ghost. NER 8/1/3
The last word. DIA 3/3
Stephens, Mary Vinson
"When we shall part." MEA 4/1
Stephenson, Daisy D.
Good tenants. AMP10-11/3
Sterling, George
"57." ALS 1/2
Afternoon. AIN 5/0
Amber. STE 7/3
Beauty renounced. ALS 4/2
Careless. BOO 8/1
The daughters of disillusion. WAN 8/3
The evening star. ALS 8/1
The first born. WAN 6/3
The flight. LYW 6/3
The fog-sea. LYW 2/3
From the heights. ALS 10/1
From the valley. LYW 3/4
Good and evil. SON 12/0
The gulls. NAT 3/22/2
The hidden pool. REW 3/2
High noon. STE 2/4
The lost nymph. REW 12/1
The midway peace. ALS10-11/3
Mirage. NAT 4/13/1
The night migration. NES 5/13/2
Ode to Shelley. SCM 7/2
Poe's gravestone. NAT 9/7/1
Princess on the headland. ALS 12/1
Problem. LYW 2/2
Pumas. NES 3/25/2
Rainbow's end. AIN 2/2
Shelley at Spezia. STE 1/3
The strange bird. OUT 3/7/3
The stranger. ALS 2-3/3
The street. STE 6/4
To Charles Warren Stoddard. LYW 4/4
To Wordsworth. WAN 2/4
To beauty. ALS 10/1
The tracker. ALS 7/3
The unconditioned. WAN 6/4
Vigil. WAN 12/3
Waste. ALS10-11/2
Wet beaches. SCM 11/3
The wild swan. SMA 4/2
The young witch. CEN 8/3
Stern, Caroline
The elm. CON 1/1
The locust. CON 1/1
Stern, Elaine
Valentine. GRA 4/1
Sterrett, Edna
My mother. LOS 5/10/4
Stetson, Marjorie Muir
November. PAG 4-5/0
Stevens, A. Borden
The choice. LAL 5/4
Love's crown. LAL 3/4
Revelation. LAL 1/4
Sacrosanct. LAL 1/4
Sacrosanct. NEP 4-5/2
Stevens, Beatrice
Deep in the hills. LYR 5/3
My love. LYW 1/3
Stevens, Eleanor Mathews
On returning from a journey. AIN 2/2
Song. AIN 10/2
Stevens, Margaret Talbott
Sorrow. INT 4-6/4
Stevens, Wallace
Another weeping woman. POE 10/1
Bantams in pine woods. DIA 7/2
The bird with the coppery, kee. BRO 12/1
Cortege for Rosenbloom. MEA 3/1
The Cuban doctor. POE 10/1
The doctor of Geneva. POE 10/1
The emperor of ice cream. DIA 7/2
Floral decorations for bananas. MEA 4/3
Frogs eat butterflies, snakes. DIA 7/2
From the misery of Don Joost. POE 10/1
Gubbinal. POE 10/1
Hibiscus on the sleeping shore. POE 10/1
A high-toned old Christian wom. DIA 7/2
How the constable carried the. MEA 4/3
Hymn from a watermelon pavilio. BRO 6/2
The load of sugar cane. POE 10/1
Lulu Gay. COT ?/1
New England verses. MEA 4/3
O Florida, venereal soil. DIA 7/2
Of heaven considered as a tomb. POE 10/1
One the manner of addressing c. POE 10/1
The ordinary women. DIA 7/2
Palace of the babies. POE 10/1
Sea surface full of clouds. DIA 7/4

The shape of the coroner. MEA 5/3
The snow man. POE 10/1
Stars at Tallapoosa. BRO 6/2
Tea at the Palaz of Hoon. POE 10/1
To the one of fictive music. NER11/15/2

Stevenson, Alec B.
Et sa pauvre chair. FUG 6-7/3
Fiddlers' green. FUG 4-5/3
The first whitethroat. COV 4/1
He who loved beauty. FUG 12/2
Meuse heights. FUG 10/2
Portrait. FUG 10/2
Rondeau for autumn. FUG 12/2
Swamp moon. FUG 2/4
Urbaine on the Planetarium. FUG 12/3

Stewart, Anna Bird
My little yesterday. PIR 5/2

Stewart, Clare
By the beach sleeping. COV 8/1
Crossing on the Seattle ferry. COV 6/0
Return. COV 8/1

Stewart, H. W.
Gum-trees. POE 11/0
Supplements. POE 11/0

Stewart, Marjory
Sometimes. COV 5/2

Stewart, Mary
A song for summer. STE 6/3

Stewart, S. D.
Now I would tell you... LYW 3/4

Stewart, W. H.
Dawn. POE 12/2
Reverie. POE 12/2

Stewart, Winifred Gray
Autumnal. MAC 11/2
The baby. WAN 6/4
Before rain. CAP11-12/2
Chimney smoke. OVM 3/4
Chromo. OVM 3/4
Convalescence. OVM 7/4
The dancer. WAN 5/4
Hummingbird. WAN 5/4
Interlude. WAN 9/3
Notes on trees for windy night. LAR 2/4
Patterns. LAR 2/4
Protest. LYW 6/2
Sky wind. LYW 10/2
Staccato. WAN 7/4

Stidger, William L.
I want to washed by God's wind. CIC 1/25/3
The sin supreme. CIC 1/11/3

Stiles, Roberta L.
Autumn. SCR 10/3
Come. SCR 5/4
Delirium. SCR 6/4
Fortified. LAL 5/4
Neighbors. SCR 5/4
On the road to town. SCR 6/4
Opportunity. SCR 10/3

Stillman, Clara G.
Dark Dream. CUU 4/3

Stillman, Mildred W.
Evangeline. AMP 12/3
Frost. CTY Aut/3
May. CTY Spr/4
To a critic. CTY Win/4

Stillson, Thelma
Freight-cars. EVM 11/0
Garden song. EVM 11/0

Stillwell, Ethel Brooks
Rain at dusk. AMP 2-3/3
The return. LYW 6/2

Stockbridge, Dorothy
Entreaty. AIN 2/0

Stockdale, Allen A.
Godstow. EME 4/3
To knowledge or to death. EME 4/3

Stockett, M. Letitia
Discovery. COV 6/0
The fallow fields. COV 3/1
Free. POE 4/3
Moonrise. COV 8/2
Pegasus. COV 1/1
A song. COV 2/2
To a musician. COV 1/2
Wedding song. COV 6/0

Stockton, Peter
My bicycle and I. LIC 3/2

Stockton, Roscoe K.
Moon-dawn. AMP10-11/3

Stoddard, Anne
The faithful. BOO 10/2
To M.D.. CEN 8/0

Stoddard, Yetta Kay
Columbine. PEG 1/3
East camp. LAR 7/3
For a rose. CUU 11/2
Homage of kings. AMP 12/2
The new poet. AMP 2-3/3
Point Loma breezes. LYW 7-8/2
Spring in California (the host. AMP 2/2
Storm-vigil. AMP Aut/1
You shall sail. LYW 2/4

Stokes, Rose Pastor
O prolitariat! LIB 10/2

Stone, Eliot Kays
When the master paints... COV 9/0

Stone, Jack
Commemoration. SOV 1923

Storer, Edward

Broken image. BRO 6/2
By the shore. BRO 6/2
The carnival. BRO 10/2
Gold. BRO 6/2
Illusion. BRO 6/2
In hospital. BRO 10/2
Poor devils. BRO 10/2
Silence. BRO 10/2

Storey, Violet Alleyn
For you. HAM 3/3
Remembrance. HAM 3/2

Stork, Charles Wharton
After that hour. MIN11-12/3
Artist whim. LYW 9/2
Autumnal ecstasy. FOR 10/3
Beauty. FOR ?/0
Because I love. LYR 3/4
Cherry boughs. LYR 4/3
The forbidden rose. FRE 7/12/2
Froding's grave. SCA ?/1
Fungi. YAR 10/3
Green fire. BOO 4/2
Half-light happiness. LYW 11/1
Horizon. VOI Win/2
A lady. NOM Win/2
The meeting of Christ and Pan. FOR 4/4
Midway. FRE 3/2/1
Motion sketch. MIN 5-6/4
Naughty Nell. LYW 9/2
Ode to winter. NEW 2/27/3
On the Jewish cemetery..Prague. FRE 2/6/4
The parson o' Porlock town. FRE10/12/1
The Platonic lover. AIN 7/2
Relativity. VOI 12/2
The rose and God. POE 4/4
Shelley, for the centenary of. PHI 1/3
The stupendous flower. STE 1/4
"Sweet custom is the chiefest. AMP Aut/1
Symphony in D minor. FUG12/20/2
To Heifetz. LYW 11/1
To Joseph Severn. FRE 2/23/1
To Rodin. VOI 12-1/4
To one who has suffered. MEA 12/3
To trees at night. VOI Win/2
To whom it may concern. VOI 7-8/3
The troubadour of God. LYR 2/2
Truancy. LYW 11/1
Wake me to life! VOI Win/2
Were I a lark. FRE 2/13/4
Wine and song. AMP 4-5/3
Your outward self. AMP 6-7/3

Storm, Julia
Up, up and away. LOS 5/10/4

Storm, Marian
The dancing fern. NES11/26/1
David. NER12/20/2
"The gate of heaven." NES 4/14/3
Spring in Orizaba. NER 5/7/4
Vain counsel. NEW 7/23/4

Stowell, Robert H.
The gypsy voice. WAN 11/3
The last faun. WAN 11/3
Slave of song. WAN 1/4

Stragnell, Sylvia
Burial. LIB 8/2
Exhalation. LIB 12/2
Mezzotints. LIB 10/2

Strandberg, Betty
Desert spring. LAR 4/4

Strange, Michael
Lines. BOO 1/3

Stratton, Porter Gene
The heart of the world. COV 8/3
Oh Lord--Lady. COV 8/3
Ox-heart cherries. COV 8/3

Straus, Edna Adelaide
At St. Roch's Chapel. DOU 3/2

Street, Mary Dallas
Adam speaks. REW 4/2
Gabriel in April. REW 4/3
To C.S.J.. REW 11/1
Today. REW 7/2

Strobel, Marion
Admonition. POE 3/2
After these days. POE 3/3
Anodyne. POE 2/1
Anticipation. POE 3/0
Boomerang. POE 3/3
A bride, to D.K.A.. POE 3/3
Daily prayer. POE 3/2
Dialogue. POE 3/3
Encounter. POE 3/3
Ennui. POE 3/0
Frightened face. POE 3/2
Full-blown. POE 3/3
The gestures you make. POE 3/3
Growth. POE 5/4
High dive. POE 2/1
I give smiles. POE 2/1
I talk with myself. POE 3/3
I would pretend. POE 3/2
In reply. BOO 4/3
In the tropics. POE 5/4
Kindness. POE 2/1
L'envoi. POE 3/2
The last ritual. POE 3/0
Let me play net. POE 3/0
Little things. POE 2/1
Marriage-caprice. POE 2/1
Miserere. POE 2/1
The night. POE 3/2
Pastoral. POE 3/3

Penitent wife. POE 5/4
Pitiful in your bravery. POE 3/3
Portrait of a friend. POE 5/4
Pretty penny. POE 5/4
The silence stirs again. POE 3/2
Spring day. POE 3/0
Spring morning. POE 3/2
Story of a life. BOO 10/3
Story-teller. POE 5/4
Tonight. POE 3/2
The tragic few. POE 5/4
Trio. DOU 5/3
Tropical pool. POE 5/4
Two liars. POE 5/4
Two sonnets. POE 3/0
We have a day. POE 3/2
Without words. POE 2/1

Strode, Muriel
Confidence. LAR 8/3

Strong, Helen Clark
I am not hard to satisfy. COV 5/2

Strong, Katharine
Bobolinks. COV 6/0

Strong, L. A. G.
Lowery cot. FUG 2-3/3
Walkhampton. FUG 2-3/3
The wise man, ante porcos. CEN 8/2

Strong, William
The unmasking. SCM 8/1

Strother, H. Dana
Solitude. POA 9/1

Stryker, Carrie Woodward
Gardens. LYW 7-8/2
When spring appears. LOS 5/10/4

Stuart, H.
Bull-fight. POE 4/3
For a dancer. POE 4/3
Helen. POE 4/3
Munich. POE 4/3
Summer. POE 4/3

Stuart, Henry Longan
The faint heart. FRE12/12/3
Requiescit. FRE 1/30/4
Song at parting. FUG 5/9/3

Stuart, John Rollin
The poet. GRA 4/2
Search. GRA 8/2

Stuart, Muriel
In the orchard. POE 11/2
In their image. POE 11/2
The seed-shop. POE 11/2

Stuns, J. S.
Youth's illusion. LAR 7/3

Sturdy-Smith, Marguerite
A confession. CTY Win/3
Dear little hands. CTY Aut/2
The flight of youth. CTY Spr/2
Red and white. CTY Spr/3
To Lucille. CTY Spr/3

Sturges, Lucy Hale
Crucible. MEA 9/2
The desert. LYW 10/2
Kara-non. PEG 5/3
Kwacho-Shoji San, Ayame, Momij. LYW 4/3
Night's end. VOI Sum/2
Noon. LYW 5/2
Romance. LYW 5/2
Temporal. LYW 5/2

Sturges, Lucy H.
Afterglow. WAV 3/4
Cho-Cho-San. LYW 3/4
Kingfisher. VOI10-11/3

Sturges, Oliver T.
My wife's friend. PAG 8-9/1

Sturges-Jones, Marion
Desolation. PAG10-11/1

Sturgill, Vergil Leon
I have known. LAR 10/3
March. LAR 4/3
Spring on the plains. LAR 3/4

Suckow, Ruth
Beauty. POE 6/1
Grampa Schuler. POE 6/1
The odd ones. POE 6/1
Prayer at timber-line. POE 6/1

Sullivan, D. C.
The fight to survive. NEP 4-5/2

Sullivan, Maurice S.
Charlemagne. LYW 12/2
Telegraph poles. ALS 8/1

Summers, Llewelyn
Saying it with flowers. LIC 12/1

Summerville, Frank
Evening moods in cameo. SOV 1923
Just life. GUL 7-8/3

Sumner, Charles G.
Ho, ho, hum. LAR 8/3
Reclaimer. LAR 10/3
Sun and shade. LAR 9/3

Svorn, Teodora
Grandmere. NOM Spr/2
Grandmere. PAG10-11/1
Nocturne. PAG10-11/1
To--. PAG10-11/1

Swain, Y. F.
Carmel Mission. WAN 12/3
Eternal. WAN 7/4
Helen. WAN 12/3
Inversion. WAN 12/3
Lady to church. WAN 2/4
Moon of Carmel. WAN 12/3
Renunciation. WAN 3/4

Swartz, David Lester

The Wisconsin dells. AMP 4/2

Swartz, Elsa E.
To a deserted house. LAR 3/4

Swartz, Roberta Teale
Babel. SOV 1923
The Hawthorne tree. POE 8/3
The other voice. BOO 9/3

Swearingen, Mabel
Chime of Christmas bells. POA 1/2

Sweet, Ione M.
Futility. GUL 5/3
I have dared dream! GUL 6/3

Swerig, Vivian
Muted. POE 6/4

Swett, Margery
The city. LYW 2/2
Finis. LYW 2/2
In a doorway. LYW 2/4
The new frontiers. LYW 1/3
Patience. LYW 2/2
Play me a little moon. GUL 9/3
Song of an impudent day. POE 3/3
The storm. LYW 2/2

Swift, Ivan
Circles. STE 4/2
Descent. POE 9/1

Swift, Walter B.
The night express. AMP 8/2

Swigert, Minerva Florence
The bee and the butterfly. SCR 8/3
The three arts. INT 1-3/4

Symons, Arthur
Alvisi contarini. DOU 12/1
Body's bloom. DOU 6/1
By the sea. NES 6/16/3
A masque of shadows. DOU 6/2
Song. DOU 1/2
Trees in Paris: 1890. DOU 1/2

Taggard, E. Vashti
Watchman and star. LYW 12/2

Taggard, Genevieve
Afternoon. POE 2/1
Angular. MEA 1/2
Beach cabin. MEA 1/2
Boys and girls. POE 6/1
Child tropics remembered in Ne. LYW 6/2
Dedication. MEA 6/1
Desert woman remembers... MEA 11/2
Drouth. POE 2/1
Dying away song. VOI Aut/1
Elegy in dialogue. MEA 3/4
Endless circle. POE 2/1
Flags flying. BOO 2/4
For a shy lover. NAT 11/9/1
Found. POE 2/1
From the sea. POE 6/0
Hard girl. NAT 1/23/4
Ice age. MEA 3/1
Immindent doom. NAT 1/23/4
Just introduced. BOO 2/2
Little Hamlet. MEA 1/2
The long magic. MEA 1/2
Lost. POE 2/1
Married. POE 2/1
Moods of women. LYW 12/1
Moonrise mockery. POE 2/1
Neither Jesus nor Prosperpine. VOI 6-7/3
Old unhappy women. VOI 3-4/4
Only the frost. NES 12/8/3
Outer circle. LYW 5/4
A parable of paradise. NAT 2/20/4
The poet in the basement. MEA 9/1
Premonition in a mist. VOI 3-4/4
The quiet woman. LIB 9/1
Runner. VOI 12/2
Sea-change. POE 2/1
She comes after years to the o. LYW 12/1
Spring touch. MEA 1/2
Supper silence. BOO 7/4
Tropical girl to her garden. POE 2/1
Walking Market Street. VOI Aut/2
With child. LIB 12/1
Woodsman. NAt10/24/3
Zenith. POE 2/1

Tagore, Rabindranath
Once when we were both togethe. NAT 8/24/1
Three specimens reproducing... MEA 6/1

Tague, Harrell N.
The gay white ships of hope. YAR 5/4
When all earth has sunk away. YAR 11/3

Tainter, Lila Munro
Introspection. PEG 3/3
Success. PEG 3/3

Tallis, Grey
Dead bird. NOM Sum/2
Life. NOM Spr/2
Portrait of a mother. NOM Spr/2
Rain. NOM Sum/2
Red mountain. NOM Sum/2

Tanaquil, Paul

Ancient. LYW 12/2
Escape. VOI Spr/3
The lover. POE 2/2
Moon. NOM Aut/3
Moondown. POE 5/0
Nous n'irons plus au bois. VOI Aut/1
Pedant. VIO Sum/2
Pour elle. NOM Aut/3
The return of the prodigal. LYW 7-8/2
Seeking and finding not. COV 1/2
She reasons. COV 3/4
To a blind girl. LYR 11/2
Two men. LYW 10/1
Undone. VOI Spr/3
Words. COV 1/2

Tandy, Jennette
I wish. POE 11/3
Machines. POE 11/3
Planting. POE 11/3
Sunday afternoon. POE 11/3

Tanenbaum, Florence
Baal - Moloch. LIB 1/2
Mortgaged. LIB 6/2

Tate, Allen
Battle of Murfreesboro (1862-1. FUG 10/2
Bored to Choresis. WAV #5/2
Calidus juventa? DOU 2/3
The date. FUG 2-3/3
Elegy for Eugenesis. FUG 10/2
Euthanasia. DOU 5/2
First epilogue to Oenia. FUG 12/3
The happy poet remembers death. FUG 4-5/3
Hitch your wagon to a star. DOU 12/2
Horatian epode to the Duchess. FUG 10/2
Lityerses. LYR 6/4
Long fingers. REW 7/3
Mary McDonald. FUG 2-3/3
Non omnis moriar. FUG 10/2
Nuptials, to J.C.R.. FUG 12/2
Parthenia. DOU 7/2
Perimeters. FUG 2-3/3
Poem for my father. VOI 3-4/4
Portent. DOU 3-4/3
Prayer for an old man. FUG 12/3
Procession. FUG 6-7/3
Resurgam. MOR 4/3
The screen. FUG 6-7/3
Sonnet (to a portrait of Hart. DOU 3-4/3
Stranger. DOU 10/2
Teeth. FUG 2-3/3
These deadly leaves. FUG 12/2
To Oenia in wintertime. FUG 10/2
To a prodigal old maid. WAV #5/2
Tousellled. FUG 2/4
The wedding. FUG 12/3
William Blake. DOU 7/2
You left. FUG 4-5/3

Tate, Orley Allen
Red stains. AMP Aut/1

Taylor, Dwight
Some Pierrots come from behind. BOO 5/2

Taylor, Eletha Mae
Duse in La Citta Morte. VOI 5-6/4
Our suburb. AMP 3-4/4
A rainy day. AMP 4-5/3
The sea's lullaby. AMP 10/2
Soft winds. AMP 2/2
Twilight, I think of you. AMP 3-4/4
Winter. AMP 12/3

Taylor, Eugene C.
The adventurer. AMP 10/2

Taylor, Frances Beatrice
"My guests" COV 1/0

Taylor, Lucile L.
The dancer. PAD10-11/1
The phantom. LYW 12/1

Taylor, Marian Warner
Birth through death. COV 5/1

Taylor, Nell
Maid of Nagasaki. AMP 4-5/3
Narcisi in a glass bowl. AMP 6/2

Teasdale, Sara
Absence. SCM 12/3
Arcturus in autumn. NER 12/5/3
Autumn dusk. POE 4/4
Bells. COV 9/0
The beloved. SCM 12/3
Blue stargrass. SCM 8/1
Compensation. BOO 4/0
The conflict. EVM 9/0
The crystal gazer. YAR 10/1
A December day. POE 4/4
"The dreams of my heart" COV 9/0
Drifting sand. VAN ?/3
Effigy of a nun. BOO 5/1
Egyptian kings were buried. NES 3/3/3
Epitaph. POE 4/4
Evening. NER 8/24/1
Foreknown. NER 12/5/3
Frost. NER 12/5/3
Full moon, Santa Barbara. BOO 12/1
The hour. SCM 12/3

I could snatch a day. POE 3/4
I shall live to be old. RHY 1/3
"I shall not go back." SCM 12/3
"I thought of you" BOO 4/0
If death is kind. CEN 3/0
In flight. POE 4/4
In the end. COV 9/0
June night. BOO 3/0
Land's end. SCM 12/3
"Like barley bending" CEN 3/0
"A little while." COV 9/0
Lovely chance. HAM 5/0
May. COV 9/0
The mystery. EVM 9/0
Never again. NER 12/5/3
Not by the sea. HAM 12/1
"Oh the day of fire and sun" BOO 3/0
On the South Downs. POE 4/4
A reply. CEN 1/3
The sea-lover. SCM 8/1
"She who could bind you." POE 4/4
Sleepless night. CEN 3/2
The solitary. YAR 10/1
Those who love. SCM 8/1
Tired. CEN 1/4
To Eleanora Duse... POE 8/3
Twilight. BOO 12/1
The unchanging. CEN 3/0
When death is over. BOO 3/0
Winter sun. BOO 12/1
Wisdom. CEN 6/2
The wise woman. CEN 9/1
Words for an old air. SCM 8/1

Temple, Beatrice
Looking toward summer. SCR 5/3
To a friend. SCR 5/3

Temple, Mary O.
A beautiful gray day. CTY Win/2
Face it squarely. CTY S-A/1
Willows and palms. CTY Spr/2

Tenny, Ruth
Lullaby of the outcast. POE 12/2
Noon in the temple. POE 12/2

Terry, Edith
California sunset. LOS 5/10/4

Thanhouser, Marian
At night. POE 9/1

Thayer, Mary Dixon
At dawn. COV 1/4
The brush. COV 1/4
Divination. SAT 7/14/3
Happiness. COV 2/3
A knight of the grail. COV 7/4
New York. COV 2/3
Prelude. COV 2/3
To a beggar. SAT 12/9/2
Vision. SAT 2/10/3
Voices. AMP 6-7/3
The wandering minstrel. SAT 6/2/3

Thew, Vivienne
Orange blossoms. AMP 2-3/3
Seasons. LYW 10/3

Thom, Benjamin
Albert Perkins. DOU 8/2
John Doe and the ghost of Solo. DOU 5/3

Thomas, Andrew Walter
Laughing pansies. INT 4-6/4

Thomas, E. H.
Smilin' Nell. LAR 3/4

Thomas, E. Wilkins
Ego. NER 7/12/2

Thomas, Edith
The starward way. CIC 12/7/2

Thomas, Edith M.
Escape. HAM 10/1
Feuille - morte. HAM 5/2
"I dreaded to be pitied" SCM 6/0
Intimate stranger. HAM 7/1
So many joys. CIC 3/16/2
"Tell me your dream" HAM 1/1

Thomas, Elizabeth H.
Autumn. AMP 12/3
In December. MEA 1/4
A pink white apple tree. AMP 8/2
Shore. MEA 11/3

Thomas, Jack C.
Lassitude. PAG 12/1

Thomas, Margaret Loring
Fog. VOI 7-8/3
Lines. CUU 9/2

Thomas, Martha Banning
Babblers. DOU 4/2
Blind man's bluff. HOL 2/4
Fore-light. COV 9/1
Lodo. MEA 6/2
Lucy. MEA 6/2
Miss Anna. MEA 6/2
Old houses. COV 10/2
The other garden. NEV 10/2
The other side. HOL 11/2
Reward. LYW 7-8/3
Wind-mother. NET 10/2

Thompson, Basil
Albert Perkins. DOU 4/4
Armament. DOU 4/4
Barataria way. NAT 4/9/4
Caprice. DOU 4/4
Coda. DOU 4/4
Dubious beneficence...winds. DOU 4/4
The first son of my mother. DOU 4/4

Gaelic boon. DOU 4/4
Gewgaw. DOU 4/4
In the tent hence. DOU 4/4
John Doe &...ghost of Solomon. DOU 4/4
Lines written on the fly leaf.. BOO 10/3
Live oak and lion. DOU 2-3/4
The lorn knight. DOU 4/4
Metaphysician. DOU 4/4
Now that you slipt away. COV 7/4
The Panurge. STE 12/2
Poetaster. NAT10/10/3
Prudence. DOU 4/4
Rebuke to the certain. DOU 4/4
Revealment. LYR 7/2
Rhyme of reasoning. NER12/26/3
Rhyme of the straight & narrow. BOO 7/4
Rhyme of the struck lad. CEN 12/3
Searcher of the skies. COV 7/4
Six cravens and a seventh. DOU 4/4
Souvenir. DOU 4/4
Spent rockets. DOU 2-3/4
Stored against ennui. DOU 4/4
The swamp spirit. DOU 4/4
Timothy spied a goblin. DOU 4/4
Two in a mad house. DOU 4/4
Variation on an old theme. DOU 4/4
The visionary. FOR 3/4
We twain. WAV 6/3

Thompson, Kathyrn
Poems. DEP 3/4

Thompson, Ralph M.
Proposal. REW 7/3

Thompson, Roy T.
Boy in the surf. LYW 7-8/2

Thompson, Susan
Prairie night. LYW 6/3

Thomson, O. R. Howard
Evening. COV 4/2
February 23, 1922. WIL 2/24/2
In memoriam H. Douglas Spaeth. PEN 5/16/0

Thomson, P. H.
"Once upon a time" GRI 8/0

Thore, Katharine Parker
The Mohawk Trail. POE 11/3

Thornton, L. M.
The change. LAR 12/3

Thorp, N. Howard
"Light, stranger, light" POE 8/0
The little cow-girl. POE 8/0
Old Hank. POE 8/0
Old Paint. POE 8/0
Pecos Tom. POE 8/0
Sky-high. POE 8/0
What's become of the punchers? POE 8/0
Women outlaws. POE 8/0

Thorpe, Rose Hartwick
When night comes. AMP 5-6/4

Thurston, Charlotte W.
The living presence. LYW 9/3
Unsettled-probably fair. AMP 1-2/4
The vanished presence. LYW 11/3

Thurston, Helen
Butterflies. LYW 9/1
Cobwebs. LYW 9/1
Thistledown. LYW 9/1
Woodland sketches. LYW 6/2

Tietjens (tr.), Eunice
The red fish. POE 11/0
Spring. POE 11/0

Tietjens, Eunice
Fire. POE 2/2
Neanderthal. CIV 4/3
To Nijinski. MEA 6/1
To a picture...tired Siegmund. POE 8/3
A woman speaks. CIV 4/3

Tilden, Ethel Arnold
Essence. POE 4/4
In bluebell time. GOH 6/4

Tinckom-Fernandez, W. G.
The broken idol. NES 4/9/1

Titus, Ira
My flower. WAY ?/0

Tompkins, Eufina C.
Mirage. POE 2/0

Toner, Edythe
Longing. POA 1/2

Toogood, Granville
The gypsy dreams. COV 6/4

Toomer, Jean
Georgia dusk. LIB 9/2
Georgia portraits. MOR 1/3
Harvest song. DOU 12/2
November cotton flower. NOM Sum/3
Storm ending. DOU 9/2

Torrence, Ridgely
The apples. NAT 1/3/0

Torrey, W. O.
The old freight way. NOW 7/3

Totheroh, Dan
Poems of the tropic sea. WAN 6/3

Tourney, Rupert
After reading the poet's pack. STE 10/2

Towle, Eugenia
Neighbors. LAR 2/4
The river. LAR 2/4

Towne, Charles Hanson
The advance guard. MUN 3/2
A ballad of the circus. CEN 4/0
"Buy my sweet lavender." SCM 12/2
Enigma. HAM 3/2
The grass. BOO 8/2
In April. HAM 4/2
In the world's cathedral. CEN 10/0
The inarticulate. SCM 7/3
London. AIN 4/2
Spring and the angels. BOO 3/2
Tides. HAM 9/0
Wisdom. SCM 5/4
Wonder. CEN 2/2
Towne, Mary Emma
Colorado calls. AMP10-11/3
Townsend, Estil Alexander
Episcopacy. SCR 3/3
Goddardized. SCR 3/4
He and I. SCR 9/2
Hoping. SCR 6/4
Mary Lee. SCR 2/4
Measurement. SCR 6/4
Pretty maid. SCR 5/4
Smyrna. SCR 9/2
The stolen kiss. SCR 9/2
The three. SCR 11/2
War heartless. SCR 8/3
Would 'twere a dream. SCR 6/4
The woven robe. SCR 4/3
Townsend, Florence Hartman
The call. LAR 12/3
The desert dweller. LAR 11/3
A plea. AMP 12/3
Spring memories. LAR 4/4
Townsend, Georgina S.
His will. LYW 10/3
Townsend, Mildred
Evening. SCR 4/4
My doll. SCR 7/4
Yellow breast. SCR 3/4
Tracey, Tom
A room in Greenwich Village. PAG 8-9/1
Tractman, Judith
Be at peace. MEA 5/4
Complexity. LIB 5/2
Immortality. COV 3/3
Orchestration. LYW 3/3
Release. LIB 8/2
Second song of release. LIB 9/2
Silhouette. LIB 9/2
Trapnell, Edna Valentine
Cherry-bloom. SMA 4/2
Ghosts. COV 10/2
Happiness. COV 5/2
Inland. COV 3/0
The net. COV 3/0
The sphinx. EVM 9/0
There's no turning back... COV 12/3
Time's picture book. COV 3/3
Trask, Sherwood
Sing, cornbelt men. LIB 1/2
Trausil, Hans
The cat. MEA 3/2
In the subway. NES 4/7/3
Traver, Olive Young
Youth has not flown. LYW 12/3
Treadwell, Sara
Payment. COV 6/0
Tree, Iris
The fog. POE 2/3
Wintry alley. POE 2/3
Trent, Lucia
Martha. AMP 1-2/4
Suggested by an old guitar. LAL 5/4
Trigg, Emma Gray
Conquered. COV 3/2
Green mist. REW 4/2
A pretty woman. REW 10/3
To the wind from the sea. AMP 4-5/3
Trombly, Albert Edmund
An afterword. COV 3/0
A boy's hands. MID 12/1
Byron. VOI 12/2
The dead master. TEM Aut/1
End of the year. LYW 1/3
Facets. POB Win/1
The fields. MID 12/1
Fisherman. LYR 7/3
Footfalls. POB Win/1
Gentile. COV 9/2
The log house. LYW 3/2
"The man with the hoe." STE 6/2
Mrs. Neighbor. TER 4/0
Napoleon. ALS 7/3
November in Texas. LYW 11/2
Orchestral. TER 4/0
Out of your manly heart. STE 6/2
A pine squirrel. TER 4/0
Play. ALS 1/2
The ranchman. TER 4/0
Red rose. POB Win/1
Renan. VOI Sum/2
Smoke. TER 4/0
Soaring and groveling. TER 4/0
Stardust. POB Win/1
Table waitress. TER 4/0
Texas Rangers. OWE 2/2
The three children. POE 7/0
To certain trees. MID 12/1
Walls. MID 12/1
Troth, John T.

Ballad of the 'Steve Girard'. COV 4/1
Fear. COV 9/2
In Woodlands Cemetery. COV 4/3
In the wake of the storm. AMP 6-7/3
Little rivers. PAR #3/4
O, I am stabbed by beauty. COV 9/2
Prescience. AMP Aut/1
Semper ridens. COV 4/3
The ultimate tryst. COV 3/0

Troy, Daniel W.
As the band goes by. COV 6/0
It does make a difference. COV 2/1
Luella was right, at that. COV 9/1

Troy, William
After Actium. YAR 3/4
Aria for a flute. YAR 11/3
Prophecy. YAR 1/4
Roads. YAR 12/3
The wind that passes. YAR 2/4

True, Alida Cogswell
Life's eventide. GRA 11/2
"Shaker meeting" GRA 3/1

Trueblood, Crestes
The world. MEA 9/2

Trueblood, Orestes
First love. MEA 1/2

Trueblood, Paul Graham
Autumn. LAR 11/3

Trusler, Harry R.
Miracles. AMP 12/3

Ts'en Sheng
A song of white snow. NAT 8/30/2

Ts'eui Tu
A solitary wild goose. FRE 1/4/2

Ts'uei Hao
Passing through Hua-Yin. CIC 6/19/4

Ts'uei T'u
On New Year's Eve. CIC 6/19/4

Ts'uei-Hao
The yellow crane tower. FRE 1/4/2

Ts'ui Hu
Inscribed where once some one. MEA 6/2

Tsu Yung
One seeing the snow peak of Ch. FRE 1/4/2

Tu Ch'inniang
The gold-threaded robe. FRE 1/4/2

Tu Fu
Bidding General Yen farewell... FRE 8/1/3
A drawing of a horse by Genera. NES10/29/1
A hearty welcome to vice prefe. NES10/29/1
A letter to Censor Hau. NES10/29/1
Marching to war. FRE 4/5/2
A night abroad. NES10/29/1
Night in the watch tower. NES10/29/1
A night vigil in the left cour. NES10/29/1
On a moonlight night. FRE 8/29/3
On leaving the tomb of Premier. NES10/29/1
Seeing Li Po in a dream. FUG 7/4/3
A song of a prince deposed. NES10/29/1
A song of an old cypress. FRE 8/8/3
A song of dagger-dancing... NES10/29/1
A song of war chariots. NEW 11/2/1
Staying at the general's headq. NES10/29/1
To Li Po at the sky's end. NES10/29/1
A view of T'ai-Shan. FRE 8/15/3
The war chariot. MEA 6/2
With her beauty. FUG 6/27/3

Tu Hsun-He
A sigh in the spring palace. FRE 1/4/2

Tu Mu
By the Purole cliff. BOO 12/1
The garden of the golden valle. BOO 12/1
I climb to look-out cemetery... BOO 12/1
In the autumn night. BOO 12/1
A letter to Han Cho... BOO 12/1
A mooring on the Ch'in-Haui Ri. BOO 12/1
A night at an inn. BOO 12/1
Parting. BOO 12/1

Tucker, Beverley Randolph
Today, based upon...Sakskrit t. REW 1/2

Tull, Jewell Bothwell
Foolish bird. POE 10/2
Gender. POE 10/2
God-like. POE 10/2
Gray river. POE 10/2
October. POE 10/2
Seven ages. POE 7/4
Sum. POE 10/2

Tunstall, Virginia Lyne
After long years. LYR 1/2
Alone. LYR 7/1
Autumn gardens. LYR 10/2
The char-woman. LYW 5/4
The charwoman. LYW 4/3
Credo. LYW 7-8/3
The derelict. PER 1/3
Evening on the harbor. LYR 6/2
The flame eternal. COV 12/3
The goog gift. LYR 12/2
If I must remember. REW 7/4
Immortality. LYR 5/1
Let me go back. LYR 11/3
Lilies. GYP #2/4
Lost youth. REW 1/4
Mignonette. PEG 5/3
Miracle. NOM Aut/2
November roses. LYR 12/1
Old April. LYR 5/4
The old spinner. SMA 8/2
Pain. LYR 7/2
Parting. LYR 11/1
Philosophy. LYR 9/3
A prayer for crippled men. LYW 10/3
Questing. LYR 4/1
The recumbent statue of Lee. NOM Sum/3
Red tulips. COV 12/3
Return. VOI 12/2
The rider. GYP #2/4
Sacrament. LYR 9/1
Sonata appasionata. LYR 3/2
Songs for April. LYR 4/2
Spinster songs. LYW 9/2
Tenebois lex. CAW 4/3
There is no song. COV 12/3
To the discus thrower. LYR 6/3
Unanswered. REW 7/3
The unknown soldier. NOM Spr/2
Unprotected. LYR 4/3
Wind in the night. COV 12/3
Wind song. PEG 5/3
Winds of spring. LYR 6/1
Winter wind. VOI Win/2

Tuomey, Honoria
An old style Valentine. OVM 2/4

Turbyfill, Mark
Apples. MIL 12/2
Charm. POE 6/4
Fire and snow. PRA 1-2/3
"He will secretly cherish it." NOM Sum/3
The intangible symphony. POE 6/1
On a dune. CAP 10/2
Personal theme with nature acc. NES 6/24/2
A personal theme. NES 6/24/2
Phantasy. POE 6/4
The physician before dawn. MOR 1/3
Poems: Corphee and Mask. MIL 10/2
The power of nothing. POE 6/1
Repletion. POE 6/1
The sea storm. POE 6/1
Spectres of spring. YOB 1/2
Subject and object. POE 6/4
Things not seen. POE 6/1
Velocity. POE 6/4
Weather caprice. POE 6/4

Turnbull, Belle
At the concert. PAR #4/4
Colorado Easter. LYW 4/4
The gallant warrior. LYW 5/4
Incident of the hawk-watch. POE 7/4
Man ponders his problem. POE 7/4
Moment of withdrawal. CAP11-12/2
Momentary respite. OVM 4/4
Mountain mad. VOI 3-4/4
Mountain road. MEA 2/4
One man. POE 7/4
Prairie wife. TEM Win/3
Song for female voices. VOI 3-4/4
To a mountain meadow. POE 7/4
Wet mountain valley (August). AMP10-11/3
A woman's diary. LYW 7-8/3

Turner, Alva N.
Coming of June. POE 5/3
The philosopher. POE 1/4

Turner, Ethel
After rain. WAN 3/4
Aquamarine. WAN 9/3
Boats in the mist. LYW 7-8/2
Come, little wildings! AMP 4-5/3
The dark. LYW 2/4
Emily Bronte. WAN 3/4
Evanescence. WAN 6/3
Extravaganza. WAN 9/3
Lagoon. WAN 6/4
Noon. VOI Sum/2
Of Rupert Brooke. POE 6/4
Simpleton. TEM Win/3

Turner, Frances Wright
October. GRA 10/1

Turner, L. Lucile
Against the wind. WAN 3/4
Before the gathering...clouds. WAN 3/4
He comes to attack. WAN 3/4
In the north. WAN 3/4
My goal. WAN 3/4

Northward they are walking. WAN 3/4
Songs of the crow and the owl. WAN 3/4
Their voices could be heard. WAN 3/4

Turner, Nancy Byrd
John Masefield. VOI 8-9/3

Tuttle, Morris M.
To a hero of the great strife. BEL ?/2

Twitchell, Anna Spencer
I known. COV 1/1
A late spring. COV 3/1
Lost soul. NER 9/1/0
Quatrain. POE 2/1
Rain. POE 2/1
Song. COV 1/1
Unfailing. POE 2/1

Twombly, Albert Edmund
Orion. LYR 11/3
Outlaws. PAR #2/3
Rio Grande valley. POE 10/3

Tyler, Morris
Coelum non animum mutant... YAR 10/3
Doubt. YAR 1/4
Lament. YAR 12/3
A night ride. YAR 3/4
Secreta. YAR 11/3
To a gargoyle. YAR 3/4

Tyler-Cope, Helen
The hills of New Jersey. CTY S-A/1
In September. CTY Aut/2
You're just a bit of heaven. CTY Spr/2

Tynan, Katharine
The pine-wood. DOU 5/3
Song of going. CAW 1/0

Tynes, Mary Pollard
My aim. AMP 5-6/4

Tzara, Tristan
Cycle de 5 crimes. LIR A-W/4

Uerkvitz, Herta
Moon madness. LYW 1/2
Mud. LYW 1/2

Uncle Billy (pseud). See Billy

Underwood, Edna Worthley
Dances of flame. LYW 1/2
Improvisations from old Chines. LYW 5/2
The tigers. CUV 11/3

Underwood, John Curtis
Aria. LYW 6/2
Burros. LYW 3/4
Chemistry. EVM 4/1
The critic. LYW 1/3
Interval. LYW 6/3
The last divide. LYW 1/3
Waiting-mist. LYW 6/2

Underwood, Pierson
Brown as any thrush is. BOO 4/3

Underwood, R. S.
Vainglory. AMP 3-4/4

Underwood, Wilbur
Pierrot (Verlaine). WAV #4/2
To death (Baudelaire). WAV 12/2

Unna, Sarah
Completion. COV 2/0
Roads. POE 3/2

Untermeyer, Jean Starr
Anti-erotic. BRO 12/1
Bad weather. REW 3/2
From the day-book of a forgott. POE 11/1
Gothic. DOU 10/1
Lake song. CEN 9/1
Mater in extremis. MEA 8/2
Mist. BRO 12/1
The passionate sword. BOO 8/1
Rescue. MEA 8/2
Song of a woman. LIB 5/2
Spring night at Lachaise's. LIB 12/2

Untermeyer, Louis
Auction Anderson Gallerils. NER ?/0
Bereaved. SCM 2/0
Book review. NER 6/4/4
Boy and tadpoles. CEN 10/0
Child and her statue. RHY 2/3
Child dancers. NER 6/15/1
Country school room, Adirondac. CEN 11/2
D.H. Lawrence. NER 8/11/0
The dark chamber. NER 7/23/4
Daughter of Jephthah. CEN 3/2
Design for a perfect world. LIB 5/2
Dialogue in a grave. LIB 12/2
Dorothy dances. BOO 11/1
A fabulous critic. NER10/11/2
Five trees. NER 9/20/2
Flushed tanagras. MEA 1/3
Ghetto prostitute. PRA 1-2/3
He goads himself. YAR 4/2
Inhibited. MEA 1/3
Matinee. DIA 2/0
Matter. CEN 12/0
Monologue from a mattress. POE 3/2
The mother. REW 7/2
Mozart. YAR 7/0
Playground. NER 1/10/3

Portrait of a revolutionary. YAR 7/0
Portrait of an old cathedral. YAR 7/0
The rescuing wave. BOO 2/3
The single song. NES 7/15/2
Stand with me here. NAT 3/29/2
Steel-mill. MIL 12/2
The struggle. HAM 5/3
Tangential. FUG 2-3/3
Two women. REW 12/1
Variations on a modern theme. NER 2/15/2
Walls against Eden. CEN 7/14/0
With a volume of Heine. DIA 2/0
You said. NES 1/27/3
The young men. NES10/29/1

Updegraff, Allan
The daily round. POE 2/0

Upper, Joseph
Darkness. SCR 5/3
Dreams reward me. SCR 5/3
Excuse. WAN 1/4
The fruit of Lemuria. WAN 6/4
Hermitage. AMP Aut/1
Infection. OVM 2/4
Leave-taking. WAN 6/4
Query. OVM 2/4
Shower. OVM 2/4
Street lamps. AMP 10/2
Sunday afternoon. WAN 4/4
Triumph. TEM Aut/1

Urch, Marion Chisnell
Stone. GUL 9/3

Urmy, Clarence
California woodlands. MUN 3/2

Uschold, Maud Elfrid
Apprentice. MEA 12/3
Leaves. MEA 12/3
Morning song. NOM Sum/3
Nostalgia. PAR #3/4
Sorrow. MEA 12/3

Vail, Lammon
A child in the dark. COV 2/2

Vail, Lawrence
Cannibalistic love song. GAR 1-2@

Valier, Edma M.
The eternal Christmas. SIJ 12/3

Valliant, Wilsie May
When skys grow pale. CIV 5-6/4

Van Cise, Ethel
Discovery. LYW 5/4
San Diego Bay. LYW 12/3

Van Doren, Carl
Pascal D'Angelo. NAT 1/25/2

Van Doren, Mark
Afterward. VOI 5-6/4
Alfalfa coming. SCM 4/4
Alteration. NAT 3/19/4
Ambush. MEA 6/4
Communication. VOI 5-6/4
December. VOI 5-6/4
Immortal. MEA 7/4
Louise Brogan. NAT10/31/3
Marriage. NES 5/3/4
Mountain house. VOI 5-6/4
Old age. CEN 1/4
Pigeon. MEA 1/4
Rain-crow. MEA 1/4
River snow. MEA 1/4
The spring in the pantry. BOO 7/4
Spring thunder. NAT 4/30/4
Traveling storm. CEN 8/3
Two mothers. VOI 5-6/4
Water wheel to mend. DOU 2-3/4

Van Dusen, Washington
Beauty at home. AMP 6-7/3
Memories of Roosevelt. AMP 5-6/4
Song of dawn. FAR 6/2

Van Dyke, Henry
Candelabra. SCM 10/0
Malgre. SCM 10/0
Promise time. SCM 10/0
The red bridge at Nikko. SCM 10/0
The repose of Nara. SCM 10/0
Salute to the trees. SCM 5/1
The spirit of Japan. SCM 10/0
Wild azaleas. SCM 10/0

Van Dyke, Kathryn Donaldson
The unrequited lover. AMP 2-3/3

Van Nostrand (Jr.), J. J.
Elegy. WAN 6/4

Van Rensselaer, Mariana G.
Asked of my age. HAM 1/2
Of a beautiful poem. NOA 6/1
The ultimate harvest. HAM 9/1
Youth and I. SCM 4/2

Van Slyke, Berenice. See Slyke

Van Wyck, William
El Camina Real. LOS 5/10/4

Van de Poel, Romanie
Contemplative. CTY Win/2
The last word. CTY Spr/2
Song sparrow. CTY Win/2

Vance, Paul L.
Empty arms. LOS 5/10/4

Vandercook, John W.
Comparison. PAG10-11/1

Varney, John
Beauty not mine. HUE 7/19/4

Vaughan, Malcolm

Coast of Georgia. MEA 9/2
Deep desire is memory. MEA 9/2
When all the world considers y. MEA 10/2

Vedder, Miriam
April evening. LIB 2/2
She will take thee. MEA 1/3
Silent. MEA 12/1
Yesterday I told the truth. COV 3/0

Verder, Daniel H.
Books and life. NET 8/9/2
Life. ATC11/15/3
A November song. ATC11/15/3

Verlaine, Paul
Chanson d'automne. NOM Spr/3

Verry, Ethel
A father. POE 4/4
The house-to-house seamstress. POE 4/4
A lady. POE 4/4

Viereck, George Sylvester
Respite. LIB 9/1

Vildrac, Charles
A friendship. DIA 5/1
An inn. DIA 4/0
A landscape. OUT 4/21/0
The one song. DIA 5/1
To be a man. DIA 4/0

Villiers, George
Blessed are the moments. ATM 4/3
Values. ATM 4/3

Vinal, Harold
Alien. GRA 1/1
April. TEM 6/1
At midnight. LYR 8/1
At night. COV 9/0
At parting. COV 10/4
Beauty will burn. NOM Sum/2
Bees in Eden. VOI 12-1/4
Blizzard. VOI 12-1/4
Buried. GRI 5/1
Calendar. EME 1/4
Change. VOI 6-7/3
Cherish my love. LIB 1/2
Colored stones. PAL Spr/3
Decoration. VOI Sum/2
Departure. GRI 5/1
Distances. LYW 7-8/2
Dryad. LYW 1/2
Early loves. LYW 1/2
Earth lover. VOI Spr/2
Earth sorrow. S4N 12/2
Elf child. FUG 4-5/3
Envy. LYR 2/3
Esplanade, Boston. WAN 9/3
Evanescence. PAG11-12/0
Farm boy. FOR 4/4
Fishermen. FUG 6-7/3
Flight. MEA 6/2
Fog. COV 10/4
Forgotten. POE 6/1
Fountain tassels. VOI 12-1/4
Friday nights. OUT 9/6/2
Futility. CAP11-12/2
Ghost walk. VOI 12-1/4
Glimpses. COV 9/0
Gone. GRA 4/2
The house of dust. PAG 8-9/1
Hurts. STE 1/4
I shall feel. COV 6/2
Immigrant. OUT 5/9/3
Invocation. TEM 6/1
Island born. COV 10/4
Islander. COV 10/4
Italian. NOM Spr/3
Judas. MEA 6/4
Last days. GRA 4/2
Last of April. GRA 4/2
Little song. VOI Win/2
Luigi walks through the crowd. EME 1/4
Memories. NEN 3/28/1
Mercy. VOI 12/2
Miser. PAG 2/1
My own. COV 9/0
New England. STE 12/3
Night memory. NOM Spr/2
Nocturne. LIB 3/2
Of mariners. COV 6/3
Old things. LYR 2/2
Pallette. EME 1/4
Pause. GRA 3/1
Pity. GRI 5/1
Pods in autumn. NER11/28/3
Recurrence. EME 1/4
The return. GRA 4/2
Salutation. COV 6/4
Sea born. LYR 8/3
Sea folk. CAS 1/3
Sea longing. COV 7/1
Sea madness. PIR 3/3
Sea memory. LIB 2/2
Sea mood. COV 6/2
Sea nearness. VOI Win/2
Sea pool. NER 6/13/3
The sea remembers. LYR 5/2
Sea urge. TEM Aut/1
Sea weeping. COV 9/2
Second mowing. VOI 8-9/3
She sews. DOU 5/2
Ship epic. VOI 12-1/4
Snow nocturne. LYW 1/2
A song for April. LYW 9/1
Song. SPT 8/25/0
Sonnet. ALS 11/1
Sonnet. GRA 5/1
Sonnet. LYW 12/3
Sonnet. NOM Sum/2

Sonnet. TOW 1/1
Spring beauty. LYW 4/2
Spring flame. GRA 4/2
Talisman. NEN 4/6/1
Tempo. NEN 4/6/1
To November. SPT 11/1/0
To Persephone. VOI Win/2
Tokens. BOO 1/2
Tornado. VOI Sum/2
Tracks. MEA 11/3
Trees in April. VOI Spr/2
Unbound. SAU 7/1
Until. PAG 12/1
Vera Fokina as Salome. PAG 5/1
Walls. EME 12/2
Water news. EME 1/4
When the crows go. COV 10/4
When you came back. WAV 6/2
White peacock. FOR 12/3
Will beauty make me forget. VOI Spr/2
You came to me. LIB 9/2

Vincent, Clarence
Life's summons. CON 5/17/3

Vincent, Paul
Death. WAN 10/3

Vines, Sherard
The bull. POE 5/0

Vinton, Eleanor W.
Inspiration. GRA 6/2
Spring mist. GRA 4/2

Voigt, Paul
Sorrow. CTY Spr/4

Von Freytag-Loringhoven, Else
Affectionate. LIR Win/2
Chill. LIB 10/2
Loss. LIB 10/2

Von Nardoff, Betty
Fat women. GUL 9/3
June shore. S4N 12/2

Von Wiegland, Charmion
Flights. LYW 11/3
The lotus of Isis. BOO 10/3
The street of prostitutes... GUL 5/3
Wind prints of a dancer. LYW 4/4

Voris, Virginia
Dawn. LIC 12/2

Voss, Elizabeth
In the waterfall. AMP 10/2
My wish. CAW 9/2
A song of life. AMP 4-5/3

Vote, Carrie Leimer
Called home. SCR 9/3
Your picture. SCR 9/3

W.,E.H.
To the match-lighter. CAS 3/3

W.,W.J.
A greater love. SCR 7-8/2
Twaddle. SCR 7-8/2

Wade, Harmon
Little boy. VOI Sum/2
Old days. AMP 8-9/3
Song for a contralto. AMP 12/2

Wade, Otis
Clair de Lune. WAN 7/4
Youth. WAN 3/4

Wadhams, Beatrice
Delphine. LIC 4/2
A flower reverie. LIC 2/2
A friend in need. LIC 3/2

Wadleigh, Wallace
To Wisconsin. AMP 4/2

Wagenhals, Margaret H.
The beggar. COV 3/4

Wagner, C. L. H.
The D-X hound. RAD 5/17/4
A thief. LAL 5/4

Wagner, Charles A.
Announcement. PAG10-11/1
Colors. PAG 12/1
My soul. NOM Sum/2

Wagner, Madge Morris
Rocking the baby. OVM 5/4

Wagstaff, Blanche Shoemaker
Gift. AIN 5/0
I will take the lone path. MUN 4/2
When these keen fires. LYR 4/4

Wainwright, Virginia
August memories. AMP 8/2

Wakeley, Charles Russell
World voices. CIC 11/3

Wakeley, Charles R.
In the aftermath. CIC 7/6/2

Waldron, Marion Patton
Your soul in my two hands. CEN 3/0

Waldron, Winifred
Arepeggio: spring. POE 3/3

Waley, Arthur
Early snow, a No play. POE 3/0

Walker, Francis I.
At the gates of life. POA 9/1

Walker, Martha
Chinese life and scenes. DEP 3/4
The deserted temple. DEP 3/4

Wallace, Edna Kingsley
Loneliness. COV 1/4
O singing wind blow through me. COV 1/4

Wallace, Grace
The account. LYW 3/1
Bourrico. LYW 9/2

Like three gold temples. COV 1/4
A preference. LYW 7-8/2
Visitors. LYW 3/1

Wallach, Sidney W.
Fantasy of the week. MEA 5/4
Old woman selling fruit. DOU 7/4

Walleser, Joseph
Betrayed. GRI 2/1
The three witches. GRI 8/0

Wallingford, L. A.
A present day saint. CAW 7/1

Wallis, Jessa Eula
Always hungry. CTY WIN/3
Premature. CTY WIN/3

Wallis, Jessie Eula
The night prowlers. CTY Sum/3

Wallis, Keene
A day as a wage. LIB 8/1
Gospel with banjo and chorus. POE 10/0
Poet on a flat car. MEA 5/1

Wallop, Gerard
Acceptance. POE 5/3
Burial bitterness. SCM 3/2
Morning song. POE 5/3
The singing boy. POE 5/3

Waln, Nora
At the altar of heaven. SCM 11/1
Baby's bath. SCM 11/1
Behind the walls. SCM 11/1
The emperor's birthday. SCM 11/1
Golden lilies. SCM 11/1
Hatamen Street. SCM 11/1
My teacher. SCM 11/1
Shackles. SCM 11/1
A wedding dress. SCM 11/1

Walpole, John Lawrence
The heart of Maryland. CIV 5-6/4

Walsh, Ernest
Bridges. POE 1/4
Collapse. POE 1/2
The fickle lover. POE 1/2
I ask for a friend. POE 1/2
In hospital. POE 1/4
Introspection. POE 1/4
Life. PEG 1/3
Sonnet. POE 1/2

Walsh, Margaret Mansfield
Pax hominibus. AMP 12/3

Walsh, Thomas
In Santo Domingo of Bogota. BOO 3/4
In the Quinta of Bolivar. BOO 3/4
Tequendama. BOO 3/4
To the conquistador... BOO 3/4

Walton, Anne
Sol-ill-o-quce. LAR 10/3

Walton, Edna Lou
Alabama. PAL Sum/3
At dawn. TER 10/1
Bridal sleep. POE 5/4
Crisis. POE 8/1
Despair. POE 8/1
Divorce. VOI 7-8/3
Dramatics. MEA 12/3
Finality. MEA 4/1
For mother on her birthday. TER 4/1
Four poems. PAL Sum/3
From a promontory. POE 5/0
Fuchsias. LYW 9/3
The goal. COV 3/1
Hands. TER 10/0
A hidden rhythm. POE 5/4
I am so unsure. COV 7/4
I have come in to myself now. VOI Win/2
I met three lovers. POE 5/0
I should like to live... NAT 4/27/1
I will run then alone. VOI Sum/2
I would be free. POE 8/1
I, who love beauty. TER 4/1
In recompense. POE 8/1
In silence. LYW 12/1
Indian love songs. COV 2/0
Indian prayer. POE 5/0
Insanity. MEA 4/1
Into the stillness..your grief. TER 10/0
Lift up your eyes to darkness. TER 10/1
Locked room. TER 10/1
Love. COV 3/1
Moon child. LYW 9/2
Morning and night. POE 5/0
Navaho poems. MEA 6/1
Navajo songs. NAT 4/17/0
Now more than ever divided. POE 8/1
One spring. POE 5/0
Patterns. COV 3/1
Pink petals. TER 10/0
Portrait. POE 5/4
Prayer against witchcraft. LYW 9/2
Prayer for harvest. COV 2/0
Reflections of a paralytic. COV 3/1
She who was I. TER 4/1
So it befell. POE 8/1
Sometimes when I sit....quiet. COV 12/3

Sometimes when I am restless. COV 12/3
Spring. WAN 4/4
Strength. POE 5/0
Suite for Iola. TER 10/0
They have built...many houses. TER 10/0
Though we protest. MEA 12/3
To a Madonna. VOI Sum/2
Truth absolute. LYW 12/1
Under an umbrella. TER 10/0
Upon reading..Browning letters. LYW 12/3
Warning. TER 4/1
When I think. MEA 6/4
When I write of love. MEA 6/2
Whence? COV 11/2
Winter roses. POE 5/4
Without figures. POE 5/4
Without grief. POE 8/1
You. MIN 3-4/4

Wang Ah-Shih
Night time in spring. POE 8/2

Wang Ah-shih
Evening house top: idle glance. MEA 6/2

Wang Ch'ag-Ling
In her quiet window. NAT 11/2/1

Wang Chang Ling
From the west window. FRE 4/5/2

Wang Chi
Futility of war. SCR 11/4

Wang Wan
A morning under Mount Pei-ku. FRE12/21/1
A song of Liang-chou. NAT 11/2/1

Wang Wei
Answering Vice-Prefect Chang. POE 2/2
The beautiful Hsi-Shih. POE 2/2
In a retreat among bamboos. POE 2/2
In my lodge at Wang-ch'uan. POE 2/2
Lines. POE 2/2
A message to Poai Ti. POE 2/2
Mount Chung-nan. POE 2/2
My retreat at Chung-nan. POE 2/2
On the way to the temple. POE 2/2
A parting. POE 2/2
A song at Wei-ch'eng. POE 2/2
A view of the Han River. POE 2/2

Warburg, James Paul
The dark star. CEN 1/1
Fame. CEN 9/0
The still flame. CEN 1/1

Ward, Bernard D.
Salve regina. MAG 5/2
Spring. MAG 4/2

Ward, Mary Armantine
Awakening. COV 2/3
The carpenter. COV 2/3
The teacher. MEA 1/4

Ward, Mary B.
Farmer's wife. NOM Spr/4

Ward, May Williams
Apices. PAR #2/4
De corporibus. STE 4/4
Grade crossing. VOI 7-8/3
Perennial. LAR 12/3
The restless tamed. LYW 2/4
Song of the plains. LYW 9/3
The tender plant. LAD 2/4
Upon reading Sandburg... LYW 9/3

Ward, Wayne
Hollyhocks. CIC 3/27/4

Ware, Richard D.
John says he's dead. GRA 3/1

Warner, Eva E.
Footholds. CIC 5/25/2
The infinite urge. CIC 5/11/2
Mother or Jesus. CIC 5/3/3

Warren, G. O.
"I reached up for your heart" DIA 3/1

Warren, Robert Penn
Adieu sentimentale. VOI 7-8/3
Crusade. FUG 6-7/3
The romance macabre. VOI 7-8/3
Vision. AMP 12/2

Warvelle, Effie Bangs
The wind. COV 1/1
Winter flowers. COV 1/0

Washington, H. Wyatt
April magic. COV 4/2
Geese. COV 4/3
It's shiftin' time. COV 4/3
Paradise of flowers. COV 4/4
Somebody's yard. COV 4/3

Wasson (Jr.), Ben
Dissection. LYR 6/4
Song for a dream. LYR 11/3

Wasson, Ben F.
Cyril Sand. PAG10-11/1
Fanny Slag. PAG10-11/1
Lucinda Ann Smith. PAG10-11/1

Waterbury, Florence
Mathematics. SCM 7/1

Waterman, Mildred
Small songs. AMP 3-4/4

Watkins, Eleanor Preston
North wind. LYW 7-8/2

Watson, Annah Robinson
The call of dawn. MEC 1/1/2

Watson, Evelyn M.

The Canyon Cascade. LYW 10/2
The five cent Jew's harp. AMP 5-6/4
Winter moonrise. SCM 1/3

Watson, Virginia
April and I. HAM 4/2
The galleons. HAM 3/0
Keys of the city. NOA 8/3
The pine tree. HAM 6/1

Watson, William
The peace of God. CIJ 2/4

Wattles, Willard
And the two Christs answer. COV 7/1
From the Parthenon I learn. BOO 8/3
Good neighbors. OUT 3/29/2
Last night. COV 3/2
Let all beauty. COV 3/2
Night of tacit-absolving. BOO 12/1
Not even sworded Thoas. CPV 3/2
Requiescat. OUT 3/1/2
Sister Euphrosyne. COV 3/0
So much of beauty. OUT12/21/1
When I first felt. COV 3/2

Wauchope, George Armstrong
Sunset over Pisgah. SOU 7/3

Waxman, Percy
Memory. BOO 5/3

Way, Isabelle Stewart
Weariness. SCR 9/3

Weatermax, Ruth
Fishing. POA 9/1

Weaver, Bennett
Early autumn. MID 8/1
The house. MID 8/1
Lost. MID 8/1
Out to sleep. MID 8/1
To father. MID 8/1
"When the drift comes in-" MID 8/1

Weaver, John V. A.
Dilemma. POE 11/2
Drug store. POE 2/0
Fantasy. BOO 7/3
Lost spring. BOO 9/3
Nocturne. POE 2/0
Picture ahead. POE 11/2
She dwelt among the untrodden. BOO 5/3
Transplanted. NER 11/9/1
Two ways. BOO 12/1

Webb, Charles Nichols
Real romance. AMP 4-5/3

Webb, Charles Nicholls
Chang Mow: through the stream. AMP 4/2

Webb, Margaret Ely
Trails. LYW 4/3
The woods are still. LYW 3/4

Weber, Kate
Prophecy. CIJ 2/4

Webster, Louise
The journey. LYW 2/4
Lament. NOM Spr/3
The point of view. LYR 2/4
The reckoning. COV 9/2
Return. NOM Win/2
Still, starry nights. COV 9/2
A woman. UNI10/12/2

Webster, Martha
At broad bar. DOU 2/2
Dune-daughter. WAN 10/3
Finale. WAN 10/3
Gas well blow-out. LYW 3/4
Let it be kelp. WAN 10/3
Love at first sight. LOS 5/10/4
A voice in the night. MEA 11/3
A wash-piece. LYW 6/3

Webster, William
A murmur. AMP 2-3/3
Respite. AMP 12/3

Weddell, Alexander
Revelation. REW 1/3

Weeks, Raymond
The hunchback'song. MID 8/1
Not like the flowers my love. MID 8/1

Wei Chauang
A night thought in Chang T'ai. FRE12/21/1

Wei Ying-Wu
At Ch'u-Cho on the western str. FRE12/21/1
Farewell to Li Ts'ao... FRE12/21/1
A greeting on the Huai River. FRE12/21/1
Meeting my friend Feng Cho in. FRE12/21/1
Mooring at twilight in Yu-Yi d. FRE12/21/1
A poem to a Taoist hermit... FRE12/21/1
A poem to secretary Yuan 1st... FRE12/21/1

Weimar, Edward William
A sonnet. OUT10/27/0

Weinberg, Katherine Gertrude
Autumn. AMP 6-7/3

Weldon, Robert Wylie
The wife..civilian,shell shock. NAT 3/26/4

Welles, Merrick
The fool. HAN 4/4
Nazimova as Salome. HEA 7/4

Welles, Winifred
Actual willow. NER 2/27/4
Ah Gabriel--. MEA 1/2

Anger. MEA 5/2
The black nun. VOI 12/2
Cliffs. NOA 1/1
Cloth of gold. NER 3/7/3
Clump of grass. VOI 12-1/4
Consecration. BOO 8/2
Diana. MEA 3/1
The driftwood harp. NOA 9/0
Driftwood. COV 2/0
Dwelling. NER 2/27/4
Exile. COV 2/0
Harlequin crucified. NES 10/8/2
Harvest dust. NER 5/24/2
Hunting dogs. MEA 12/2
Indian pipes. MEA 3/2
Jealousy. COV 12/0
Lace shroud. MEA 11/3
The last night of winter. NES 3/11/2
Mist shell. VOI Spr/2
Moors. NER 5/23/3
Open grave. MEA 12/2
Overtones. VOI Spr/2
The poppy room. COV 9/1
Proud shanties. NER 2/27/4
Revelation. MEA 5/1
Second growth. HAM 1/0
Silence. COV 6/2
Silver fog. POE 5/2
Silver for Midas. MEA 3/2
Strange laughter. MEA 12/2
Suicide. MEA 5/2
A thing of wonder. MEA 3/2
This delicate love. NER 2/6/4
White death. MEA 12/2
White fear. MEA 2/2
Winter apples. NER11/15/2
With a red geranium. VOI 12-1/4
Women and orchards. COV 12/0
Worship. COV 8/0

Wellman, Esther Turner
Nocturne. AMP 12/2
A Spanish home. AMP 2-3/3

Wells, Carolyn
The beloved face (Lincoln Memo. HAM 2/3

Welsh, Cecilia M.
The miracle. LYR 9/2

Wen T'ing-Yun
Near the ferry at Li-Chou. FRE 1/4/2
A sign on a jade lute. FRE 1/4/2
To a friend bound east. FRE 1/4/2

Wendell, Roland M.
Karl Vondell, color sergeant. SOV 1923

Wentworth, C.
The mountains. PAG 8-9/1

Wentworth, E. S.
The mordant. MEA 5/2

Werfel, Franz
The good man. NAT 3/14/3
An old woman passes. POE 12/2

Werner, Flora T.
Past. PAG 12/1

Werner, Marguerite Edwards
Before words come. POE 3/3

Wescott, Glenway
The chaste lovers. POE 9/1
Coyotes. POE 10/3
Evening illusion. POE 10/3
Foresight. POE 8/3
The free and the bound. POE 10/3
Gifts of the river. POE 10/3
The hunter. POE 9/1
Magnolias and the intangible h. DIA 6/3
Mountain. POE 10/3
Named Flamingo. DIA 9/3
Natives of rock. DIA 12/1
Old style of garden. LIR Spr/4
Ominous concord. POE 9/1
The poet at night-fall. POE 9/1
To L.S.. POE 9/1
Without sleep. POE 9/1

West, Alvin
Earth, my heaven. MEA 6/2

Western, Grace
Grieg, 'Nocturne.'. LAL 5/4

Weston, Edward
Ballade. S4N 12/2

Weston, Mildred
A portrait. POE 5/2

Westy, Pal
Hail, Lariat. LAR 12/3
The sand squall. LAR 12/3

Wetjen, Albert R.
The unknown soldier. LAR 8/3
The wreck of the Bengal prise. LAR 9/3

Wetterau, Anna M.
Worship. AMP 6-7/3

Wharton, Edith
Lyrical epigrams. YAR 1/0
Mistral in the maquis. YAR 1/0
The young dead. YAR 1/0

Wheeler, Claude H.
To Ruth. PAG 8-9/1

Wheeler, Ermine B.
Counterpoint. GUL 9/3

Wheeler, Mary H.
Canterbury bells. GRA 1/1
The minutes. GRA 11/0

Wheelock, John Hall
By the gray sea. NES 6/17/2
Exultation. COV 4/2
The fish hawk. SCM 8/2

Haunted earth. YAR 10/2
In the dark city. POE 7/2
Legend. SCM 1/2
The lion house. NES 8/12/2
Mirror. ALS 5/1
My lonely one. FRE 7/0
Night has its fear. ALS 6/2
Noon. OUT 5/3/2
Noon: Amagansett Beach. OUT 7/2/4
O happy heart! BOO 2/2
Panther! Panther! SCM 10/1
Plaint. ALS 3/1
The poet tells of his love. SCM 8/0
The sorrowful masquerade. POE 1/1
Starless morning. LYR 10/1
This quiet dusk. CEN 5/4
Three poems. COV 4/1

Whicher, George Meason
An epistle to Stephen. SCM 3/0
Wych-hazel. GRI 8/0

Whitaker, Robert
The soul's summer. LYW 7-8/2

Whitcomb, G. Faunce
Fragment. GRA 1/1
To dawn. GRA 3/1

Whitcomb, George Faunce
Aftermath. VOI 12/2

White, C. J.
Via Dolorosa. AMP 6-7/3

White, Eliot
The water lily. NEU 7/23/2

White, Florence
The night flyer. AMP 2-3/3

White, Florence Branch
Three sonnet poems. AMP 5-6/4

White, Florence
Love's portion. TEM Aut/1
Revelation. AMP 8/2

White, Grace Hoffman
Easter. MIN 5-6/4
A Japanese print. MIN 5-6/3
Spring ghosts. MIN11-12/3

White, Hal Saunders
Strangeness. FOR 7/4

White, Heber
The fiddle on the wall. LAR 4/4

White, Hervey
Aftermath. HUE 7/5/4
From songs of friendship. HUE 6/21/4

White, Hinton
The conqueror. BOT12/23/2

White, Michael
Platonic friendship. LAL 1/4

White, Nancy Ellen
May moon. LYW 5/2
World wonder. LYW 2/2

White, Owen P.
Realism. STE 12/2
Repartee. STE 12/2

White, T. P.
The tree. GRA 6/2

White, Venita Seibert
Mothers. MAC 2/3

White, Viola C.
Provincial. NAT 11/1/2

Whitelock, William Wallace
A statesman. MUN 5/2

Whiteside, Mary Brent
After all splendors. HOL 10/3
The ancient secret. HAM 3/1
The casement. COV 11/2
The challenge. DOU 1/2
Clay. VOI Spr/2
The coming. SVG 1/4
Consolation. LYW 11/1
Content. AMP 6/2
Dedication. COV 11/2
Dust. SVG 2/3
The eternal quest. COV 10/1
Eve. SVG 12/1/2
From the Acropolis. STE 5/4
Guests. LYW 2/2
The high road. SOU 8/3
Houses. LYW 11/2
Hunger. ALS 8-9/2
Journey. LLYW 5/2
The last evening. TEM Aut/1
Leaves. LYW 11/1
Lost trail. HOL 9/3
The minor poet. LYW 4/4
The nearer gift. HOL 12/3
New poems. NEN 3/28/1
Old selves. HAM 1/2
Old trees. HAM 8/0
Paper flowers. FRE 6/13/3
The passing. VOI Aut/1
The path of the star. SOU 12/3
The pool in the wood. VOI Aut/1
Poprtrait of a lady. COV 7/3
Sea rhythm. LYW 3/4
The seeking. LYW 5/4
Stone mountain. SOU 9/3
Three sonnets. LYW 10/3
To a poet. HAM 11/3
Treasure. IND 9/1/3
Unbelief. COV 7/3
The unknown road. HAM 1/4
Who has known heights. HAM 12/2

Whitesides, George M.
Confession. SCR 11/3

Whitford, Robert Calvin
Lament for Midkiff. KNO 3-4/1

Whiting, Herbert R.
Ascension. CIC 7/3/4

Whiting-Baker, A. E.
Little summer song. BOO 9/3

Whitley, Isadore B.
Insomnia. WAV 3/4
Quiet interior. WAV 3/4
Shadows. WAV 3/4
Whitmarsh, Esther A.
Life everlasting. POE 10/0
Whiton, Juliet
My books. SCM 12/0
Whitsett, George F.
Beauty. ALS 8-9/2
City sea. ALS 10/1
Dance of the sycamores. ALS 11/1
Daylight at the country club. ALS10-11/2
Days drowned. ALS 8/1
An epitaph. ALS 3/2
Evening on the farm. ALS 5/2
Forge. ALS 12/1
He came to me. ALS 5/1
Its slave. ALS 5/1
Portent. ALS 9/1
The seven o'clock symphony. ALS 2/1
Skyscraper. ALS 1/2
Song of life. ALS 4/1
Steel mill at night. ALS 2/1
Strange things happen in the w. ALS 6/2
Tide moon. ALS 3/1
Unknown. ALS 8/1
When the dark races come. ALS 9/1
Whittaker, George S.
The absent voice. SCR 7/4
Cactus blossoms. LAR 4/4
Ecstasy of night. LAR 3/4
The sea. SCR 7/4
Whittier, Mary Iva
House of dreams. GRA 10/1
Wickham, Anna
Code. NER 1/25/2
King Alfred on the peasant wom. POE 7/2
The last round. NER 1/4/2
The muddle. NER 1/4/2
A poet advises a change of clo. POE 7/2
Song of Orphelia the survivor. MEA 8/2
Weapons. NER 1/4/2
The winds. NER 1/4/2
Woman to the male psychologist. NER 1/4/2
Wooing. MEA 8/2
Widdemer, Margaret
Admiration. BOO 9/2
At autumn. BOO 9/2
A ballad of Queen Elizabeth. VOI 6-7/3
A ballad of the mid-Victorian. NES 1/13/3
Before my heart was broken. HAM 3/2
Behind the hills. AMP 2/2
The bird misunderstood. BOO 9/2
Bird on tree. BOO 9/2
The breaking. BOO 2/1
Clear sight. OUT 3/12/4
Coup de grace. WAN 8/3
Cowardice. COV 11/1
Currant bushes. HAM 8/2
The daughter. COV 5/3
First lover. COV 7/4
Glamour. LYW 2/4
Hill sunset. LYW 4/3
The Hoboken grackle and the ho. BOO 9/2
Holly carol. LYR 12/2
Imri Swazey. BOO 9/2
Inevitability. BOO 9/2
Irony. HAM 5/3
Loves. OVM 7/4
Mimes. LYR 2/2
Mistake. NES 4/1/2
Oh bird!!! BOO 9/2
Oiseaure. BOO 9/2
Old love. AIN 3/0
Omission. HAM 12/1
A path in Cyprus. VOI Spr/2
The pigeon house. COV 3/1
The prisoners. CON 5/17/3
Rambuncto. BOO 9/2
Revisitants. DOU 9/2
Romantique. POE 4/3
Songs from a masque. COV 12/2
To a young man. BOO 5/4
To the younger set. WAN 8/3
Words. OUT 2/7/3
Wiegand, Frances
Departing youth. LAR 12/3
A thought for a poet. LAR 4/4
Wisdom. LAR 12/3
Wiggin, Dorothy Pettit
Half-gifts. COV 5/1
Wilbur, Harriette
The postman-a pantoum. COV 8/0
Wilcox, Almira Richardson
Scars. LYW 10/3
Wilder, Amos Niven
Logos. DOU 7/4
Wilder, Charlotte Elizabeth
Hollows. COV 9/1
Wilder, Charlotte E.
The last hour. POE 7/4
Wildman, Marian E.
Youth sings. UNV 4/3
Wiley, Harley R.
My horse. SCM 12/0
Wiley, Mildred

The supper bell. CTY Aut/2
Wilkie, Isabelle
Evening in the Berkeley hills. WAN 1/4
Incompatibility. WAN 4/4
Wilkinson, Elizabeth Hays
The far traveller. AMP 6-7/3
Wilkinson, Florence
Don Juan in Portugal. POE 11/1
Her death. POE 4/0
The hope of heaven. POE 4/0
Pawnbrokers. BOO 2/4
Speech. POE 4/0
Wilkinson, Marguerite
Colors. COV 2/0
The empty throne. CIC 6/7/3
Finis. CIC 6/4
The first gray hair. COV 11/1
Food. COV 2/0
The great dream. COV 2/2
Guilty. CIC 6/28/3
An oath in April. AIN 3/0
Oblation. CIC 6/5/4
A proud song. MEA 1/4
Scatheless. FOR 1/4
Scornful answer. COV 11/1
Shelter. OUT 1/11/2
The Somerset farmer. NOA 3/1
This shall be the bond. SCM 1/0
Trees. COV 2/0
Waking thought. CIC 6/5/4
Weather. COV 2/0
When first I heard thy call. CIC 5/1/4
"Your way is glad with roses." OUT 6/18/4
Willard, Edna Constance
Resonance. PEG 3/3
Willard, Pierrepont
Along the Bayous. LYW 4/1
Decision. LYW 7-8/2
Willcox, Charles
A garden in winter. COV 2/0
Willcox, Louise Collier
Wings. LYR 10/1
Williams, Claire
The proof. COV 8/0
Williams, Edward
Crosses. CIC 5/1/4
Williams, Eleanor
Love. GUL 6/3
Williams, Florence Rosing
Sometimes. LAR 2/4
Williams, Gusty
"A wish, not small." MES 7/4
Williams, Hamilton
The sunny mind. MUN 1/2
Williams, Harriet
Night. STE 12/3
Williams, Hazel Wyeth
After school. CTY Spr/3
All on a summer's day. CTY S-A/1
Bring on your spring! CTY Spr/2
The ceiling. CTY Win/4
The friendly dark. CTY Sum/3
Going back. CTY Spr/2
A Jersey piper. CTY Spr/3
Now the day is over. CTY Win/3
A picture. CTY Win/3
Salutes in season. CTY Aut/2
Sunshine. CTY Spr/2
Thoughts on a ferry-boat. CTY S-A/1
The tugs. CTY Win/2
Where are you. CTY S-A/1
Woodman in the city. CTY Spr/4
Williams, Mary
The passing of Joaquin Miller. AMP 2-3/3
Williams, Oscar
The actor. NOM Sum/2
After I am dead. COV 10/1
At love's door. LYW 12/3
Because. POE 7/1
Being. CAP 10/2
A bleak day. DOU 10/1
The bubble. GRI 2/1
The bubble. POE 7/1
A call. STE 11/2
Chiarascuros. POE 9/0
The children. NOM Aut/2
Cinquain. PAG 8-9/1
The clouds of death. LYR 4/2
Clouds. GRI 3/1
Cobwebs. POE 7/1
The corn. PIR 4/1
A cry. NOM Aut/2
A crying. GRI 6/1
Darkness like a bird. VOI Spr/2
The darkness. GRI 2/1
Dead trees. BOO 2/3
The earth. GRI 6/1
The end. DOU 10/2
Failure. MID 3/1
Frost nocturne. COV 2/1
Frost nocturne. GRI 2/1
The golden fleece. POE 7/1
Grey. POE 7/1
How many? MID 1/1
If one should ask. GRI 5/1
In the subway. CAP 10/2
Man. MID 1/1
Maybe. PIR 5/2
Mood. POE 9/0
Motes. POE 7/1
The mouse. PAG 8-9/1
My greatness. POE 9/0
Never. GRI 5/1

O my love. POE 9/0
Oblivion. DOU 9-10/1
The ocean. GRI 2/1
The old man. EVM 9/0
The old perplexity. NAT 7/27/1
On death. GRI 1/1
Only the hope, the desire. GRI 5/1
Outcast in the night. COV 10/1
Painter girls. DOU 2/2
The pane of dreams. VOI Spr/2
The pane of dreams. WAV 3/4
Presences. DOU 2/2
Pursuit. VOI Spr/2
Rains. POE 7/1
A reason. COV 10/1
The return. POE 7/1
Revenge. POE 9/0
Rhapsody. VOI Aut/2
The rose that tripped a wind. STE 10/2
Ruminations. NAT 1/24/0
Silence. MOR 1/3
The sky. GRI 5/1
Snow nocturne. MID 3/1
Song. GRI 5/1
Spirit of all things. DOU 12/1
The subway is lit. POE 7/1
The sun. VOI Aut/2
To life. VOI Aut/2
To one unknown. POE 9/0
The traveler. GRI 5/1
The voice of death. DOU 9/2
The voice. ALS 2/2
A walk in the woods. VIO Aut/1
Wandering. WAV 6/2
When at last. GRI 2/1
While I talked. DOU 3/2

Williams, Wayland Wells
Country club portraits. BOO 11/3
Once on a grey beach. FUG 6-7/3
Rapid transit. S4N 12/2
Striding the blast. YAR 7/0
Two men. FUG 6-7/3
Where beauty lodges. YAR 1/2

Williams, William Carlos
Blizzard. DIA 8/0
Bull. DIA 2/2
The desolate field. DIA 8/0
Fish. BRO 4/2
Full moon. DIA 1/4
A goodnight. POE 1/1
The jungle. DIA 2/2
The lonely street. POE 1/2
Poem. DIA 6/3
Portrait of a lady. DIA 8/0
Portrait of the author. COT ?/1
Spring storm. DIA 8/0
Sprouts. POE 1/2
St. Francis Einstein of the da. CON Ad#/2
Three poems. DIA 8/3
To waken an old lady. DIA 8/0
When fresh, it was sweet. DIA 12/2
The widow's lament in springti. POE 1/2
Wild orchard. POE 1/2
Willow poem. DIA 8/0

Williamson, Estella M.
The violincello. LYW 4/1

Williamson, George
The nameless one. POE 5/4

Williamson, William Hay
To my valentine. WOW 2/0

Willian, Ruth H.
Circumstance. LYW 10/3
Kin. LYW 10/3
To an old lover. LYW 10/3

Willis, Winifred Lockhart
Heart of the woods. NET 8/5/3

Wills, Jesse
Consider the heavens. FUG 2-3/3
In the observatory. FIG 12/3
To Jones: of Brown, Schwartz &. FUG 4-5/3

Wills, Ridley
Calvary. FUG 12/2
De senectute. FIG 12/3
The experimentor. FUG 2-3/3
I gloat. FUG 12/2

Willson, Dixie
One star. MAC 2/3

Wilson (Jr.), Edmund
G.H.Q., January 1919. POE 11/0
Not here. POE 11/0

Wilson, Albert Frederick
Black loam. CEN 9/2
Blackberry briars. NAT 4/12/2
Concentrics. CEN 9/2
Vespers. CEN 9/2
Woodrow Wilson. POE 9/0

Wilson, Arden M.
"Tired business men" COV 6/0

Wilson, Caroline Crosby
The deserted house. LIB 9/1
October graveyard. COV 10/3
On a chilly day in spring. COV 3/2
To Judelle. COV 10/3

Wilson, Charlotte Joy
Sleep. LYW 4/3

Wilson, Edmund
Gluck in New York. NER 3/31/0
The Olympians. SCM 1/3
Quintilian - a ballad. DOU 5/2
Stucco and stone. DOU 9/2

Wilson, Ethel Brodt
All the blues in one. OVM 6/4

Clouds and rain. OVM 4/4
If I could stay. WAN 5/4
Possession. OVM 4/4
Sleeping out. OVM 4/4
Waiting. OVM 4/4
A whisper of color. OVM 4/4

Wilson, Irene H.
There is no wind. COV 10/1

Wilson, John French
At grandfather's, victory. COV 10/2
Blue moonlight. COV 7/0
Candles until dawn. COV 7/1
The captive. COV 7/0
Citadel. COV 4/4
In the night. COV 4/2
Moonlight. COV 7/0
Nocturne. AMP 6/2
Rain. COV 7/0
A song at Armageddon, 6/2/17. COV 7/0
Sonnet. COV 7/0
To the rebels. COV 4/4
Winter afternoon. COV 7/0

Wilson, Kathryne
The basket woman. SUN 7/3
On a famous poem. AMP 12/2

Wilson, Margaret Adelaide
I kissed my love today. LYW 3/4
The quail's grace. LYW 10/2
When I was happy. LYW 5/4

Wilson, Marie
Alone. GRA 11/2

Wilson, Nell G.
The eucalyptus to the lupines. AMP 5-6/4

Wilson, R. H.
Aphorisms. SCR 9/2

Wilson, Stanley Kidder
Choice. NES 2/25/2
What poet can be sure? COV 8/0
Where do you read my letters? COV 8/0

Wilson-Howell, Jennie
Testimony. BOT 3/17/3

Wing, Eleanor Evans
Sonnet. SCR 8/3

Wing, J.
Chinese poems. BRO 11/1

Winke, Charles
Liberation. AMP 8-9/3
Milwaukee. AMP 4/2
Vision. AMP 8-9/3
Wisconsin, an experiment in de. AMP 4/2

Winship, Charles
"Oh, do not let your singing j. LYR 9/2
The shrine of spirit. MUN 5/2
Unification. LYW 3/4

The usurer. LYW 10/3
The waiting dusk. LYR 7/3
Your voice. LYR 11/2

Winslow, Alice C.
Autumn wind. GUL 9/3

Winslow, Anne Goodwin
Actuality. FRE 8/29/3
The answer. NOA 8/3
The birth tokens. FRE 9/12/3
The caretaker. HAM 6/2
Choral. YAR 4/3
Classic dancing. FUG 8/30/2
Dandelions. LYR 5/2
Free forms. FRE 7/12/2
Intrusion. FUG 7/25/3
The lesson. FRE 3/28/3
A new anthology. HAM 1/2
The outdoor theatre. FRE 3/14/3
Santa Maria degli Angeli. NES12/30/2
Spring song (after Isaiah). FRE 4/26/2
The steed. FRE 8/16/2
The thief. LYR 8/2
Three characters. FRE12/12/3
To his teacher. FUG 3/17/3
Twelfth night. FRE 5/31/2
Two songs of returning. FUG 3/17/3
The unregretting. FRE 3/14/3

Winsor, Mary
The May king (A.M. Palmer). NER 6/2/0

Winters, Dorothea
Love's house. NOM Spr/4

Winters, Yvor
Apocalyptic harvest. BRO 11/2
Ballad of men. POE 12/0
Ballad. POE 12/0
Chicago spring. POE ?/2
The crystal sun. DIA 10/3
Death goes before me. POE 12/0
The dry year. POE 5/3
The far voice. POE 12/0
"The fragile season." POE 9/2
Fragrant bones. MIL 10/2
Hawk's eyes. POE 12/0
Hill burial. MIL 10/2
The immobile wind. POE 12/0
Jose's country. MOR 7/4
Lament, beside an acequia,... POE 9/2
Late winter. POE 9/2
The little deity alone in the. POE 9/2
The mule corral. MIL 10/2
The precincts of February. DIA 7/3
The priesthood. POE 12/0
The schoolmaster and the quere.

POE 5/3
The schoolmaster at spring. POE 5/3
The schoolmaster writes to a p. POE 5/3
The silent days. POE 9/2
Song for a small boy who herds. POE 12/0
Statis autumn. POE 5/3
The stone mountain. MIL 10/2
Two songs of advent. POE 12/0
The walker. POE 12/0
Where my sight goes. POE 12/0

Winton, G. B.
The thrush. CIC 6/28/3

Wintrowe, Norine
At the theatre. COV 12/2
Night thought. COV 7/4
Rose jar. GRI 6/1
Sacrement. COV 7/4
Searchlights. MID 9-10/1

Witherbee, Mary Chase
The brook. CIM 6/11/4

Wolf, Howard Paulus
Ichabod Crane. STE 3/4
To the Arthur Machen... STE 2/4

Wolf, Robert L.
Giddy. NAT 7/30/4
His house. MEA 3/1
A pagan reinvokes...23rd Psalm. NAT11/28/3
Prologue for the modern male. POE 12/3
The public. NES11/17/3
The son. NAT 3/14/4
Tableau. MEA 7/4

Wolfe, Ian M.
Wild apples. COV 10/0

Wolfe, Walter B.
Amritam. PAG 12/1
Au soleil. GRA 3/1
Avidya. PAG 12/1
Caesura. GRA 5/1
Grosbecks. GRA 4/2
Jack Frost. GRA 3/2
Kleidoscope. AMP 1-2/4
Prometheus. GRA 11/2
Reflets dans l'infinite. GRA 2/2
Rythms. PAR #2/4
Sadhana. PAG 12/1
Sannyasin. PAG 12/1
Sasseopeia. LYW 2/4
To a hamadryad. GRA 7/2
Traumerei. APM 2/2

Woliston, Mary R.
Fetters. COV 10/3

Wones, H. C.
Morning. LAR 9/3

Wood, Anna Hamilton
Futility. CIV 3/4
The half-sinner. CIV 7-8/4

Wood, Annabel
Winter - Milwaukee downer. AMP 4/2

Wood, Charles Erskine Scott
A fallen pine. POE 2/4
First snow. NES12/22/3
Lay me on the hill-top. POE 2/4
To his mare. POE 2/4
War. ALS 4/2
The water-hole. POE 2/4

Wood, Clement
At dawn. NOM Spr/3
At twilight. AMP Aut/1
Brotherhood. SVG 1/3
Canopus. NAT 6/22/1
The changeling. VOI 8-9/3
Chinaberries. VOI 8-9/3
The crooked street of dreams,. NES 12/3/1
Culture. NAT 3/1/2
De Lawd's baptizin'. COV 10/1
Eagle sonnets. NAT 12/7/1
The fire burns low. STE 7/4
The gold hour. NOM Spr/3
The golden kiss. COV 7/3
I walked an hour. AMP 4-5/3
A last taper. AMP 12/3
The man beneath the sky. COV 7/1
Mists. WRE 5/2
Oh Jubilee! NAT 1/24/3
A prayer in time of blindness. SVG 2/3
Ragle sonnets. NAT 12/7/1
The silver hour. COV 7/2
The singing shadows. SCM 11/2
Sparta. BOO 7/2
Their words were strong words. GUL 9/3
Time. SVG 10/2
To a starry lover. PAR #2/3
Two sonnets. YAR 1/3
Wandersoul. COV 3/2
Weirdwoman. COV 1/3
When earthlifts skyward. AMP 9/3
Where does the tall sun-. LYR 7/2
You. COV 7/4

Wood, Jane D.
The rag. CIC 7/6/2

Wood, Lora Person
Song of the poplar tree. VER 5/3
The thief. VER 10/2

Wood, Narcisse
Antinous. LYW 9/2
Tapestry. LYW 7-8/3

Wood, Narcisse
Praising her hands. POE 12/3
Woodall, Allen Earl
The dream of the Yengeese poet. SCR 9/3
Woodberry, George Edward
America. TEM Aut/1
Experience. OVM 7/4
Woodberry, Laura G.
The lighthouse. AMP 8/2
The marsh. COV 1/1
North shore sounds. AMP 8/2
Snowflakes. COV 1/1
The wind is in their feet. VOI Aut/2
Woodbury, Benjamin Collins
Chores. VOI 3-4/4
Woodhull, W. S.
The dilenttante. COV 1/1
Woods, Bertha Gerneaux
The foster child. NET 1/6/1
Woods, Charles Coke
The philosopher. PER 4/2
Woods, Edna Hamilton
Three poems. COV 3/1
Woods, William Hervey
Comes great heart. SCM 1/2
Country-bred. SCM 6/2
The poet's holiday. SCM 5/3
Serenity. SCM 9/2
Woodward, Louis Burton
Why I teach. EME 2/3
Woolsey, E. G.
Faith at Forty-second Street. NES 6/3/2
Woolsey, Gamel
Gay street. NES 5/6/2
Hugh Early. CAP 5/3
Woolson, Elinor C.
Youth. CIC 2/21/4
Worth, Kathryn
Mistake. AMP 8-9/3
Unfillment. AMP 10/2
Worth, Patience
Jesus-shepherd. STE 11/3
Mecca. STE 11/3
My bird of hope. STE 11/3
Pierrot. STE 11/3
A poem for Gloria's room. STE 11/3
Worthen, Samuel C.
The flag at half-mast. GRA 12/1
Worthington, George
Sonnet to a young co-worshippe. REW 4/3
Wright, Cuthbert
On the title page of Thais. FRE11/14/3
Wright, Donald
Garden piece. BOO 9/2
Wright, Harold Holston
Kinship. POE 4/0
A letter. POE 4/0
Pastel. POE 4/0
Wright, Muriel
Stranded. PAG10-11/1
Wrynn, Anthony
Admonition in autumn. DIA 3/3
He wove his nest...the portico. DIA 10/3
Heat. MEA 11/2
Orpheus. MEA 11/2
Prelude. MEA 11/2
Proud. DIA 10/3
Seaward. MEA 11/2
To my mother. RHY 6-7/3
Wyckoff, Dorothy
Of glow-worms. NAT 2/28/3
Wylie, Elinor
All souls. YAR 1/3
Atavism. POE 4/1
August. NER 8/25/0
Benvenuto's valentine. YAR 4/3
Beware! NER 1/25/2
Bronze trumpets and sea water. NER 4/27/1
Castilian. NER 11/2/1
Demon lovers. NER 6/14/2
Drake's drum. BOO 4/3
Drowned woman. NER 6/21/2
The eagle and the mole. NER 4/13/1
Eipitaph. NER 5/24/2
The fairy goldsmith. CEN 8/0
"Fire and sleet..." POE 4/1
Francie's fingers. OUT 6/14/2
Full moon. NER 6/28/2
Gifts at meeting. MEA 7/2
Golden bough. NES 12/1/3
The good birds. NAT 7/12/2
Heroics. NER 6/28/2
The innocents. NER12/26/3
King's ransom. NER 9/19/3
"Les Laurier sont coupes" COV 5/0
Let no charitable hope. NES 7/1/2
Lilliputian. OUT 6/1/4/
Little sonnet. NER 5/10/2
The lost path. CEN 11/0
Lucifer sings in secret. NES 3/17/3
Madman's song. CEN 10/0
Minotaur. NER 6/13/3
Nebuchadnezzar. NER 12/7/1
Nonchalance. NER 8/24/1
Now that your eyes are shut. OUT 6/14/2
Parting gift. OUT 6/14/2
The Pekingese. CEN 4/2

The Persian kitten. POE 6/3
Phases of the moon. POM 1922
Pity me. MEA 3/2
Poor earth. NES 2/18/2
Preference. MEA 7/2
Pretty words. BOO 10/1
The prinkin' leddie. CEN 8/1
Profession of faith. NER 2/6/4
The Puritan's ballad. DOU&RHY1/3
Quarrel. CEN 12/2
Romance. CEN 5/3
Sea-blue eyes. CEN 6/1
Self-portrait. NER 3/29/2
Shepherd's holiday. CEN 10/3
Silver filagree. POE 4/1
Simon Gerty. LIB 3/2
Sonnet. VOI Sum/2
Three wishes. NER11/23/1
The tortoise in eternity. NER 4/13/1
Twelfth night. YAR 1/3
Unwilling admission. NER 12/5/3
Velvet shoes. POE 4/1
Viennese waltz. CEN 9/3

Wynne, Annette
If a dream should break. COV 9/0

X.,X.Z.
Gift weighing. SCR 7-8/2
A sad farewell. SCR 12/2

Yantis, Amee
El Rosario. LAR 9/3
San Antonio River. LAR 4/4
Silence and the great hurt. LAR 3/4

Yarnell, Esther
Black night. LYR 8/2
Color. LYW 10/1
"I have climbed the dark hills. LYW 7-8/2
The sky-rocket. LYW 10/1
A wraith. LYR 8/2

Yawor, Nahum
Ahhhh! CAP 10/2
Vacant. CAP 10/2

Yeats, John Butler
Autumn. MEA 7/1

Yeats, William Butler
All Soul's night. DIA 11/0
Ancestral houses. DIA 1/3
Demon and beast. DIA 11/0
Easter, 1916. DIA 11/0
The gift of Harun-al-Rashid. DIA 6/4
The heart replies. DIA 6/4
I see phantoms of hatred... DIA 1/3
The jay's nest by my window. DIA 1/3
Leda and the swan. DIA 6/4
The lover speaks. DIA 6/4
A meditation in time of war. DIA 11/0
Michael Robarts and the dancer. DIA 11/0
My descendants. DIA 1/3
My house. DIA 1/3
My table. DIA 1/3
On a political prisoner. DIA 11/0
The road at my door. DIA 1/3
The rose tree. DIA 11/0
The second coming. DIA 11/0
Throughts...present state of t. DIA 9/1
Towards break of day. DIA 11/0
Under Saturn. DIA 11/0

Yeed, Dick
A sucker. CTY Win/3

Yeh Shih
On being denied admittance to.. POE 8/2

Yenny, Cordelia
Caged. SCR 6/4

Yoemans, Horace
To a--. LAR 3/4
A wish. LAR 12/3

Yoffie, Leah Rachel
A cry of the foreign-born. COV 9/0
Faith. COV 9/0
The lost vision. COV 3/4
A voice. COV 11/3

Yothers, Merrill Arthur
To the Columbia. LAR 5/3

Young, Barbara
A certain woman. KAN 3/14/3
The cross of every day. NEW12/10/2
The doors. NEW11/26/2
Extra muros. NEW 12/3/2
The harp. NEW 9/22/2
I met a shining woman. NEW 7/8/3
In through my window. NEW 11/5/2
Lady April. NEW 4/15/3
"Long live the king!" NEW 2/18/3
My windows. NEW 9/13/2
Sanctuary. NEW 5/20/3

Town waif. NEW 7/29/3
Via Victoria. NEW 4/30/3
Viae novae. NEW 1/3/3

Young, Duncan Francis
I'se gwine ter lib in town. CTY Win/2

Young, Jessie M.
Lead me. CTY Sum/3
Llano Estacado. CTY Win/4
My dad. CTY Spr/4

Young, Roland
Lakewood. SCM 1/4
Pittsburgh. SCM 1/4

Young, Stark
The egoist. NER 4/16/4
For a wawside inscription. NER 4/16/4
Ranchman's manicure. NER 4/16/4
Romantic. NER 4/16/4
To a rose at a window of heave. SCM 9/2

Yuan Chen
An elegy. FRE 1/4/2

Yuan Chieh
A drinking-song at Stone Fish. FRE 3/15/2
To the tax-collector... FRE 3/15/2

Yukio Ozaki
Fate. FRE 11/9/1
Threatened. FRE 11/9/1

Yukio Ozaki (tr.)
Autumn reflections. FRE 11/9/1
The consequence. FRE 12/7/1
Is't possible. FRE 11/9/1
Love's lesson. FRE 12/7/1
Memory. FRE 11/9/1
No reservation. FRE 12/7/1
Overcome by confession. FRE 11/9/2
A splendid sin. FRE 12/7/1
Transmuted. FRE 11/9/1
When beauty dies. FRE 11/9/1

Zagat, Helen
To a talented child of the Eas. SVG 2/3

Zaturensky, Marya
Amaryliss sings in the shade. LIB 11/1
Elegies over John Reed. POE 3/4
A ghetto poet. NER 6/30/0
Indifference. LIB 2/2
Memories. POE 9/1
An old tale. POE 9/1
The poet seeks a new beauty. LIB 6/2
Portrait of a Russian novelist. BOO 2/3
A Russian Easter. POE 4/0
Russian peasants. POE 4/0
She longs for the country. POE 9/1
A song for vanished beauty. POE 9/1
Song of a factory girl. POE 9/1
Song. LIB 9/2
The spinners at Willowsleigh. POE 9/1
"Young girl takes her place.." POE 8/3

Zausmer, Emanuel
Lyric. POE 11/3

Zeigen, Frederick
Mist. CUV 11/3

Zeigler, Mary Morton
Jane A. and Maria E.. LAL 1/4

Zeiss, J. Roy
Enchantment. GRA 6/2

Zimmer, Henry
Christ in..blessed sacrament. MAG 9/3
Shrines. CAW 7/2
To Margaret. MAG 3/2

Zuheir, Abu
Poems. STE 2/3

Zukofsky, Louis
The faun sees. PAG 8-9/1
Glamour. RHY 3/3
Louis XIV chamber. VOI 8-9/3
Mood. PAG10-11/1
Of dying beauty. POE 1/4
This earth. RHY 3/3

Zulen, Pedro S.
Love beyond. AMP 8/2

Zumwait, Imri
The Nazarene. CIC 2/15/3